# CRITICAL SOCIAL ISSUES IN AMERICAN EDUCATION

## Transformation in a Postmodern World

*Second Edition*

Edited by

**H. Svi Shapiro**
**David E. Purpel**
*University of North Carolina, Greensboro*

LAWRENCE ERLBAUM ASSOCIATES, PUBLISHERS
1998    Mahwah, New Jersey                    London

Lawrence Erlbaum Associates, Inc., Publishers
10 Industrial Avenue
Mahwah, NJ 07430

Cover design by Kathryn Houghtaling Lacey

**Library of Congress Cataloging-in-Publication Data**

Critical social issues in American education : transformation in a
    postmodern world / edited by H. Svi Shapiro, David E. Purpel.
    — 2nd ed.
            p.  cm. — (Sociocultural, political, and historical
                        studies in education)
    Includes bibliographical references and index.
    ISBN 0-8058-2540-1
1. Critical pedagogy—United States. 2. Education—Social as-
    pects—United States. 3. Education—Political aspects—United
    States. I. Shapiro, H. Svi. II. Purpel, David E. III. Series.
LC196.5.U6C75    1998
370.11'5—dc21                                    97–47079
                                                    CIP

Books published by Lawrence Erlbaum Associates are
printed on acid-free paper, and their bindings are chosen for
strength and durability.

Printed in the United States of America
10  9  8  7  6  5  4  3  2  1

# Contents

# Preface

This volume is predicated on the following assumptions: Educators must see their work as being in the eye of a vast social storm; education and teaching are inseparably linked to the crises of the social order—cultural, moral, political, economic, ecological, and spiritual. It is impossible to make sense of what is happening educationally if what is happening is not placed in the context of the stresses, strains, and contradictions of both our national and our global society. Issues such as the growing administrative control over teachers' lives, allegations about the mediocrity of American schools, the crisis of funding, concern about what is called *excellence*, the impoverishment of increasing numbers of children and adolescents, fears about moral degeneration, bitter contention over the nature of the curriculum and of school knowledge, and widening disparities in educational achievement among ethnic and racial groups all must be seen, at the same time, as both critical issues in American education and as metaphors for the larger human and societal situation. This awareness is what we have tried to convey in this book. What happens in school, or as part of the educational experience, is only a part of a larger process—a process that raises profound questions about the direction and nature of the society we inhabit.

We attempted to organize the readings in this book in a thematically meaningful structure. The five sections offer a useful way to make sense of the crises and concerns that confront us. Each section is preceded by a brief essay (except the last) that provides some background to the readings. Still, the organization must be viewed as only a heuristic measure. In the real world, issues do not come neatly and conveniently packaged or compartmentalized. One problem or crisis flows out of and into another, forming interrelated aspects of a social totality. Whether one aspect of this totality ought to be seen as fundamental (as in some way, determining all others) is the subject of much intellectual controversy. Those who assert that the key is found in capitalism, patriarchy, modernity, or elsewhere dispute where the lion's share of the blame must go. Reflections of this debate can be found in the pages of this book.

The volume broadly follows the lines of our earlier edition, although many of the readings are new. We addressed some issues that emerged in the last 4 years as being especially salient such as welfare reform, the construction of sexual identities, violence, the pursuit of national standards for schools, the notion of education as caring, and the growth of inequality. However the overarching concerns that shaped the first edition—the influence of capitalism, social justice, marginality and differ-ence, and the political and moral nature of curriculum—continue to shape the work. Perhaps the most significant departure is in the final section in which David Purpel and I offer directions for a new and radically different public discourse on education.

The readings in this collection represent, important, sometimes seminal state-ments on critical social and educational issues. They offer a perspective on both the long-range and the more immediate problems and issues we face as a national and global community, and they provide a consideration of these concerns at both an applied and a theoretical level. We hope the reader experiences the disjunction between readings that deal explicitly with education and those whose concerns are broader, not as something jarring, but as moments of a connected dialectic—a vehicle for moving between the distinct, but very related aspects, of a single social world. Most of all, however, we hope readers feel they gained something by giving up a trivializing, narrow discourse that dominates so much of professional educa-tion for one that is broader in its sweep, even if this broader vision is also sometimes a dispiriting one. It is hard to dispute that the pages of this volume are filled with a terrible commentary on the human condition. Yet, as we often found, attempting to connect the field of education to the most serious and pressing concerns of humankind, however overwhelming this sometimes feels, ultimately elevates and ennobles the perceptions that educators have of their work. We hope this conviction is borne out by those who make use of this text.

We wish to acknowledge the importance of our students in the cultural studies program. Their passion for a critical understanding of our world and their courage to venture along often difficult personal and professional paths in pursuit of transforming our culture continues to inspire us as to the possibilities of real social and educational change in bleak circumstances.

—*Svi Shapiro*
*Greensboro, NC*

# Introduction

In this volume, our goal is to provide a focus for thinking about education in the context of a society that now, in the final decade of this millennium, is faced with a range of critical, sometimes catastrophic issues and problems, such as poverty and growing social injustice, racism and sexism, and other forms of exclusion; the depersonalization of social and political life; the moral and spiritual decay of the culture; and the ecological deterioration of the planet. Our concern is not only for American society (although this is the emphasis), but also for the larger global community.

We start from the conviction that as both citizens and educators we dare not ignore these issues and problems. Educational discourse in both professional and public circles has become narrow and trivial. This volume is offered as part of our continuing efforts to resist and transform the assumptions and concerns of such discourse. For education to become a humanly vital, ethically responsible endeavor, infused with a serious commitment to democratic values, we must understand its connection to the urgent and pressing issues laid out in this text. These issues represent what we believe to be the most critical issues that we and our children face as we move into the 21st century.

This volume is intended to work on two levels. First, we are concerned with developing an awareness concerning how education is connected to the wider structures of social, cultural, political, and economic life. Any attempt to apprehend the nature and purpose of education in the United States requires us to grasp the interrelatedness between schooling and the larger culture. The readings were selected to heighten understanding of these links. For example, some of the chapters examine how educational reform was a response to popular movements concerned with equality and social justice. Others explore how changes in education are connected to the restructuring of American labor and the decline of U.S. manufacturing industry. Further readings discuss ways in which the process of schooling legitimizes the hierarchies of social class, race, and gender and transmits the dominant ideology.

It is important to add here that we have come to appreciate the debilitating and demoralizing effects on students of critical analyses that only criticize. Empowering human beings for the purpose of social change requires, we believe, not merely brilliantly insightful criticism, but also the vision of alternatives that can be positively embraced and ultimately, worked for. Such description helps us to re-image the future and to make in Maxine Greene's words, "the strange familiar."

Thus, on a second level, our goal in this volume is to encourage not only a critical examination of our present social reality, but also a serious discussion of alternatives—of what a transformed society and educational process might look like—through what Henry Giroux calls a "language of possibility." This volume provides elements of what might be termed a new paradigm for conceiving of our social, cultural, economic, political, and moral worlds.

The major theme of this text—that education is intimately connected to the major social concerns and issues of our time—challenges the conventional, shallow terms of educational discourse. What is perhaps unusual about the collection is that we have included not only chapters specifically about education, but also those that provide a broader social perspective. In this way, we hope to maintain a dialectic between the issues and problems of education and those of the larger society. This volume includes pieces by authors who are influential both inside and outside the field of educational studies.

This collection is intended to focus on issues we believe to be crucial aspects of a growing world crisis. In this context, a word is in order about what this volume is *not*. The readings are not offered as a contribution to the preparation of impartial social scientists nor are they meant to titillate detached, aloof, uninvolved voyeurs of a catastrophic global condition filled, as it is, with human suffering of enormous proportions. What we intend, in presenting these readings, is to increasingly challenge educators to define education as a political and ethical activity explicitly connected to the making of a world in which such suffering is reduced, if not eliminated. Indeed, the fact that professional and theoretical discourse about education is not centered on the immense problems confronting humanity indicates the degree to which it has been trivialized. This discourse is concerned with such issues as merit pay, achievement test scores, homework, and the like—rather than with the looming issues confronting all of humankind today.

Some people concerned with teacher education would argue that the primary value of teaching educators about social issues is to make them more "well-rounded." Yet, our view is quite different. We believe that as educators and future educators, we must understand what is happening around us (and as a consequence, in us and to us) because these larger issues are the ones we must actively address in our work. In a world in which 40,000 children die each day from starvation—over 500,000 a year—any other kind of education represents a failure of our deepest human responsibilities.

Many of the students we taught find disturbing, even shocking, our efforts to deliberately connect the work of teachers to an ethically committed, politically charged pedagogy. This link flies in the face of many teachers' best liberal instincts about the moral neutrality of what is taught and the impartial role of teachers. Our primary response to those teachers is to point to the substantial literature about schools that clearly demonstrates education is a human practice that always has been and always will be a moral and political practice. We believe that education is always (and everywhere) about the business of legitimizing and reproducing existing social relations, values, and ways of life—or about working to oppose them. Shaull[1] expressed it well:

> There is no such thing as a *neutral* educational process. Education either functions as an instrument which is used to facilitate the integration of the younger generation into the logic of the present system and bring about conformity to it, or it becomes "the practice of freedom," the means by which men and women deal critically and creatively with reality and discover how to participate in the transformation of their world.

Our volume is specifically organized to raise awareness of what is at stake in this country and in the world as we move into the 21st century. More than this, however, we hope that it cries out for the need for us to act as citizens and as educators to address the pain, the dilemmas, and the crises that pervade our national life and the life of the planet. Through consideration of the issues addressed in this volume, we hope to contribute to increased awareness and greater human commitment. We are not suggesting that simple, easy answers are always available, nor are we arguing that policy choices can be merely "read off" from ethical commitments. Yet, this is not to say that there are no responses or solutions to the problems and crises discussed in this text. We believe that there are. The most honest stance we can take—one that is neither simplistically hopeful nor bleakly hopeless—is to alert our readers to the often contradictory demands and pulls of the modern (or perhaps more accurately, postmodern) condition. Thus, one consideration guiding the selection of the readings in this volume is what we perceive to be some of the most difficult dilemmas of our time: the free-market economy versus democratic and egalitarian values; the assertion of cultural differences versus community; social justice and responsibility versus individual freedom; moral commitment versus the uncertainty of truth or knowledge; full employment versus the end of the work-oriented culture.

The issues raised in this volume have shaped and will shape the present and future condition of all our lives—our hopes, fears, anxieties, and dreams. Addressing these issues is not simply a matter of referring and deferring to the experts, for we all know a great deal about them (even if, as Michael Polanyi noted, we frequently know "more than we can say"). Antonio Gramsci, the Italian Marxist philosopher taught us to recognize that in the often-maligned (especially in academic circles) common sense of people, there are penetrating insights into the nature and workings of our social reality. Gramsci, and those influenced by him, tell us that in dealing with our lived world, we are all unavoidably philosophers and social scientists. This world in crisis is the world in which all of us struggle to survive, produce meaning, and derive joy. The crises we are concerned with are not just faraway events depicted on the television evening news but also are mirrored in our families, sexual relations, the quality of life in our neighborhoods and communities, and the nature of our work experiences. It must be added, however, that although we all know about and have something to say about these matters, in the classroom, students are often unable to speak up. Many voices are never heard. Such silence, as those who espouse critical pedagogy or study the lives of the disempowered have made abundantly clear, is also an important dimension of the crisis. It is the consequence of a world—especially schools—that systematically devalues and excludes the voices of many individuals.

Of course, taking seriously the voices of students certainly undermines the teacher's possibility of covering the curriculum. Yet, this is a problem that does not worry us too much because covering a prescribed number of text pages or topics or sequencing the topics in the right order are problems more relevant to bureaucrats than to teachers. Our concern for the readers of this book is of a different type. Through these chapters, we hope that students confront the truly critical issues that face us as individual human beings, as citizens of U.S. society, and as members of a global community—and consider what are, or ought to be, the consequences of these issues for education. We tried to assemble, here, more than just another reader in the social foundations of education. Our goal is to offer a set of readings that demands a critical encounter between the reader and education's social and cultural functions at this important historical moment.

This volume developed out of our work as teachers in the social foundations of education. Specifically, it reflects themes and concerns that formed an important focus of the work in a course for graduate students entitled "Critical Social Issues in American Education." Although students come to the class for a variety of reasons and with diverse emotions, by the end, most admit that it represented a significant and influential departure in the way they learned to think about and approach their work in the field of education. Quite apart from the idiosyncratic qualities of the course and the teacher, it is clear that the changes students experience point to important issues in the nature and discourse of educational studies—issues that in turn, raise fundamental questions about the relevance or adequacy of these studies to the extraordinary conditions that we and our children face today as members of both a national and global community.

The language of educational studies is frequently devoid of any serious or sustained engagement with the concept of society. Such studies are a stunning example of what Jacoby so aptly termed "social amnesia." The focus in these studies of the educational process, it appears, are individuals abstracted from their positions within a historically constituted culture; human beings unrealistically stripped of the results of their lifelong immersion in a socially constructed world. The amnesia that Jacoby referred to is "forgetting" that we come to be who we are through a process in which our very subjectivity is shaped in the institutions of our social world. We are gendered, speak a language, are situated as members of a social class and race, and assume the characteristics of a national or other cultural community. None of these aspects are separated from the relational or social nature of human existence. Indeed, the very predilection to see our individuality apart from its social context is an important manifestation of our social consciousness. It is part of a national ideology that mystifies and distorts the nature of human identity, and is an aspect of a social consciousness that denies its own existence. It is the consequence of a national culture that has historically demanded personal self-sufficiency, promoted an aggressive individualism, and celebrated those who, in search of better things, could appear to tear up their historic ties and communal dependencies.

Our apparently asocial consciousness, however, is not merely intellectually bogus. More important, it is politically crippling. It denies us full awareness of the way in which all of our lives are embedded in social relationships structured through and around conditions of power. From the bedroom to the classroom, office, or factory, social relationships imply political relationships. It should be added, in our particular world, these relationships are generally hierarchical, implying the systematic control of some human beings by others.

What kind of an educational discourse ignores, denies, or forgets the social and political nature of human existence? It is, in fact, one that most students in the United States are exposed to. It is one that puts overwhelming emphasis on psychological perspectives and explanations—(e.g., in the study of learning theories, human development, instructional methodologies, or curriculum planning). Such discourse focuses on the individual student or on the student in interaction with the teacher or the texts and materials that form the curriculum. The theoretical discourse most likely acknowledges a sphere of influence on the student that includes the family and the school as an institution, but little is said about the wider circles of influence that shape human lives, constitute the very conditions and meanings of educational practice, and form our understanding of what school is meant to accomplish in this culture at this particular moment in history.

The limited, circumscribed, nonsociological perspective of most educational theorizing reifies our school world. It teaches us to accept as a given most of what appears in the world. Notions of childhood and adolescence, the roles of student and teacher, the kinds of knowledge considered valid and valuable— all the areas that constitute the educational world—become unquestionable facts of life, not social practices that can be challenged or even transformed.

Not to locate schooling in the larger culture or society is to attempt to grapple with educational issues with an arm tied behind one's back. It is a fraudulent intellectual endeavor that disables those whose business is education and who study education so that they might in some way apprehend the real universe in which they work. Semester after semester, we are confronted by individuals whose often considerable time spent as students in a university department of education has made them social amnesiacs—individuals whose studies in education have excluded any substantial intellectual encounter with their society or culture. Such students are seriously disempowered by a professional discourse that disconnects them from any critical interrogation of the culture that shapes their existence as well as the social circumstance of the young people they will teach. Any expectation that educators truly address their human and ethical responsibilities requires an understanding of the unprecedented, indeed cataclysmic, social forces transforming our world. It requires, at a minimum, some development of what one of our greatest social critics C. Wright Mills called a "sociological imagination." Painfully, we are only too aware of how little opportunity is usually offered to students in professional educational training to acquire this. Nonetheless, the stakes in human lives are too great to abandon the attempt. However limited or blocked the opportunities, our children's future and the fate of the earth are in question; only if educators themselves become educated to the cultural conditions that surround and shape our work is change toward a more just, democratic, and compassionate world possible.

## Notes

1. Richard Shaull, "Introduction" in Paulo Freire, *Pedagogy of the oppressed* (New York: Continuum, 1988), p.15.

# I

▼▼▼▼▼▼▼

# THE FUTURE OF CAPITALISM: CONTRADICTION AND CRISIS

A peculiar feature of American society is that relatively few people, including educators, are willing or able to name the social and economic system in which they live. Whether we choose euphemisms (e.g., "the free enterprise system") or names that avoid the issue of economics altogether ("democratic society"), we shy away from the term *capitalism*. Yet, any attempt to understand or grasp the nature of our world that does not situate our lives in a capitalist society is doomed to irrelevance. It is, after all, in capitalist institutions that most of us spend our hours at work; it is through the market that most of the resources that enable us to survive or flourish are allocated; our national and global life is increasingly dominated by the investment decisions of transnational corporations; and our cultural values and belief systems, in no small measure, serve and legitimize capitalist social relations and practices. Consider, for example, the pervasive effects of advertising, whose subtext is always the need to buy or consume more in order to address such fundamental human concerns as sociability, sexuality, security, femininity and masculinity, or physical well-being. No attempt to address present and future issues in education can be successful if schooling is not related to capitalism. Sociologists of education, in recent years, have documented how schools in the United States (and elsewhere) reproduce the unequal, hierarchical, and competitive structures of capitalist institutions, especially those of the workplace. Schooling simply cannot be understood unless its relationship to capitalist society is recognized. Schools, in the language of critical social theory, are cultural sites that attempt to socialize children in the reigning values, beliefs, meanings, and knowledge required to live and work in this kind of society. Schools are important vehicles for shaping subjectivities compatible with the demands of the corporate world. Of course, schools are not the only avenue for socialization. The mass media, for example, also clearly exert enormous influence. Nonetheless, the powerful role of schools in transmitting capitalist values (such as the emphasis on personal achievement and success, competitive individualism, and the distinctions between work and play) is undeniable.

Although schools are shaped by, and encoded with the imperatives of the wider social and economic system, this is not a fully synchronized process. Schools and other institutions do not work together as a well-oiled machine, each part seamlessly supporting every other part. On the contrary, American society contains explosive conflicts and contradictions. Indeed, as is evident from the readings in this volume, we are in a period of profound instability and crisis, all of which deeply affects education. The readings point, for example, to how the intensified deskilling of labor, the collapse of traditional manufacturing work, the fiscal crisis of the state, the erosion of communal stability, deepening ecological problems, the undermining of moral values, and the spread of violence create crises and dislocations that education is more often called on to address. Yet, it should also be clear that education is far from being only a means to paper over these cracks in the system. It is also an important force in raising demands regarding the unmet promises of American life especially around issues of social justice, democratic rights, and accountability. It is possible to argue that public education, in particular, exists at the intersection of these conflicting demands and expectations of society and will increasingly be subject to the strains and stresses of contradictory social, economic, and political pressures. All of this is documented in the readings in this section as well as elsewhere in this volume.

In chapter 1, Charles Derber describes, in vivid terms, the "wilding" behavior that now grips American life. By "wilding," he means the epidemic of uncontrolled, unconstrained self-interest that increasingly permeates all aspects of our society, bringing with it enormously destructive consequences to our material, moral, and communal existence. In his chapter, Derber considers how this "culture of wilding" has triggered widespread violence that has undermined civic life. In addition, he looks at the disintegration of stable family life with its catastrophic effects on the emotional and material well-being of children. Finally, he considers how this culture of self-interest is leading to an abandonment of society by the country's political leadership. The consequences of this are the destruction of the nation's physical and social infrastructure and the serious erosion of support for institutions concerned with the quality of public health, social services, and education.

In chapter 2, Richard Brosio examines the effects of the profound changes that have occurred in the economy since 1970. These changes, he argues, have meant a tremendous increase in the power of capital to reshape and restructure the nature of work, education, and much else in the society not only here in the United States, but also throughout most of the world. Among its consequences is a proliferation of dead-end, low-wage work and a drastic decrease in the number of stable, middle-class jobs. Indeed, the increased global power of corporations means greater insecurity and impoverishment for many workers who are more vulnerable to the easy mobility of capital around the world. In this same period of economic change, the language and policies of educational reform have more often sought to gear schooling toward big business's industrial and technocratic needs. Brosio argues that reforms have shifted the concerns of education from an earlier commitment to equity for the disadvantaged to the production of a workforce suited to the new international corporate order.

In a similar vein, Svi Shapiro, in chapter 3, looks at the educational policies and discourse of the Clinton administration. He asserts that its central emphasis is on the notion that public education exists to service the needs of corporate America; education is more and more defined in terms of preparing kids for the job market. With this, an almost obsessive concern with the competitive nature of education is developed; the language of performance and accountability pervade schools forcing educators to focus increasingly on test scores and rankings. Shapiro argues that such an emphasis reinforces the uncritical and uncreative character of public education. More significant, it moves education further from a concern for the development of those skills and attitudes that are needed to renew a democratic culture. It does little to link education to the crucial struggle for a more socially responsive, ethically sensitive citizenry capable of addressing our eroding communal relationships and disintegrating civic purpose.

For Phillip Slater (chap. 4), too, schools (and other social institutions) are moving further away from teaching democratic attitudes and behavior and toward greater authoritarianism. The thrust of current educational practices—the obsession with product, with SAT scores, and with grade point averages—is part of a process of discouraging a critical and creative approach to knowledge and reality among young people. The emphasis on the basics expresses an agenda that squelches exploration, discovery, and "putting together old facts in new ways." In this environment, students do not have to think, only remember. Democracy, says Slater, requires independent minds, but school, for most students, is a passive affair that demands little in the way of active or creative learning. In addition, college is not very different. With few exceptions, higher education is a continuation of this authoritarian pedagogy. Its dehumanizing approach to learning is one that emphasizes a bureaucratic and hierarchic approach to knowledge. It insists on students following the most conventional and rigidly policed approaches to so-called truth and understanding.

Finally, in chapter 5, David Korten analyzes the social and ecological crises facing our nation and our world and offers a vision for restructuring our economic and cultural priorities. After nearly 50 years of international development, says Korten, which have led to tremendous growth in the global GNP, "unemployment, poverty, and inequality continue to increase, the social fabric of family and community is disintegrating, and the ability of the ecosystem to support human life is being destroyed" (p. 7). At the same time, the largest corporations have gained a monopolistic control over global markets, finance, and technology, while governments are increasingly forced to pander to these powerful forces. Korten argues that human interests are better served if market economies serve as adjuncts to a *social economy* founded on values of cooperation, sharing, trust, and mutual obligation. This economy would give much greater priority to ensuring that all people have the opportunity to contribute to meeting the needs of family and community, consumption patterns would be regulated by concerns for human equity, and consumption and production constrained by sensitivity to environmental resources.

All of the chapters in this section reject the widespread assumption that education and schools can be understood as phenomena separate from their social and economic contexts. Although professional studies in education continue to emphasize the psychological or developmental life of students, or the internal organizational structure of schools, they egregiously fail to come to grips with education as a part of the social world. Such studies offer little to the struggle for a public discourse that consciously attempts to discern how education could or should address itself to the social, cultural, economic, or political crises that beset the nation and the world. These chapters reflect the development of a powerful set of analyses that attempt to explicate education's connection to the institutions of capitalism and the state. We hope these works encourage educators to begin defining the nature and purposes of their practice in ways that confront its political character.

# 1
▼▼▼▼▼▼▼

# Killing Society:
# The Ungluing of America*

Charles Derber

*A nation never falls but by suicide.*

—Ralph Waldo Emerson

The wilding epidemic has brought American society to a critical divide. American cities and families, for several decades in a state of decline, are now beginning to unravel rapidly. If the forces behind American wilding are allowed to grow, it is possible that the fabric of American social life will decompose.

A degraded individualism, especially in the economy, lies at the root of this decline. Adam Smith, the first great economist of the modern age, articulated the idea of the "invisible hand," the mysterious market mechanism that automatically translates the selfish ambition of each person into the good of all. Always a problematic doctrine, the idea of an invisible hand has now been spun into a dream with almost surreal dimensions. In the good society, a market society, Americans now learn, the supreme virtue is to concentrate feverishly on one's own interests, for by doing so one not only maximizes one's chances of getting ahead, but also performs what George Gilder, whose book *Wealth and Poverty* is discussed in Chapter Three, calls a great "gift" to society. As with the Ik, goodness, in practice, means "filling one's own stomach"; the difference is that an Ik does not pretend that such "goodness" is good for any one else.

An American Dream that does not spell out the moral consequences of unmitigated self-interest threatens to turn the next generation of Americans into wilding machines. In a pattern already visible today, Americans could

---

turn, not only on each other, but on society as well, too self-absorbed to make the commitments and observe the moral constraints that hold stable communities together. There is already abundant evidence that a wilder generation of Americans is assaulting and abandoning society, allowing the guarantees of civilized behavior and the most vital social institutions to languish and die as they pursue their own selfish dreams.

The breakdown of society that I describe in this chapter—violence on the streets, family dissolution, chaos in government—is a cause as well as a consequence of the wilding crisis. The wilding culture poisons families, workplaces, and neighborhoods, which in their weakened form are fertile spawning grounds for more wilding. There is no first cause in this chicken-and-egg causal chain; the wilding virus creates social breakdown and simultaneously grows out of it.

## CIVILIZATION AT THE BREAKING POINT: WILDING IN THE STREETS AND THE UNRAVELING OF SOCIETY

America's culture of wilding, at its extreme, is triggering an epidemic of bizarre and terrifying violence. The new violence constitutes a direct assault on society, undermining the social infrastructure that sustains civilized life.

In November 1989 the *New York Times* reported that ten teenage girls were arrested and "charged with jabbing women with pins in dozens of unprovoked attacks on the Upper West Side over a one-week period." The girls "thought it was fun to run down Broadway," Deputy Police Chief Ronald Fenrich said, and stick "women with pins to see their reactions." The girls expressed some remorse, Fenrich said, although mainly "they were sorry they got caught." Meanwhile, the neighborhood residents, although they had seen more vicious crimes, told reporters that they found the pinprick attacks an "intolerable invasion, both because of the cavalier manner in which the attacks were carried out, and because rumors spread early that it was possible the jabs had come from AIDS-infected needles."[1]

American cities have always been violent places, but the pinprick attacks are emblematic of a new, more menacing violence and a more profound breakdown of social life. Like the expressive wilding in Central Park, it involves taking pleasure in the inflicting of pain and complete indifference to the sensibilities of the victims. For the potential targets—anyone walking the street—the message is to remain hypervigilant and assume that every pedestrian is a potential threat.

The new phenomenon of bystander killings carries a similar message: that no place is safe and that society has become too weak to offer protection. In 1987, Darlene Tiffany Moore, a visitor to Boston, was killed by a stray bullet from nearby gang shooting while sitting on a front porch. By 1990, so many Bostonians had been hit by randomly ricocheting bullets, often inside their own homes, that 47-year-old Dorothy Ingram "sleeps on the floor, fearing stray bullets may come through her windows at night."[2]

The sheer volume of violence is also new. A resident of Ingram's neighborhood says that "the past whole year of 1990 has been killing, killing, killing; somebody got shot, somebody got stabbed. That's all I've been hearing since 1990 began." There is a new expression in Boston neighborhoods, "twenty-four-and-seven-kids," referring to children whose mothers keep them in the house twenty-four hours a day, seven days a week, because they fear for their safety.

The horrifying image of children killing children has helped define the 1990s. In October 1994 two Chicago boys, ages 10 and 11, threw a 5-year-old child, Erik Morris, to his death from a 14th floor window. The reason: Erik had refused to steal candy for them. Erik's 8-year-old brother had desperately tried to save him but was overpowered by the bigger boys.

A month earlier, Chicagoan Robert Sandifer, age 11, was killed by two boys, ages 14 and 16, who feared that Sandifer would squeal about their gang activities to police. Sandifer, shortly before his own murder, had killed a 14-year-old girl, Shavan Dean, when he fired a volley of bullets into a group of teenagers playing football. Young Sandifer was buried with his teddy bear.

On Halloween night, 1994, a 16-year-old killed Boston's youngest street-violence victim, Jermaine Goffigan, murdered on his ninth birthday. Only a few hours before his death, Goffigan's third-grade class had thrown him a surprise birthday party. Like Shavan Dean, another complete innocent, Goffigan had the misfortune to be in a crowd of kids mistakenly shot up in a mass gang shooting.

Children themselves are terrified in many neighborhoods. 14-year-old Chirll Rivers is a Boston student who says she's scared: "I don't want to die. You have to watch your back every day. Someone could mistake you for someone else and shoot you. I could be the wrong person."[3] Another kid, forced to walk home from a youth program after a van broke down, collapsed in a panic, crying "I can't walk home, I just can't walk home. Someone got killed on my street, I'll get killed too." The *Boston Globe* reported that this youth got home, running all the way, but in the next eight days, three young men did not have the same luck, killed on the same street, while a fourth was fatally shot through the window of his mother's apartment." The result of this unprecedented epidemic of violence, the *Globe* said, was that increasing numbers of city youths are arming themselves, carrying small knives and pistols tucked into their waistbands or inside their coats."[4]

Omaha Police Chief James Skinner consoled Bostonians that they have plenty of company. "Yes, you're suffering. Yes, it hurts," Skinner said, "but Boston is not alone, it's not unique." In 1990, New York City Mayor David

Dinkens had to order increased police funding after the *New York Times* reported at mid-year that nineteen cabbies had already been murdered, that four children had been killed within a single week in their apartments by stray bullets (called by the tabloids the "Slaughter of the Innocents"), and a sleeping baby had been wounded when a bullet came through the wall of his apartment. Describing it as an unacceptable surge of violence, Dinkens had to take money away from schools, city hospitals, and public transportation to finance additions to the 26,000 police officers already on the force. Felix Rohatyn, the financier known as the man who helped save New York from bankruptcy in the 1970s, feels that far more needs to be done, saying "there is no part of the city where the quality of life is acceptable." Perhaps influenced by the fact that his wife had been robbed three times in the previous few years, once by a bicyclist who ripped a gold chain off her neck on Madison Avenue and another time by a thief who stole her wallet from her handbag on Fifth Avenue, Rohatyn said "there is a qualitative difference today. . . . What you feel is the constant threat of something that's going to happen to you. It's not civilized life to consider yourself lucky when you've been mugged but haven't been killed." Rohatyn says it would not be difficult for him to relocate his business to Denver, but knows that there he would not find things much better.

Many Denverites, like Philip Connaghan, a machine-shop owner, feel they are in a "war for survival." After his shop was burglarized eight times in two years, Connaghan rigged up a shotgun booby trap (a single-barrel shotgun propped up and attached to a tripwire) that led to the death of Michael McComb, who was shot when he tried to break in to Connaghan's store. Connaghan was fined $2,500 and ordered to pay $7,000 restitution to McComb's family, but he received overwhelming support from Denver residents fed up with crime.[5]

In Philadelphia in 1995, District Attorney Lynne Abraham says that "all of our cases now are multiple gunshot executions, houses set on fire and six children burned to death. This," she says of Philadelphia, "is Bosnia."

## SUBURBS, SMALL TOWNS, AND NATIONAL PARKS: NEW WILDING TERRAINS

It is not only city life that is being subverted by the new wilding. In November 1994, six teenagers from Abington Township, a quiet, middle-class suburb of Philadelphia, went on their own wilding spree when they savagely beat Eddie Polec, age 16, to death with clubs and baseball bats. Law-enforcement officials said this might have been part of a "fun outing," although there were reports that the murder was retaliation for the alleged rape of an Abington girl.

One Abington mother, expressing the shock of the community, said, "These are suburban kids—you don't figure them to go bad. It's not their character to be a rough group of kids." An Abington father and Rabbi, Aaron Landes, said, "There was a presupposition we lived in a kind of safe cocoon because we lived in suburbia. There are many families who have struggled to buy a home in suburbia to avoid the urban ills for their children." But suburbs have become cauldrons of both street and domestic violence, including an explosion of child-abuse and neglect cases among educated and professionally successful suburban parents.[6]

Priscilla Dillon, a social worker whose caseload is in Weston, Wellesley, and other posh suburbs of Boston, says that the frequency of suburban "family cris[e]s has escalated by 50% in the last five years." The kids, she says, "act out the frustrations of the family by running away, drinking, doing drugs, confusion. The only difference is that they are not publicized as much they are in the inner city." Suburban social workers say the suburban ethos of success triggers the problem; some highly successful parents "are quite absent from their kids' emotional development" and others, who "have very, very high standards for their children," put "undue pressure" on them to replicate their parents' success.[7]

Some suburbanites are beginning to question the myth of suburbia as haven. Stephen Lutz, a 17-year-old student at Abington High, recently renamed "Murder High," aptly concluded: "Maybe we can learn violence is not a city thing. It's not a suburban thing. It's not an Abington thing. It's a society thing. It can touch you anywhere."[8]

Violence is spreading not only to suburbs but to small towns as well, where crime is growing at an alarming rate. In 1993, the small town of Ayer, Massachusetts, had a higher rate of aggravated assault than either Boston or Worcester, and in 1994 small towns in Massachusetts were experiencing the largest crime rate increases in the state. In the new climate, the traditional friendliness of small towns, ironically, is becoming a spur to crime. In Kewanee, Illinois, a tiny, close community, Roger Harlow, a 48-year-old Sunday school teacher, was arrested and charged with over eighty-five bur-glaries in December 1994, mostly in homes of his friends and business acquaintances. Harlow would invite friends out to lunch and arrive late after stopping to burglarize their homes. Darrell Johnson, a country club and Elks associate of Harlow, said, "I'm mad at myself, too, for leaving the house open. Not anymore."[9]

Even our national parks are becoming violent places. Paul Crawford, a national-park ranger who now wears a .357 magnum revolver on his hip alongside his billy club and handcuffs, says, "Fighting, stealing, killing, we get it all. People drop their guard when they come to the parks, and that's why the criminals follow them here." John C. Benjamin, a district ranger, agrees. "I thought I'd be out here protecting the environment," Benjamin says. "I had no idea I would be breaking up bar fights, investigating murders and making reports on assaults."[10]

National park officials in Washington have called for bulletproof vests for their rangers. "Things have gotten a lot more intense," says Robert C. Mariott. "It used to be that we'd run into a belligerent drunk occasionally. But now," says Mariott, rangers routinely "run into people who are confrontational and violent." Ranger Robert L. McGhee was shot to death in Mississippi after "making a traffic stop on a park road." Drug rings have been uncovered in several national parks, and officials say that the parks have become stalking grounds for bands of thieves hunting automobiles, camera equipment, and jewelry.[11]

People come to national parks to restore their faith in society. A Detroit truck driver says one of the reasons he likes camping is that in the park he "can leave things in the tent. . . . It's not like the city, where you have to lock everything up." But Jenn DeRosa, a New Jerseyite who camped across the country with her friend Steve Grillo and had her bicycle, money, and all her credit cards stolen, today prepares for camping as if she were a hardened inner-city dweller. "I feel pretty safe," DeRosa says, because she now carries a knife.[12]


## THE MURDER CAPITAL OF THE WORLD:
## CRIME IN AMERICA

All over the country, people are plagued by an intensifying fear of violence. The Figgie Report, a national survey on fear of crime, indicates that four out of five Americans "are afraid of being assaulted, robbed, raped, or murdered." An estimated 90 percent of Americans lock their doors, and more than half "dress plainly" to avoid attracting the attention of violent criminals. Over 50 million households stock guns, including a rapidly growing arsenal of automatic assault weapons, to ward off attack.[13]

Violence has always been endemic in the United States, but national statistics suggest we are entering a new era. In 1990, violent crime in America hit a record high, including 23,348 murders, prompting Delaware Senator Joseph Biden to dub it the "bloodiest year in American history." Private security expenses—for walled or wired homes, guns, and armed guards—rose from $20 billion in 1980 to $52 billion in 1990. Thirty-four percent of the American population said they felt "truly desperate" about rising violence.[14]

In 1993, violent crime hit another peak, rising over 5.9 percent from 1992 to about 11 million reported cases—an astonishing rate of 51.5 cases per 1,000 people over the age of 12. Although FBI statistics showed a 3 percent decline in violent crime over the first half of 1994, a period of economic recovery, a special Justice Department report issued in late 1994, based on lengthy interviews with 100,000 Americans, concluded that violent crime was actually still rising. The study revealed that official FBI data severely under-represent American violence, with over half of all crimes not reported to law enforcement agencies. In 1995, compared to 1955, the rates of robberies and aggravated assaults have gone up sixfold, rapes have tripled, and the overall major-crime rate has quadrupled.[15]

The epidemic is most severe among youth. Gang violence against the young has been the fastest-growing type of killing in the nation, increasing 371 percent from 1980 to 1992. The percentage of people charged with murder who are under 18 has also been growing explosively, increasing 165 percent between 1985 and 1993, as has the percentage of victims who are teenagers and younger children. Psychologist Charles Patrick Ewing reports a burgeoning epidemic of murders by juveniles—in 1995, about 4,000 homicides. "I'm terribly pessimistic," Ewing said. He showed that the number of murders by youths doubled between 1984 and 1990 and will likely "quadruple by the end of the century." Youth suicide is also at a near all-time high: In 1995 it was more than double the rate of 1970. Paul Bracy, director of the Massachusetts Department of Health's Office of Violence, says flatly that the "youth violence we're experiencing in this country has never been to this level before." The *Journal of the American Medical Association* reports that the toll is enormous, with almost four out of every five deaths among youth between 15 and 24 years of age due to accidents, homicides, and suicides.[16]

The murder rate in 1995 will be about two-and-a-half times that of 1960. As a Senate Judiciary report noted soberly, "We are by far the most murderous industrialized nation in the world." British, Japanese, and Germans kill each other one-tenth as often as Americans do.[17]

## DOMESTIC VIOLENCE RUN AMOK: WILDING IN THE KITCHEN AND THE BEDROOM

One of the remarkable things about Ik society is the complete unraveling of the family. Consumed by the desperate quest to get food, an Ik views family obligations as "insane." Family members, the Ik believe, are either "burdens" or competitors, in either case an obstacle to filling one's own stomach. The Ik are quick to cast off old parents and children, whom they view as "useless appendages." Bila, an unexceptional Ik mother, frequently took her baby to the fields, hoping a predator would take it away. When a leopard finally made off with it, she "was delighted. She was rid of the child and no longer had to carry it about and feed it."[18]

An extreme wilding culture spells death for the family, as it does for society as a whole. The family is ultimately a set of demanding social obligations and commitments, requiring a sense of moral obligation and a robust capacity to think beyond oneself.

America's own wilding culture seems at first blush to be reinforcing the family rather than subverting it. Wilding has made the outside world a dangerous place. To protect themselves, journalist Chris Black writes, "citizens have hunkered down with their nuclear families and turned their homes into suburban bunkers against the threats" outside. Sociologist Ray Oldenburg says that as the sense of community erodes and the city streets become scary, "we have replaced the ideal community with the ideal private home." Americans try to keep off the streets, spending time with family rather than friends, watching videos at home rather than venturing out to the movies. Marketing consultant Faith Popcorn calls the trend "cocooning"—escaping into the warm bosom of one's own family and home in order to tune out the rest of the world. The family, in Christopher Lasch's phrase, beckons as the only "haven in a heartless world."[19]

Families, however, are always more a mirror of the outside world than a barrier against it, and wilding on the outside is helping to unglue the American family, turning it into an unstable and increasingly heartless haven. As Americans harden themselves to survive on the streets and compete at work, they make more conditional family commitments and may be becoming more indifferent or violent toward the people to whom they are closest. Taking violence as one indicator, veteran researchers Richard J. Gelles and Murray A. Straus report: "The cruel irony of staying home because one fears violence in the streets is that the real danger of personal attack *is in the home*. Offenders are not strangers climbing through windows, but loved ones, family members."[20]

In 1995, approximately 5,000 Americans murdered someone in their immediate family—about half of these killing a spouse and the other half a parent, child, or sibling—accounting for almost 25 percent of all murders in the country. A staggering number of Americans are physically assaulted by family members each year, including over 1.5 million elderly victims, over 2 million children, and more than 2 million wives who are severely beaten by their husbands. In America a wife is beaten, the FBI estimates, every thirty seconds, and over 40 percent of the most brutally beaten, according to researchers William Stacey and Anson Shupe, are pregnant at the time. The fantastic obsession with the O.J. Simpson case partly reflects the epidemic of expressive wilding in the form of spousal abuse that is poisoning America in the 1990s.

As for children and the elderly, the greatest threat comes not from strangers, the *Boston Globe* reports, "but overwhelmingly from their families," where new forms of abuse are on the rise. Despite all the publicity on TV and milk cartons about strangers snatching kids, the *Globe* notes, there are no more than 300 such cases a year, whereas there are now "more than

160,000 family abductions annually, and nearly 60,000 youngsters expelled from their homes and refused reentry." Typical of elderly victims, who get less public attention than battered spouses and abused or abandoned children, is a 77-year-old California woman who told police her son repeatedly "hit her on the head with beer bottles," a 71-year-old Massachusetts man who "suffered a six-inch gash in his forehead when his son struck him with a frying pan," and an 80-year-old California grandmother who was imprisoned by her grandsons. She was "isolated from all outside contact" while they cashed her Social Security checks and depleted her bank account.[21]

Representative Edward R. Roybal of California, reporting a House Aging Committee finding of a 50 percent increase in family violence against the elderly from 1980 to 1990, calls it a "crisis of epic proportions." Similarly, official statistics show astronomical increases of anywhere from 100 to 400 percent since the mid-1970s in the rate of child abuse. It is impossible to be certain that family violence is increasing, for the figures may simply reflect better reporting techniques. Nor do we know that the modern American family is more violent than families throughout history, which have often been "cradles of violence." In ancient civilizations, including the Greek and Roman, as well as among the Gauls, Celts, and Scandinavians, newborn babies were routinely drowned in rivers, abandoned as prey for birds or other predators, and buried in dung piles. One historian concludes that a large percentage of eighteenth-century European and American children, subjected to routine beatings and indentured labor, would be considered battered children today.[22]

## THE UNGLUED FAMILY: DIVORCE, SINGLES, AND THE SOCIOLOGY OF THE HEART IN THE "POSTMARITAL" ERA

Whether or not it is becoming more violent, the American family is clearly becoming a less stable institution; the traditional bonds between spouses and between parents and children eroding so rapidly that some fear the nuclear family may not survive the next century. Senator Patrick Moynihan, reviewing evidence that only 6 percent of black children and 30 percent of white children will grow up with both parents, says we are already in a "postmarital" society. "The scale of marital breakdown," writes historian Lawrence Stone, "has no historical precedent that I know of, and seems unique. There has been nothing like it for the last 2,000 years, and probably much longer."[23]

At least three long-term, unambiguous trends signal a dramatic ungluing of the family as we have known it: sustained high rates of divorce, a precipitous increase in the number of single-parent households, and an extraordinary increase in the numbers of Americans living outside of any family structure. Demographer James R. Wetzel reports that divorce rates are now holding steady at double those "of the average for the 1950–1964 period, and about triple the average of the 1920s and 1930s." Wetzel estimates that "more than half of all marriages contracted during the 1970s will end in divorce." Among young people marrying today between the ages of 18 and 24, approximately 75 percent will divorce. Marriage is no longer "for better or for worse," but on average for about seven years, after which time a declining number of divorcees will remarry, with an even higher probability of divorcing again for those who do. This decisive breakdown in permanent relationships may be, as Stone suggests, the most important revolution of modern times, a "watershed in the culture of the West."[24]

The number of single-parent households is another revolutionary development, with about 15 million such families in 1994. This is almost triple the number in 1950 and, remarkably, is nearly one-third of the number of "normal" families, that is, the approximately 50 million traditional households with two parents and children. The number of mothers raising children without a husband present has exploded from about 3.5 million in 1950 to approximately 12 million in 1994, including a rapidly growing number of white as well as black women. In 1995, the Census Bureau reported that 30 percent of all families, and 63 percent of black families, were headed by single parents. Demographer Thomas Exter projects a continued mushrooming of such "incomplete" families, with numbers estimated to soar another 16 percent by 2000.[25]

Perhaps the most dramatic signal of family unraveling is the number of Americans living outside any family system. "Families were the order of the day early in the twentieth century," Wetzel writes, and as late as 1940, only about 7.5 percent of Americans lived outside of a family. Today, almost 30 percent of households are made up of single or unrelated people and about 25 million Americans now live alone.[26]

The ungluing of the family has been visible for decades, but in the last two decades has been accelerating at an extraordinary pace. The number of single mothers, for example, rose 53 percent from 1950 to 1970, and then increased an astonishing 98 percent between 1970 and 1989. The number of never-married mothers exploded tenfold during the same period, and the percentage of babies born out of wedlock mushroomed from about 5 percent of all births in 1960 to about 27 percent in 1994, constituting over 1.2 million newborns, more than one out of every four births, in that year alone.[27]

The same trends are taking place in European countries and Japan, but the rate in America is out of whack. The U.S. divorce rate is higher than any other country's: four times higher than Japan's, three times higher than England's or France's, and two times higher than Denmark's or Sweden's. The percentage of single-parent households in America is also the highest: almost four times higher than in Japan, almost three times higher than in

Sweden, and two times higher than in England. Moreover, the American rate of increase in single parents far outstrips that of any other country.[28]

Family ungluing, particularly divorce, reflects some positive developments—such as the new freedom of economically independent women to leave bad marriages. But it also reflects the most radical individualistic currents of the modern era, currents far more powerful in America than anywhere else. Traditional family obligations are becoming too confining for a growing segment of Americans. Lawrence Stone argues that since 1960 American "spouses are being traded in almost as cheaply and easily as used cars," reflecting "a moral and cultural shift to untrammeled individualism." This is consistent with a long-term cultural revolution in which people withdraw some of their attachments to their communities in order to gain more freedom for themselves. As early as 1853, Horace Greeley warned of rising divorce as a by-product of an American individualism evolving into virulent egotism, "wherein the Sovereignty of the Individual—that is the right of every man to do pretty nearly as he pleases . . . is visibly gaining ground daily."[29]

As individualism intensifies, the balance of commitment can tilt so far toward the self that the family and other building blocks of society decompose. When individualism turns into rampant wilding, as among the Ik, the family is shredded, leaving atomized individuals to prey upon each other. In the Reagan-Bush-Gingrich era, as the line between individualism and wilding blurs, the American family suffers its own form of abandonment, strained to the breaking point not only by acute economic pressures but by the burden of its members' self-preoccupation. Americans converted to the reigning ideology of "looking out for number one" are proving ready to sacrifice not only outsiders but their kin on the altar of their own needs and pleasures. Divorce court judge Edward M. Ginsburg concludes that the people passing through his courtroom are so committed to putting their own happiness first that it sometimes reminds him of Rome "just before it all came undone." Ginsburg muses that the role of the family has changed from caring for children to being "eternally in love and having a good time."[30]

Abandonment is a thread common to divorce and broken households. Both reflect choices to preserve the self and enhance personal happiness at the expense of the family unit, a choice that may be rational when no children are involved, but frequently proves catastrophic when they are. L. J. Weitzman, in her study of the children of the divorced, finds that they tend to feel abandoned, often traumatically so. They, indeed, are an abandoned population, if only because divorce is typically "financially a severe blow" for children, who lose the full economic as well as emotional support of two parents. Disruptions such as sale of the family home "adds to the trauma of children," Laurence Stone notes, "who may find themselves suddenly deprived not only of their father but also of their home, their school, their friends, and their economic comforts." Summarizing research findings, *Newsweek* concludes that "divorce has left a devastated generation in its wake."[31]

The experience of stepfamilies shows that the family, once dismantled, is not easily put together again. Testimony to the new age of serial marriage is the fact that one-third of all children born in the 1980s live with a stepparent and more than 7 million kids now live in stepfamilies, often composed of conglomerates of children from several past marriages. Sociologist Frank Furstenberg says that "one of the consistent findings in research is that stepparenthood does not recreate the nuclear family. It does not put the family back together again, in Humpty-Dumpty fashion." Researcher Nicholas Zill says that, psychologically, kids in stepfamilies "most resemble kids in single-parent families—even though they may be living in two-parent households." These children often "feel they've been cast in an outsider role," says Zill, who adds that as a group stepchildren have more emotional and developmental problems and "are more likely to be victims of child abuse, especially sexual abuse." Furstenberg notes that in the stepfamily it is problematic "whether the people we count as kin can be counted on." For one thing, second marriages break up more frequently than first marriages, at an extraordinary 60 to 70 percent divorce rate. "Remarriages are very fragile," says Johns Hopkins researcher Andrew Cherlin. "These couples have gone through one bad marriage and they're determined not to go through another. Their antennae are up . . . and they're prepared to leave." Moreover, many stepparents can truly not be counted on as parents. Esther, a high-school senior in Chicago, says of her stepmother, "It's like having a permanent guest."[32]

The abandonment of children is clearest in single-parent households, whose meteoric upsurge reflects the rise of a generation of young men, themselves abandoned by society, who feel little responsibility for their progeny. The psychological neglect is compounded by economics. According to Senator Moynihan, 55 percent of children in single-parent households live in poverty, and they constitute the core of the 500,000 children who go to sleep homeless every night, the one in four children who have dropped out of high school, and the 14 million children without any health insurance. Ultimate casualties of family disintegration and of the broader wilding culture and the economic policies at its source, the worst off of these children are called by *Newsweek* "American untouchables," reflecting a journalist's reaction to the sight and smell of filthy, impoverished infants and his feelings of shame at "resisting the affections of a tiny child whose entire being seems to emanate pathology." The plight of these victimized children should not obscure the struggles of one-parent children at every income level. Many, like Andy, age 11, do not live in poverty, but live disrupted lives. When he was removed from his mother after she became abusive, Andy went to live with his aunt; but when her residence was sold and she could not bring Andy to her next home, it was left unclear where he would live next.[33]

Within the two-parent household, and at the higher income levels, the larger wilding culture may be leading to a more invisible emotional sabotage of the family and abandonment of children. *Newsweek* opened its special issue on the family with a critique of affluent professionals who prize their careers or BMWs more than their children. The fact that many upper-middle-class young people are taking longer to get college degrees, are flitting across careers, and are waiting longer before getting married and less time before getting divorced, suggests that they find it increasingly difficult to make, in sociologist David Popenoe's words, a "commitment of any kind." This may reflect aborted emotional relations with professional parents too consumed by their own career drives to invest time in their children, who get expensive stereos and cars instead of love. Although most expect to get married and have children of their own, "the prospect fills them with dread."

Summarizing research findings, Kenneth L. Woodward maintains that these children appear to constitute a generation that has "grown accustomed to keeping their options open. There are so many choices to make—in relationships, careers, and consumer goods—that they hate to limit their freedom." Many of these young people, beginning to suffer from their inability to make commitments, are flocking to codependency groups, a rapidly proliferating self-help movement focusing on the emotional devastation wreaked in dysfunctional families, a condition now said to include as many as 90 percent of American families.[34]

Dr. Benjamin Spock, America's best-known "family doctor," sees a direct connection between the undoing of the family and the values of the Reagan-Bush era. "By far the most disturbing force in America today," Spock says, "is excessive competitiveness. It keeps people obsessed with their jobs and with personal advancement," at the expense of feelings for others. Spock argues that the effects on the family are devastating, because it destroys the ethos of kindness and care upon which loving families depend. Spock has put his finger on the essential wilding drama of the current era: unmitigated self-interest inevitably means abandonment of the family and, ultimately, as among the Ik, all social commitments.[35]

## FALLING BRIDGES, POTHOLES, AND PEELING SCHOOLROOM PAINT: THE ABANDONMENT OF SOCIETY

"The limo from the Honolulu airport is a lumbering, battered Buick," writes journalist Tom Ashbrook, noting his first impressions after returning from a ten-year sojourn in Asia. "The doors don't close properly. The seats are stained and torn. The suspension is dropping, cockeyed. The music is mushy.

The paint is extravagantly scarred. The passengers are fat." Images of Japan still in his mind, Ashbrook is deeply concerned.[36]

In Honolulu, Ashbrook again records his impressions. "Hello Occident. Cracked highways, no service. Hotel is heavy on glitter and self-promotional hype, light on everything else. Construction quality shabby. Rusting metal-work. Cheap materials. . . . Rich next to poor. Slick by shabby. Twitchy bag ladies and a legless panhandler croaking 'Aloha.' . . . Korean cabdriver complains road repairs take ten times longer than in Seoul."[37]

"An American homecoming," Ashbrook groans, "is a journey into shades of disarray." It is downright "scary for a recent returnee." Ashbrook learns that his brother-in-law "sleeps with a large pistol in his nightstand and an alarm system that can track a burglar room by room." Turning on the radio, Ashbrook hears of "Los Angeles drivers taking potshots at one another on the freeway, American schoolchildren scoring at the bottom of the First-World heap in key subjects. Drug lords reigning over urban fiefs, Alcoholics Anonymous and its ilk as a new religion. Wall Street sapping the economy." Fresh into his hotel, Ashbrook's son flicks on a Saturday morning cartoon; "Hey fella! This is America," booms the wisecracking voice of an animated hero. "I've got the right to not work any time I want."[38]

The comparison with Asia is too disheartening for Ashbrook. "While veins of efficiency and competence feel ever-expanding in Asia, they appear to be contracting in the United States. Our cracked highways and rusting bridges seem physical reflections of falling standards, organization, simple care in the performance of jobs—of lost resolve." Ashbrook concludes that a "returning American comes home with trepidation," hoping that his or her sense of the breakdown of America "is exaggerated, fearing that it might not be, subtly prepared to accept it as fact."[39]

Ashbrook is seeing the unmistakable signs of a breakdown in both the physical and social infrastructure necessary to keep a society together. America's physical infrastructure, its grid of roads, bridges, railways, ports, air-ports, sewer systems, and communication nodes, is in near-terminal disrepair. This is no surprise to the folks in Covington, Tennessee, where a bridge over the Hatchie River collapsed, sending seven motorists to their death; nor to people in upstate New York, where the collapse of a bridge killed ten people. Nearly half of Massachusetts' twenty-seven bridges are officially "substand-ard." Two-thirds of these are so badly broken-down that they need to be replaced. Moreover, 70 percent of Massachusetts roads are rated "fair" or "poor." Almost everywhere "the nation's roads are crumbling . . . existing highways go unrepaired while new ones seldom advance beyond the blueprint stage. Forty percent of the nation's bridges have serious deficiencies. Air-ports, like highways, are strained beyond capacity, while potential mass transit options go unexplored. Water delivery systems are so antiquated that some cities still transport water through nineteenth-century wooden pipes."

California Democratic Representative Robert T. Matsui says, "The problem is absolutely catastrophic"; perhaps an understatement given the price tag of repair estimated at over $3 trillion, which is three times the size of the annual federal budget and more than the entire national debt. Rebuilding the national infrastructure, Massachusetts Transportation Secretary Frederick P. Salvucci says, "is the greatest public works challenge since the pyramids were built."[40]

As the physical infrastructure collapses, the social infrastructure is being starved, creating an emergency in the provision of affordable housing, jobs at a liveable wage, basic health care, education, and the social services required to sustain the fabric of civilization. The crisis of affordable housing has now yielded "over three million homeless people," writes journalist Michael Albert, "who wander our backstreets eating out of garbage cans and sleeping under tattered newspapers in bedrooms shared with alley-rats." About 14 percent of Americans have fallen through gaping holes in the social safety net and are poor, partly reflecting the unpleasant reality of an economy in decline churning out a high proportion of extremely low-wage jobs: 44 percent of the new jobs created during the 1980s pay less than $7,400 a year, which is 35 percent less than the poverty-level income for a family of four. Over 36 million Americans have no health insurance. This includes one-fifth of all American children, contributing to America's life expectancy being lower and the infant mortality rate higher than in all Western European countries and some Eastern European countries as well. Meanwhile, the collapse of American public education is yielding an average American high-school student who not only has difficulty locating France, Israel, or the United States itself on a map, but scores lower across the board than students in virtually all the other advanced industrialized countries. This is well-understood by American parents who shun the public school system when they can afford to do so. An estimated nine out of ten Boston parents send their children to parochial school or any place other than a Boston public school.[41]

Parents recognize that American public schools are literally disintegrating. A 1995 report by the General Accounting Office showed that 25,000 U.S. schools housing 14 million children need extensive physical rehabilitation, including New York city schools with exposed asbestos, rotting roof beams, and broken plumbing, Montana schools where water leaks led to collapsed ceilings, and the New Orleans school where termites ate books on library shelves and then the shelves themselves. The Education Infrastructure Act, approved by Congress in 1994, allocated $100 million to help fix the problem, but the new Republican Congress sought to cut the funding; it wouldn't have made much of a dent anyway since the GAO estimates it would take $112 billion to do the job, more than a thousand times the amount originally allocated.[42]

This abject unraveling of the entire social fabric is the ultimate manifestation of the new wilding culture, an abandonment of society consciously engineered by the country's political leadership and passively endorsed by the majority of voters. The cost of maintaining and reconstructing its physical and social infrastructure is well within the reach of the world's still richest country; however, in what may be the greatest act of domestic-policy wilding in this century, recent presidents, while continuing to pour billions into the Pentagon's coffers, have refused to support the public spending that would halt and reverse the crumbling infrastructure. This refusal is rationalized under the umbrella of "free market" ideology, to wit rolling back taxes, deficits, and "big government." In contrast, Western European countries such as Belgium, France, West Germany, and the Netherlands, less wealthy than the United States, have managed to preserve much of their social infrastructure by spending a substantially higher percentage of their GNP on health care, education, and a wide range of other social programs.[43]

## THE END OF GOVERNMENT? THE THIRD WAVE AND POLITICAL WILDING

"No new taxes" is the ultimate symbol of the new public-policy wilding, a thirty-second sound bite powerful enough to catapult two presidents into the White House. Cynically fueled by politicians, the so-called tax revolt has created the political space leaders need to defund society, and reflects the war in Americans' hearts and minds between their commitments to society and to themselves. Refusing taxes has become the respectable political vehicle for lashing out at and ultimately abandoning both government and society itself. Future historians may come to view American leaders playing the tax revolt as a sequel to the emperor playing his violin as Rome burned.

While tax cuts were at the heart of the 1980s Reagan Revolution, the tax revolt reached its full head of steam in the 1990s. Newt Gingrich and his Republican colleagues who took over Congress in 1995 put tax-cutting at the center of their Contract With America, proposing to cut $220 billion over five years. The Contract spelled out tax cuts for business investment and capital gains which, as the *New York Times* observed, would not only reward the speculative short-term investments that are sapping the economy, but would shower 30 percent of the tax savings on less than 2 percent of the richest Americans—those making $200,000 or more—and 47 percent of the savings on the richest 10 percent, thereby accelerating the "trickle-up" to the super-rich begun in the 1980s.

To pay for the tax cuts, Republicans proposed $200 billion worth of cuts in education, housing, health, welfare, and other social spending. Liberal critics noted that this meant the poor and the working class—especially poor children—would be paying for the tax cuts. Science, music, lunch programs, and sports in the public schools, health clinics, food stamps, child-care centers, legal aid, and cash income assistance to the poor could go the way of the Edsel. Gingrichites proposed to cut Medicaid, the only source of medical care for 36 million poor and elderly Americans, by as much as $125–200 billion over seven years, to be followed by huge cuts in Medicare, the lifeline of the middle class elderly. These cuts not only punch more and bigger holes in the collapsing infrastructure and safety net, but threaten to terminate the federal government's legal obligation to prevent starvation, illness, and death among dispossessed populations, the subject of our next chapter.

The Contract's tax and spending cuts were part of a systematic plan to dismantle much of the federal government itself. Gingrich described this as part of the historic Third Wave revolution, conceived by futurists Alvin and Heidi Toffler, that would sweep away central government and "devolve" power and resources to state or local governments. Despite the faddishness of the Tofflerian perspective and the dangers of "states' rights movements," which have historically helped preserve segregation and intolerance, Gingrich translated Third Wave "devolution" into a recipe for "zeroing out" a remarkable array of the most socially protective parts of the government. Among the hundreds of agencies targeted for extinction or zero public funding were the Department of Education, the National Public Broadcasting Service, the Department of Housing and Urban Development, the National Endowment for the Humanities, the National Endowment for the Arts, much of the Environmental Protection Agency, and the Federal Drug Administration.

The attacks on the EPA and the FDA make clear that the tax-cutting revolution of the mid-1990s was a wedge designed not to reform but destroy government. The new Contract with America would effectively end the capacity of the EPA to regulate by mandating prohibitively complex or expensive forms of cost-benefit analysis and compensation to property owners, essentially gutting prospects for the Superfund, meaningful enforcement of the Clean Air and Safe Drinking Water Acts, and threatening many of the other environmental, health, and workplace regulations put in place since the New Deal. EPA chief Carol Browner said, "This is about shutting us down, there can be no mistake." As for the FDA, Gingrich has called it "the leading job killer in America" and dubbed FDA Commissioner David Kessler, appointed by President Bush, a "thug." Renowned *New York Times* columnist Anthony Lewis, reviewing the FDA's role in saving Americans from the Thalidomide tragedy, which led to the birth of over 10,000 deformed babies in Europe, recognized the wilding side of the tax-cutting and spending revolution, saying that although there is a need for regulatory reform, "there are some things that a civilized society needs government to do. One of them is to protect its citizens from untested drugs that may do terrible harm."[44] Another is to protect Americans from contaminated meat; as President

Clinton said in 1995, the proposed deregulation would make it difficult to "stop contaminated meat from being sold." Clinton was referring to the recent case of Eric Mueller, a 13-year-old Chicago boy who died after he ate a hamburger with toxic levels of *E. coli* bacteria.

While Speaker Gingrich was leading the assault on the national government, more than thirty states were planning to cut taxes and radically downsize their own governments, led by rising Republican stars such as New Jersey Governor Christine Whitman, New York Governor George Pataki, and Massachusetts Governor William Weld. Whitman gave the GOP response to President Clinton's 1995 State of the Union address to showcase her own 30 percent cut in the state income tax, which critics charged would gut many of New Jersey's crumbing public schools, shut down hospitals and mental-health clinics, undermine the solvency of New Jersey's pension system, and lay off thousands of public employees. Pataki, also elected on the basis of radical tax-cutting fever, is cutting billions in state funds for New York's rotting schools and its increasingly punitive welfare and Medicaid programs. Promising to change "Taxachusetts" into a business paradise, Weld slashed capital gains and business taxes while proposing to cut within months thousands of welfare mothers and their children off the rolls forever. While Whitman, Pataki, and Weld parrot the praises of Tofflerian devolution, they seem unaware of the irony that their programs are undermining the very state and local services that could conceivably replace the federal ones sledge-hammered to death by the Gingrichites.

Although in his 1995 State of the Union address President Clinton repeated his rhetorical commitment to a "New Covenant" for social reconstruction, in practice he rushed to join the Tofflerian and tax revolutions, entering into competition with Republicans to see who could cut taxes and government faster. Not only did he propose his own multibillion dollar tax cuts, targeted largely to the educated middle class rather than the rich or poor, but he also sponsored, in the name of "reinventing government," an unprecedented Democratic war on government itself. Among the agencies that the Clinton administration proposed to eliminate, privatize, or radically shrink were the Federal Aviation Administration, the Department of Transportation, the Interstate Commerce Commission, the Department of Energy, the Department of Housing, the General Services Administration, and the Office of Personnel Management. One hundred and thirty programs, including many for education, scientific research, environmental protection, and welfare would be terminated. As one Washington observer noted: "You expect to see Republicans, when they are in power, do this—it's what they've been pushing for years. But to see Democrats doing it, and to see the competition between the White House and the Congress as they race to privatize—it's amazing."[45]

Making government the enemy has dangerous consequences. The right-wing terrorists who blew up the Alfred P. Murrah Federal Building in

Oklahoma City on April 19, 1995, were influenced by a quarter century of relentless attacks on government by politicians such as Ronald Reagan, Newt Gingrich, and Pat Robertson, talk-show radio personalities such as Rush Limbaugh, and the militant anti-government ideologues who lead the "patriot militias" of the 1990s. Oklahoma bombing suspect Timothy J. McVeigh is not an isolated psychopath but a devoted disciple of extreme right-wing militia movements which have caught fire from Montana to Massachusetts. Such militias teach not only hatred of Jews, Blacks, and immigrants, but a perverted individualism that sees drivers licenses, public schools, and social security cards as extreme infringements on personal freedom. They preach that government is the ultimate enemy of the people and should be demolished through bombings or other acts of sabotage of government installations. McVeigh and thousands of other militia militants are the bastard stepchildren of the conservative free-market fundamentalism that captured much of the nation in the 1980s and mid-1990s, and horrific wilding such as the Oklahoma City bombing will continue until the nation repudiates the extreme antigovernment ideology that is the hallmark of the Gingrich era. Tax cutting can serve the public interest only if it preserves the social infrastructure and protects the poor and middle class, who in the current tax revolution are paying more to support new business depreciation, capital gains, and offshore tax credits for the rich. As for government downsizing, the *New York Times*, noting that only 1 percent of the federal budget goes to welfare for the poor, proposes that human lives and much more money can be saved by slashing corporate welfare, including the billions of dollars now subsidizing agribusiness, oil, and mining industries and the billions more lost in outrageous business tax loopholes.

Jill Lancelot and Ralph De Gennaro suggest a "green scissors" approach to both tax cutting and government pruning which would eliminate tax credits for companies and government programs that are ruining the environment at public expense. For starters, they suggest ending costly give away programs to the big mining corporations, such as the 1995 deal in which the Chevron and Manville corporations sought to pay $10,000 for national forest land in Montana estimated to be worth $4 billion in platinum deposits. To add insult to injury, such publicly subsidized mining deals lead to massive pollution which ends up costing taxpayers an estimated $30 billion more to clean up.[46]

The assault on government is an intimate, perhaps suicidal, wilding dance between leaders and voters. Politicians and business conservatives are orchestrating the dance, according to Bob Kuttner "channeling the raucous popular energy of the tax revolt into an orderly drive for systematic limitations on the welfare state and reductions in taxes on the well-to-do." The rich are using legitimate grievances by overtaxed home owners and working people to reduce their own obligation to society. This proved to be such a fortuitous political recipe for the affluent that it has become the bible of the

Republican Party; however, what has proved to be a guaranteed ticket to
elected office may prove disastrous to society as a whole, for it is doubtful
that a society can survive when those governing it become accessories to its
breakdown.[47]

Ordinary voters are, at minimum, being willingly seduced to dance. John
Powers argues that "cafeteria-style government is on the rise in Massachusetts as more taxpayers believe that they need pay only for what they order.
Yes for plowing, no for schools. Hold the bridge repairs." Powers believes
that Massachusetts voters may be breaking faith with their constitution,
defined as "[a] social compact, by which the whole people covenants with
each Citizen and each Citizen with the whole people." In the tax revolt each
voter is for himself or herself. Elderly and childless couples vote against
raising taxes for schools. The young seek to ration health care for the elderly.
And the well-to-do are prepared to cut back social services for the poor
because in their eyes such programs are wasteful and create dependency.
"Whatever happened," Powers asks, "to the common good?"[48]

Suzanne Gordon, an Arlington, Massachusetts, writer watching her neighbors acquiesce in the closing of one junior high school, two branch libraries,
and the cutback of 30 percent of the city's work force, sees the emergence of
the "No Cares Cohort"—a "vast group of professionals between the ages of
about twenty-five and forty. A lot of them don't have children till they're older,
so they don't have to worry about taking care of them. They're young and
healthy, so the disastrous decline in our health care system doesn't affect them.
If they're married or living with someone, they're probably co-workaholics.
. . . They are as removed from the social contract as those minority kids the
system has truly abandoned." Gordon concludes that "our town is crumbling"
because these residents are content to "sit idly by," with many "sucked into a
swirl of antigovernment, antihuman frenzy. . . . The spirit of generosity seems
to have been executed in Massachusetts, if not in the nation as a whole."[49]

Yet substantial majorities of taxpayers continue to tell pollsters they
support earmarked spending for public universities, universal health care,
and other specifically targeted social services, even as they vote against
general tax increases, suggesting caution in proposing that voters have turned
wholesale into mean-spirited Scrooges. Many voters say that they want to
continue to help those truly in need but see government programs as a
gigantic hoax and a waste, subsidizing bureaucrats rather than the poor. The
public response is as much an attempt to deliver a swift kick to an overfed
public bureaucracy as it is an abandonment of the needy.

My own interviews with about thirty Massachusetts voters suggest that
suburbanites, affluent and geographically insulated from city life, most
closely fit the "mean-spirited" image. Many seem prepared to see the cities
abandoned if their own comfortable lives could be preserved. The wilding
ethos of the suburbs and the more affluent urban neighborhoods expresses

itself less as a frenzied, "antihuman" rage than as an increasingly thick wall that makes the suffering of others emotionally tolerable. Most of the voters I interviewed believe that the larger society may be in danger of falling apart, but find, nonetheless, a remarkable capacity to enjoy their own lives. That a growing segment of the population is hell-bent on having a good time even as they recognize that the ship may be sinking is one of the most telling marks of the new wilding culture.[50]

## NOTES

1. Craig Wolf, "Ten Teen-Age Girls Held in Upper Broadway Pinprick Attacks," *New York Times*, November 4, 1989, p. 27.
2. "Fears Rise of a City Consumed by Violence," *Boston Globe*, March 15, 1990, p. 12.
3. Ibid.
4. Ibid. Sally Jacobs, "As Streets Turn Deadly, Youths Revise Their Survival Code," *Boston Globe*, February 24, 1990, p. 1.
5. "Gang Violence Afflicts Cities Nationwide," *Boston Globe*, March 26, 1990, p. 10. Sam Roberts, "No, This City Is Not the One He Helped Save," *New York Times*, April 12, 1990, p. B1. "Booby Trap Death Brings Fine," *New York Times*, August 22, 1990, p. 8.
6. Michale Janofsky, "A Youth's Fatal Beating Sends Ripples Through Philadelphia," *New York Times*, December 5, 1994, p. A16.
7. Linda Matchan, "Suburban Strife," *Boston Globe*, October 28, 1991, pp. 1, 6.
8. Charisse Jones, "An Act of Youthful Savagery Stuns a Suburb," *New York Times*, November 19, 1994, p. 1.
9. "Friendliness May Have Been Ruse for Burglaries in Small Town," *New York Times*, December 25, 1994, p. 21.
10. Dirk Johnson, "In U.S. Parks, Some Seek Retreat, But Find Crime," *New York Times*, August 21, 1990, pp. 1, A20.
11. Ibid.
12. Ibid.
13. Richard J. Gelles and Murray A. Straus, *Intimate Violence* (New York: Simon and Schuster, 1988), p. 18.
14. Paul H. Robinson, "Moral Credibility and Crime," *Atlantic Monthly*, March 1995, pp. 72–78.
15. Ibid., p. 72.
16. Peter S. Canellos, "Killings by Young Believed on Rise," *Boston Globe*, August 13, 1990, pp. 1, 18. "Boston Tries to Stem Tide of Violence Among Young People," *Boston Globe*, February 25, 1990, p. 31.
17. "Record U.S. Murder Rate Seen," *Boston Globe*, August 1, 1990, p. 1.
18. Turnbull, *Mountain People* (New York: Simon and Schuster, 1987), pp. 133–4, 136.
19. Chris Black, "The High Cost of a Gimme-Gimme Culture," *Boston Globe*, August 26, 1990, pp. A15–16.
20. Gelles and Straus, *Intimate Violence*, p. 18.
21. "Poll: 1 in 4 Jailed Killers Was Friend, Kin of Victim," *Boston Globe*, July 30, 1990, p. 5. William Stacey and Anson Shupe, *The Family Secret* (Boston: Beacon Press, 1983), pp. 2–3, 31, 66. Ethan Bronner, "For Youths, Family More a Threat than Strangers," *Boston Globe*, May 3, 1990, p. 1. Robert A. Rosenblatt, "Abuse of the Elderly, Most Often in Family, Is Soaring, Panel Says," *Boston Globe*, May 1, 1990, p. 10.

22. Lloyd de Mause, (Ed.), *The History of Childhood* (New York: Psychohistory Press, 1974).
23. Patrick Moynihan, "Toward a Post-Industrial Social Policy," *The Public Interest*, Fall, 1989. Lawrence Stone, "The Road to Polygamy," *New York Review of Books*, March 2, 1989, p. 14.
24. James R. Wetzel, "American Families: 75 Years of Change," *Monthly Labor Review*, March 1990, pp. 4–5, 9. Desiree French, "Second Marriages," *Boston Globe*, September 19, 1989, pp. 61–62. Stone, "The Road to Polygamy," pp. 12–15.
25. Wetzel, p. 9. Thomas Exter, "Look Ma, No Spouse," *American Demographics*, March 1990, p. 83. See also Constance Sorrentino, "The Changing Family in International Perspective," *Monthly Labor Review*, March 1990, p. 50.
26. Wetzel, "American Families," p. 11.
27. Ibid. Associated Press, "Over a Quarter of Babies Were Born to Unwed Mothers in '88, Study Finds," *Boston Globe*, June 14, 1991, p. 6.
28. Sorrentino, "The Changing Family," op. cit., pp. 46–47.
29. Stone, "Road to Polygamy," p. 15.
30. Edward Ginsburg, cited in Barbara Carton, "Divorce: What the Judge Sees," *Boston Globe*, May 22, 1991, pp. 79, 81.
31. L. J. Weitzman, *The Divorce Revolution* (Glencoe, IL: Free Press, 1985). Stone, "Road to Polygamy," p. 14. Jerrold Footlick, "What Happened to the Family?" *Newsweek* Special Issue on the Family, 1989, p. 16.
32. Barbara Kantrowitz and Pat Wingert, "Step by Step," *Newsweek* Special Issue, pp. 24, 27, 34.
33. Jonathan Kozol, "The New Untouchables," *Newsweek* Special Issue, p. 52.
34. Kenneth L. Woodward, "Young Beyond Their Years," *Newsweek* Special Issue, p. 57.
35. Dr. Benjamin Spock, "It's All Up to Us," *Newsweek* Special Issue, p. 106.
36. Tom Ashbrook, "A View From the East," *Boston Globe Sunday Magazine*, February 19, 1989, p. 16.
37. Ibid., p. 71.
38. Ibid., pp. 71–72.
39. Ibid., p. 76.
40. Philip Mitchell, "Saving State Roads," *Boston Globe*, March 1990, p. 11. "Aging Roads, Bridges, Get Scant Notice," *Boston Globe*, April 11, 1990, p. 20.
41. Michael Albert, "At the Breaking Point?" *Z Magazine*, May 1990, p. 17. Susan DeMarco and Jim Hightower, "You've Got to Spread It Around," *Mother Jones*, May 1988, p. 36. Irene Sege, "Poverty, Disease, Poor Education Imperil Nation's Youth, Panel Says," *Boston Globe*, April 27, 1990, p. 6.
42. William Honan, "14 Million Pupils in Unsuitable or Unsafe Schools, Report Says," *New York Times*, February 1, 1995, p. A21.
43. "Consensus Fuels Ascent of Europe," *Boston Globe*, May 13, 1990, p. 19.
44. Anthony Lewis, "Reform or Wreck," *New York Times*, January 27, 1995, p. A27.
45. Michael Kelly, "Rip It Up," *New Yorker*, January 23, 1995, pp. 32–39.
46. Jill Lancelot and Ralph de Genero, "Green Scissors Snip $33 Billion," *New York Times*, January 31, 1995, p. A21.
47. Robert Kuttner, *Revolt of the Haves* (New York: Simon and Schuster, 1980), p. 10.
48. John Powers, "Whatever Happened to the Common Good?" *Boston Globe Sunday Magazine*, April 1, 1990, pp. 16–17, 38–42.
49. Suzanne Gordon, "Our Town Crumbles as Residents Idly Sit By," *Boston Globe*, February 24, 1990, pp. A1, A22.
50. These interviews were skillfully carried out by Boston College graduate students David Croteau and Mary Murphy.

# 2

▼▼▼▼▼▼▼

# End of the Millennium: Capitalism's Dynamism, Civic Crises, and Corresponding Consequences for Education

Richard A. Brosio

Radical democrats have regarded the capitalist system as the most important determinant of what occurs—or does not occur—within our complex social–cultural lives. Most struggles for the enhancement of human dignity have taken place on terrains that are importantly established by capitalist power and the class-State; furthermore, democratic struggles have been conducted importantly and necessarily against capitalism. Because I regard the historical regime of capital to be of such causal, if not determinative, importance in relation to civil society (including schools and education in general), my focus is on its power and the continuing reactions to it. I maintain that from its inception, capitalism has caused a response by those who insisted that the economy should be a moral one that serves human needs. This insistence is made by the many who are often described as ordinary men and women, workers, proletarians, minorities, popular forces, and/or subaltern people. This historic struggle is presently characterized as one that insists on the construction of a moral economy, bona fide participatory democracy, respect for diversity, and the broadening of social justice to include everyone. As these progressive changes are achieved, it is more possible for educational experiences to occur that permit and enhance the development of each student to her or his full potential as a human being. Let us turn our attention to an analysis of the radical changes that occurred in the national and global capitalist economies beginning in the 1970s as well as some corresponding consequences for education.

I

Most of the world's economies have undergone basic, structural changes
that have been socially disruptive since 1970. The responses to the threat
facing the Western world order, which was developed during the aftermath
of World War II, are complex and ongoing; moreover, the education communities in the United States and elsewhere have become important parts
of those responses. Fundamental changes in the economy influence and bring
powerful pressures to bear on persons and institutions throughout society,
including schools. Economic changes brought intense pressures to bear on
less powerful and dependent institutions such as schools. These pressures
were directed at convincing or forcing the educational communities to march
correspondingly along the paths chosen by those who are mainly responsible
for the ongoing changes. These pressures, of course, were resisted; however,
much time and energy had to be spent in order to contest such powerful
pressures.

The historical record demonstrates that the capitalist system always featured patterns of economic expansion, interruptions, malfunctions, reces-
sions, and depressions. These dynamic, but disruptive, ups and downs derive
from the lack of any long-term trustworthy mechanism that is capable of
bringing the private aims of capital into equilibrium and accord with the
social needs of the community as a whole. According to Heilbroner, "these
anarchic properties of capitalism follow from the deepest social and historical
properties of the system, and not from circumstantial accidents."[1] Many
observers see intrinsic conflict between the horizontal tendencies of democracy and egalitarianism and the vertical hierarchical realities of contemporary
capitalism. Unfortunately, mainstream economists tend to obscure the deep
political—even ethical—nature of most economic questions. Under conditions of advanced capitalism, the central government (State) must often
interfere in the workings of a "market system" that consistently causes social
problems considered to be intolerable in a democratic system. However,
governmental interference in the economy occurs most often on terms favorable to corporate interests. The State often acts as a partner of powerful
private interests that are seemingly uninterested in the social consequences
of their actions.

The anarchic nature of capitalism and its fundamentally nondemocratic
nature gave rise to corporate power that, in may cases, acts as a private
government. The current form of corporate power most responsible for the
profound economic changes is the multinational corporation. Technology
and capital are introduced into pre-industrial countries and zones without
regard for the needs and desires of the majority of citizens in the new market
areas. Native peoples are attracted, or forced, to new occupations, often
with little regard for their health, security, or self-esteem. All factors are

subservient to the requirements of capital, as represented by the multinational corporation. Governments of countries penetrated by Western culture or other multinationals are pressured to adopt policies that answer to the demands of economic efficiency. These corporations are able to avoid national jurisdiction because they are powerful and are based in many different countries. Such great centralization of private power means exploitation for many of those who are subject to it.

The social relations underlying the pattern of capital accumulation were seriously altered beginning around 1970 because of contradictions in the capitalist system and specifically because of the disruptions and challenges occurring during the 1960s. As we know, the upheavals of the 1960s did not lead to a general breakdown of the system itself; however, the result was a structural crisis of world capitalism. A *structural crisis* is one in which it becomes impossible to expand or reproduce the system without a transformation or reorganization of the basic characteristics of production, distribution, and management as well as their translation to different kinds of social organizations.[2] The structural crisis caused profound alterations in economic and social life, as we shall see.

The late 1960s and early 1970s were a time of the weakening of American predominance in economic, political, and social terms. The defeat in Vietnam is a spectacular manifestation of this erosion. There were many reasons for the weakening of U.S. predominance—for example, the growing competition of other capitalist powers, the dramatic emergence of the Organization of Petroleum Exporting Countries (OPEC) power with resulting skyrocketing petroleum prices, the growing deficit and balance of payments problem, and the crisis of the dollar. The emerging parity of Soviet military power exacerbated the crisis for the West. In addition to Vietnam, there occurred mounting resistance by other oppressed people around the world. The 1970s and 1980s crises in Central America are examples of such resistance, as is the great movement of Black power that eventually deconstructed the worst features of an institutionally racist South Africa. In addition to problems abroad, it appeared (for a time) that Western capitalist democratic societies lost a good deal of control over, and allegiance of, members of their own societies. The radical, if not revolutionary, action by American, French, and Italian youth in the late 1960s frightened the establishments in those countries. The political right has assigned other reasons for the troubles. The following are some of those alleged reasons: the cost of the welfare state, an uncooperative, lazy, and incompetent workforce; and the high cost of gains achieved by popular forces since the Great Depression.

The profound economic changes are also characterized by tearing apart the pact between labor and management, which was established during the 1930s and 1940s. This pact or compromise between popular forces and capitalists created conditions that helped cause an acceleration of growth, one that seemed to eliminate class conflict in developed societies of the northern hemisphere. It was thought by many observers that a comparative respite in the long historical battle between the popular forces and those who exercised power over them was developing into a new world order—one within which the prospects for capitalist expansion seemed limitless and the Leftists no longer posed a realistic threat.

The pact between popular forces and capital in the developed core countries, including the United States, featured a significant redistribution of wealth, power, and access, all of which were importantly caused by a weakening of the disciplinary power in worker–boss relations. The social welfare institutions that were put into place during the structural world crisis of the 1930s were kept—and even improved on—during and after World War II. Capital was forced to validate and sanction, in law, the gains achieved by labor in the workplace. However, it is not the case that capital ever accepted American labor as a codetermining partner in formulating economic policy. Capital has always been too strong and labor has always been too weak to achieve anything remotely similar to a partnership. Despite gains made by labor and popular forces, capital is able to exercise predominance throughout most of the industrialized societies.

In spite of this fact, capital was responsible for precipitating the crisis that began in 1970 as it declared war on the gains so painstakingly achieved by popular forces. By the time of Thatcher's victory (as prime minister) in Britain and Reagan's presidency in 1980, we witnessed a new class war, one launched by capital and its allies against the achievements that were commonly called the "welfare state."[3] As was seen, capital developed the multinational corporation in order to get around the restrictions imposed on business, profit, and bossism by the achievements of labor, popular forces, and the political Leftists. Berquist thought that it was in order to protect and develop the activities of the multinational corporations—for the transnational investment of capital on an unprecedented scale—that the whole political, military, monetary, and financial superstructure of the postwar capitalist order was created. The multinational corporation was a product of domestic class struggle that was forced on capitalists by the victory of labor, popular forces, and the Leftists during and after the Great Depression structural crisis of the 1930s.[4] The equilibrium established in the world after the Depression and World War II remained in place until the end of the 1960s. Domestic peace in the United States rested importantly on a foundation of steady economic growth and government transfer payments that grew in absolute terms and as a percentage of the national budget. These transfer payments, chief among them being Social Security, enhanced working-class and middle-class security. As long as no one asked for more than a little security and a little more income each year, the political system could respond without causing basic changes in structure and authority. Questions concerning equitable distribution of wealth, income, and power were not part of the agenda—except for a few Leftists and mainly during the 1960s. There was little opposition to the massive transfer of capital abroad in search of new markets, lower labor costs, and higher profits. The American people were insistently told that our entry in the world economy was both inevitable and good for everyone—or least for those with talent and energy. Although it is admitted that many persons and firms might suffer during the transition to high-tech internationalism, there has been too little discussion about nondemocratic decision-making and how this may have been the initial and chief cause of the crisis.

The transformation from a dominant production economy to a service one has profound consequences for the organization of American society. First, it provides employment for many women. Second, many high-wage jobs in unionized production industries were lost. Third, the hourly pay in many new jobs is very low. Fourth, many of the new positions are dead-end jobs. Last, these new service jobs, characterized by temporary and part-time employment and women workers, are less protected by union agreements and benefits than those in the old manufacturing industries.[5] Many of the new jobs produce the frivolous products characterizing contemporary retail capitalism. These jobs support the fundamental assertion of contemporary advanced capitalism—the primary requirement for individual self-fulfillment and happiness is the possession and consumption of consumer goods. Furthermore, these new jobs make a mockery of the contention in our civilization that human beings develop their personhood through useful work that transforms potential to bona fide human usefulness.

Many observers sounded the alarm that movement toward middle-class status has stopped in the United States and that we are seeing the emergence of three rather distinct societies. The first is characterized by comfortable suburbs, occupied by the rich, middle class, and some of the highly skilled, (mostly) White workers. The second society consists of ghettos, barrios, and places in which deskilled workers and their families live. According to Davis, this second society features:

> "citizen" rights to a minimal social safety net [but] this enlarged low-wage working class would remain politically divided and disenfranchised, as unions continue to be destroyed and the influence of labor and minorities within the political system declines. With fading hopes of entry into the norm of consumption defined by the boutique lifestyles of the . . . "secure" employment status of the shrunken core workforces of the great corporations, this [second] sector of the nation will increasingly encounter social degradation and relative impoverishment.[6]

The third society consists of irregularly employed workers without citizen rights or access to the political system at all—a society of illegal aliens or

guest workers. Inside the materially comfortable confines of the first society
of yuppie comfort and professional management values, an enlightened psychologically oriented management of human relations prevails, whereas a
more authoritative environment is dominant in the second society. The third
society is described as a *free-fire zone*. Those fortunate persons in the first
society have geared up to defend their advantage over those who have been
cast out from the luxuries of consumer capitalism in America.

This protected favored class supports policies that seek to crush revolutions abroad, which seem to threaten their privileges. The Reagan administrations demonstrated how important defense was viewed by those who have
the power to make decisions in this country. The single, most important
investment trend in the economy was for national defense. Military spending
lay at the heart of the American economy in the 1970s and 1980s; furthermore, even with the end of the Cold War in the late 1980s, the United States
maintains a huge defense establishment and military capabilities. As was
seen, Desert Storm demonstrated our leaders' willingness to use this fire-
power. Military spending is highly compatible with the purposes of contemporary capitalism because it does not interfere with existing areas of profit
making. Furthermore, it does not challenge the class structure or seriously
affect income redistribution possibilities, mainly because of who does—and
does not—enjoy the pay and profit from these jobs. Social spending would
have powerful consequences for all of these things; therefore, it has been
resisted by the defenders of the status quo.

The Reagan administrations made it clear all along that the problem of
inequality was no longer a concern of the federal government. The Clinton
administration has not reversed this development; in fact, the president's
signing of the Republican-led welfare reform bill into law in August 1996
signifies the end of the New Deal commitment for the federal government
to assist the most unfortunate among us. These policies resulted in a redistribution of wealth upward. A drive by the newly rich occurred, initially
under the auspices of Reaganism, to increase social and economic inequality.
More specific, the drive was to expand low-wage jobs, reduce tax overheads
for the rich (and becoming rich), and provide a union-free environment.
Although the rhetoric of the Reagan alliance was against big government,
the real goal was to bring it even more solidly on the side of capital—and
to remove its support from the Left coalition and the welfare payments called
"social wages." The recent administrations and their allies in Congress have
made possible huge profits and salary increases for those who command the
heights of corporate power. "As collective bargained wages were increasing
at less than three percent per annum, a leading firm of management consultants . . . was reporting that the average salary of corporate CEOs had
skyrocketed forty percent since 1980, from $552,000 to $775,000. Similarly
. . . the share of management in the national income had increased from

16.5 percent in 1979 to almost 20 percent in 1983."[7] These facts either reflect a tremendous increase in merit or a riot of hoggishness. The percentage of personal income derived from interest has nearly doubled in the 1980s, rising 24% in the first years of the Reagan administration alone. These trends have not been stopped or rolled back during the first Clinton administration.

## II

Let us direct our focus more specifically to a description and analysis of the corresponding consequences for education, consequences caused by the profound economic changes described. These changes had a continuing impact on education and schooling from the outset; however, the specific educational response became most evident by the time of the famous national education reports in the 1980s. We begin with attention to the national blue-ribbon commission reports.

In the early 1980s, national attention was given to the supposed need for educational reform. The language of this reform was marked by terms like *educational excellence, higher academic standards, harder work, back to basics, emphasis on science, math, and technology, ability to compete internationally, teacher competency*, and so forth. These concerns resulted in a number of policy reports, all of which called for reforms that were presented as being able to improve the quality of American education.[8] An overview of the policy reports includes the following: (a) the need to combat students' abandonment of the core curriculum; (b) warnings against lowered graduation requirements; (c) dangerous grade inflation; (d) disastrous decline of scholastic aptitude scores; (e) poor American comparisons with students from other industrial nations; (f) some 25 million American adults who were thought to be functionally illiterate; (g) about 13% of American 17-year-olds being functionally illiterate, with the rate jumping to 40% among minority youth; and (h) business and military leaders complaining that they were required to spend millions of dollars on remedial education and training.

The reports' underlying assumptions appear to be based on the fear that the United States was being overtaken by other nations in commerce, industry, science, and technology.[9] The reports emphasized tougher curricular standards and courses. They proposed more rigorous grading, testing, homework, and discipline. These recommendations were seen against an atmosphere of emergency, urgency, risk, global competition, unilateral disarmament, and so forth.

> All of the reports are concerned that the schools are pressed to play too many social roles, that schools cannot meet all these expectations, and they are in danger of losing sight of their key role of teaching basic skills and the core

academic subjects (math, science, English, foreign language, and history or civics), new skills for computer use, and high-level skills for the world of work and technology. The reports consider the restoration of academic excellence to be the overriding national aim.[10]

In general, the skills that are accentuated in the reports are geared to industrial, business, technocratic, and military needs. Furthermore, some reports advocate that industrial and business leaders participate with school personnel and especially administrators for the purpose of school planning, budgeting, and so on and that courses be conducted realistically about the world of work. Finally, to quote from the report by the National Commission on Excellence in Education, *A Nation At Risk*, " 'If an unfriendly foreign power had attempted to impose on America the mediocre educational performance that exists today, we might well have viewed it as an act of war.' We have in effect, 'been committing an act of unthinkable, unilateral education disarmament.' "[11]

These reports reflect the shift from an earlier commitment to equity for the economically disadvantaged, bilingual, handicapped, and racially discriminated-against youth to an emphasis on those who can easily be helped to become the qualified elite needed for the new business order of contemporary international competition and the disciplining of labor. According to Carnoy and Levin, "the educational response to the economics crisis was to reject the pattern of equality and democratization of education that had characterized the three previous decades in favor of shifting support to private schools and to more advantaged students who were preparing themselves for college careers."[12] The structure and content of the reforms tend to correspond to particular changes in the contemporary workplace.

Apple wrote that the nature of the crisis the reports were responding to is, most importantly, an economic crisis, but looming behind it, lies a crisis in authority relations and of ideology. For the authors of the reports, *economic problems* are those defined by business and industry. The corporate sector that came to dominate American society since the mid-19th century and that pushed the logic of short sighted, "bottom line-ism," deskilling, and subtle domination to new heights is curiously left off the hook for the monumental problems sketched for us by the reports. The current economic crisis is structural and is the most serious since the 1930s. In order to solve it—in an advantageous way for capital and other dominant interests—the educational sector must be made to help prepare the conditions for capitalism's greater control over workers as well as the possibility for greater profits. The gains made by popular and democratic forces must be rolled back. Americans must be educated to see that these former gains are too expensive. We must be made to see that current realities do not allow the preference for democratic and personal rights over capital, property, and profit.

According to this logic, good curricula become those that have easily testable results. Good learning becomes the accumulation of discrete skills and facts that can be evaluated by objective tests. This is a victory for technique as well as for the children of those who make the most important decisions in our country. Berman is convinced that American public schools "have lost any semblance of a coherent philosophy, common purpose, or shared direction."[13] Not one of the educational reports offers the possibility of an emancipatory, democratic, empowering education for students. The proposed reforms seem to hitch students to the purposes of the corporations and the mostly procapitalist central government, with very little intellectual encouragement to think beyond the one-dimensional society, characterized by many consumer choices for some people. The alleged reforms were developed in reaction to the victories achieved by popular and democratic forces in the school and society. As a result of this reaction, American schools are being asked to concentrate more attention and resources on gifted youngsters and to encourage them to excel in math, science, and technology, so that U.S. capitalists can re-establish their economic predominance. Some critics argued that the search for gifted students will worsen the stratification of schools according to social class, race, ethnicity, gender, region, and so forth.

The national reports are seen as attempts by the so-called reformers to lock schools and students into the narrow confines of human capital theory: direct attempts to make the educational system more responsive to the immediate needs of the capitalist-dominated workplace.[14] For example, the widespread concentration on computer use and computer literacy is only part of the larger shift proposed by conservatives in this country. This conservative agenda or discourse has argued for a school atmosphere that emulates so-called market conditions. Schools are to present a Darwinian jungle picture to students so that they come to realize the relevance of social Darwinism. The fit will survive, and fitness is determined by the curricula proposed by the national reports. According to Aronowitz and Giroux, the emerging school is saying, "If you don't learn, 'we' the school will not punish you, *life* will."[15]

Although the members of the national commissions represent many social and professional points of view, the crucial question is to understand which points and agendas are finally represented in the reports. Shapiro argued that, "finding evidence in the reports of diverse, or even oppositional statements concerning what is required in education is not . . . [the] issue here. Such evidence does not refute my claim that the real significance of the educational reports has to do with attempting to remedy the capitalist crisis of falling productivity and the decline of U.S. capital in the world."[16] The fact that there exists popular support for some of the reforms does not allow us to equate popular with authentic democracy, nor with authentically progressive reform. Students of education and society are aware of Rightist populism and how those who fight to maintain control are often successful at converting legitimate grassroots issues into what is best for the maintenance of the status quo.

Because the current crisis of global monopoly capitalism is primarily responsible for the present economic changes, the educational reforms proposed and enacted have corresponded to the economic crisis as defined by capital and its allies. Had the present economic crisis been defined by other social classes, groups, and alliances, the pressure on the educational system would have been different from what we witnessed. Whether or not the reforms of the 1980s will get the school back in sync with the needs of capital remains to be seen.

The 1980s reforms did not take critical citizenship education seriously. There is neither encouragement for teachers to become the kind of critical intellectuals who understand what the underlying assumptions of this status quo are nor about their commitment to educate students about what they discovered. The current reforms speak of fixing up certain losers in the American Darwinian race, but there is no mention of the unfairness of the contest itself. All of the reforms are ones that the secure middle and upper classes can live with and profit from. The programs proposed and enacted surely allow the sons and daughters of the privileged—those who have money, power, and access—to increase their lead over those who have been victimized by social-class, racial, ethnic, and gender inequities. The reforms do not send supplies to those who wish to encourage democratic empowerment and the civic courage to establish such participation. The participation suggested and spoken by the current reforms speak of inclusion in the credentials race, the one-upmanship race, and the right to score well in the merchandise and investment markets of capitalism. It does not speak of the kind of participation that allows de jure democratic power to become de facto by its necessary intrusion into the economic realm—a realm that continues to be mainly controlled by capital and its allies in the State and elsewhere. Those of us who seek bona fide progressive reform must focus our attention on the economy and the power of capital. The following text describes and analyzes, thus far, the crisis of American democracy itself.

III

The following analysis called "The Ruthless United Statesian Economy" represents an update of what was presented thus far in this chapter. Societies here and elsewhere continue to be colonized, saturated, and subjected to capitalism's totalizing logic; furthermore, we have seen the reappearance of ruthless economic policies in countries that feature formal democratic political systems as well as capitalist economies. In a passage that provides great sensitivity to the concrete and human results of post-Cold War shock therapy and triumphant capitalism, Chomsky wrote the following:

> Child poverty in the U.S. is off the scale. Poverty altogether is. The U.S. has the most unequal distribution of wealth of any industrial country, and that has been radically increasing in recent years. . . . New York City has as high a level of inequality as Guatemala, which has the worst record of any country for which there are data . . . [Child poverty and infant mortality are consequences of] social policy. Take . . . family leave . . . most civilized countries nurture that. They want parents to be with children when they're little . . . [The U.S. policy for bonding and care is nonexistent.] That's part of the war against children and parents and in general against poor people that's carried out under the rubric of "family values." The idea is, only rich people should have state support. They have to be subsidized by massive transfer payments. . . . Incidentally, it's not only children who are suffering [from] poverty, but also the elderly. . . . Again, that's a phenomenon unknown in industrial societies, and . . . in poor societies, because there they have support systems, extended families. . . . But we're [the U.S.] unusual. *Civil society has been basically destroyed* [emphasis added]. There is a powerful nanny state, but it's a welfare state for the rich. That's an unusual system, and it comes from having a highly class-conscious business class and not much in the way of organized opposition.[17]

The underdeveloped countries, many of which do not enjoy even minimum political freedom and civil rights, have long suffered as a result of neo-imperial policies being imposed on them by the rich nations of the West and North. The communist and former communist countries also endured hardship as well as inadequate protections against governments that were not (and still are not) bona fide democratic regimes. Having said this, we turn to a more specific description and analysis of how Americans are faring under the so-called "New World Order."

Lorton, who is a member of the American Federation of Government Employees, explained what organized labor's issue priorities should be in response to capital's attempt to foist a new ruthless regime on workers. He argued that there must occur a revival of an insistence on reduced hours at work for those who were forced into overtime, partly in order to reduce workforces in the name of efficiency. Lorton believed that corporate downsizing has only begun. Drawing from Rifkin's work, he asserted that only about 5% of major U.S. corporations actually underwent downsizing and re-engineering so far. He feared the advent of "workerless factories." Unless organized labor can achieve a 30-hour work week, by the beginning of the 21st century, there is little hope of avoiding chronically high levels of unemployment in the United States. Lorton explained the sequence of corporate downsizing as follows: Computers and automation are introduced in place of many workers; profits increase; the remaining workers are forced to work longer hours; this also leads to greater bottom-line profits; the employed workers are frightened by the existence of a growing army of the unemployed, underemployed, and poorly paid; and management's drive to increase profit is camouflaged by terms like *continuous improvement, total quality management, process technology,* and so forth. In Lorton's view:

> While the real purchasing power of the average wage has declined since the 1970s, the average American worker now works 164 hours per year more than he or she did in 1975. That means that in barely two decades the corporations have been able to squeeze a whole extra working month out of the average American worker, but are actually paying less in real terms. . . . This does not even count the additional personal, family, and community strains [conditions that wise educators realize are responsible for many student problems experienced in school and elsewhere] brought on by increased hours of work.[18]

Although productivity significantly increased during the most recent economic upheavals and restructuring, the living standards of most Americans have not improved. Workers who are categorized by U.S. government statisticians as production and nonsupervisory workers saw their earnings fall by 18% between 1973 and 1995. "By contrast, between 1979 and 1989 the real annual pay of corporate chief executives increased by 19 percent, and by 66 percent after taxes."[19] Since the early 1970s, when capital began its push to reorganize the economy, output per person in the private, nonfarm sector rose by 25%; however, increases in real wages have not matched these productivity improvements. Head explained that "this is the first time in American postwar history that the real wages of most workers have failed to increase during a recovery."[20] Many mainstream economists and economic commentators warned about the growing inequalities as a major threat to U.S. society. Rohatyn alerted us to an " 'advanced capitalism' whose 'harsh and cruel climate' imposes 'stringent discipline on its participants.' [In his view,] 'what is occurring is a huge transfer of wealth from lower skilled middle-class American workers to the owners of capital assets and to a new technological aristocracy with a large element of compensation tied to stock values.' "[21] The newly emerging, ruthless United Statesian economy—importantly driven by the application of information technology to work of all kinds—is threatening even those who have been (historically and recently) considered safe in somewhat protected sectors of labor. It is no wonder that social class status anxiety, which afflicts so many people in the United States, fuels a hope, an insistence, that expert use of computers and information technology, in general, provide the advantage over the competition for their daughters and sons as they make their way through the increasingly vocational hurdles of the K through 12 school system. It has not been generally realized by these advocates of computerization that this window of opportunity for them and their children may close sooner than they think. As we know, "re-engineers" learned to combine the skills of certain specialists, clerks, middle managers, et al. into software.

The political Rightists sought to blame the victims of the latest economic-work restructuring for their poor pay, difficult working conditions, and unemployment. It is argued that their personal and family values are not adequate for success. Many educators are convinced that unemployment is mainly caused by inadequate vocational training in secondary schools. This conviction serves to exonerate those who control the command heights of the political economy for the dire straits all too many workers find themselves in presently. Head argued that as lean production methods in Japan reached higher levels of productivity, the need for skilled labor declined. In fact, the so-called "integrated" worker of lean production teams need not have many skills at all. Head explained that when he visited Nissan and Honda plants in Europe, the personnel managers told him that they gave very little importance to educational and vocational qualifications for those who were to work on the shop floor.

> What they were looking for . . . were dexterity, enthusiasm, and an ability to "fit into the team." . . . In a well-known account of lean production in the world auto industry . . . [it was argued] that increased reliance on less-skilled and lower-paid workers was one of the chief selling points of the new system. One advantage of lean production . . . is that it "dramatically lowers the amount of high-wage effort needed to produce a product . . . and it keeps reducing it through continuous incremental improvement."[22]

Educators beware.

My experiences with contemporary workers of many kinds—primarily in the human and retail services—convinced me that one can hardly get any good help these days. Obviously, my use of the Rightist criticism of labor intends a different reading; however, the stupidification of all too many American workers is apparent to many of us who are attentive to workers and their worlds of work. Contrary to the current conventional wisdom, school vocational programs—whatever name they operate under—are not the cure for stupidification, deskilling, unemployed, or underemployed. As is seen, for the most part, schools are criticized by capital and its allies when they do not operate in sync with capitalist and other Rightist imperatives. Much of the current school talk about the need for schools to prepare skilled workers is based on faulty assumptions (e.g., that there are many high-skill jobs to be filled and that job skill can best be taught in schools). The current dominant K through 12 school discourse concerning the need to turn students over to the undemocratic and irrational capitalist world of work demonstrates that capitalist hegemony is alive and well—even among those who allegedly devoted their professional lives to the Deweyan development of the whole person.

Nissen and Seybold argued that the current conventional wisdom about schooling, jobs, and the global economy holds that there exists a skills shortage. Although these claims are superficially plausible they do not correspond to reality. Conservative think tanks, like the Indianapolis-based Hudson Institute, clamored for a transformed public education that better serves the current demands of employers. There are calls for partnerships with business, public responsibility for formerly private-funded training, and of course, a market-driven approach to K through 12 public education.[23] The Indiana Governor's (Evan Bayh) Workforce Proficiency panel assessed skills and proficiencies required (demanded) by employers in the state's major industrial occupations. Nissen and Seybold admitted that there is a type of skills upgrade required for many jobs today; however:

> it is far from that envisioned by proponents of the "skills upgrade" thesis. Basic literacy and numeracy are the critical skills which many Indiana high school graduates lack, but employers require. Here, the woefully poor public school system must do better, but this is not a highly specialized or skilled training we are talking about . . . Most of the "skills" which employers find inadequately developed in today's job applicants are actually *attitudes*, not really skills. Thus, workers should have the "skill" of being a good team member, of being honest with the employer, of faithfully reporting to work punctually, of internalizing the company's attitude toward profitability and customer satisfaction, and so forth. This is not genuine skill being sought, but rather worker attitudes and personal characteristics most useful for company profitability. The truth about skill requirements for jobs of the future is a matter of much dispute, but much evidence indicates that growth in skill requirements beyond basic numeracy and literacy will actually slow down.[24]

As critical students of U.S. schooling have long recognized, the K through 12 schools served as an efficient selecting and sorting machine with regard to the head–hand dichotomy; moreover, proper acceptance and deference were built into this preparation for highly unfair, stratified workplaces. Nissen and Seybold reported that "the dirty secret of present educational reform, known to all but rarely stated, is that employers generally don't want or need a highly trained workforce."[25] In the labor studies writers' view, Braverman's thesis[26] is highly relevant in today's ruthless United Statesian economy, namely that market mechanisms of capitalism do not automatically favor or develop job enrichment and increased skill levels. In fact, the reverse is true. Nissen and Seybold pointed to the U.S. Department of Labor findings concerning the 10 occupations most likely to grow by over a half million jobs between 1992 and 2005. Without denigrating anyone's occupation, Nissen and Seybold listed the following: retail personnel, cashiers, general office clerks, truckdrivers, waiters and waitresses, nursing aides, orderlies, janitors, cleaners, such as maids and housekeepers (not of their

2. CONSEQUENCES FOR EDUCATION

own households), and food preparation workers. Only two of the top occupations listed by the Department of Labor are realistically called high-skill jobs that require extensive training and/or education—registered nurses and systems analysts.

Another of the most recent and ironic examples of worker vulnerability is the elimination of jobs at the Bell-Atlantic sites in Pennsylvania. Noble explained that workers referred to themselves as "Information-Highway Roadkill" in reference to ruthless job elimination in a giant telecommunications industry, supposedly one of the sites where the new good jobs were to be created by the information highway.[27] The "re-engineering" technological aristocracy is closely linked to small groups of top executives; moreover, because of the weakness and or absence of unions, this elite coalition experiences little effective opposition to reforms that fail to benefit everyone in the capitalist work organization. Despite public relations and euphemistic terms intending to soften and/or disguise what will happen to jobs under re-engineering toward lean and mean criteria, the reformers do not ordinarily operate as though workers have legitimate interests that should be negotiated (with compromise being central to such negotiation). There is too little recognition here of the moral need for managers and bosses to be accountable to a democratically constructed view of the common good.

It seems likely, if not obvious, that more and more workers in the United States will be forced to work in a new kind of mass production, capitalist economy, with the odds stacked against them (i.e., they will be forced to accept the verdict of a ruthless market with little citizen-worker protection). A Manpower CEO revealed that a person with a high school diploma can be trained in basic computer skills in only 2 months. There are still jobs for machinists, electricians, plumbers, and so forth, but as Head explained, the demand for such workers is rising at a slow rate and it seems unlikely that their wages earn much more than the inflation rate. There is a demand and high pay for the new technical aristocracy. As we learned from the recent Caterpillar Inc. strike conducted by the United Auto Workers, the company could use temporary help agencies to replace nearly all of the striking shop floor workers. The Clinton administration's claim that job training is a sufficient solution to the problem of static or falling real wages and unemployment does not hold up well under investigation. Growth alone does not result in social and economic justice for the mass of workers in the United States. As we know, the stock market suffers when employment increases.

The capitalist offensive of the last 25 years aimed at increasing profits—as well as the necessary socioeconomic, political, educational, and cultural conditions to achieve this goal—lays bare that the central problem with the U.S. economy is the maldistribution of wealth, not the failure to increase it. The need for powerful countervailing forces is obvious to those who understand the power of capitalism, its allies in the government, and the various

Rightist activist groups. Unmistakably, the central, state, and local governments must be pressured by voters and activists to craft better conditions in which unions and other progressive forces can flourish. The Reagan and Bush administrations were vehemently and effectively anti-union; the Clinton "New Democrat" administration is not actively engaged in trying to enhance the power of organized labor. This administration's leadership role with regard to North American Free Trade Agreement (NAFTA) and General Agreement on Tariffs and Trade (GATT) left union members deeply suspicious of Clinton. Citizen-workers must be part of an educative process by which they again come to realize (as they first learned in the 1930s) that politics, direct action, and ultimately legislation are their/our only opportunity with regard to forcing a human face on the ruthless United Statesian economy. One hopes that were this series of informed collective actions to occur, the experience of engagement and struggle would convince enough people that capitalism, as a system, must be overcome.

In conclusion, the last few years of the second millennium feature many problems, but some possibilities, for educators and others who seek to construct a participatory democracy as well as a just society that features good schooling for all and continuing education that allows us to understand and act on the social and physical world(s) in which we live. Although the K through 12 institutional school and postsecondary education are places of great importance for progressive democrats to struggle upon for a more inclusive, participatory, and just society, these sites must be seen as inextricably connected to extramural ones—including the larger civil society, government, and of course, the capitalist system. It must be said that such a struggle is difficult. Any serious student of educational history realizes that progressive school reform is difficult to achieve. When it is accomplished, it will be due to committed persons participating in broad coalitions outside of school politics. This is not a project for just brave educators and their students; furthermore, it will surely fail if limited to a 5-year plan or becoming the best by the year 2000. The actors must be committed to the struggle for the duration—a very long march.

The democratic imperative upon schools in the U.S. has been most effective when it has taken the form of common-sense *opposition* to education as mere vocational preparation and *support* of education for broad personal development. Educators, parents, and students have a long and rich record of seeking to promote school practices that are based upon inclusion, fairness, enrichment, individual and personalized instruction, and citizenship, as well as understanding why the art of Mozart, Dizzy Gillespie, [Astrud Gilberto] et al. is "relevant." All of the [effort] must be encouraged and continued. Two cheers for what has been done, but the third cheer awaits the overcoming of the capitalism that we endure.[28]

## NOTES

1. Robert L. Heilbroner, *Marxism For and Against* (New York: W. W. Norton & Company, 1980), p. 132.
2. Manuel Castells, *The Economic Crisis and American Society* (Princeton University Press, 1980), p. 8.
3. Frances Fox Piven and Richard A. Cloward, *The New Class War: Reagan's Attack on the Welfare State and Its Consequences* (New York: Pantheon Books, 1982), passim.
4. Charles Berquist, ed., *Labor in the Capitalist World Economy* (Beverly Hills, CA: Sage Publications, 1984), p. 9.
5. Emma Rothschild, "Reagan and the Real America," *The New York Review of Books* 28, no. 1 (February 5, 1981), pp. 12–13.
6. Mike Davis, *Prisoners of the American Dream* (London: Verso, 1986), p. 304.
7. Ibid., p. 234.
8. The five national reports on education published in 1983 were: (a) *Academic Preparation for College* (The College Board), (b) *Making the Grade* (Twentieth Century Fund), (c) *Educating Americans for the 21st Century* (National Science Foundation), (d) *Action for Excellence* (Education Commission of the States), and (e) *A Nation At Risk* (The National Commission on Excellence in Education).
9. Allan C. Ornstein and Daniel U. Levine, *An Introduction to the Foundation of Education*, 3rd ed., (Boston: Houghton Mifflin Co., 1984), pp. 464–65.
10. Ibid., p. 468.
11. Ibid., p. 471.
12. Martin Carnoy and Henry Levin, *Schooling and Work in the Democratic State* (Stanford, CA: Stanford University Press, 1985), p. 260.
13. Edward H. Berman, "The Improbability of Meaningful Educational Reform," *The Education Digest* 52, no. 2 (October, 1986): p. 2
14. Carnoy and Levin, *Schooling and Work in the Democratic State*, p. 223.
15. Stanley Aronowitz and Henry A. Giroux, *Education Under Siege* (South Hadley, MA: Bergin & Garvey, Pub., Inc., 1985), p. 191.
16. Svi Shapiro, "Reply to Stedman," *Educational Theory* 37, no. 1 (Winter 1987), p. 77.
17. Noam Chomsky, *Class Warfare: Interviews with David Barsamian* (Monroe, Maine: Common Courage Press, 1996), pp. 34–5.
18. Brad Lorton, "Our Time Famine: Labor's Issue in the 21st Century," *Labor News* (Indiana) 31, no. 1 (April 1996), p. 19.
19. Simon Head, "The New Ruthless Economy," *The New York Review of Books* 43, no. 4 (February 29, 1996), p. 47.
20. Ibid. The U.S. economy entered its sixth year of recovery from the recession of 1990-91.
21. Ibid.
22. Ibid., p. 48.
23. For more on school-business partnerships see, Richard A. Brosio, "The Present Economic Sea Changes And The Corresponding Consequences For Education," *Educational Foundations*, no. 3 (Fall 1987): 4–38. See especially, "Examples from Indiana," pp. 29–30.
24. Bruce Nissen and Peter Seybold, "Labor and Monopoly Capital In the Labor Education Context," *Monthly Review* 46, no. 6 (November 1994), p. 42.
25. Ibid., p. 43.
26. See Harry Braverman, *Labor and Monopoly Capitalism: The Degradation of Work in the Twentieth Century* (New York and London: Monthly Review Press, 1974).
27. David Noble, "The Truth About The Information Highway," *Monthly Review* 47, no. 2 (June 1995), pp. 47–9.
28. Richard A. Brosio, *A Radical Democratic Critique Of Capitalist Education* (New York: Peter Lang Publishing, Inc., 1994), pp. 538–39.

# 3

▼▼▼▼▼▼▼

# Clinton and Education:
# Policies Without Meaning*

Svi Shapiro

Even by the conventional criteria of education professionals, the Clinton administration's first-year efforts at education reform have been modest. This is not to say that some of your priorities are unimportant. Certainly, for example, the shift in emphasis toward early childhood needs is welcome and overdue. We have come to recognize the United States' shameful record in immunization against childhood diseases, and the crying need for more resources and a more systematic approach to addressing the public health crisis of young children. In addition, we welcome the attempt to direct more resources to the funding of Headstart programs, given the increasing impoverishment of America's children. Your initiative to make college loans more available is also welcome. We are supportive of Secretary of Labor Robert B. Reich's attempts to establish effective job-training programs. And we appreciate the administration's proposals to encourage more flexibility and innovation at the local level in teaching and educational programs, since the dead hand of educational bureaucracy is widely recognized for its enervating effect on reform and experimentation.

Your proposals represent a significant shift in outlook, if not in outlays. The actual increases in funding in education proposed by your administration are, in fact, disappointingly small. The 1994 budget included only a small increase in discretionary spending over the Bush administration's last allocations. This year's budget will provide a modest increase in these funds (although it is true that education would be one of only a handful of agencies to receive *any* increase). Yet it is clear that this administration is concerned

*Reprinted from TIKKUN MAGAZINE, A BI-MONTHLY JEWISH CRITIQUE OF POLITICS, CULTURE, AND SOCIETY. TIKKUN, 251 West 100th Street, 5th floor, New York, NY 10025.

about redressing the social neglect of the Reagan/Bush era, and we support this greater sensitivity to the needs of the young, the recognition of the gross inequities that exist in the funding of school programs and resources, and your attention to families' growing difficulty meeting the costs of higher education.

Despite this turn in mood, rhetoric and, to a more limited degree, resources, however, I am both wary and disappointed with your emerging approach to both the language and policies of education. However serious the crisis of jobs in this country is—and you rightly have identified the erosion of meaningful, secure, and decently rewarded work—your attempt to define the value of education primarily in *vocationally related* terms is misguided. As Tom Hayden stressed in a recent issue of TIKKUN ("Running in Place," January/February 1994) the core of your administration's reform pragmatism "is subsumed within a larger ideology which promotes corporate expansion. 'Making us competitive again' is only the current slogan of this worldview." According to this view, clearly articulated in the writings of Labor Secretary Reich, the core of America's problems is the failure of "our" corporations to be effective players in the world market. Reich's solution is vigorous state action to lay the human groundwork for a rejuvenated American economy. This means greatly expanded government initiatives and investment in research and development, and in education, oriented to what the economists call the enhancement of "human capital," including development of apprenticeship programs and greater investments in vocational training.

The most alarming feature of your approach to education is the greatly increased emphasis on the notion that public education exists to service the needs of corporate America, *that education is preeminently about preparing kids for the job market*. Of course, this view of the purpose of schooling was not invented by Reich or other members of your administration. From its inception, public education has always been seen, and served, as a training ground for employers concerned about prospective employees having the right technical skills and, even more important, the right attitudes to authority and alienating work. But it is disappointing and dismaying that your administration is attempting to relegitimate this educational philosophy by framing the public discourse of education in economic terms.

It is easy to forget, in the constant reiteration of this discourse and its association with images of electronic super-highways and new computer technologies, that there is another American tradition and language concerning the purpose and meaning of education—one that connects people, especially the young, to the making of a democratic culture. It is about creating and nurturing the individual's capabilities to live critically aware, humanly sensitive, and socially responsible lives. In the press of powerful class interests, racism, and the widespread influence of positivist values, this paradigm has never been dominant in the public struggle to define the goals of education. It does persist nonetheless in the ideals, and sometimes the practices, of American educators. Sadly, there is little room in the ideological framework of expanding markets and corporate development for an educational philosophy that might emphasize this democratic tradition.

Let me remind you, however, that there does not have to be an unbridgeable divide between work preparation and democratic education. Indeed, some of the most interesting recent ideas about the rejuvenation of the American workplace have emphasized the importance of allowing employees to assume much more decision-making power. Experiments in decentralized management, quality circles, job rotation, and cooperative decision-making have questioned the traditional, hierarchical form of corporate control as the means to higher productivity. Where workers share in the power over the work process there are clear gains in product quality, and other beneficial results such as reductions in absenteeism.

The value of more democratically structured workplaces suggests that public education must do more than teach workers how to use machines or to master technology. Our schools need to educate individuals in cooperative work, collective responsibility, negotiation of priorities, and conflict resolution. In such settings, workers will need to consider critical economic and human issues that include the environmental impact of particular production decisions, the effects on workers' security and labor of the adoption of specific technologies, or the consequences of investment decisions on employees and their communities.

If you are to take the possibility of more democratically managed workplaces seriously, you must urge the adoption of a different approach to decision-making in schools. Schools will need to become what John Dewey many years ago called "laboratories of democracy"—places where students of all ages begin to experience empowerment in their everyday lives. In this sense, work-related education becomes not simply job training, but a genuine form of critical, cultural education where the broad human, social, economic, and environmental consequences of one's work can be, and often are, in question.

And to take seriously the notion of school as a place where democracy is learned—not merely through books but as a matter of experience—means to confront how thoroughly disempowering today's typical American schools are. Contrary to our myths, our public schools are not places where young people learn what it means to live and work in a democratic environment.

The linchpin of "Goals 2000"—the major education bill of your administration in 1994—is the push for national standards and methods of assessment throughout public education. Yet nothing is more likely to reinforce the uncritical and uncreative character of public education than this added emphasis on so-called "performance standards." Such an approach to education will, in all likelihood, exacerbate the trend toward conformist teaching in the nation's schools. It is destined to increase the concern with tests and testing among teachers and educational administrators, while further increasing the levels of boredom and alienation already so pervasive among students. This is the latest consequence of the educational reform movement that began in the early 1980s with the publication of the report, "A Nation At Risk," which blamed America's economic decline on failing schools. It has, as a result, managed to turn public education into what education critic David Purpel has dubbed "public evaluation."

Increasingly, schools and schooling are dominated by a concern with testing. During the 1980s and '90s, the number of standardized tests administered to students during their pre-college years has increased by almost 400 percent. The laudable notion of public accountability in education has been reduced to the obsessive and destructive charting of test numbers. Teachers are compelled to "teach to the test" in order to ensure their jobs. Not surprisingly, the result for teachers is work without creative, imaginative, or intellectual content. Like many other forms of contemporary labor, teaching has been progressively deskilled, as education administrators and policymakers insist on the use of what radical scholar Michael Apple has called "teacher-proof" curricula that will mechanistically produce the desired results.

As we have striven to keep up with the Japanese, we have placed evergreater emphasis on the competitive nature of education; one result is an obsessive concern with how students, schools, and their administrative units are doing vis-à-vis one another. As the language of performance and accountability in education pervades our schools, educators, parents, and kids focus on test scores, ranking, and the need to get ahead.

And, of course, there will be no surprises in such a system about which segments of the population will come out on top. Educational achievement in this sense has always mirrored—and legitimated—our grossly inequitable social structure. Vast differences in the material and cultural resources available to different groups will ensure that success in schools reflects the deep inequalities between races and classes in American society.

Viewed through the prism of hopes, expectations, and opportunities, America's children attend schools that can only be described as worlds apart. Family socioeconomic background is the primary predictor of educational achievement. Increasingly, minority children attend schools that are physically dilapidated, overcrowded, with the greatest problems of teacher turnover, gangs, and violence. Your administration's emphasis on national standards will heighten the degree to which education is understood as a contest for a limited supply of rewards; school will become a place that emphasizes winning and losing—getting ahead of one's neighbor, whether that neighbor is across the street, the town, or across the world.

But beyond the moral implication of this increasing emphasis on testing and performance in the discourse of schooling, you should be concerned about its equally deleterious effects on pedagogy. Tom Popkewitz, a radical critic of schools, is probably correct when he observes that more and more power is being given to teachers to decide less and less. The attempt to authorize national performance standards across the curriculum of elementary and secondary schools represents a continuation of a 1990 Bush administration initiative calling for the establishment of "world-class" standards for what students should know and be able to do in five core subject areas. Four years later you have proposed setting up a national panel that would review and certify the standards in these and additional areas (the arts, civics, English, foreign language, geography, history, and science).

This effort comes at a time when many states are introducing similar policies. At the last count, at least forty-five states are planning, developing, or implementing new curriculum standards. In their present form, the content and evaluation standards often run to hundreds of pages, and elementary teachers teaching several subjects would be confronted with thousands of pages of regulations and standards. The job of translating these standards into the everyday work of teaching would likely fall to curriculum supervisors at the state or district level—a paradoxical development, given the parallel attempt in public education to shift more administrative power to classroom teachers. Talk of empowering teachers rings hollow when the very heart of the teaching process—the design and conceptualization of the curriculum—is removed from teachers' purview: Decisions about what to teach, when to teach, and how to evaluate students' work fall under the control of one's supervisors. For those of us who argue that schools need to be places that model democratic values and nurture a democratic culture, this trend signals an antithetical authoritarian and dehumanizing view of education. It is not only teachers who suffer as a result of these policies. Study after study in recent years has noted the pervasive boredom and alienation of students toward the ostensible primary purpose of schools—academic instruction. This alienation is reflected in the popular culture—just about every recent popular movie and television show depicting adolescent life conveys the disdain, irrelevance, and meaninglessness that kids feel toward school. For those of us who watch these portrayals, humor and fascination is tempered by great sadness about what they reveal of kids' cynicism toward learning and the school experience.

Yet their cynicism is easily understandable. In a world in which a 1991 federal survey of U.S. high school students reported that 27 percent had "thought seriously" about committing suicide (including 8 percent who had made an attempt), the daily grind of school subjects is, to a large extent, existentially without meaning or purpose. Much of what goes on in the classroom is disconnected from the lives, interests, dreams, fears, anxieties, and concerns of young people. School is felt to be the real venue of trivial pursuit.

Without the intensifying drumbeat of warnings about the current job market and the fate of those who do not possess the necessary credentials to enter the competition, how many students would actually spend time in school? If we actually measured the levels of school drop-outs to include not only the third or so who physically drop out, but also those who mentally and emotionally do so, we might have to recognize the utter futility of policies and talk about higher levels of performance, more content, and academic excellence.

Such hollow education-speak is rooted in what the great Brazilian educator Paulo Freire called the "banking method" of education. Freire noted how much of the educational process treats students not as active producers of knowledge, but as empty vessels who we attempt to "fill up" with curriculum material. Kids, however, experience this content as remote and abstracted from their real lives. It is, in a real sense, meaningless knowledge; reified information that might be memorized by students and regurgitated in a subsequent test or examination, but has little use as a means to help students gain some critical understanding of the world that confronts them.

Freire and other educators have noted that this concern with transmitting subject matter and covering content has little to do with educating people in ways that might begin to empower them or imbue their lives with meaning. Indeed, it does the opposite, by teaching students that successful schooling requires an altogether passive and uncritical attitude toward the words of teachers and texts. Classrooms are rarely places where students learn to question the taken-for-granted assumptions and beliefs of the culture. They are seldom spaces where they learn the meaning of democratic values by challenging social myths or realities. Nor are they places where knowledge is actively constructed by students as they bring their own lives and experiences into a dialogue with the understandings of others. They rarely create situations where individual and communal meanings can be forged out of the voices, memories, and wisdom of other human beings.

The language of increased content, higher levels of performance, and improved test scores—sadly, the language of your administration's educational policies—will only continue and exacerbate this confusion of schooling with some genuine, humanly liberating, and meaningful education. It will ensure that many students (especially older ones) will continue to find school deadening and oppressive; a place where their own lives in all of their particularity and difference will find little resonance in the curriculum that confronts them.

This lack of connection is especially acute among those for whom schools have historically offered little—the poor, minorities, and working-class students. For them, the oppressiveness of schooling is compounded by an even more stark separation of the classroom from the culture of the streets and the neighborhood. It is a gap that has been documented in the ludicrous and/or minimal images of such groups in textbooks, in the inattention of the curriculum to their experiences, history, and lives, and in the ways that schools track and exclude students from less favored backgrounds. The documentation makes clear how schools create cultures that silence and invalidate students—a process that, not surprisingly, frequently produces in students hostility and resistance to the official culture of schools. In this sense, the poor educational performance of minority students is a deliberate response to a school experience that continues to demean and exclude them.

The greatest disappointment of your administration's approach to education is not in what you've proposed, but in what is missing. Your approach is overwhelmingly technocratic in its stress on making systems more effective and efficient and its view of education as an investment in human capital, ensuring that talent is not wasted. Educationally, it is an approach without heart or soul, a discourse about education that accepts liberalism's excision from it of moral and spiritual concerns. It is a language that reduces the education of the young to skills, knowledge, and competencies, one that accepts a disastrously limited view of what it means to nurture a new generation for a world in crisis and pain. It is a view of education that bears none of the marks of your own formative "educational" experiences; of what it means to grow up in a time when the real curriculum meant grappling passionately with the life and death issues of one's world. Nor is there any sense of why for your own child you and Hillary would choose a Quaker school, part of an educational tradition based in progressive moral concerns and commitments. It is one of the profoundly instructive political lessons of our time that the Right has been so willing and able to invoke moral claims and purposes in its social and cultural agenda—a process that has been analyzed with great insight in the pages of this magazine. The Left, in contrast, continues to defend church-state separation and academic freedom and offers a view of education that is largely bereft of spiritual affirmation or moral conviction. While we understand the demagoguery surrounding the Right's appeals to family values and its intolerance of those whose lives do not fit some preordained condition of virtue, or the hypocrisy of those who call for religious prayer in school while they sanction a more callous social order, we cannot dismiss the popular hunger for such talk. We, and even more our children, face a world that is spiritually desiccated and ethically a wasteland, where communal purpose and individual meaning are absent for so many. In this context, the Right has been correct in arguing that education must be connected to some moral purpose or vision.

It is indeed time to say that education is about more than higher test scores, advancing industrial productivity, and improving human capital. Real educational change should be linked to the struggle for a politics of meaning, asserting clearly that at the heart of the educational enterprise are questions of human purpose and social vision—what does it mean to be human, and how should we live together? Education, at its core, is *not* about the trans-mission of information or skills, but is the quest for lives lived together more fully and meaningfully. While the issue of our children's economic futures is legitimate and must be addressed, education encompasses far more. And you, like most parents, know it.

Whatever else it may be expected to accomplish, education's role in shaping human consciousness and communal purpose must be affirmed and reaffirmed. Education must be understood as a cultural act—an important means through which we, and especially the young, develop a sense of what our lives are about and what it means to live with others in community. Through it we may learn how to envision our future and decide what values and beliefs we might live by.

The struggle for a politics of educational meaning is thus not fundamen-tally a battle for the passage of one sort of policy or another so much as the struggle for a new language of educational purpose. It is the struggle to change the public discourse of education to reshape the moral and social commitments that underpin our educational work. And in this we call upon you, a progressive president, to act as a force in the re-articulation and affirmation of our nation's educational goals. Politics here is to be understood not in its instrumental, legislative sense, but as pedagogy—attempting to influence and reshape the concerns, hopes, and aspirations of citizens.

You can use your presidency as a bully pulpit, to make clear to the nation that education is about more than grades, test-scores, or even jobs. The character of our community, the vitality of our democracy, and the sense of individual purpose and meaning depend on it. And there is nothing especially radical about such ideas. They are deeply rooted in American traditions of public education—traditions that have always linked education to the quality of communal and civic life.

If you champion this vision, it will be vying with a number of competing possibilities. We have, for example, seen the repressive and intolerant versions recently articulated by Pat Robertson, Bill Bennett, and their followers. Yet they have tapped into themes such as the erosion of community and the decline of personal responsibility that have a wide and resonant appeal and must be understood as speaking to critical moral dimensions of our lives and the lives of our children. These same themes can and ought to be central to the struggle for a new progressive language of educational purpose. Indeed, you have shown a remarkable ability to harness them to other areas of social policy, though, sadly, not yet in education.

It is clear, for example, that across a wide spectrum of American life there is a deep sense of the socially irresponsible nature of our culture—we see the irresponsibility mirrored in the callous and ubiquitous use of guns, the fathers who refuse responsibility for their offspring, the rapacious corporate behavior that produces toxic environments, and the Wall Street speculators making millions of dollars as they destroy the livelihoods of American workers. There is a strong and growing sense of the decay of communal values and concerns, and the need to address this by infusing a sense of care and mutuality into our shared life.

This crisis of responsibility is deeply rooted in the structures and practices of our society, yet I believe there is potentially wide support for a model of schooling concerned to develop an attitude of care for others (as well as for our natural environment). It is an attitude that might start with the value of helping the sick, the elderly, or those who are alone, and extend to the value of addressing the effects of social injustice whether among the poor, those with AIDS, the homeless, immigrants, the handicapped, or the victims of discrimination on the basis of race or other forms of identity. At the core of this educational goal is the regeneration of the sense of meaningful and concerned citizenship among the young—offering a different vision of social life from the now-pervasive sense of apathy, disinterest, and cynicism.

Your recently enacted national service plan is a small but important step toward expanding civic engagement and awareness among young people. If you stress the ethical impulse behind this program, not just the fact that it may help pay college tuition, it can become a valuable part of an educational vision centered on the renewal of our civic life.

In this context of civic concern and social responsibility there is a place for discipline. The debate over discipline, although often expressed in unduly restrictive and punitive ways, resonates through a wide cross-section of the adult population. A progressive, ethically infused, educational process needs to help redefine what discipline might mean. It does not translate into simply exerting control, managing behavior, or exacting a mindless compliance with the rules of the institution. None of this is good for the nurturing of a democratic culture where thoughtful and questioning behavior are prized, and dissent encouraged.

Yet the deep salience of the discourse of discipline stems from Americans' sense of the world as increasingly chaotic, insecure, and threatening, concerns that cut across the political spectrum. The leading advocacy group for young people, The Children's Defense Fund, in its most recent annual report argued that epidemic poverty, joblessness, racial intolerance, and family disintegration have been eclipsed by the "greater crisis of children killing children." The report notes that between 1979 and 1991 almost 50,000 children were killed by guns, a figure equivalent to the number of Americans killed in the Vietnam War.

In this context, discipline means acting in ways that are mindful of the needs and rights of others. It arises from social standards and moral behavior that resist the disregard for human life shown on our streets, just as it opposes wasteful and unrestrained consumerism and the irresponsible destruction of the Earth and its resources. Inculcating this sort of discipline requires teaching methods that contest the indifference, callousness, and self-indulgence of our individual and collective behaviors, conveying the importance of acting with regard to limits and with respect for human life (indeed, of all life).

The call for education stressing community, meaning, and moral purpose is rooted in a rich tradition of educational thinking and practice. It must be built around curricula created out of the desire to address the concerns and hopes of students' lives through the process of critical reflection, teachers who encourage young people to pursue questions of personal meaning and moral commitment, and classrooms in which the fundamental concern is the cultivation of human care and sensitivity to our neighbors and to the Earth.

Critical to the notion of a politics of meaning is the belief that so-called ordinary people are deeply concerned with issues that go beyond questions of income, material interests, and economic rights. Among these are questions of community, the meaningfulness of our lives, the care and dignity in our treatment at work or at home. They are issues that speak to the nature of our moral and spiritual lives, or more accurately, to the present crisis in these dimensions of our lives. It is deeply disappointing that in your tenure as president, you have not yet sought to connect education—that part of our society whose concern is explicitly and uniquely with the development and well-being of the young—to these concerns. Instead, you have relied on a vision of our future focused on jobs, markets, and technology with little to offer on more fundamental matters—identity, connection to others, or the meaning of democratic life.

We have not seen the last of Pat Robertson's Christian Coalition or of William Bennett's call for a "curriculum of virtue." And there are others waiting in the wings ready to respond to the crisis of meaning through education with prescriptions that are equally or more coercive and reactionary. This is the time for you and those in your administration to widen the focus of your educational lens, to transcend its limited technocratic and corporate view of what is really at stake and to begin to reclaim the moral vision and human concerns that must be the heart and soul in educating a new generation. In making this point to educators, I often recall the words of one principal who, at the beginning of each school year, sends this note to the teachers in her school:

> Dear Teacher:
> I am a survivor of a concentration camp. My eyes saw what no man should witness:
> Gas chambers built by *learned* engineers. Children poisoned by *educated* physicians. Infants killed by *trained* nurses. Women and babies shot and burned by *high school* and *college* graduates.
> So I am suspicious of education.

My request is: Help your students become human. Your efforts must never produce learned monsters, skilled psychopaths, educated Eichmanns.

Reading, writing, and arithmetic are important only if they serve to make our children more humane.

# 4

# Learning the Ropes*

Philip Slater

> *[Schools are] machines for forcing spurious learning on children in order that your universities may stamp them as educated men when they have finally lost all power to think for themselves.*
> —George Bernard Shaw

> *In the education of our young people it is not enough to teach them their "duty,"* . . . *there must be created for them . . . a world of high purpose to which their own psychic energies will instinctively respond.*
> —Mary Parker Follett, *The New State*

Cultural patterns are imbibed in infancy. What the child learns in the mini-society of the family is often accepted as the way the world is, even in the face of radically new experiences later in life. A child raised in an authoritarian family—where unquestioning obedience is demanded, discipline is severe, the parents secretive, and the child encouraged to hate various kinds of strangers—may grow up, even in a democracy, believing that authoritarianism is normal and psychological slavery a sign of character and moral rectitude.

People brought up in this way are uncomfortable with democracy and never really accept its premises. Yet they are too well trained in obedience to rebel overtly against their society's principles. Their solution to this dilemma is to pay the most fervent devotion to the words and subvert the principles themselves. We see this a great deal today: self-proclaimed super-patriots talking raptly of democracy while opposing its principles in practice.

---

## THE AUTHORITARIAN FAMILY MYTH

In our society it has long been believed that at some time in the past this strict authoritarian family was the norm, but that at some recent date some benign or misguided (depending on your viewpoint) person persuaded American parents to become "child-oriented" and "permissive." What is peculiar about this myth is that it has existed ever since the Pilgrims landed. There is no time in the history of our nation when Americans didn't believe that previous generations were brought up with a severity only recently abandoned—each generation believing itself to have newly discovered, or been newly victimized by, "permissiveness."

Foreign visitors to American shores, on the other hand, exclaim with horrified unanimity—from 1650 to the present day—that American children are spoiled, overindulged, demanding, intrusive, and rowdy—even in the "best" families—and that their presence makes intelligent adult discourse impossible.

In each period there have been many individual families structured on authoritarian lines (several million, after all, would still be a tiny minority today). But most American parents have tended to act from a conviction that children represent the future, and should be allowed to grow into that future with as little archaic baggage as possible. This conviction is based on a realistic assessment of American conditions. Ever since the first settlers arrived, parents have noticed the ease with which their children were able to adapt to life here, having known no other. They spoke the language better, understood the culture better, felt more at home with technological change and the increasingly man-made environment.

It is folly, in other words, to bring up children in rigid accordance with some parental formula when conditions are changing so rapidly that by the time the children grow up that formula may no longer apply. Children will always be better adapted to a changing environment than their parents—less committed to obsolete agendas. The democratic family—like democracy itself—is a system that maximizes the availability of agenda-free individuals. In a democracy, as Follett says, the goal of education is to train citizens in "the power to make a new choice at every moment."

In the past decade this characteristic American child-orientedness has undergone a severe decline. According to a recent congressional study, we now stand last among industrialized nations in providing for our children.

## "THE PEOPLE ARE CHILDREN"

Authoritarian individuals like to use the parent-child relation as a model for political relationships—the rulers seen as parents who guide, protect, and discipline the silly, unruly masses, who are so very likely to do the wrong thing because the simple creatures don't know what's good for them.

This analogy is badly flawed, for the authoritarian ideal is static—masters remain masters and slaves remain slaves—but children grow up and in time supersede their parents.

Democratic families try to facilitate this process and prepare their children for self-mastery. Authoritarians resist it in both the family and the body politic. Authoritarian parents try to maintain social inequality even with middle-aged children, and authoritarian rulers are antagonistic to anything that will help the public "grow up"—such as the exposure of secrets or the expenditure of funds for education.

This difference reflects the contrasting educational goals of democrats and authoritarians. In a democracy, the fundamental goal of education is *development*. For authoritarians it is *obedience*. What authoritarians want children to learn is their "place" in society. The idea of children becoming curious, creative, or original gives them hives.

To the authoritarian mind the world is permanent and fixed—any departure from their rectilinear concept of it is seen as decay. Society is a series of slots, and education a process of molding people to fit into those slots. To the authoritarian, children are not complex beings of infinite and uncharted potentiality—they are simply a sloppy throng of round pegs in desperate need of being squared up.

## THE "BASICS" IN AN AUTHORITARIAN SOCIETY

This is the reason why authoritarian educators call for "a return to basics," and the elimination of "educational frills." The "basics" are the basics of two centuries ago, the "frills" are attempts—some successful, some not—to involve students in the present and the future. Underlying these so-called frills is the idea that the natural curiosity and motivation of the student should be kept alive at all costs. For boredom is the greatest enemy of learning, and when the brightest students find school boring—as they usually do in traditional authoritarian schools—it is an incalculable loss.

But there is a hidden agenda in this concern with "basics." What characterizes "the basics" above all is that they are fixed and arbitrary. The student is told how to write, how to spell, how to add and subtract, what to read and how to interpret what is read. There is very little room for exploration, for discovery, for putting together old facts in new ways. There is no need to think, only to remember. It is the intellectual equivalent of boot camp.

The call for "a return to basics" has a covert message, which can be translated simply as "we should spend less money on education." The authoritarian senses intuitively that an ignorant populace is more likely to be an obedient one. Less money for education means larger classes. Larger classes mean that less time will be spent learning and more time keeping order. Students in such classes will learn little except how to take orders and how to keep quiet.

Children learn by doing. This is how we learn to walk and talk, to ride a bike, to drive a car. We don't learn by sitting straight in a chair and having someone tell us how to do it. "As we perform a certain activity," Mary Parker Follett reminds us, "our thought towards it changes and that changes our activity." But in a large, authoritarian classroom there is very little opportunity for doing, only for rote repetition and the application of un-analyzed principles and formulae. There is little true education here—students are merely taught to take a great deal of nonsense on faith. This will prepare them to live in the kind of society in which authoritarians feel comfortable—where people know only what their ruler chooses to tell them and authority is never questioned—but it is an abominable preparation for life in a free democratic society.

A first-grade teacher once told me about going into a new school and finding the students all sitting mutely at their desks. "It was so *quiet*! How can they learn anything if they're not talking?" Her response was based on the democratic approach of learning by doing, by experimenting and testing the world and making knowledge your own.

Democracy is based on participation, and if students are not in a position to participate, what are they being prepared for? Democracy also depends on informed and independent minds, and how can they inform themselves if they are taught from their earliest years to remain passive no matter what nonsense is being stuffed down their throats?

The thrust of our current educational system—the obsession with product, with SAT scores, with grade-point averages—leads naturally to the mentally moribund college student who asks continually, "Will this be on the exam?" and thence smoothly forward to the bureaucrat who wants everything in writing so he can "cover his ass," and who trusts only what can be quantified and manipulated statistically. The kind of bureaucrat who can't see people in front of him—only their files, ID numbers, and constructed résumés. The kind of bureaucrat who is skilled at finding flaws and imperfections, but couldn't recognize a new idea if it bit him on the neck and drew blood.

Early in 1989 the National Assessment of Educational Progress reported that students taught by traditional methods were unable to reason or think for themselves, and that teachers would have to become less authoritarian for more sophisticated learning to occur. This was no news to good teachers, and will probably be ignored by the authoritarians who so often make educational policy.

The middle-class American child has at least a chance of receiving an education in which this kind of active, participatory learning is possible. But most working-class children are packed into classrooms that are run like boot camps and help track them into authoritarian work situations. Our educational system—despite all the rags-to-riches myths attached to it—seems designed to maintain a rigid class structure with as little movement between the classes as possible. Our schools—especially as crippled by the authoritarian policies of the last decade—seem designed to keep people stuck in the social stratum into which they were born.

The Carnegie Foundation for the Advancement of Teaching found in a recent study that more than two-thirds of the nation's teachers instruct children who live in poverty, who are undernourished, in poor health, abused, or neglected. This is a sorry record for a democracy, for a nation that believes itself to be child-centered, for a nation that pretends to believe in the future.

## EXTRACURRICULAR "BASICS"

School isn't the only way children learn. The world is brimming with information, available to any active, curious person. Even TV, our most loathed and yet most used source of information, probably gives the child more information in a week about the society he or she lives in than the average authoritarian school does in a year. It is a distorted and unreal picture, but in comparison with the average American history text it comes off rather well. Both contain more fantasy than reality, but the TV fantasies are at least current.

The big problem with TV (as so many critics have pointed out) is that, like the authoritarian school, it encourages passivity. If participation is the soul of democracy then anything that encourages spectatorship is to be viewed with mistrust, and it cannot be denied that TV has replaced innumerable participatory activities. While the *content* of TV is ambiguous from a democratic viewpoint, the *process* of TV watching is inherently destructive to democracy.

Another unfortunate trend is the increasing bureaucratization of athletic activities for children (Little League, etc.). When children play by themselves they are training for democracy. The uncertainties and imperfections of available playing fields ("if it hits the tree it's a double"), and the fluctuating numbers of players ("you got Louie so we get the extra player") call for the continual making, modifying, and discarding of rules. This is done collectively, by agreement. No adult is around to hand down edicts or resolve disputes. All free play, physical and otherwise, is democracy in action, and has been since the beginning of time.

Much of this is now gone. Adults have usurped the play of children and converted it into an authoritarian activity. Adults establish the rules and enforce them; there is no democratic negotiation. In many contests I have seen, the adults seem more obsessed with the outcome than the players. They scream with rage over the failings of their own and other people's children. The games do not seem to be played for pleasure, only to win—perhaps to bring some vicarious triumphs into the unsatisfying lives of the parents. The children learn to be competitive and follow orders—excellent training for the army—but they do not learn how to live in a democratic society. From a democratic viewpoint, the intrusion of adults into the play of children must be deemed an unqualified disaster.

Children raised with a basically democratic vision can survive many authoritarian experiences without altering that vision. I myself was educated in traditional schools, and although I was intensely bored, I can't say I was marked by it. It was simply a waste of time and a lost opportunity for learning. I played the game and succeeded, but it never once occurred to me that there was any connection between the avid reading I did on my own and what went on in school. (Like many people, I developed an almost permanent loathing for authors whose books we had to read in school.) That school could be a place where ideas were exchanged—where you could think and talk about important questions—was inconceivable.

For me the authoritarianism of school was balanced by the democracy of play. But if *all* a child's experiences are framed in an authoritarian mode, some of it will begin to rub off; and it is disconcerting that the typical American childhood seems to be drifting in that direction.


## ADVANCED "BASICS"

For the rapidly decreasing number of Americans who are able to afford it, college is supposed to restore a modicum of democracy to the educational process, but this is true in only a very small number of settings. For students at many universities—especially the larger ones—college is simply high school all over again, one more dehumanizing bureaucracy. As Baritz points out, "higher education is as bureaucratic in its form and substance as the military."

Authoritarianism in education takes forms so familiar to us that it seems almost persnickety to call attention to them. My intent is merely to show how deeply and comfortably embedded we are in our authoritarian past, not to argue that this or that pedagogical custom will stunt growth or engender political masochism. Each may in and of itself be harmless.

The most obvious authoritarian holdover in education is the obsession with ranking—with placing individuals above and below one another on some sort of scale. We do this first of all by the system of consecutive classes—first grade, second grade, junior, senior, etc.—which takes no account of the fact that people do not learn in numbered increments, but in bursts, and at uneven and unpredictable rates. Nor is intelligence measured out in years, or in accumulated obedience. Yet people are defined this way, by category ("she's a senior"). And within each "class" (the word itself is revealing) students are ranked by grades, and defined as such ("she's an A student").

In addition, the material to be learned is arranged in artificial categories, and artificial rankings are created within these. This system is a vestige of the slaveholding tradition of keeping information hidden from the subject classes—protecting it with esoteric jargon. Medicine, law, and many of the sciences, for example, disguise very commonplace ideas in Greek and Latin terminology whose only function is to hide understanding from the "common" people.

## ACADEMIC BORDER GUARDS

The division of knowledge into departments or disciplines is a holdover from feudal real estate customs and the obsession with classification that afflicted the medieval clergy. James Gleick, in his book on chaos theory, points out that this system is a serious impediment to scientific progress and tends to block the acceptance of new ideas. Scientific revolutions, he observes, tend to arise from people "straying outside the normal bounds of their specialties." Chaos theorists—the current revolutionaries in science—were all interdisciplinary mavericks, and all met with resistance and hostility. For years their interests were considered illegitimate, their research proposals turned down, their thesis prospectuses rejected, their articles refused for publication.

Each discipline, furthermore, is structured hierarchically, so that the student is forced to learn the material in certain order. In many cases this order is completely arbitrary. There are some areas of knowledge that presuppose others, but this is the exception rather than the rule. The main function of this rigid control is to ensure that the student learns to look at reality through the lenses of that particular discipline—absorbing its conventions, prejudices, and worldview.

This is not a conscious goal, of course. Most academics sincerely believe that there is only one path to the truth and the student must be led carefully along it. But fashions change, even in the sciences, and the truth of one decade becomes the quackery of the next, as when doctors say, without a shred of embarrassment or diminution of arrogance, "Oh, we no longer do that operation—we *now* believe . . ." or a scientist says, "No reputable biologist (chemist, physicist, paleontologist, or whatever) thinks *that* anymore."

But the discarding of useless academic fashions and outmoded theories would take place a lot more quickly if students weren't required to absorb information in quite so controlled a manner. Learning at a university is a little like being taken through the spook house at an amusement park—one has the sense of going on a long twisting road, but when you turn the lights on it's just one little room with a lot of corners and a winding bit of track. To turn on the lights—to learn things in the "wrong" order—would shake up traditional arrangements of ideas. It is no accident that some of the most creative and radical thinkers in every era have been self-educated.

This turnstile approach to education—which says, in effect, that if you want to go to New York or San Francisco you must first spend specified amounts of time in Memphis, Indianapolis, Oklahoma City, Butte, and Phoenix—is not only cumbersome but demotivating. Why not let the student go where he or she wants?

It will be objected that the analogy is unfair, since you don't have to know Butte to understand San Francisco, but you do have to know math to understand physics. But a person who plunges into physics, eager to learn, and discovers this need, will approach math with a very different attitude than one who is simply told that you must learn X before we will even let you look at Y. No one had to persuade me to take statistics in graduate school once I had tried to make sense out of some research data without it.

Adults as well as children learn by doing—by trying things out, making mistakes, failing, and trying again. This is the democratic approach to learning. The authoritarian way is to say, "We already know the Truth, and hence every conceivable error that can ever be made, and we will save you from the humiliating experience of failure; simply follow our directions and we will lead you along the Only True Path."

Most of these hierarchical arrangements are completely arbitrary. It is rarely necessary to have had an introductory course in sociology or psychology or political science or history or literature or anthropology to understand the "advanced" courses in these subjects. One might in fact learn a great deal more freed from the stultifying effect of each field's hoary preconceptions and unexamined conventions. Introductory courses are notoriously tedious, save on those rare occasions when some eager assistant professor, unacquainted with the rules for getting ahead in a university, goes out of his or her way to make it exciting.

There are dedicated teachers in every university—trying in every possible way to arouse, enhance, or facilitate the desire to learn—but they have a hard time of it. Their popularity, the excitement they create, is looked upon with suspicion by their more traditional colleagues. They have trouble getting tenure because they are more interested in teaching than in writing and research; and universities, like all bureaucracies, tend to reward those activities that can be quantified and will enhance their image. Hence those who write a great deal and regard teaching as an unpleasant ancillary chore (and I must admit I was one of these) find their path to tenure smooth, while the dedicated teachers are scorned and cast out. Their very success with students is held against them. They are accused of either entertaining or being manipulated by the students and of "lowering academic standards."

4. LEARNING THE ROPES

The assumption underlying these accusations is that learning should be arduous, tedious, and unpleasant, and that if students enjoy it and are excited by it something underhanded is going on and should be squelched as quickly as possible. Knowledge must be doled out sparingly, lest the wrong people get hold of it and use it in the wrong way. Authoritarians love to say that "a little knowledge is a dangerous thing." But *no* knowledge is the most dangerous thing of all.

## THE IVORY FORTRESS

By virtue of their transience, students tend to have little power in the system that is supposed to serve them. In the university they constitute an inferior subject class, and they are approved of by the society as a whole only if they are inconspicuous or very far away. Americans feel deeply for students who march and demonstrate in China and Prague, but are extremely critical of those who do it in the United States or Latin America, although they are, of course, exactly the same breed of troublesome idealists saying exactly the same things. Some of the people who were horrified by the events in Beijing in 1989 were cheering when riot troops and helicopters attacked, clubbed, gassed, and shot American students during the sixties.

Even some liberal academics—ardent supporters of democracy in Mississippi and self-determination in Southeast Asia—found these notions reprehensible when students in the sixties began to apply them to their immediate environment. They were irate when they saw their carefully controlled environment unraveling—when students flocked to marathon teach-ins on world events, deserting their tidy classes.

Academia seems to act as a kind of insect trap for obsessive-compulsive personalities—it attracts them in larger numbers than other institutions and they tend to accumulate there. They prefer a tightly ordered environment over which they have complete control. They like to design things on paper and hate to see them altered. A faculty debate on the issue of whether a science requirement should consist of six credits or eight can go on for months, with the bulk of Western civilization brought in to justify positions on either side.

## LICENSE FOR MEDIOCRITY

Many of those concerned about the decline of democracy in America have singled out the professions for particular attention. James Fallows comments on the trend toward a kind of Mandarin order—based on educational tracking and credentialing—in place of the free-ranging, unbounded, self-defining democratic initiative that created the promising society America once was.

It is always tempting to attribute wisdom to people who claim it—especially when they have banded together and agreed to attribute it to each other. This is the problem with professional licensing—it tells us that our own criteria for evaluating competence are of no consequence, that we should rely exclusively on the criteria the professionals themselves have set up. One becomes an expert by taking certain courses and/or being approved by other experts. A profession is a kind of union against the consumer—a device for ensuring that the consumer cannot choose a healer or legal adviser simply on the basis of past performance at a price established in a free and open market.

As Fallows points out, there is often very little relationship between the skills required to obtain credentials and those required to practice effectively in the field. Professional licensing systems make it possible for many individuals too incompetent to practice in a free and open democratic market to make a good living simply by going to school and passing examinations.

Fallows observes that once a professional passes the initiation tests demanded by his particular sodality, his or her competence may never again be subject to review. Once having entered the hallowed fold, the licensed tend to be immune from later scrutiny.

Not only may they diminish in skill, knowledge, and morality without fear—some professionals are inclined to believe that their certification entitles them to exercise their "expert" status in areas in which they have no particular experience or competence. Doctors, for example, are viewed by many naive people, including themselves, as competent to speak with authority on virtually any subject; and even a Ph.D. has a range of credibility far beyond whatever particular assemblage of meticulous details gave rise to it.

What is dangerous is the claim made by professionals that they know better than we do what is good for us. And this is dangerous only if we believe it. Many people, for example, will consult a doctor or a lawyer on the recommendation of a colleague—though such recommendations are usually made on the basis of personal friendship, obligation, or hearsay. Unless the referring professional has actually been treated or represented by this colleague, the recommendation is usually worthless.

Can one trust the recommendation of a doctor, for example, when doctors will not criticize a colleague to "outsiders" even when he or she is guilty of gross negligence or lethal incompetence? A demented gynecologist was recently slapped on the wrist for performing crippling and grotesque operations on the vaginas of women without their consent—supposedly to enhance their sexual response, but actually creating incapacitating pain. Despite the fact that surgeons for miles around not only knew what he was doing but were kept busy (and well-paid) trying to undo the damage he had wreaked, he was able to mutilate hundreds of women over a twenty-two year period without ever being challenged by another doctor. This demonstrates the limits of "medical ethics," or the ethics of any group placed beyond the reach of democratic controls.

Intelligent people select a professional on the only reasonable basis on which one can make such judgments: the reports of satisfied customers combined with one's own experience. It is the wearer, not the shoemaker, who is the best judge of whether or not the shoe fits—a fundamental democratic principle that the medical profession seems to have forgotten.

I place particular stress on medicine because it is the most powerful stronghold of authoritarianism in the United States today, outside of the military. Where else can one find such rigid insistence on titles and deference? Doctors complain about the high cost of malpractice insurance, but a Harvard study found recently that only one out of ten patients injured by medical negligence ever files suit, so successfully has the industry managed to overawe the nation with its authority. American doctors have established a monopoly over the healing art that is unparalleled in the Western world—to the point where competitors can actually be jailed for "practicing without a license."

Fallows is particularly concerned with the way educational tracking has begun to create a special Mandarin class in our society. He points out that the IQ test is the most common device used to *class*-ify individuals in this way. Since the test is largely one of familiarity and comfort with middle-class urban culture, it is primarily a measure of social standing—immigrants and people from rural areas do poorly until they become acclimated, for example, whereupon their scores shoot up dramatically.

Tests—IQ or otherwise—measure the ability to take tests and often very little else. Fallows points out that people who have been determined by IQ test scores to be morons or imbeciles have subsequently become successful managers and professionals. A fundamental principle of democratic education is that people develop uniquely, unevenly, erratically, and continually. Only in an authoritarian society are a priori decisions made about a child's future. In a true democracy, competence is demonstrated, not scored. Fallows observes that "America was built by people who broke out of categories, defied probabilities, and changed their fate." Has this democratic potentiality been permanently stifled in our society today?

# 5
▼▼▼▼▼▼▼

# Sustainable Livelihoods: Redefining The Global Social Crisis[1]

David C. Korten*

In March 1995, the World Summit for Social Development will bring together heads of state and government in Copenhagen to "agree on a joint action for alleviating and reducing poverty, expanding productive employment and enhancing social integration." These are fundamental needs that stem from a growing global social crisis. Of the three needs, attention is likely to focus on expanding employment as the solution not only to unemployment, but also to poverty and social disintegration. Indeed unemployment—a clear, universal and growing problem—is almost certain to be a focus of political concern and action at local, national and global levels for many years to come.

This paper presents an argument, emerging out of discussions among a number of grassroots citizen organizations, that attempting to solve the world's employment crisis using conventional job creation measures—such as economic stimulus packages that encourage increased consumption and offer incentives to large investors—cannot work. To the contrary, such measures will almost certainly deepen the global social crisis and increase the stress on an already overburdened environment. We need to look in a very different place for a solution to our collective social crisis that will lead more directly to eliminating deprivation and mending the social fabric that has fallen into an advanced state of disintegration.

A suggested starting point is to focus not on the need for jobs—defined by an English dictionary as "a specific piece or work, as in one's trade; an activity performed in exchange for payment"—but rather on the need for

*From: Korten, David C. *Sustainable Livelihoods: Redefining the Global Social Crisis.* May 10, 1994. pp. 1–7. Reprinted by permission.

sustainable livelihoods—defined as "a means of living or of supporting life; of obtaining the necessities of life." In light of current realities it is wholly unrealistic to expect that any available policies will result in providing adequate and satisfying jobs for everyone in the world who might want or need one. However, assuring everyone an opportunity for a satisfying and sustainable livelihood by which they may obtain the necessities of life—even while significantly reducing traditional welfare assistance programs—is entirely within our collective means.

## WHY CONVENTIONAL SOLUTIONS DO NOT WORK

Nearly fifty years of international development effort have focused public policy and resources on efforts to accelerate the growth of monetized economies. These efforts have achieved a five-fold increase in global GNP since 1950. Yet unemployment, poverty, and inequality continue to increase, the social fabric of family and community is disintegrating, and the ability of the ecosystem to support human life is being destroyed—all at accelerating rates. Left without adequate opportunities for productive employment, a major portion of humanity is marginalized from the mainstream social, political and economic processes of the societies in which they live, and more than a billion people are consigned to lives of abject poverty. The tragic irony is that while a wide range of essential needs go unmet, hundreds of millions of people have been forced into unproductive idleness or meaningless work.

These economic failures have gripped the world in a deepening social crisis every bit as severe as the parallel environmental crisis. Both crises result from misplaced priorities that are in turn a direct consequence of confusing means with ends. Very simply, we have defined our goals in terms of growing economies to provide jobs—a means—rather than developing healthy sustainable human societies that provide people with secure and satisfying livelihoods, an end. Consequently, the economic growth of the past twenty years has primarily benefited a tiny elite while leaving the rest of humanity, present and future, with the bill. It is time to recognize that we are getting the wrong answers because we are asking the wrong questions.

### Deregulation and Globalization: A Race to the Bottom

The obsessive quest for economic growth has provided the impetus for recent economic policies geared to the deregulation and the integration of local markets into a single global economy. As local economies have been globalized, economic power has shifted from smaller, locally rooted producers to powerful global corporations beyond the reach of government regulation and freed from accountability to the public good. These corporations have in turn used technological advances to shed jobs by the hundreds of thousands—producing ever more of what existing markets will absorb with ever fewer workers. They have similarly taken advantage of economic integration to move production to wherever wages, working conditions, taxes and environmental standards allow them to produce at the lowest cost for sale wherever markets exist. The result is to push down wages, weaken the implementation of environmental standards, and reduce their taxes below their fair share of costs of the public facilities they use. Returns to a small number of investors are increased relative to returns to labor, steadily widening the gap between the wealthy and most everyone else. Growing numbers of workers do not earn enough to buy the products they produce, ultimately narrowing the market for the products of the companies that employ them.

All the while the largest and wealthiest corporations are gaining and strengthening monopolistic control over global markets, finance, and technology by buying out, squeezing out, or forming strategic alliances with their competitors. These efforts are often aided by the ability of these corporations to promote favorable legislative treatment for themselves through generous political contributions to those who make the laws. Smaller enterprises that continue to be the primary source of new jobs and technological innovation survive only by filling specialized market niches or servicing the needs of larger corporations on terms largely dictated by the latter. With goods and capital flowing freely across national borders, governments lose the ability to manage what used to be national economies, bargain away their ability to collect taxes, and become increasingly irrelevant.

These processes have combined with population growth and migration to create a growing employment crisis in nearly every nation in the world—depriving people everywhere of the personal security of either an adequate livelihood or a secure social support system. A vast global pool of unemployed, underemployed and underpaid workers competing with one another for ever-scarcer jobs, assures that wages will be kept low.

Governments at all levels typically respond to the resulting crisis by offering investment incentives to global corporations searching the world for the lowest cost production sites. By responding to a real need in an obvious way, each locality in turn joins a race to the bottom that pits localities against one another in a global competition for a declining pool of good jobs. A few localities emerge as temporary winners, creating the illusion that such competition is the path to economic security.

In unregulated globalized markets, capital becomes rootless, impatient, and controlled by entities that have no commitment to place or people. Those who make decisions regarding the use of local resources live in distant places wholly insulated from the local consequences of those decisions. Markets respond to money and to those who have money. The most fundamental needs of the poor are ignored for the simple reason they do not have money. Few companies, aside from those selling soft drinks and tobacco, prosper by targeting the poor. The ability of governments to manage national and local economies in the public interest, raise taxes for public needs, and hold inequality within reasonable bounds becomes impaired. More of the costs of production, including environmental and social·costs, are passed from the producer onto the community. Toxic contamination, chronic health problems, hunger and malnutrition, deteriorating public infrastructure, increased deprivation among the poor and growing inequality are evident consequences.

A Full World: Destroying Our Nest

Every bit of material and energy used by the human economy comes from earth's ecosystem. Every waste particle discarded by the human economy is returned to earth's ecosystem. The meaning of the term "environmentally sustainable" is quite clear. Activities that depend on turning the earth's stored energy and materials into wastes faster than the ecosystem can recycle them is inherently unsustainable. Current unsustainable consumption reduces the opportunities available to future generations. A substantial portion of the activity we count as economic growth is in sectors such as oil, petrochemical, metal, agriculture, public utilities, road building, transport and mining that involve heavy demands on materials, space, soil and energy and generate enormous wastes. Furthermore, as a general rule, the more resources an activity consumes—for example driving a car versus riding a bicycle—the more it contributes to GNP and to employment.[2]

It is evident that the environmental demands of many human activities have reached or exceeded what the ecosystem can sustain. Most of the world's cultivatable land has already been appropriated and the soils of much of the currently cultivated land are being depleted. Many of the world's historically most productive fisheries are collapsing. More and more localities face severe shortages of fresh water. Much of the world's grasslands are heavily over-grazed. Pollution of the atmosphere is thinning the ozone layer and creating a risk of massive climate change. Garbage is accumulating faster than we can find ways to dispose of it, while chemical and radioactive wastes are rendering more and more areas of the earth's surface unusable. And each day adds more people to the global population than were added the day before.[3]

In an open market economy scarcity is an inconvenience for the rich. It is a disaster for the poor. It has been said that the free market is the most efficient human institution ever devised for assuring that when resources get scarce the rich will get them. In the name of economic growth and job creation, livelihoods are being destroyed at an alarming rate as stable sub-sistence communities are evicted from their lands to make way for dams, mines, golf courses and luxury resorts, agricultural estates, and forest plantations—or their forests, water sources, and fisheries are mined for quick profits by powerful corporate interests.

Roughly 80 percent of the burden on the world's environmental resources is created by the consumption of the 20 percent of the world's population who earn 80 percent of global income. Much of that consumption—especially for transportation and packaging—is enormously wasteful. Encouraging those with money to consume more than they really need intensifies the competition for limited environmental resources between those who produce luxuries for the rich and the poor who depend on the same resources for survival.

In the end, there are too few people in the world with consequential discretionary income to make a dent in the world's unemployment by increasing their consumption even if they were to devote their total income to wasteful extravagance. The main consequence would be to increase the burdens placed on the environment at the cost of further displacing those whose subsistence depends on those same environmental resources—as is already happening.

## Development: Strengthening the Market and Weakening Community

Functioning, caring families and households are the foundation of functioning, caring communities, which in turn are the foundation of functioning, caring societies. The strength of the family or household, the community, and the society is dependent on the strength of mutual, cooperative relationships—the social economy. Unlike market economies, which tend to join people in purely impersonal and instrumental relationships—social economies create a dense fabric of relationships based on long-term sharing and cooperation.

Traditionally most of the productive and reproductive activities that provided people with their basic needs for food, shelter, clothing, child care, health care, education, physical security and entertainment were carried out within the framework of the social economy, largely outside of the market. A substantial portion of production/consumption activities took place within a single household or took place between people who related directly to one another. The productive activities of the social economy met most of the basic needs of its members, the very conduct of these activities served to maintain the social bonds of trust and obligation, "the social capital," of the community.

Social economies are by nature local, non-waged, non-monetized, and non-market. Therefore, they are not counted in national income statistics, do not contribute to measured economic growth, and are undervalued by policy makers who count only activities in the market economy as productive contributions to national output. A considerable portion of the economic growth of recent decades is simply a result of shifting functions from the social economy, where they are not counted in GNP, to the market economy, where they are.

Shifting a basic function like child care, health care, food preparation, entertainment, or physical security from the social economy to the market economy produces no necessary improvement in well-being. To the contrary, because the energies once invested in developing and maintaining family and community relationships have been redirected to generating sufficient income to meet needs the social economy once fulfilled. Left without consequential functions, the social capital on which the social economy is based erodes, social bonds are weakened and whatever economic gains, if any, may have been achieved by shifting functions to the market economy are more than offset by the costs of the resulting insecurity, crime, mental depression, violence, and suicide.

## Conventional Solutions Can Only Make the Problems Worse

It should by now be evident why conventional job creation policies do not work. The efforts by large corporations to improve their bottom line through downsizing renders already highly educated and skilled workers jobless, while government sponsored training programs prepare people for jobs that do not exist or pay too little to provide basic sustenance without government supplements. Capital investment incentives encourage the purchase of more advanced labor saving technologies that allow companies to reduce employment even further. Government fiscal policies aimed at strengthening demand by reducing taxes or increasing government spending often encourage more waste of environmental resources for non-essentials, while depriving the truly needy of their use.

For a given locality efforts to place more money in the hands of consumers may only increase the demand for imported products—creating foreign exchange deficits and increasing pressures to sell-off environmental resources such as timber at bargain prices to make up the difference. Reducing trade barriers in the hope of increasing export sales may only displace more locally produced products with imports while encouraging the export of plants, equipment, and jobs to localities that offer cheaper labor. Offering subsidies to firms to locate in a particular locality only moves jobs around, it does not create them. The best that most of these measures accomplish is to further increase corporate profits at the public expense.

Ultimately, many current public policies are self-defeating. A global economy that depends on consuming environmental resources faster than they can be regenerated destroys its own resource base. A global economy that pays its workers too little to buy the products they produce destroys its own markets. A global economy that displaces the functions of households and communities destroys the social fabric. A global economy that destroys its resource base, its markets, and the social fabric cannot long survive—nor can the corporations whose profits depend on these self-destructive dynamics. Dealing with the world's social crises requires a more holistic approach that views the development of healthy societies to be the goal, deals with the market economy as one of several means to realize that goal, and returns economic and political control to people.

## REGENERATING THE SOCIAL FOUNDATIONS OF HEALTHY SOCIETIES

A strong and vibrant social economy is a necessary foundation of a healthy human society. For this reason, the regeneration of social economies is fundamental to any successful effort to address the world's proliferating social crises. Taking appropriate steps requires understanding the nature of social economies and why they have become so dangerously eroded.

### Undervaluing the Social Economy

The fact that a market economy depends on a strong social economy to maintain the ethical structure, social stability, and personal security on which the smooth function of a market depends is routinely overlooked by economic policy makers. To the contrary, the destruction of the social economy to advance economic growth is not only accepted, but applauded by most economic planners—much as they applaud economic activities that advance economic growth by depleting natural capital.

Why isn't the important output of the social economy recognized in economic statistics? One explanation is that this output is harder to count. Another is that women have traditionally had the primary role in the productive and reproductive activities of the social economy, while men have had the dominant role in the monetized market economy. When male economists decided to develop a measure of economic output, they assigned more importance to things produced in the pursuit of money, traditionally the world of men, than to what was produced as an act of love, mutual obligation, or service to family and community, traditionally the world of women. As any economist will cheerfully point out, economics is about money—not love.

It is hardly surprising that predominantly male economic policy makers using indicators that recognized only the male dominated market economy were inclined to believe that moving women into the money economy constituted a real contribution to improved national output and well-being. Many women, eager to escape the inferior status assigned to their roles in the social economy and to have a wider range of opportunity for economic participation, readily embraced the logic of the male dominated market place.

## Where Markets Are Inefficient

As productive and reproductive functions have been transferred from the social economy to the market economy, more and more of the return from productive activity has been shifted away from the actual producers to those who perform overhead functions that add no real intrinsic value. When family and community members work directly with and for one another there are no taxes, management salaries, lawyers fees, stockholder dividends, middlemen, brokers, transportation costs and other overhead expenses. The full value of the goods and services produced is shared and exchanged within the family and the community among those who actually created the value.[4] The result is an extraordinarily efficient use of resources to meet real needs.

Indeed, in many sectors the market economy's overhead costs are so high that, even with two wage earners and longer work hours, many households cannot now adequately meet needs once met quite satisfactorily by the social economy. With no parent in the home, children are sequentially cared for, if at all, by nurseries, day-care centers and schools. Parents, or more often a single impoverished female parent, are left with little time, energy or encouragement to do more than function as income earners and night guardians. The modern urban home has become little more than a place to sleep and watch television—if the household can afford one. High rates of deprivation, depression, divorce, teenage pregnancy, violence, alcoholism and drug abuse, crime and suicide are among the more evident consequences in both high and low income countries.[5]

In general, public policy proposals intended to correct these indicators of serious social dysfunction take no account of the fact that they are a direct consequence of the destruction of the social economy, which is in turn a consequence of the same unsound economic policies commonly favored by efforts to increase employment.

## Restoring Roots, Balance and the Social Economy

The market is an important and useful human institution for meeting certain needs to which it is well suited. Unfortunately, we have lost sight of a basic reality that market economies best serve the human interest when they functions as an adjunct to a robust social economy founded on values of cooperation, sharing, trust and mutual obligation. Market economies are most likely to serve such a supportive function when:

- They are primarily local in character—augmented by, rather than dependent on, trading relationships with more remote localities;

- Capital is rooted in local ownership and most production is carried out by small enterprises;
- Strong democratically accountable governments set the goals and provide a regulatory framework for the market's socially productive function; and,
- A strong and politically active civil society holds government accountable to the public interest.

When any of these conditions are not met, the market is likely to undermine the social economy and reduce human security. A globalized market tends to negate all of these conditions. The result is enormous social inefficiency—as the world is now experiencing.

We must find more holistic approaches to dealing with poverty, unemployment and social disintegration based on restoring the bonds of community and healing the planet. This requires a search for economic policies that strengthen rather than displace the social economy. In addition, such policies must accomplish what contemporary social economies have failed to do—support gender equity and a sharing by women and men of responsibility for the functions of both the social and market economies.

## EVOKING IMAGES OF SUSTAINABLE SOCIETIES

It is time to move beyond competing globally for a finite pool of formal *jobs* and think more creatively about ways of engaging people in *sustainable livelihoods*—meaningful productive activities meeting real and otherwise unmet needs of households and communities in ways that are socially and environmentally sustainable. This shift in perspective recognizes that the economic systems of healthy sustainable societies must do a great deal more than provide a favored few with jobs to earn money to buy things they don't need to stimulate the economy to provide a favored few with jobs to earn money to buy . . . etc.

In a more holistic vision, sustainable societies:

- Provide all people an opportunity to contribute meaningfully to meeting the needs of family, community and society;
- Give first priority to meeting the basic needs of all and provide them security against involuntary deprivation;
- Live within their means and discourage consumption patterns beyond an equitable per capita share of sustainable ecosystem output;
- Structure production process so that environmental resources are used in sustainable ways; and,

- Contribute to maintaining a strong and dynamic fabric of cooperative human relationships.

Our modern concept of a "job" is imbedded in a complex set of values, institutions and relationships that are leading us into ever deeper social and environmental crisis. The concept of a "sustainable livelihood" is similarly imbedded in a complex, but quite different, set of values, institutions and relationships suited to a sustainable post-modern society. While there are groups all around the world working to create the future within their local settings and who are seeking out appropriate guidelines for policy and constructing possible scenarios for a sustainable future, these remain speculative and fragmented. We are of necessity engaged in an act of creation, not replication.

For most of us, the topic of jobs brings to mind primarily images of people working in the plants and facilities of world's largest transnational corporations for which localities around the world are competing. The term "sustainable livelihoods" is meant to evoke very different images of people and communities engaged in meeting individual and collective needs through the cooperative use of local resources in environmentally sustainable ways.

As the unfolding image takes on ever greater definition, we may begin to discern an organizational structure that links the local with the global in a multi-level system of human habitats organized as continuously self-renewing, self-governing, self-reliant eco-communities. Household eco-communities might be clustered into neighborhood eco-communities, clustered into village eco-communities, clustered into regional eco-communities, and so forth, to the level of a global eco-community. A system goal would be to concentrate decision-making authority at local rather than global levels, with the result that those who make decisions would be more likely to bear their primary consequences and it would be more difficult for one group to pass the environmental or social costs of its decisions onto another group.

Since the few examples we have in our modern world of societies that practice sustainable living are found among remote peoples and cultures, often living under primitive conditions, there are those who dismiss any talk of sustainability as calling for a return to living in trees and caves and hunting wild animals. It is an uninformed charge that bears no relationship to the vision of those who point to the need for economic justice and a balanced relationship between people and environment as necessary conditions for the survival and continued progress of our species.

The challenge is to make full, but selective, use of our technical and organizational capabilities in taking a new evolutionary step toward the creation of human societies that define their well-being not by the size of their garbage dumps, but rather by their success in assuring the physical security of all their members and in achieving ever higher levels of intellectual, social, cultural and spiritual development.

## ECO-COMMUNITIES: POSSIBLE SCENARIO[6]

The ideal of neighborhood and village eco-communities envisions the melding of human and non-human systems in co-productive processes of continuous regeneration by recycling sewage, solid waste and even air through fish ponds, gardens and green areas to produce much of the local requirement for food, energy, clean water, fresh air and recreational spaces. Generally we think of such processes entirely in terms of rural areas, however, proponents of rural agriculture and ruralized urban design believe that even urban spaces can be made far more self-reliant than at present. Urban agriculture, urban aquaculture, repair and reuse, and the intensive recycling of wastes would provide new sustainable livelihood opportunities, while renewing family and community ties, decentralizing administration, and allowing greater sharing of family responsibilities among men and women.

With time we may find traditional types of cottage industries existing side-by-side with urban agricultural and recycling activities and with electronic cottage industries of the high technology age. Family support services such as community-based day care, family counselling, schools, family health services, and multi-purpose community centers could become integral neighborhood functions, engaging people in livelihoods within easy walking distance of their homes. Many eco-communities may issue their own local currency to facilitate local transactions and limit the flow of money out of the community.

Continuing the current trend toward home-based part-time employment, many households might combine salaried employment with urban subsistence agriculture, recycling and voluntary community service—leading to a return to the multi-functional home that serves as a center of family and community life. This would be consistent with the call to design human habitats such that residential, work, recreation and commercial facilities are within walking distance of one another, reducing much of the energy and other environmental costs of transportation.

Promoting sustainable livelihoods rather than jobs will not in itself change the powerful and deeply imbedded values and institutional structures that sustain the present economic system, but it will suggest that we recognize the need for unconventional solutions—a first step toward corrective action. At last we might begin to ask the right questions.

What is the prospect for such a fundamental redirection? While we must continue to hope that there are enlightened power-holders willing to come forward and provide real leadership, our major hope for change is found among ordinary people all around the world who are awakening to the basic reality that the mega-institutions that have consolidated their hold on the instruments of economic and political power do not, and will not, serve their interests.

## TAKING BACK RESPONSIBILITY

January 1, 1994 was the inaugural day of the North American Free Trade Agreement (NAFTA), an agreement intended to complete the integration of the economies of Mexico, Canada, and the United States. The corporate elites of the three countries congratulated themselves on the new opportunities the merger created to expand their profits and market share. Among the most jubilant were the 36 Mexican businessmen who own 39 Mexican conglomerates that collectively account for more than 54 percent of Mexico's Gross National Product.

The indigenous peoples of Chiapas State in Southeastern Mexico on the border with Guatemala took a strikingly different view of this new step toward economic integration and globalization. Calling NAFTA a death sentence for the people of Chiapas, some four thousand Indians celebrated the occasion by launching an armed rebellion against the Mexican government. Mexican political analyst Gustavo Esteva called it the first revolution of the 21st century. Unlike most revolutions of the 20th century, it was not aimed at capturing state power. Its goal was rather to secure the right of people to govern themselves within the borders of their own communities. They demanded only greater local autonomy, economic justice and political rights.

The Chiapas rebellion was only one of the more visible manifestations of similar social forces that are emerging almost everywhere in the world with a potential to redefine the face of politics and economics well into the 21st century. These social forces grow out of two realities that give a distinctive quality to this moment in human history.

- **Institutional Legitimacy and Local Responsibility.** In democratic societies, it is expected that the institutions in which political and economic power have been vested derive their legitimacy from being duly constituted by and accountable to the sovereign people, conducting their operations according to an appropriate code of morals and ethics, and producing desirable consequences for the whole. The world's dominant mega-institutions—both public and private—currently fail on all three counts and their legitimacy in the eyes of the public is at a near historic low.

  Reform is becoming less and less an issue. They are simply too big, too distant, too beholden to special interests and too costly to respond in any useful way to the broader human interest. Instead of looking to them for solutions, the impulse of those who have been discarded or marginalized by the globalized economy is increasingly to dismiss such mega-institutions as hopelessly unresponsive and get on with taking back responsibility for their own lives. In the spirit of earlier frontier communities, they are saying, "If our needs are to be met we will have to get together and figure out how to meet them for ourselves."

- **Global Interdependence.** Modern communications technologies have created awareness nearly everywhere that all people share one fragile planetary ecosystem and are suffering in similar ways from the failure of the mega-institutions that govern the planet. This awareness—along with the ability for instantaneous communication through phone, fax, and computer—has created a foundation for cooperation and solidarity among the world's people wholly without precedent in human history. A sense that the well-being of each increasingly depends on the well-being of all is beginning to take hold as the foundation of grassroots alliances aimed at strengthening local control and the rights and well-being of ordinary citizens everywhere.

The emergent social forces find expression in local initiatives aimed at regenerating local economies, ecosystems and communities. As people reclaim responsibility, they are also reclaiming their sovereignty, reasserting their basic rights over local resources, challenging the abuses of absentee corporations, and telling nonperforming governments to reduce their tax burden. They are also beginning to reach out in search of new alliances, both nationally and internationally, with those engaged in similar self-help initiatives.

These countless initiatives and the cooperative networks that are melding them into a growing political force are the building blocks of a process of globalization-from-below that may well result in a bottom-up reconstruction of our dominant political and economic institutions. As this process unfolds, it will become increasingly clear that the mega-institutions that have broken free from their own roots cannot long survive. Floating in space they can only consume themselves while the people they have abandoned work to fill the gap left in the social ecology with new institutions rooted in place and community.

When the heads of our governments gather for the Social Summit in 1995, we might hope that at least a few among them will recognize that the path to a more promising human future lies with the people and the process of globalization-from-below through which the seeds of new and strongly rooted human institutions are being planted and nurtured. Perhaps at least one or two may speak not of jobs, but of sustainable livelihoods. While a small step, it may give us hope that the people are not entirely alone in their historic struggle to regain control of their local political and economic space.

## NOTES

1. This paper was produced as a cooperative undertaking that involved important contributions from a substantial number of the contributing editors of the People-Centered Development Forum. It also benefited from extensive critical feedback from participants in a joint

PCDForum-IGGRI workshop organized in conjunction with the 21st Global Conference of the Society for International Development held in Mexico City in April 1994.

2. Jan Tinbergen and Roefie Hueting, "GNP and Market Prices: Wrong Signals for Sustainable Economic Success That Mask Environmental Destruction," in Robert Goodland, Herman E. Daly, & Salah El Serafy, *Population, Technology, and Lifestyle* (Washington, DC: Island Press, 1992), pp. 52–62.

3. Sandra Postel, "Carrying Capacity: Earth's Bottom Line," in Lester R. Brown, *et. al., State of the World 1994* (New York: W. W. Norton & Co., 1994), pp. 3–21.

4. Edgar Cahn and Jonathan Rowe, *Time Dollars* (Emmaus, Pennsylvania: Rodale Press, 1992).

5. Clarence Shubert, "Creating People-Friendly Cities," PCDForum Column #72, April 5, 1994.

6. This section is based on *Ibid.*

# II
▼▼▼▼▼▼▼

# SOCIAL JUSTICE:
# PROMISES AND DESPAIR

One of the most enduring phenomena of the American experience is the story of people continuing to press for a greater measure of justice in their lives. Indeed, the struggle occurs in the daily grind of work, school, and home life as individuals constantly look for ways to resist the processes of dehumanization and subordination. In a variety of ways, people continually fight for more dignity, more control over their lives, and more resources with which to live. They do so as workers, consumers, students, members of minority groups, women, oppressed sexual groups, people marginalized by virtue of age, disability, or illness, and so on. As the slogan of the women's movement, "the personal is political" has taken hold, the struggle for more equality involves increasing dimensions of the self, moving into areas of life hitherto unimaginable.

Despite the ebb and flow of these struggles their essential continuity should come as no surprise. Our egalitarian faith is, after all, an inescapable component of the republican discourse of the nation. It is a much proclaimed virtue, deeply rooted in both the naturalistic social philosophies and the Judeo-Christian values that structure the culture's official language. Perhaps what ought to be considered more surprising is not the impulse toward greater equality, but the way in which this impulse is tempered, "cooled-out," or accommodated to the existing hierarchical social relations. It is this fact that is an important dimension of the readings in this part of the volume. In contrast to important elements of conventional educational discourse that emphasize the way schooling facilitates upward social mobility, our concern is with the way that egalitarian discourse is reconciled with the massive inequities of our social, economic, and political lives. What must be faced and understood is the coexistence of powerful movements of the disadvantaged, demanding redress for the unmet promises of the society, with the continual—indeed, intensifying—injustices produced by the divisions of class, race, gender, and other social distinctions. As all of our authors make clear, these unmet promises are more than moral or philosophical abstractions. The United States is moving with alarming speed to an era marked by grotesque disparities of income and conditions of life. It becomes increasingly difficult to escape an awareness of the millions of our fellow citizens (including an unprecedented number of children) who are without adequate shelter, food, or other basic provisions of life such as medical insurance. The fact that this continues, despite what is claimed to be the longest peace-time economic recovery, indicates that the massive poverty is no aberration, but a deeply structured, enduring aspect of our social reality.

Beyond presenting the harsh reality of social injustice in contemporary America, we wish to pursue two related questions. The first is concerned with how this situation has come to be—what are the social, economic, and political dynamics of inequality in this country. In addressing this issue, we look at the conditions that produce disproportionate degrees of poverty among women and children as well as among people of color. Second, we are concerned with the nature of the ideology that manages to reconcile quite spectacular levels of inequality with the value of a (formally) democratic culture. (In these questions there is, of course, a clear overlap with issues and questions raised in the previous part).

As the readings make clear, in answering these questions, the role of public schooling has been, and continues to be, central. It is quite simply the key institution in the practical process of social differentiation and selection and the heart of the ideological process through which inequality is made to seem legitimate.

Christine Sleeter and Carl Grant, in chapter 6, provide us with powerful insights and data on the intimate relations among education, class, race, gender, and disability. Their message is of a society that is, on the one hand, committed to the notion of education as a primary tool for reducing inequality and on the other hand, has adopted educational practices that perpetuate and validate inequality. They offer compelling evidence of the degree to which wealth and poverty are linked to an education that seems determined to preserve an existing class system. In a time of enormous sensitivity to and awareness of cultural and social diversity, the authors see the schools as unresponsive, developing policies and practices that amount to "business as usual." They see a school system that continues to maintain grouping and hierarchical policies and practices that work against women, the poor, people of color, and the disabled.

The notion that the public schools are primarily an institution for providing equal opportunity is a crucial component of our vision as a democratic society. Jeannie Oakes, in chapter 7, helps to clarify the assumptions that underlie this claim by focusing on the role of student tracking and inequality. Of course, this paradox of schooling in America is not essentially new. It reflects persistent and deeply rooted assumptions about human abilities and the role of schools in providing equal opportunity. Notwithstanding whether the political pendulum swings to the left or right, schools are fundamentally organized around the differentiation of educational experiences, according to the belief that children possess quite fixed individual abilities. Schools, it has long been assumed, can act in a fair and unbiased manner to decide which students have the capacity for achieving excellence. As a result, and despite the inequalities of American society, equal educational opportunity appears as both a possible and valid means through which to stage the competition for adult positions in the social and economic hierarchy. Despite the plethora of data that clearly shows how educational success favors the already privileged, a complex ideology that merges democratic sentiments and meritocratic notions functions to make schooling appear as politically and ethically legitimate.

For the most part, educational reforms that sought to equalize educational opportunities remain at the level of changing, or remediating, individual students rather than challenging the assumptions about ability or success built into the process of schooling. Present school reforms centered around the drive for excellence, says Oakes, only serve to intensify such assumptions and prejudices. The practices of excellent schooling are, she says, clearly reflective of the "Anglo-conformist" values that historically served to discriminate against youngsters who are poor or are members of ethnic minorities. The failure of disadvantaged children continues to be seen as a matter of their own deficiencies—social, economic, educational, and linguistic—not of the schools' inadequate response to them. Children, says Oakes, continue to be seen as entrants into an equal, fair, and neutral competitive process.

The absurdity of any such assumptions about the fairness of the system is powerfully underlined by Stan Karp in chapter 8 on school finance. Karp notes the enormous disparity of public support of schools among and within states, particularly where the local property tax is the primary funding source. Here, once again, one finds social ambivalence. There is an apparent cultural consensus that our democracy requires equal access to educational opportunities as reflected in and augmented in specific, seemingly clear judicial and legislative decisions to redress inequalities.

Yet, in spite of court orders and special legislative sessions, we continue to tolerate a political reality in which obscene disparities in resources for school districts persist. It is a reality that Karp believes does not even meet the discredited standards of separate and equal and indeed, is a reality in which racial segregation and class differences are maintained, if not legitimated.

Harold Hodgkinson (chap. 9) provides even more disturbing evidence on how schools are involved in social and economic inequality, focusing on school performance, race, and income level. His contribution to the debate offers the provocative and controversial idea that those committed to reducing inequality should accept the data that suggests it is poverty and not race that is the best predictor of school failure. His is a compelling and eloquent argument on the alarming growth of poverty among children and the even more alarming public indifference to this suffering. According to Hodgkinson:

> We have more effectively segregated people by wealth than we ever did by race: 37% of America's wealth is owned by only 1.5% of the people, yet one-quarter of our youngest children live in poverty. . . . Questions of income distribution are usually political suicide for politicians, but when youth poverty rates are destroying the future of their entire society, one must wonder whether there can be any long-term winners. (p. 166)

These millions of poor children, of course, are often enrolled in schools with limited resources and overwhelmed teachers who share the anguish that accompanies our social reluctance and inability to end poverty. Mark Stern's chapter (chap. 10) was written during the recent Congressional debate on welfare reform and the subsequent law that was enacted reflects that there are indeed strong forces in our society that seek to punish the poor rather than deal with the structures that produce poverty. His position is that this law not only seeks to stigmatize those on welfare, but also fails to distinguish between those who rely on welfare on a temporary basis from those who do so perennially. Many would have us believe that those on welfare do not have the proper values or are somehow lacking in character, but Stern insists that the problems are far more complex than differences in attitudes toward responsibilities. Indeed, he maintains that the difficulties of the welfare system are deeply rooted in far-reaching cultural and lifestyle changes that permeate all aspects of American society. Moreover, he is distressed that the new law "reinforces the myth that a huge gap separates welfare recipients from the mainstream" and refers to the new legislation as an "intolerable hypocrisy" (p. 174).

Like those found in the previous section, the readings here reflect a critical account of the purpose of schooling in the United States. The authors in this part insist that the real nature and purposes of education can only be grasped if we view schools as cultural and political sites that give legitimacy to the way social relations are organized in this society. From this perspective, all our talk about education's connection to the realization of human potential is a denial or avoidance of the real work of the school, which is inseparable from the economic, cultural, and social differentiation of students.

# 6
▼▼▼▼▼▼▼

# Illusions of Progress:
# Business as Usual*

Christine E. Sleeter
Carl Grant

Picture the following class: Of its total number of 30 students (15 girls and 15 boys), 21 are White, 5 are African American, 3 are Hispanics (2 Mexican Americans and 1 Cuban American), and 1 is second-generation Asian American. Two of the African-American students, 1 Hispanic student, and 4 White students come from families who live below the poverty line, while another 4 White students are from upper-income homes. These socio-economic status distinctions are not readily visible, however, because most of the students are clad in jeans and cotton shirts or T-shirts. Nevertheless, a glance at home addresses and at the free-lunch roster suggests the students' socioeconomic status. The students' families vary widely: Whereas only 2 students come from families in which the father but not the mother works outside the home, 9 are from single-parent families (6 of which live below the poverty line), and both parents of the remaining 19 students hold or have recently held jobs at least part-time. Most of the students grew up speaking English, but 2 of the Hispanic students speak Spanish at home, and 1 White student speaks French at home. The students' academic skills vary widely: Two spend part of the day in a learning disabilities class, 1 is in a class for the mentally retarded, 1 is in a gifted program, and 1 is in a speech therapy program.

How does a teacher teach such a wide variety of students? What sort of curriculum is taught? Are all students taught the same curriculum? What teaching strategies are used? How are students grouped for instruction, or are they grouped at all? How are they seated? You may find two conflicting images forming in your head—one depicting how you believe a teacher

*From: Sleeter/Grant, MAKING CHOICES FOR MULTICULTURAL EDUCATION, 2/e © 1994. Reprinted by permission of Prentice-Hall, Inc., Upper Saddle River, NJ.

should teach these students, the other depicting how most teachers really do teach them.

Where does one find this class of students? We based our hypothetical class on statistics describing the composition of public schools in the United States in the early 1990s (National Center for Education Statistics, 1991). Actually, student composition varies widely across the country, even within the same city or the same school. But given the diversity of America's students, schools, and classrooms, the same questions persist: How do teachers actually teach their students, and how should students be taught?

These are the central questions this book addresses. We recognize, however, that schools do not exist in a vacuum. They are, instead, quite closely connected to the society they serve. Therefore, when considering what kind of education would best serve America's increasingly diverse student population, we also need to consider the nature of the society in which schools exist. This chapter first will briefly discuss the nature of society in the 1990s as it relates to race, language, culture, gender, social class, and disability. Then it will synthesize recent research to provide a portrait of how teachers actually teach America's diverse student population. Finally, it will provide the framework used in subsequent chapters to address alternative approaches to teaching.

## SOCIETY TODAY

People are seeing contradictions today related to sexism, racism, and bias against people with disabilities and gay people. In some cases, it seems that race, gender and bias against a disability are no longer major societal problems. We see increasing numbers of White women and African-American men as mayors of large cities. An African-American male serves as governor of a state that claims the first permanent English settlement in North America, was one of the 13 colonies, and became the 10th state of the United States of America. Also, of the women elected to Congress, 39 have been White (34 in the House and 5 in the Senate), 10 have been African American (9 in the House and 1 in the Senate), and 1 has been Asian American; and Hispanic, Asian-American, and Native-American political clout is growing. Additionally, several African Americans have leading roles in television entertainment, and it is becoming rather commonplace to see people of color and both sexes reporting the news or hosting television programs in large urban television markets. One can think of additional illustrations of progress in the late 1980s and the 1990s. Women and minorities as astronauts are no longer big news; the U.S. Supreme Court has an active female member and its second African-American justice. In addition, a review of many newspapers and magazines suggests that many Americans now are hearing more about "diversity" in regard to both national and international matters than they have heard in their lifetimes.

However, these indications of progress obscure the larger picture. In spite of such examples, which involve only small numbers of people, there is considerable evidence that U.S. society is still battling problems of racism and sexism and is very stratified on the basis of race, gender, and disability. In fact, stratification based on socioeconomic status is a prominent feature of U.S. society and one that social policy in the last four decades has made little sustained attempt to change.

In the past few years, Americans have been reminded repeatedly that the population of the U.S. is rapidly becoming more racially and ethnically diverse. In 1990, the U.S. population was 12.1% African American; 9.0% Hispanic; 2.9% Asian or Pacific Islander; .8% Native American, Eskimo, or Aleut; 3.9% other races; and 71.3% non-Hispanic White. In the 1980s, 6 million legal immigrants joined the U.S. population, and the 1990s will probably see an even larger wave of immigrants. Most immigrants are from areas other than Europe. About 43% of the Hispanic population are immigrants from the 1970s and 1980s, and fully 70% of the Asian population are immigrants from those two decades (Riche, 1991).

This diversity certainly enlarges the pool of diverse cultural resources that exists in the United States, at the same time as it provides for a good deal of misunderstanding and resentment. In addition, the growing racial diversity of the United States underscores the urgent need for our nation to come to grips more seriously with racism. While European immigrants have been able to blend in with the dominant population after a generation or two, non-Europeans continue to be visibly distinct from EuroAmericans and thus experience American racism, a situation that causes disillusionment even among those who came to the United States full of hope and optimism. When considering racism in society, Americans often cite improved racial attitudes as a sign of progress. Indeed, attitudes have improved, according to a Gallup poll taken in 1990. In 1963, when Gallup asked Whites if they would be inclined to move out if a Black family moved next door to them, 45% said they would. Presently, only 5% respond in the affirmative when asked that same question. In contrast, Gallup (1990) has reported no significant change since the late 1970s in public opinion about African Americans' success in achieving equal opportunities. The perception of how well African Americans are treated in their communities has not improved since that time. Sixty-three percent (63%) believe that African Americans are treated the same as Whites, while 24% say that African Americans are treated "not very well" or "badly." However, in a study analyzing racial attitudes toward residential integration, Bobo, Schuman, and Steeh (1986) found that there is evidence of a steady progressive trend toward acceptance of the goal of residential integration and toward support for enforcement of black's housing rights. These changes are lent further credence by expressed white willingness to take part in integrated living situations that involve more than a token black presence. On the other hand, support for enforcing blacks' rights to free residential choice is well below that for the principle itself. Indeed, respondents proved to be quite willing to endorse the principle and express reluctance to enforce it. (p. 165)

The last four decades may have brought about improved White attitudes and improved access to facilities such as schools, but African Americans, Hispanics, and Native Americans are still distinctly subordinate economically and politically. For example, in 1990, although the average educational attainment of African Americans was only slightly below that of Whites (12.2 years and 12.6 years, respectively), the median income of African-American families was only 60 percent of the median income of White families and had improved little in over a decade. Hispanics with at least a high school diploma were more than 2½ times as likely as Whites to be living in poverty in 1988, and in 1990 Hispanic males earned a lower annual earning rate than either Whites or African Americans (U.S. Department of Commerce, Bureau of the Census, 1991). As Table 6.1 shows, education does not pay off equally for members of different racial groups: Being White has measurable economic and employment advantages.

People of color continue to experience poverty and unemployment disproportionately. For example, Figure 6.1 shows the poverty rate since 1959 for persons based on race. Data on Native Americans are not reported as systematically as they are for other groups, but many tribes experience devastating poverty and unemployment. For example, in 1980 the poverty rate for Native Americans was 27.5% overall, although on the Rosebud and Navajo reservations it was 51.4% and 52.4% respectively (Tippeconnic, 1991).

Children are particularly hard-hit by poverty. As Table 6.2 shows, for example, in 1988 the percentage of African-American children living below the poverty line was 3 times that of White children, and Hispanic children

TABLE 6.1
Earnings of Full-Time, Year-Round Workers, Age 25 and Older (1989)

| Education Attained | Annual Earnings | | |
|---|---|---|---|
| | White | Black | Latino |
| 4 years high school | $24,755 | $19,813 | $20,567 |
| 1–3 years college | $29,498 | $22,813 | $25,620 |
| 4 or more years college | $43,314 | $32,046 | $38,559 |

SOURCE: U.S. Department of Commerce, Bureau of the Census, *Population Survey*, March 1990, Table 6.

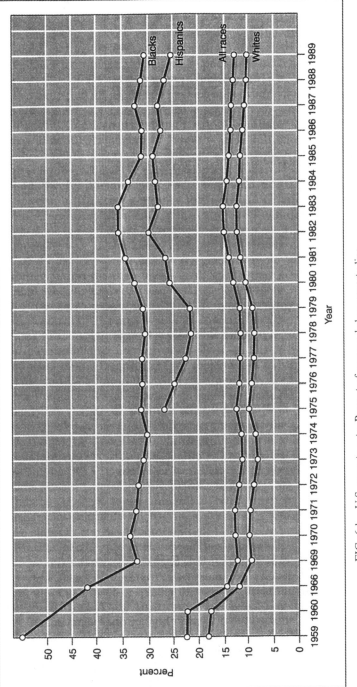

FIG. 6.1. U.S. poverty rate: Percent of persons below poverty line
SOURCES: U.S. Department of Commerce, Bureau of the Census, *Current Population Reports*, series P-60, No. 168 and earlier reports; U.S. Department of Commerce, Bureau of the Census, *Statistical Abstract of the United States* (111th ed.), 1991.

TABLE 6.2
Children Under 18 Living in Poverty: 1960–1988

| Year | Percent of children in poverty | | | | Percent of children in poverty living with female householder | | | |
|------|-------|-------|-------|----------|-------|-------|-------|----------|
|      | Total | White | Black | Hispanic | Total | White | Black | Hispanic |
| 1960 | 26.5  | 20.0  | 65.5  | —        | 23.7  | 21.0  | 29.4  | —        |
| 1965 | 20.7  | 14.4  | 47.4  | —        | 31.7  | 27.0  | 49.7  | —        |
| 1970 | 14.9  | 10.5  | 41.5  | —        | 45.8  | 36.6  | 60.8  | —        |
| 1975 | 16.8  | 12.5  | 41.4  | 34.5     | 51.4  | 41.7  | 70.1  | 42.9     |
| 1980 | 17.9  | 13.4  | 42.1  | 33.0     | 52.8  | 41.3  | 75.4  | 47.1     |
| 1981 | 19.5  | 14.7  | 44.2  | 35.4     | 52.2  | 42.0  | 74.3  | 48.5     |
| 1982 | 21.3  | 16.5  | 47.3  | 38.9     | —     | —     | —     | —        |
| 1983 | 21.8  | 17.0  | 46.2  | 37.7     | 50.0  | 39.3  | 74.5  | 42.5     |
| 1984 | 21.0  | 16.1  | 46.2  | 38.7     | 52.4  | 41.8  | 74.9  | 47.2     |
| 1985 | 20.1  | 15.6  | 43.1  | 39.6     | 53.8  | 43.0  | 78.4  | 49.6     |
| 1986 | 19.8  | 15.3  | 42.6  | 37.1     | 56.6  | 45.7  | 80.5  | 49.5     |
| 1987 | 20.0  | 15.0  | 45.1  | 39.3     | 56.9  | 46.0  | 79.0  | 47.2     |
| 1988 | 19.2  | 14.1  | 43.5  | 37.6     | 58.7  | 49.7  | 78.4  | 48.7     |

SOURCE: U.S. Department of Commerce, Bureau of the Census, "Poverty in the United States: . . . ,"
Current Population Reports, series P-60, various years, March.

were over 2.5 times as likely as White children to live in poverty (Ogle, Alsalam, & Rogers, 1991). Also, children of color living with two parents were more than twice as likely to be poor as White children living with two parents (National Commission on Children, 1991).

The gap in employment has not improved, either: Whites continue to have the greatest access to available jobs. In 1989, only about 55 percent of all African-American recent high school graduates were employed, compared to about 75 percent of White recent high school graduates. In fact, White dropouts were almost as likely to be employed as African-American high school graduates (Ogle, Alsalam, & Rogers, 1991). There are several reasons for this phenomenon. Racial discrimination in hiring is one of them. In spite of affirmative action, a study by the Urban Institute found that when African-American and White candidates with the same qualifications applied for the same jobs, African Americans were interviewed only 80% as often as Whites; 15% of the Whites were ultimately offered jobs while only 5% of the African Americans were offered employment (Dervarics, 1991). Another reason for the employment gap is that jobs increasingly are not located where people of color live. After World War II, millions of people of color moved to urban areas to take manufacturing jobs, which are now being exported to Third World countries. Job openings increasingly are located in suburban areas. People of color find it difficult to relocate, largely because of housing discrimination. Two studies of housing discrimination conducted by the

Department of Housing and Urban Development (HUD) in 1987 and 1988 found that African Americans face housing discrimination in both rental and sales markets 59% of the time, and Hispanics, 56% of the time. When people of color are matched with White home-seekers on factors such as income and family size, over half the time the White home-seekers are given more options and better chances to locate housing.

Mare and Winship (1984), after studying racial inequality and joblessness among Black youths, observed that this gap is widening because Black youths are both staying in school longer and joining the military in greater numbers—thus no longer having a "head start" in the labor market for unskilled or semiskilled jobs. Their study suggests that "worsening labor force statistics for Black youths do not denote increasing racial inequality, but rather persistent racial inequalities previously hidden by race differences in other aspects of young adulthood" (p. 54).

As a result of differential access to jobs, housing, and health institutions, other estimates of quality of life vary according to race. For example, in 1988, 88.5% of White Americans were covered by health insurance, while 80% of African Americans and only 74% of Hispanic Americans were similarly covered. The percent of all Americans without health insurance rose from 13.6% to 14.0% between 1989 and 1990 (U.S. Department of Commerce, 1991a). Moreover, Whites enjoy a longer life expectancy than Americans of color. Native Americans are especially short-changed on life span, the average life expectancy for Native Americans being six years less than that of other groups of color (U.S. Department of Health and Human Services, 1985). As life expectancy for the general population increases, a racial gap persists (Figure 6.2).

People of color are also more likely than Whites to be imprisoned. In 1990, jail inmates were 47.4% Black, 13.3% Hispanic, .8% Native American and Alaskan Native, .3% Asian and Pacific Islander, and 3.7% not known, while 34.5% were non-Hispanic White. However, as of December 31, 1990, of the 2,356 prisoners under sentence of death, 943 (40%) were Black, 38 (1%) were listed as "other races," and 1,375 (59%) were White (U.S. Department of Justice, *Correctional Population In the U. S.*, National Prison Statistics Series, 1990).

People of color are also still locked out of much of the political system, even though increasing numbers of big-city mayors are men of color. Since 1971 there have been only two African-American U.S. senators; the number of other senators of color has fluctuated between two and four. Between 1971 and 1993, the number of African-American congresspersons increased from 12 to 39, but still constituted only 9% of the House of Representatives, a significant underrepresentation for the 12% of Americans who are Black. Four percent (4%) of the House in 1993 was Hispanic; Hispanic representation had grown over the decade but still underrepresented the 9% of

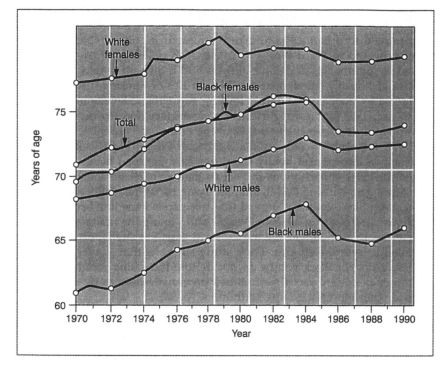

FIG. 6.2.  Life expectancy at birth.
SOURCE: Division of Vital Statistics, Center for Health Statistics, U.S.
Department of Health and Human Services, 1985, U.S. Government Printing
Office.

Americans who are Hispanic. There are 2 Asian senators and 6 Asian
members of the House. There is 1 Native American senator in Congress.
The year 1984 had the first Black presidential candidate, but his White
constituency was small and his support of the Democratic nominee was
considered a liability by many Whites.

Women, too, are still distinctly subordinate, both economically and politically, in spite of recent gains. Women are participating in the labor market
in ever-growing numbers. However, the earnings of full-time working women
are only about 71% the earnings of full-time working White men. This wage
gap has fluctuated over the last three decades and appears to be shrinking
currently as women enter male-dominated fields (Table 6.3). As Table 6.4
shows, this gap exists between men and women who have attained the same
levels of education. A number of studies have examined human capital factors
(e.g., work experience, evidence of work commitment) that might explain
this differential; but taken together, Treiman and Hartman (1981) report
that these "factors usually account for less than a quarter and never more
than half of the observed earnings differences" (p. 42). One major institu-

TABLE 6.3

The Wage Gap over Time: Earnings of Full-Time Female Workers
Compared to Each Dollar Earned by Full-Time Male Workers (1955–1990)

| Year | Female earnings per dollar of male earnings | Year | Female earnings per dollar of male earnings |
|------|------|------|------|
| 1955 | 63.9¢ | 1979 | 59.6¢ |
| 1959 | 61.3¢ | 1980 | 60.2¢ |
| 1960 | 60.8¢ | 1981 | 59.2¢ |
| 1962 | 59.5¢ | 1982 | 61.7¢ |
| 1965 | 60.0¢ | 1983 | 63.8¢ |
| 1967 | 57.8¢ | 1984 | 67.8¢ |
| 1970 | 59.4¢ | 1985 | 68.2¢ |
| 1972 | 57.9¢ | 1986 | 69.2¢ |
| 1973 | 56.6¢ | 1989 | 68.0¢ |
| 1975 | 58.8¢ | 1990 | 71.0¢ |
| 1977 | 58.9¢ | | |

SOURCE: U.S. Department of Commerce, Bureau of the Census, U.S. Department of Labor Statistics, *Employment and Earnings*, 1991.

tional factor perpetuating this situation is that "women are concentrated in low-paying occupations and, within occupations, in low-paying firms" (p. 42). Women are making substantial inroads into some high-paying, traditionally male occupations, such as law. Nevertheless, over 60% of female workers in 1991 were concentrated in low-paying "pink collar" ghettos, such as clerical work, nursing, teaching, day care, health services, and domestic service (U.S. Department of Commerce, Bureau of the Census, 1991d), and often their median weekly earnings in these occupations were less than men's (Table 6.5).

TABLE 6.4

Average Earnings of Full-Time, Year-Round Workers,
by Educational Attainment and Sex (1987)

| | Average Earnings | |
|------|------|------|
| | Men | Women |
| Less than 8 years | $16,863 | $10,163 |
| Eight years | $18,946 | $12,655 |
| 9–11 years | $21,327 | $13,136 |
| Completed high school | $24,745 | $16,223 |
| 1–3 years college | $29,253 | $19,336 |
| 4 years college | $38,117 | $23,506 |
| 5+ years college | $47,903 | $30,255 |

SOURCE: U.S. Department of Commerce, Bureau of the Census (1990). *Statistical Abstracts of the United States 1990*. Washington, DC: U.S. Government Printing Office, p. 455.

TABLE 6.5
The Wage Gap Between Men and Women

| Basic Data—U.S. Dept. of Labor Occupations | Women's Median Weekly Earnings | Women's Median Weekly Earnings as a Share of Men's Wages | Men's Median Weekly Earnings |
| --- | --- | --- | --- |
| Computer Programmers | $573.00 | 83% | $ 691.00 |
| Financial Managers | $558.00 | 67% | $ 833.00 |
| Lawyers & Judges | $834.00 | 70% | $1184.00 |
| Managers, Marketing, Advertising, & Public Relations | $616.00 | 68% | $ 902.00 |
| Personnel & Labor Relations Managers | $604.00 | 69% | $ 881.00 |
| Registered Nurses | $608.00 | 99% | $ 616.00 |
| Secretaries, Stenographers, & Typists | $341.00 | 88% | $ 387.00 |
| Teachers, College & University | $620.00 | 77% | $ 808.00 |
| Teachers, Elementary | $513.00 | 89% | $ 575.00 |
| Waiters & Waitresses | $194.00 | 73% | $ 266.00 |

SOURCE: *U.S. News and World Report*/U.S. Department of Labor.

As women increasingly become heads of households, this persistent wage gap contributes heavily to the growing pauperization of women and children. In 1990, while the average married-couple family with the wife in the paid labor force earned $39,996, and the average unmarried male earned $22,489, the average unmarried female earned only $14,099 (U.S. Department of Commerce, Bureau of the Census, 1991c). Currently, about half of all female-headed households live below the poverty line. This situation heavily affects children: Women are given custody of children in about 90% of divorce cases and often must attempt to support the family on a low-wage budget. According to the National Center for Children in Poverty (1991) nearly one of every four children in the nation under six years of age is poor. Additionally, children represent a declining proportion of the population, whereas the elderly represent a rising proportion (Figure 6.3). One implication of this demographic shift, according to the National Commission on Children (1991), is that "each worker will bear a greater burden of support for the nation's retirees" (p. 5).

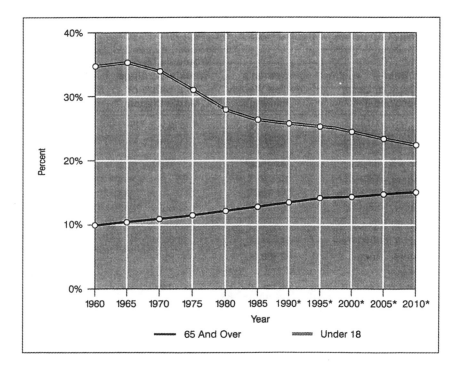

FIG. 6.3.   Growth in the elderly population.
SOURCE: U.S. Department of Commerce, Bureau of the Census, *Current Population Reports*, series p-25, no. 1018, *Projections of the Population of the United States by Age, Sex, and Race: 1988–2080* (Washington, DC: U.S. Government Printing Office, 1989), page 8, Table G.

The influx of women into the labor market is taking another toll on women as well: Because housework and child care continue to be regarded as women's responsibilities, most husbands do not yet assume an equal share of these roles, although they share more now than they did 20 years ago. Consequently, married women who hold jobs are finding themselves with less and less leisure time. For example, researchers in a 1986 study of a company in Boston found that:

> women work twice as many hours on child care and homemaking as men, even when the woman's income is greater than the man's. They also found that women are more likely to stay home if the children are sick and that married female parents spend a total of eighty-five hours a week on work, in and outside of the home, while married male parents spend sixty-five hours. (Sidel, 1990, pp. 202–3).

Because they anticipate being the primary domestic workers, many women do not enter careers that require long hours, one reason why women's earning power continues to lag. For example, "a recent detailed study by the Boston Bar Association of 2,000 lawyers in the Boston area found that women were significantly more likely than men to be single, divorced, and without children" (Sidel, 1990, p. 174). These developments and divorce settlements in which women are viewed as the primary caretakers of children are leading some female attorneys and scholars to argue, according to Gest (1991), that the landscape of the legal world needs to be redrawn to replace the "male" value system of rights, rules, and hierarchies with "female" values based upon relations, responsibilities, and caring.

Violence against women is another manifestation of women's devalued status in society. Statistics on battered women vary from 15 million physically abused women to one-third of the female population (Sidel, 1990). For example, in Wisconsin during 1991 there were 24,163 reported incidents of domestic abuse; 80% of the victims were female. Physicians were being instructed to ask more about domestic abuse when female patients showed physical injuries (Buelow, 1992). Many women regard violence against women as a power issue, the act of beating representing an attempt to reaffirm women's subordinate status.

The political position of women has improved somewhat, but is still no better than women's economic position. Although greatly increasing numbers of women have been elected to local and state offices, women still constitute only a small minority of officeholders at the state level, and an even smaller minority at the national level. Only about 14% of the state legislators in 1985 were women. In 1993, 11% of the members of the House and .013% of all U.S. senators were women. In 1993, furthermore, only 14% of the women in Congress were of color (*Congressional Monitor*, January 5, 1993, p. 6). Only one or two states at a time have a female governor. While 1984 saw the first woman nominated by a major political party for vice president, she needed to make herself acceptable to the public by emphasizing that she had fulfilled the traditional roles of wife and mother in addition to pursuing a career.

As women gained ground both in the political sphere and in the job market during the late 1970s and 1980s, a backlash grew—one that many women regard as a move to keep women in their place domestically and to protect male access to better-paying jobs. For example, Wolf (1991) analyzed the growth of the beauty industry, arguing that media are projecting an increasingly thin and perfect beauty image to women, who are responding by becoming increasingly obsessed with losing weight and changing how they look. She reports, for example, that 90% of young American women believe they weigh too much, 5% to 10% are anorexic, most would rather lose 10 to 15 pounds than achieve any other goal in life, and 150,000 starve themselves to death every year. She traces this obsession with beauty to profit-making beauty industries, beauty requirements for some careers (such as television reporting), and media images that are sold to women. The entire feminist movement itself has been cast as the "ravings" of a fringe group of women who would rather be men. As a result, contemporary young women are often ambivalent about gender issues and tend to regard equality as having been achieved, with choices now open to everyone regardless of sex (Sidel, 1990).

Sexual orientation is a gender issue that came "out of the closet" during the 1960s and 1970s. Gay and lesbian activists worked hard to redefine sexual orientation from a pathology to a civil rights issue— claiming, for example, that heterosexual couples who marry receive tax benefits that gay couples who marry do not receive. Currently, there is no national legislation that protects the rights of gay and lesbian people. While some cities, for example, prohibit discrimination in hiring on the basis of sexual orientation, in other areas of the country such discrimination is legal. Further, the 1992 Republican platform adopted a plank that specifically opposed civil rights laws protecting people on the basis of sexual orientation.

The United States is a distinctly social class–stratified society, and appears to be becoming more so. Although debates about racism and sexism have always existed, and in the last three decades have been quite plentiful, Americans have devoted much less attention to social class stratification. Yet there are tremendous inequities in the distribution of wealth. In 1989, the wealthiest 4% of the population earned as much as the bottom 51%. In 1970, the wealthiest 4% earned as much as the bottom 38%, and in 1959, as much as the bottom 35% (Barlett & Steele, 1992). In other words, more and more Americans have over the past three decades been downwardly mobile, and the gap between the wealthiest Americans and the majority has widened. As Figure 6.4 shows, between 1978 and 1986, a time of rapid change in wealth distribution, the middle class shrank and the lower class grew over twice as much as the upper class.

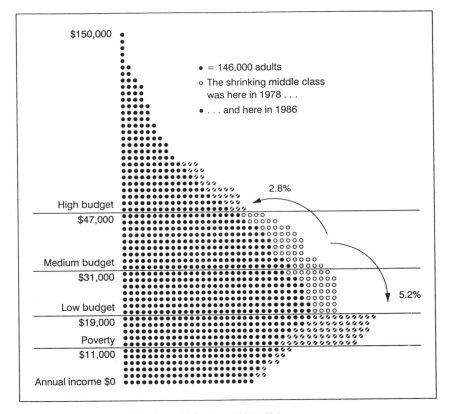

FIG. 6.4.   The shrinking middle class: 1978–1986.
SOURCE: S. J. Rose, *The American profile poster*. New York: Pantheon
Books, a Division of Random House, Inc. 1986. Reprinted by permission.

The poverty rate in the United States in 1990 was 13.5% (U.S. Department of Commerce, Bureau of the Census, 1991a). Although the United States is a relatively wealthy nation, it has not been able to rid itself of poverty. Many find it tempting to blame the poor for poverty, arguing that the unemployed do not want to work. However, our economy sustains an unemployment rate that rarely falls below 7%. This statistic means that there are not enough jobs to go around, and 7% of Americans actively seeking work are unable to find it; this figure does not include those who have given up and stopped looking. Furthermore, many of the poor are employed but are paid very low wages.

For example, Figure 6.5 shows the income of a woman with two children in Kenosha, Wisconsin, in 1991 if she is on AFDC (Aid for Families with Dependent Children), or if she is employed in a minimum-wage job. In either case, her financial resources are minimal. Try constructing a budget for her that includes rent, utilities, food, transportation, toiletries, medical expenses, and clothing.

---

Woman with 2 children in Kenosha in 1991:
What she lives on per month.

- No earned income:
  $517 AFDC + $112 food stamps
- Full-time minimum wage worker:
  $3.80/hr = $576/month + $57 food stamps
- Full-time worker: $4.25/hr = $731/month + $48 food stamps

---

FIG. 6.5. Options for mothers on welfare.
SOURCE: What welfare moms live on. *Kenosha News* Special Report, *No place to call home.* February 22, 1992, pp. 2–3.

In *The New American Poverty*, Harrington (1984) argued that there was a growing gap between rich and poor in the United States and that the middle class today was shrinking as a result of changes in the economic structure. He observed:

People who, twenty or even ten years ago, were secure in their jobs and communities now live somewhere between poverty and semiaffluence, walking the edge of an economic precipice. Their problems will be ameliorated, but far from ended, by economic recovery, if this really does come. For they, or people like them, are likely to face downward social mobility for twenty or thirty years, unless this country turns around. These are not, then, the instant "new poor" that the media discovered in that winter of American discontent, 1982–83. (p. 64)

Almost a decade later, with the U.S. economy still operating at a subpar level, Hacker (1992) in *Two Nations* points out that the economic situation for many is still very dismal. He observes that many who have jobs are employed for less than a full day's work or only for a part of the year. He also discloses that in addition to the number of men and women who are officially recorded as unemployed, at least an equal number have given up the search for a job. Because of the inability of these people to find work, the Bureau of Labor Statistics has created a category called "discouraged worker" (p. 105).

In spite of the popular belief that anyone who desires it can attain wealth through individual effort, Jencks et al. (1972) found occupation to be predicted largely by educational attainment, which in turn is predicted mainly be family socioeconomic background. In other words, children tend to grow up to occupy the same social class position as their parents. Similarly, Hacker (1992) reports that, "there is a close association between economic status and SAT scores . . ." (p. 144). Even among those with the same level of education, the children of wealthy parents are much more likely to attain high-paying jobs than are children of lower- or middle-class parents (Rumberger, 1983).

In addition, those controlling the greatest proportion of wealth tend to have the most political power. As Parenti (1978) points out, those who are most likely to sit on state and local boards, boards for college and universities, and boards of corporations are from the upper socioeconomic classes and make the rules by which society operates. For example, in the 1980s, while the paychecks of top corporation executives increased by 149%, the pay to workers at the largest corporations decreased by 5%. While the income taxes of the richest one percent of Americans dropped 25%, income taxes for the average family rose about $400 (Reeves, 1990). In their analysis of "what went wrong" with the distribution of wealth, Barlett and Steele (1992) argue that the wealthiest rulemakers on Wall Street and in Washington have constructed laws and rules for corporations that are dismantling the middle class and channeling wealth upward to a small minority.

Finally, people with disabilities constitute a subordinate group, although statistics are not kept on them nearly as much as on other groups. Historically, public concern for their welfare has risen and fallen. With the recent passage of the Americans With Disabilities Act, it is hoped that public concern will remain active, but if history is an accurate guide, this concern may wane. Federal and state laws for disabled people do make a difference in that they offer greater protection for the rights of people with disabilities and they demand that support services be expanded. However, laws and services on behalf of people with disabilities are usually made by nondisabled people and often are not as comprehensive as people with disabilities advocate. Further, disabled people as a group are overrepresented in the ranks of the poor, and they are somewhat invisible as an impoverished group because statistics on their employment and income are not widely kept and published.

Nevertheless, there are some patterns. Most disabled adults are either unemployed or employed part-time, and their earnings are often below the poverty level. For example, Hasazi, Gordon, and Roe (1985) followed up on 459 youths exiting special education programs in Vermont. The youths' employment rate was only 54%. In a similar follow-up study in Colorado, Mithaug, Horiuchi, and Fanning (1985) found an employment rate of 69%, but almost half of those employed were earning less than $3.00 per hour. In 1984, only 27.4% of disabled people were employed full-time, a decrease of two percentage points since 1972. Of those employed, the poverty rate is 26% (Habeck, Galvid, Frey, Chadderden, & Tate, 1985). Unemployment and poverty are particularly severe among disabled people of color, who face double discrimination in the job market.

Disabled people lack access to facilities and the opportunities that most citizens enjoy. For example, although mentally retarded people are no longer automatically institutionalized in most states, increasing numbers have been institutionalized in some states in the last few years (Gearheart, 1980). Zoning laws restrict where homes for deinstitutionalized retarded people can be built. Blind, deaf, and physically impaired people have legal rights to public facilities, but in practice find it difficult or impossible to get around in many buildings, communicate with public service workers, or use certain public channels of communication.

The speed with which the Americans With Disabilities Act (1990) removes these barriers will greatly impact the successful mainstreaming of people with disabilities. Disability advocates, however, are wary and issue cautions. An article in *The Disability Rag* points out that the act "drew national attention to the fact that the problems disabled people face are primarily discrimination—not health—problems" (The Americans With Disabilities Act, 1991, p. 11). However, many people working on the act's implementation still treat those with disabilities as incapable persons rather than as intelligent collaborators. Further, opposition to the act is mounting because of the costs it will incur.

In addition, there are issues the act does not solve. For example, although the act specifies that housing is to be accessible, many builders are not familiar with or interested in accessibility (Johnson, 1991), and the legislation does not address the problems of far too little low-costing housing. Chicago's Access Living, for example, refers people with disabilities to housing, but has run out of low-cost housing to which to refer people, due partly to the fact that federal funds for low-income housing have been slashed drastically ("No housing," 1990). People with disabilities are often targets of violence and hate crimes. "Data about rape, child sexual abuse, incest, sexual harassment, battery, neglect, defamation, and other forms of violence directed at disabled people indicate that they are much more likely to be targeted for violence than their nondisabled cohorts" ("Hate," 1992, p. 5). *The Disability Rag*, a disability activist publication, regularly creates attention for access and discrimination issues of which people without disabilities are usually simply unaware.

People with disabilities also bear stereotypes of incompetence. As Gliedman and Roth (1980) have noted, public images of the disabled emphasize limitations, and disabled people have no offsetting counterimage, such as African Americans have with the "Black is beautiful" concept. Many disabled people also must depend on others to articulate their concerns. Siegel (1986) has pointed out that physically disabled people represent "an extremely vocal and powerful lobby," whereas mentally retarded and emotionally disabled people are less able to express their own interests persuasively and assertively (p. 50). Recently, nondisabled people have created alternative terms such as "physically challenged" and "differently abled" to attempt to redress this image. However, *The Disability Rag* periodically editorializes against such euphemisms, pointing out that disabilities are real and present policy issues that need action to enable real choices; euphemistic terms tend to gloss over the need for action.

## BUSINESS AS USUAL

Before we discuss approaches that teachers can take to deal constructively with race, class, gender, and disability, it is important to describe what often occurs in many classrooms and schools. School, it has been observed, reflects society. Just as a few improvements in society may give an incomplete or inaccurate view of progress in reducing racism, sexism, class bias, and bias against disabilities, a few improvements in our schools are similarly misleading. In many schools, one can readily observe students of color and White students socializing; girls in classes such as wood shop and auto shop, once considered the exclusive domain of the boys; boys in home economics classes, once considered no-man's-land; Spanish spoken in mathematics classes; and students in wheelchairs attending proms and participating in many other school events. Also, in some schools the cheering squad, band, and sports teams often reflect the diversity of the student body. Moreover, it is not unusual in integrated schools for a person of color to be the president of the student council, a class officer, or a member of the queen's court.

Furthermore, most teachers and school administrators support equal opportunity and access to all courses and activities for all students enrolled in the school: They support events that recognize the contributions of people of color and women; many welcome mainstreamed special education students into their classes; most will not tolerate sexist behavior in the classroom; and virtually all support having students from different socioeconomic status attend the same school. Also, many teachers examine their curriculum materials for bias, are willing to attend workshops dealing with multicultural education, and try to avoid using any instructional materials that are obviously biased.

These examples suggest that success for all students is the order of business in classrooms and schools. However, to the discerning observer, much has been left out. Like the society we described earlier, schools are beset with problems related to race, class, gender, and disability.

Our description of "business as usual" is based on several studies published during the 1980s and 1990s in which researchers observed what actually takes place in the schools. We will describe the main patterns that emerge. We acknowledge that schools and classrooms vary, although those that vary significantly are usually few and far between. We invite you to compare this description with schools with which you may be familiar. We have organized this description into five categories: how teachers teach, what teachers teach, how students are grouped, other patterns, and student culture.

How Teachers Teach

Many studies have found strong similarities in how teachers teach (Bigler & Lockard, 1992; Cuban, 1984; Everhart, 1983; Goodlad, 1984; Grant & Sleeter, 1986; Page, 1991; Sleeter, 1992; Trueba, Jacobs, & Kirton, 1990). Cuban (1984) summarizes these well, drawing on his own research. He separates the elementary and secondary levels, acknowledging a greater diversity among elementary teachers than among secondary teachers. Cuban reports that in elementary classrooms he came to expect a number of regularities. Almost half of the teachers (43 percent) put up a daily schedule on the blackboard. If it was time for reading, the teachers would work with one group and assign the same seatwork or varied tasks to the rest of the class. If it was time for math, social studies, science, or language arts, generally the teachers would work from a text with the entire class answering questions from the text, ditto sheets, or workbooks (p. 220).

Both Cuban, in his study of 6 school districts, and Goodlad (1984), in his study of 13 elementary–middle–high school feeder systems, found that many elementary teachers deviate from this pattern by individualizing instruction, using learning centers, and using small groups. However, the majority favored teacher-centered, large-group instruction in which all students work on the same tasks and in which much of the work depends on the textbook, ditto sheets, or workbooks.

At the secondary level, there is much more uniformity. Cuban describes the main pattern as "rows of tablet-arm chairs facing a teacher who is talking, asking, listening to student answers, and supervising the entire class for most of the period—a time that is occasionally punctuated by a student report, a panel, or a film" (p. 222). Cuban found labs in science classes to offer the main variation from this pattern in academic courses: Goodlad added that vocational, physical education, and art classes involve more varied activities and much more hands-on learning. Page's (1991) study of eight lower-track classrooms in two middle-class high schools revealed that the teachers arrange the classrooms so that students can proceed in simple, step-by-step routines to learn practical skills. She posits that the teachers dominate classroom talk without being domineering, and they "teach by remote control, without calling attention to themselves as teachers" (p. 147).

These patterns have several implications for student diversity. One implication is that students whose learning style diverges from predominant teaching styles are at a disadvantage. For example, Shade (1989) argues that African American students suffer academically in schools because their learning style tends to be oriented toward cooperation, content about people, discussion and hands-on work, and whole-to-part learning, which conflicts with the independent, task-oriented, reading-oriented, part-to-whole style that most teachers employ with most students. As another example, Deyhle (1985) found that young Navajo students interpret tests as games, in contrast to White students who view tests as serious business, a result of different home socialization. Whereas White children learn early to display knowledge publicly for evaluation, Navajo children learn at a young age that serious learning is private and therefore do not exert their best effort when tested. Furthermore, Goodlad notes that the activities used in nonacademic areas, such as industrial arts, attract students who prefer active involvement in learning. This approach may help lure lower-class and minority students, more than middle-class White students, into these areas and away from academics.

A second implication is that students whose skills deviate from those of the majority present a problem for the classroom teacher, because most teachers individualize very little. The main solution schools have used has been to place such students in remedial or special education classes or to track them. This has created additional problems.

Clearly, this uniformity in teaching procedures conflicts with the mainstreaming movement. In a study of one junior high school, we found that regular education teachers modified their procedures only minimally for mainstreamed students, and they expected everybody else to learn at the same rate, through the same instruction procedures and materials (Grant & Sleeter, 1986). It seems that regular and special educators often find themselves in conflict over the intent of PL 94–142: Many regular educators view special education as a place to put students whose skills deviate significantly from the majority, while special education teachers are trying to move students from special education back into the mainstream and wish to see regular education teachers become more flexible in how they teach.

Similarly, many bilingual education teachers find themselves in conflict with "regular" classroom teachers over the specific needs of limited English proficiency (LEP) students. Although sent to other classrooms for reading, mathematics, or other instruction, LEP students are often "mainstreamed" in art, music, and physical education. Unfortunately, some teachers refuse to alter their standard approaches to meet the needs of these students. Instead, the students' language and cultural background is sometimes perceived as a handicap, and they are then "diagnosed" and treated as learning disabled (Trueba et al., 1990).

A third implication is that much instruction given in classrooms is uninteresting and alienating for many students. In our study of a junior high school, the word students used most often to describe instruction was *boring*. Goodlad (1984) describes classrooms as emotionally flat. Students who do not readily identify with schooling, with their teachers, or with the content being taught tend to become turned off and disengaged. This seems particularly true when the content is unrelated to the students' experiential background. Everhart (1983) describes an incident in a junior high classroom in which students were filling in a worksheet after reading about Switzerland in their textbooks. Not having been to Switzerland, and not having been provided experiences to develop visual, aural, or tactile imagery about Switzerland, the students discussed the weekend football game while completing an assignment that to them was merely verbal gymnastics.

Of course, there are some excellent and dynamic teachers. Unfortunately, much of the usual classroom instruction discourages some students, turns off others, and fails to engage the minds of many. Further, those who tend to become turned off, disengaged, or frustrated are disproportionately lower-class students and students of color. (Students mainstreamed from special education may also become frustrated and disengaged, but they usually have the support and help of a special education teacher.)

There is another instructional problem that occurs in some classrooms. Research has found that many teachers interact with, call on, praise, and intellectually challenge students who are White, male, and middle class more than other students in the same classroom and that they reprimand Black male students the most (Jackson & Cosca, 1974; Sadker & Sadker, 1982). For example, Table 6.6 illustrates the average proportion of questions and praise that girls and boys received in several classrooms at three different times during the year. In the first and third observations, boys received proportionately more questions and praise than girls. During the second observation, teachers were monitoring their behavior because results of the first observation had been shared with them, but by the third observation they had returned to their earlier pattern. Further, as the year progressed, boys initiated an increasingly larger proportion of student-initiated questions (Sleeter, 1992). Teachers are usually unaware that they are showing favoritism, but such bias can benefit members of advantaged social groups when it occurs.

Bigler and Lockard (1992) observed that the teachers they interviewed reported that the reason students tell parents they did "nothing" in school is "not due to the lack of talented teachers or their desire to teach, but as a direct result of too much to do, insufficient time to do it and increasing intrusion on teaching time" (pp. 63–64). Bigler and Lockard's observation would generate very little debate among researchers who study classroom life. Nevertheless, overtaxation of teachers, lack of teaching and planning time, and classroom interruptions most directly impact students who are marginalized and can least afford it.

## What Teachers Teach

Goodlad's (1984) study of 38 schools nationwide provides a comprehensive view of what teachers today are teaching. We will not provide extensive description, but rather we will note salient findings. The main finding was

TABLE 6.6
Teacher-Student Interaction: Gender Patterns

Average Classroom Composition:
   Females    46%
   Males      54%

|  | *OBS. #1*<br>*(24 classrooms)* | *OBS. #2*<br>*(14 classrooms)* | *OBS. #3*<br>*(16 classrooms)* |
|---|---|---|---|
| Who Gets Called On: | % | % | % |
|   Females | 39 | 47 | 38 |
|   Males | 61 | 53 | 62 |
| Who Gets Praised: | | | |
|   Females | 32 | 51 | 43 |
|   Males | 68 | 49 | 57 |
| Which Students Initiate Questions: | | | |
|   Females | 35 | 22 | 19 |
|   Males | 65 | 78 | 81 |

SOURCE: C. E. Sleeter (1992), *Keepers of the American dream*, London: The Falmer Press, p. 127.

school-to-school uniformity, especially at the secondary level. Goodlad summarized two subject areas as follows: "Overall, the impression that emerged from the analysis of English and language arts was one of great curricular similarity from school to school. This impression comes through even more strongly for mathematics" (p. 208). He found that teachers in both subject areas emphasized the acquisition of skills, often apart from context or real-life use. Social studies and science at the elementary level varied considerably from classroom to classroom, often being grounded in students' experiential background. For example, primary-grade social studies usually revolved around the family and neighborhood. At the secondary level, however, social studies content became increasingly alike from one classroom to another and increasingly removed from student experience. More variation was found in what was taught in the arts and vocational areas. Goodlad also found heavy emphasis on rote learning: Although teachers often said they were developing higher-level thinking skills, their tests overwhelmingly emphasized the regurgitation of memorized material.

Curricula emphasize the White wealthy male experience, although less so today than 25 years ago. In 1990, we analyzed 47 textbooks that were in use in grades 1 through 8, with copyright dates between 1980 and 1988. The analysis included social studies, reading and language arts, science, and mathematics textbooks. The results supported the following conclusion:

> Whites consistently dominate textbooks, although their margin of dominance varies widely. Whites receive the most attention, are shown in the widest variety of roles, and dominate the story line and lists of accomplishments. Blacks are

the next most included racial group. However, the books show Blacks in a more limited range of roles than Whites and give only a sketchy account of Black history and little sense of contemporary Black life. Asian Americans and Hispanic Americans appear mainly as figures on the landscape with virtually no history or contemporary ethnic experience. . . . Native Americans appear mainly as historical figures. . . . Males predominate in most books; but even in books in which females have a major presence, females of color are shown very little. One gains little sense of the history or culture of women, and learns very little about sexism or current issues involving gender. . . . Social class is not treated in the books much at all. . . . The image that books in all subject areas convey is that the United States is not stratified on the basis of social class, that almost everyone is middle-class, that there is no poverty and no great wealth. . . . Disability is ignored as well. (Sleeter & Grant, 1991, pp. 97–98).

Furthermore, there seems to be more cultural diversity in curricular materials than in the actual content teachers teach. It is important for us to point out that, although an increasing number of teachers do use culturally pluralistic and nonsexist materials, most of these teachers do not refer very often to people of color or women when talking or lecturing (Grant & Sleeter, 1986). Thus, what teachers teach when doing "business as usual" includes people of color somewhat, and in a supplementary way, but Whites still predominate; it includes White females, but males still dominate; it includes disabled people sporadically; and it virtually excludes the experience of those living below the middle class.

The curriculum responds most actively to diversity when there are non-English-speaking students. Since the Supreme Court decision in *Lau v. Nichols* (1974), schools have been required to provide help in learning English as well as instruction in the child's language while the child is learning English. Under business as usual, this seems to mean providing bilingual or English as a Second Language (ESL) instruction for as short a time as possible until minimal English proficiency is achieved. For example, Guthrie (1985) studied a Chinese-English bilingual program in California. She found that the Chinese community wanted its children to learn the Chinese language and culture, whereas the school system expected bilingual education to work toward as rapid a transition to English as possible. Debates at the federal level during the 1980s and into the 1990s support the school system's expectation: Debates revolve around how to teach English most effectively, not how to promote bilingualism. (Interestingly, however, business as usual does encourage college-bound English-speaking students to acquire minimal competence in a second, usually Western European, language.)

So far, our description suggests that all students of a given grade level are taught much the same thing, regardless of geographic region, student interest, or cultural background, except in the case of non-English-speaking students.

This characterization is only partially correct. There does appear to be a standard curriculum that most teachers use as a guide. It is not codified in a national curriculum guide; rather, it is codified in standardized achievement tests and text materials, which are more alike than different for any given subject area. Teachers tend to use the content of text materials and standardized tests as the basis for what they teach. They then modify this material to fit the average skill level of a class and, to a much lesser degree, student interest and experiential background. For example, consider the teachers in the junior high school studied by Grant and Sleeter (1986). When asked how they decided what to teach, most teachers reported starting with an idea of what students at that grade level should know in that subject area, then adjusting forward or backward to most students' current level of mastery. In this case, students were behind grade level in most areas, so teachers either retreated to earlier material or watered down grade-level material to make it simpler. Student interest rarely affected what these teachers taught.

Goodlad's (1984) study of 38 schools supports this finding. The main variation he found in content was between tracks or ability groups. Teachers beefed up or watered down content in response to student skill level. Student interest played at most a minor role in determining the curriculum. Geographic locale played no role. Student cultural background played a minor role. Because track or ability group plays the main role in determining how teachers vary both instruction and content, we turn next to how students are grouped.

How Students Are Grouped

Within school districts, students are grouped in various ways: by school, by ability group or track, by special education need, and by interest (in the form of electives). We will discuss aspects of grouping under business as usual as they relate to race, social class, gender, and handicap.

First, although schools are supposed to be racially desegregated, they do not need to be desegregated on the basis of social class. It is quite common for schools to serve primarily or solely upper-class, middle-class, working-class, or lower-class students; and schools serving different social classes are not alike. They differ somewhat in the availability of resources, such as computers (Campbell, 1984) and in the salaries they are able to offer. They differ strikingly in curriculum and instruction. For example, based on observations in five schools, Anyon (1981) reported differences that are virtually the same as those we will describe between tracks.

Racial desegregation is also less a reality than many of us would like to believe, particularly for language-minority students. Although the segregation of African American students has decreased, the segregation of Hispanic students has increased (Orfield, 1986). The majority of Hispanic students attend schools that serve predominantly minority populations. This increased segregation of Hispanic students interferes with their acquisition of English-language competence (Garcia, 1986) and is related to higher high school dropout rates. In addition, the schools that Hispanic students attend are largely inferior, reporting the highest dropout rates, lowest achievement rates, and greatest problems with teacher turnover, overcrowding, and gangs (Kyle, Lane, Sween, & Triana, 1986). As Orum and Vincent (1984) put it, "Hispanics now have the dubious distinction of being not only the most undereducated group of American children, but also the most highly segregated" (p. 26).

A second important kind of grouping is ability grouping, extensively found in elementary schools, and tracking, a pervasive feature of high schools in the major academic areas. The pros and cons of ability grouping are a continuous focus of debate among teachers, as demonstrated on the "Speak Out" page of the American Federation of Teachers' publication *On Campus* (Lucas, 1992; Mitchell, 1992). Here, two teachers argued their positions on ability grouping, one basically arguing that ability grouping can create a label that lasts a lifetime and the other arguing that talented students must not be ignored. Based on a review of research on the effects of tracking, Oakes (1985) reports that although many people assume that ability grouping and tracking are best for most students, the evidence points clearly to the conclusion that "no group of students has been found to benefit consistently from being in a homogeneous group," and those in the middle and lower groups are often affected negatively (p. 7). Her own investigation of 25 secondary schools across the country in the late 1970s found considerable tracking being used. In multiracial schools, upper-track classes were disproportionately White, whereas lower-track classes were disproportionately minority and lower-class. Upper-track students tended to receive the following: at least 80% of class time spent on instruction, considerable homework, more varied teaching activities, clear instruction, emphasis on higher-level thinking skills, and exposure to content that would gain them access to college. Lower-track students, on the other hand, received about 67% of class time spent on instruction, half (or less) the homework of upper-track students, varied materials but very routinized instructional activities, less clarity in instruction, emphasis on rote memory, and content oriented around everyday-life skills (which may seem practical but also may block access to college). Most upper-track students reported enthusiasm for school and feelings of personal competence, whereas lower-track students were often turned off to school and felt academically incompetent. These are the same sorts of differences Anyon (1981) found between upper-class and working-class schools.

These studies clearly show that students are being grouped partly on the basis of race and social class and then are taught differently. Upper-track and upper-class students are offered more instructional time, more challenge, interesting and effective instruction, opportunities to think, and preparation for college. Lower-track and lower-class students tend to receive routine and dull instruction, less challenge, memory work, and little or no preparation for college. Middle groups receive something in between. Although people often say that these groupings meet students' instructional needs and provide opportunity for advancement, lower groups for the most part are being turned off to school and are not being pushed to catch up, causing them to grow increasingly different from other groups as they proceed through school. For this reason, schools have been very accurately described as a sorting machine, slotting the young for a stratified labor market (Spring, 1976).

A third problem is the proportionately small numbers of female students in upper-level mathematics and science courses and in computer courses. It appears that although girls may take almost as many mathematics and science courses as boys, they often avoid the more difficult courses, which greatly hinders access to mathematics and science majors in college (Fennema, 1984).

A fourth aspect of grouping is special education, which in many ways fits into the tracking system, although less so for the physically, visually, and hearing impaired than for other categories. Gifted classes are still disproportionately White, whereas classes for the mentally retarded and emotionally disturbed are disproportionately African American (Table 6.7). In some schools, Hispanic students are overrepresented in special education; in some, they are placed in bilingual education whether this is appropriate or not. Learning disability classes appear to be shifting from protective areas for White, middle-class, failing children to remedial classes for students previously classified as retarded or slow (Sleeter, 1986). The nature of content and, to some extent, instruction parallels distinctions between upper and lower tracks. However, special education teachers often do a better job than most other teachers of adapting instruction to students' learning styles, skill levels, and interests and often act as advocates and helpers for their students, helping to get them through the school system to graduation (Grant & Sleeter, 1986).

A fifth aspect of grouping is vocational classes, which group students at the secondary level somewhat by interest. Even here, however, we find grouping roughly following social class, race, and gender lines. For example, Oakes (1985) found a distinct racial difference in vocational courses: Home economics and general industrial arts were by far the main vocational courses in White schools, whereas courses preparing students for specific blue-collar and clerical occupations were common in non-White and racially mixed schools. In spite of Title IX (an education amendment of 1972 that forbids schools from restricting access to courses and school activities based upon sex), one is also likely to find a gender difference, with home economics and clerical courses dominated by girls and industrial arts courses dominated by boys (DBS Corporation, 1982). Although enrollments in vocational courses depend largely on student choice, researchers find that other factors strongly

TABLE 6.7
Percentage of Students in Disability Categories by Race

|  | Enrollment by Race (%) | | | | |
|  | American Indian | Asian | Hispanic | Black | White |
|---|---|---|---|---|---|
| Total Enrollment in School System | 1 | 3 | 10 | 16 | 70 |
| *Special Ed Classifications:* | | | | | |
| Gifted & Talented | 0 | 5 | 5 | 8 | 81 |
| Educable Mentally Retarded | 1 | 1 | 5 | 35 | 58 |
| Trainable Mentally Retarded | 1 | 2 | 10 | 27 | 60 |
| Speech Impaired | 1 | 2 | 8 | 16 | 73 |
| Severely Emotionally Disturbed | 1 | 0 | 7 | 27 | 65 |
| Specific Learning Disability | 1 | 1 | 10 | 17 | 71 |

SOURCE: B. Harry (1992). *Cultural diversity, families, and the special education system.* New York: Teachers College Press, p. 62. Reprinted by permission of the publisher, ©1992 by Teachers College, Columbia University. All rights reserved.

affect what students choose. These factors include availability of courses at their school, how comfortable students feel with the gender composition that is usually in a given course, how useful students think the course will be in helping them attain what they consider is a realistic (although not necessarily desirable) future occupation, and the quality of guidance and encouragement they receive (Grant & Sleeter, 1986; Oakes, 1985; Valli, 1986).

A sixth aspect of grouping at the secondary level is bilingual education or English as a Second Language (ESL). Many bilingual programs at the secondary level are seen by local administrators as remedial in nature, designed primarily for the limited English proficiency student who needs to "catch up" or minimally develop "survival" English skills. In addition, many programs segregate language-minority students within the school, making it more difficult for them to interact with Anglo students in English or to receive exposure to the curriculum that Anglo students are being taught. In some states where graduation requirements have recently been raised, bilingual and ESL classes are not counted for graduation. With the institution of minimum competency testing (in English), many language-minority students face the possibility of not receiving high school diplomas or of receiving "attendance diplomas" that will close opportunities for postsecondary education (Fernandez & Velez, 1985).

All of this suggests that when schools operate according to business as usual, students are grouped in ways that roughly parallel race, class, and gender lines and then are taught in ways that help channel them into roles currently occupied by members of their race, class, and gender groups. Grouping is usually based on tests, teacher judgment, grades, and student choice, but as ethnographic studies of schools are revealing, all of these processes are often linked in subtle but strong ways to race, social class, and gender.

Other Patterns

Additional patterns in schools tend to mirror and help reproduce prevailing race, social class, and gender patterns. Viewing school systems from top to bottom, one finds the following staffing patterns: Superintendents are overwhelmingly White and male (95%). Twenty-seven percent (27%) of the principals in the country are women, and although they make up 34% of the elementary school principals, they only account for 12% of the secondary school principalships (American Association of School Administrators, 1989). Therefore, women and men of color in school administration tend to be elementary school principals, central office staff, or administrators charged with duties related to Title IX, desegregation, and so forth. Over

90% of teachers are White, and this percentage is increasing. Over 80% of elementary school teachers are female; mathematics, science, and industrial arts teachers are predominantly male, whereas foreign language, English, and home economics teachers tend to be female. People of color are often custodians and aides, and over 90% of secretaries are women. These patterns offer distinct role models and authority relationships for students.

In addition, the growing lack of people of color in teaching and administration means that fewer teachers are likely to identify with and advocate concerns particular to students of color. Furthermore, the preponderance of men in decision-making positions sometimes causes insufficient attention to be paid to the concerns of female students, whereas the preponderance of women at the elementary school level makes it difficult for many boys to identify with school and its requirements.

Extracurricular activities can also mirror existing societal patterns and reinforce segregation patterns, although situations vary from school to school. However, the following patterns are not uncommon. Middle- and upper-class students often dominate the activities, especially activities that are academically oriented. In racially mixed schools, especially if Whites are clearly in the majority, Whites tend to dominate. When White domination occurs, other students often feel unwelcome in activities. Students of color sometimes dominate some of the sports. At times, sports are race/class divided, with golf or swimming, for example, predominantly White and basketball predominantly Black. Boys' sports often receive a larger share of the budget than girls' sports and may receive better coaches, better playing schedules, and so forth. Probably the greatest change in extracurricular activities in the past several decades has been the development of girls' sports; the challenge now seems to be to make them qualitatively equal to boys' sports.

## Student Culture

The preceding discussion centered on what schools do. But students do not respond to schools in a mechanical fashion. Researchers are increasingly aware that student cultures develop in ways that often help reproduce existing social patterns, make it difficult to change student behavior, and reaffirm to teachers that their own behavior toward students is correct. Often, great gaps exist between how teachers and students perceive each other and how they perceive themselves.

Everhart (1983), for example, studied boys in a White, working-class junior high school. The boys entered school uncertain about occupational goals, familiar mainly with working-class jobs and ways of life. The teachers perceived the students as academically average or below average, with most of them probably headed for working-class jobs. Classroom instruction was teacher dominated, rarely individualized, and routine, emphasizing the memorization of predigested material. To an observer, it was immediately apparent that students spent quite a bit of time goofing off, investing only as much effort in classwork as they needed to get by. On closer examination, however, Everhart found that the students actively engaged in creating a culture that would help make school livable. The students saw school as analogous to the work world, and the school offered much on which to base this analogy: It was clearly dominated by authority figures with whom the students could not identify; the work was routine and unrelated to the students' daily lives; most of the students' time was structured; and students were rewarded for accomplishing prescribed pieces of work. Without consciously connecting their interpretation of school to the labor market or their future life chances, the students attempted to control whatever fragments of time they could and to build relationships with each other. To the teachers, the students' behavior reaffirmed that they were not interested in academic work and were incapable of managing substantive decisions, so there was no point in challenging them. The teachers seemed unaware that the student culture was generated partly in response to what they offered the students; and the low level of academic work, accepted by both teachers and students, helped ensure the students a working-class future.

Gaskell (1985) offers a similar portrait of working-class girls in clerical courses. The girls chose the courses for several reasons: These courses offered more hands-on learning than did college-preparation courses and were therefore more fun; the students were treated more like adults than were academic students; and the courses would help the girls secure a secretarial job before settling down to raise a family. Many of the girls did not particularly like secretarial work, but given the world they grew up in, this option seemed like a more viable alternative than college preparation. In school, they developed a culture that rejected academics (academic kids being viewed as somewhat childish rather than mature). Their culture centered around building social relationships with each other and drew on traditional patterns of femininity for guidance in how to control bosses, handle male workers, make boring work fun, and so forth. To the outside observer, it seemed that these girls were predisposed to be traditional women, that they chose secretarial work because they liked it, and that the school had nothing to do with these things. From the inside, it was found that the girls developed their secretarial culture as a way of trying to make the best of what they saw as limited career options, to cope with male co-workers, and to attain some status for themselves in relationship to middle-class, college-bound students.

Student culture has relevance to "business as usual," because it helps shape many of the decisions students make about school and because it develops as much from within the school as from outside the school. Many teachers believe that all or most of their students' values and beliefs are generated only from outside; students who fail, turn off, drop out, or choose low-ability classes are doing so in spite of the school's attempt to give all an equal chance. These teachers often blame the students' home culture or society in general.

Although society and home certainly cannot be discounted, they do not determine student behavior. In a very real sense, students determine it as they make sense of the school experience they confront every day. All the patterns described here as business as usual present students with experiences that vary somewhat according to student race, social class, and gender, among other factors; the experiences that students have outside the school give them frameworks that also vary by race, social class, and gender, and students use these frameworks to interpret school life. There has always been a gap between teachers and students, resulting at least from age and role and often compounded by differences in cultural background. This gap has been recently expanded, as an increasing number of students come from homes that have alternative life styles and family arrangements. Some teachers bridge this gap and grasp the differences in student culture and life style fairly well; many do not, interpreting student behavior as part of the natural order of things that teachers need to control and to discourage from being reproduced. As the teaching staff in the United States becomes increasingly older and increasingly White, it is quite possible that the gap between teachers and students, and especially low socioeconomic-status students and students of color, will widen to become a chasm in many schools.

## APPROACHES TO MULTICULTURAL EDUCATION

The problems we have just described have existed for a long time and have been recognized and contested by many educators. In fact, the progress that we have noted has come about largely through the efforts of educators, working in conjunction with community and social movements, to make schools, along with other social institutions, fairer and more responsive to the needs of the students.

The reforms that educators have advocated bear different names but are directed toward common practices. Some of the more common names for these reforms are *multicultural education, nonsexist education, human relations, gender fair education, multiethnic education, ethnic studies, sex equity, bilingual/bicultural education, anti-racist teaching,* and *mainstreaming.* Multicultural education has emerged as an umbrella concept that deals with race, culture, language, social class, gender, and disability. Although many educators still apply it only to race, it is the term most frequently extended to include additional forms of diversity. For this reason, we will use the term *multicultural education* to refer to educational practices directed toward race, culture, language, social class, gender, and disability, although in selecting the term we do not imply that race is the primary form of social inequality that needs to be addressed. We see racism, classism, and sexism as equally important.

Educators have not advocated a single, unified plan for multicultural education. Responding to somewhat different issues in different schools, employing different conceptual views of school and society, and holding somewhat different visions of the good society, educators over the years have constructed different approaches to multicultural education.

Gibson in 1976 reviewed advocacy literature in multicultural education, identifying four approaches that led her to ultimately suggest a fifth. The four approaches she identified were education of the culturally different, or benevolent multiculturalism, which seeks to incorporate culturally different students more effectively into mainstream culture and society; education about cultural differences, which teaches all students about cultural differences in an effort to promote better cross-cultural understanding; education for cultural pluralism, which seeks to preserve ethnic cultures and increase the power of ethnic minority groups; and bicultural education, which seeks to prepare students to operate successfully in two different cultures. She proposed, as an alternative, "multicultural education as the normal human experience," which teaches students to function in multiple cultural contexts, ethnic or otherwise (such as regional).

Pratte's (1983) typology of approaches was similar. He identified the following four approaches: restricted multicultural education, which seeks to remediate deficiencies in culturally different students and teach majority students to tolerate minorities; modified restricted multicultural education, which seeks to promote full school services for all groups and promote equality among groups within the school; unrestricted multicultural education, which seeks to remediate ethnocentrism in all students by teaching them to identify with a plurality of cultural groups; and modified unrestricted multicultural education, which seeks to prepare all students for active citizenship in a racially diverse society.

Combined, these two typologies distinguish fairly well among the various approaches to multicultural education, but they have some limitations, the main one being that neither author fleshed out the theory undergirding each approach. (Each approach occupied a page or less in a journal.) A second limitation is that both typologies were applied only to race and missed or glossed over distinctions related to gender and social class. A third limitation is that the two typologies did not quite capture the range of practices we have observed in schools. Finally, a fourth limitation is that they tended to focus on issues related to cultural diversity more than social inequality.

Based on our own work as teachers, administrators, college professors, and ethnographic researchers, as well as on extensive reviews of the literature on multicultural education (Grant, 1992a & 1992b; Grant & Sleeter, 1985; Grant, Sleeter, & Anderson, 1986; Sleeter, 1991 & 1992; Sleeter & Grant, 1987), we constructed our own typology of approaches to multicultural education. We will briefly introduce these approaches.

During the 1960s, in efforts to desegregate schools, many White educators "discovered" students of color and saw them as culturally deprived. This view was contested vigorously by those who argued that these students were different, not deficient, and that their cultural differences should be accepted by the school. This view has been paralleled by many special educators who argue that disabled students' differences should be accepted and built on. The approach that emerged—Teaching the Exceptional and the Culturally Different—focuses on adapting instruction to student differences for the purpose of helping these students more effectively succeed in the mainstream. This corresponds to Gibson's first approach and Pratte's first and second.

During about the same period, but building on the post–World War II Intercultural Education Movement, other educators argued that love, respect, and more effective communication should be developed in schools to bring people who differ closer together. This developed into the Human Relations approach, which corresponds to Gibson's second approach. It has often been applied to race, gender, and handicap.

The 1960s also saw the emergence of more assertive approaches to change the mainstream of America rather than trying to fit people into it. Ethnic studies, women's studies, and, to a lesser extent, labor studies were developed in an effort to focus attention on specific groups, raise consciousness regarding that group's oppression, and mobilize for social action. This was a portion of Pratte's second approach.

The Multicultural Education approach emerged during the early 1970s, continuing to develop as some educators have grown disenchanted with earlier approaches and as others have begun conceptualizing more complete and complex plans for reforming education. This approach links race, language, culture, gender, disability, and, to a lesser extent, social class, working toward making the entire school celebrate human diversity and equal opportunity. Both Gibson and Pratte described it as their third approach, and we have subsumed Gibson's fourth and fifth approaches under it.

Finally, the 1970s and 1980s saw the development of a fifth approach, which we are calling Education That Is Multicultural and Social Reconstructionist. In the 1990s this approach is gaining in recognition and credibility, in part because it extends the Multicultural Education approach into the realm of social action and focuses at least as much on challenging social stratification as on celebrating human diversity and equal opportunity. Pratte's fourth approach leaned in this direction.

## REFERENCES

Alsalam, N., & Rogers, G. T. (1991). *The condition of education 1991: Volume 2. Postsecondary education.* Washington, DC: U.S. Government Printing Office.

American Association of School Administrators. (1989). Personal communication.

The Americans with Disabilities Act: Where we are now. (1991, January/February). *The Disability Rag,* 11–19.

Anyon, J. (1981). Elementary schooling and distinctions of social class. *Interchange, 12,* 118–132.

Barlett, D. L., & Steele, J. B. (1992). *America: What went wrong?* Kansas City, MO: Andrews & McMeel.

Beulow, M. C. (1992, July 13). State doctors told to ask more about domestic abuse. *Kenosha News,* p. 1.

Bigler, P., & Lockard, K. (1992). *Failing grades.* Arlington, VA: Vandermere Press.

Bobo, L., Schuman, H., & Steeh, C. (1986). Changing racial attitudes toward residential integrations. In J. Goering (Ed.), *Housing desegregation and federal policy* (pp. 153–169). Chapel Hill: University of North Carolina Press.

Campbell, P. (1984). The computer revolution: Guess who's left out? *Interracial Books for Children Bulletin, 15,* 3–6.

*Congressional Quarterly Weekly Report.* (1986, 8 November).

Cuban, L. (1984). *How teachers taught.* New York: Longman.

DBS Corporation. (1982). *Elementary and secondary schools survey.* Unpublished paper prepared for the U.S. Office of Civil Rights, U.S. Department of Education.

Dervarics, C. (1991). Landmark study confirms widespread job bias. *Black Issues in Higher Education, 8*(7), 1 & 4.

Deyhle, D. (1985). Testing among Navajo and Anglo students: Another consideration of cultural bias. *Journal of Educational Equity and Leadership, 5,* 119–131.

Everhart, R. (1983). *Reading, writing, and resistance.* Boston: Routledge & Kegan Paul.

Fennema, E. (1984). Girls, women, and mathematics. In E. Fennema and M. I. Ayer (Eds.), *Women and education* (pp. 137–164). Berkeley: McCutchan.

Fernandez, R. R., & Velez, W. (1985). Race, color, and language in the changing public schools. In L. Maldonado & J. Moore (Eds.), *Urban ethnicity in the United States: New immigrants and old minorities* (pp. 123–144). Beverly Hills, CA: Sage.

Gallup, G., Jr., & Hugick, L. (1990). *Racial tolerance grows, progress on racial equality less evident.* Los Angeles: Gallup Poll News Service.

Garcia, E. E. (1986). Bilingual development and the education of bilingual children during early childhood. *American Journal of Education, 95,* 96–121.

Gaskell, J. (1985). Course enrollment in the high school: The perspective of working-class females. *Sociology of Education, 58,* 48–59.

Gearheart, B. (1980). *Special education for the '80s.* New York: Merrill/Macmillan.

Gest, T. (1991, June 17). The new meaning of equality. *U.S. News & World Report,* p. 48.

Gibson, M. A. (1976). Approaches to multicultural education in the United States: Some concepts and assumptions. *Anthropology and Education Quarterly, 7,* 7–18.

Gliedman, J., & Roth, W. (1980). *The unexpected minority.* New York: Harcourt Brace Jovanovich.

Goodlad, J. I. (1984). *A place called school.* New York: McGraw-Hill.

Grant, C. A. (1992a). *Best practices in teacher preparation for urban schools.* Paper presented at the American Educational Research Association National Conference, San Francisco.

Grant, C. A. (Ed.). (1992b). *Research and multicultural education.* London: The Falmer Press.

Grant, C. A., & Sleeter, C. E. (1985). The literature on multicultural education: Review and analysis. *Educational Review, 37,* 97–118.

Grant, C. A., & Sleeter, C. E. (1986). *After the school bell rings.* Barcombe, England: Falmer Press.

Grant, C. A., Sleeter, C. E., & Anderson, J. E. (1986). The literature on multicultural education: Review and analysis, Part II. *Educational Studies, 12,* 47–71.

Guthrie, G. P. (1985). *A school divided.* Hillsdale, NJ: Lawrence Erlbaum.

Habeck, R. V., Galvid, D. E., Frey, W. D., Chadderden, L. M., & Tate, D. G. (1985). Economics and equity in employment of people with disabilities: International policies and practices. *Proceedings from the Symposium.* East Lansing, MI: University Center for International Rehabilitation.

Hacker, A. (1992). *Two nations: Black and white, separate, hostile, and unequal.* New York: Charles Scribner's Sons.

Harrington, M. (1984). *The new American poverty.* New York: Holt, Rinehart & Winston.

Harry, B. (1992). *Cultural diversity, families, and the special education system.* New York: Teachers College Press.

Hasazi, S., Gordon, L., & Roe, C. (1985). Factors associated with the employment status of handicapped youth exiting high school from 1979 to 1983. *Exceptional Children, 51,* 455–477.

Hate. (1992, May/June). *The Disability Rag,* 4–7.

Jackson, G., & Cosca, C. (1974). The inequality of educational opportunity in the Southwest: An observational study of ethnically mixed classrooms. *American Educational Research Journal, 11,* 219–229.

Jencks, C., Smith, M., Acland, H., Bane, M. J., Cohen, D., Gintis, H., Heyns, B., & Michelson, S. (1972). *Inequality: A reassessment of the effect of family and schooling in America.* New York: Harper & Row.

Johnson, M. (1991, March/April). What builders don't know. *The Disability Rag,* 12–17.

Kyle, C. L., Jr., Lane, J., Sween, A., & Triana, A. (1986). *We have a choice: Students at risk of leaving Chicago public schools.* Chicago: DePaul University Center for Research on Hispanics.

Lau v. Nichol, 414, U.S. 563 (1974).

Lucas, L. (1992). Does ability grouping do more harm than good? Don't ignore the potential of talented students. *On Campus, 11*(6), 6.

Mare, R. D., & Winship, C. (1984). The paradox of lessening racial inequality and joblessness among black youth: Enrollment, enlistment, and employment, 1964–1981. *American Sociological Review, 49,* 39–55.

McGowan, B. (1991). *Children welfare reform.* New York: National Center for Children in Poverty, Columbia University School of Public Health.

Mitchell, B. L. (1992). Does ability grouping do more harm than good? It creates labels that last a life time. *On Campus, 11*(6), 6.9

Mithaug, D. E., Horiuchi, C. N., & Fanning, P. N. (1985). A report on the Colorado statewide follow-up survey of special education students. *Exceptional Children, 51,* 397–404.

National Center for Education Statistics, Office of Education Research and Improvement. (1991). Washington, DC: U.S. Government Printing Office.

National Commission on Children. (1991). *Beyond rhetoric.* Washington, DC: U.S. Government Printing Office.

No housing to refer people to. (1990, May/June). *The Disability Rag,* 7.

Oakes, J. (1985). *Keeping track: How schools structure inequality.* New Haven: Yale University Press.

Ogle, L. T., Alsalam, N., & Rogers, G. T. (1991). *The condition of education 1991: Volume 1. Elementary and secondary education.* Washington, DC: U.S. Government Printing Office.

Orfield, G. (1986). Hispanic education: Challenges, research, and policies. *American Journal of Education, 95,* 1–25.

Orum, L., & Vincent, A. (1984). *Selected statistics in the education of Hispanics.* Washington, DC: National Council of La Raza.

Page, R. N. (1991). *Lower-track classrooms.* New York: Teachers College Press.

Parenti, M. (1978). *Power and the powerless.* New York: St. Martin's Press.

Pratte, R. (1983). Multicultural education: Four normative arguments. *Educational Theory, 33,* 21–32.

Reeves, R. (1990, August 30). Who got what in the 1980's. *Kenosha News,* p. 10.

Riche, M. F. (1991). We're all minorities now. *American Demographics,* 26–34.

Rumberger, R. W. (1983). The influence of family background in education, earnings, and wealth. *Social Forces, 3,* 755–773.

Sadker, M., & Sadker, A. (1982). *Sex equity handbook for schools.* New York: Longman.

Shade, B. J. (1989). *Culture, style, and the educative process.* Springfield, IL: Charles C. Thomas.

Sidel, R. (1990). *On her own: Growing up in the shadow of the American dream.* New York: Penguin Books.

Siegel, S. (1986). *The right to work: Public policy and the employment of the handicapped.* Unpublished doctoral dissertation, San Francisco State University and University of California, Berkeley.

Sleeter, C. E. (1986). Learning disabilities: The social construction of a special education category. *Exceptional Children, 53,* 46–54.

Sleeter, C. E. (Ed.). (1991). *Empowerment through multicultural education.* Albany, NY: SUNY Press.

Sleeter, C. E. (1992). *Keepers of the American dream.* London: The Falmer Press.

Sleeter, C. E., & Grant, C. A. (1987). An analysis of multicultural education in the U.S.A. *Harvard Educational Review, 57,* 421–444.

Sleeter, C., & Grant, C. (1991). Race, class gender, and disability in current textbooks. In M. W. Apple & L. K. Christian-Smith (Eds.), *The politics of the textbook* (pp. 78–110). New York: Routledge.

Spring, J. (1976). *The sorting machine: National education policy since 1945.* New York: McKay.

Tippeconnic, J. W., III. (1991). The education of American Indians: Policy, practice, and future direction. In D. E. Green & T. V. Tonnesen (Eds.), *American Indians: Social justice and public policy* (pp. 180–207). Milwaukee, WI: University of Wisconsin System Institute for Race and Ethnicity.

Treiman, D. J., & Hartman, H. I. (1981). *Women, work, and wages: Equal pay for jobs of equal value.* Washington, DC: National Academy Press.

Trueba, H. T., Jacobs, L., & Kirton, E. (1990). *Cultural conflict and adaptation: The case of Hmong children in American society.* London: The Falmer Press.

U.S. Department of Commerce, Bureau of the Census. (1991a). *Current Population Reports,* series P-70, no. 29. Washington, DC: U.S. Government Printing Office.

U.S. Department of Commerce, Bureau of the Census. (1991b). *Measuring the effect of benefits and taxes on income and poverty: 1990.* Washington, DC: U.S. Government Printing Office.

U.S. Department of Commerce, Bureau of the Census. (1991c). *Statistical Abstract of the United States 1991.* Washington, DC: U.S. Government Printing Office.

U.S. Department of Commerce, Bureau of the Census. (1991d). U.S. Department of Labor statistics. *Employment and Earnings.* Washington, DC: U.S. Government Printing Office.

U.S. Department of Commerce, Bureau of the Census. (1991e). *Workers with low earnings: 1964 to 1990.* Washington, DC: U.S. Government Printing Office.

U.S. Department of Health and Human Services. (1985). *Report to the secretary's task force on Black and minority health, Vol. 1, Executive summary.* Washington, DC: U.S. Department of Health and Human Services.

U.S. Department of Justice. (1990). *Correctional population in the U.S.* National Prison Statistics Series. Washington, DC: U.S. Government Printing Office.

Valli, L. (1986). *Becoming clerical workers.* Boston: Routledge & Kegan Paul.

Wolf, N. (1991). *The beauty myth: How images of beauty are used against women.* New York: William Morrow.

# 7

▼▼▼▼▼▼▼

# Tracking, Inequality, and the Rhetoric of Reform: Why Schools Don't Change*

Jeannie Oakes

In these times of perceived scarcity, the question that most threatens American ideology surfaces at every turn: If there isn't enough to go around, who gets it? The current supply-side, trickle-down answer is clear: Those who have, shall get. In education the question has been forced by diminishing resources and the withdrawal of public support. The answer is confirmed in the recent reform reports and in policymakers' enthusiastic response to them. There is a cynical common thread that both the detractors and supporters of these reports share, and the metaphor of the swinging pendulum serves to illustrate it. Sometimes we're more conservative, sometimes more liberal; sometimes there's money and confidence, sometimes we feel poor and hopeless. Back and forth. Everyone senses that the change is illusory.

The intent of this paper is to respond to that pendulum phenomenon, for until it is understood clearly, a powerful force—as little "seen" as gravity—will continue to shape our schools. That force, present at the turn of the century, almost unchanged in the generous '60s, and with us today, is the differentiation of schooling experiences according to the belief that some children can more easily or more deservedly achieve excellence.

Current school reform proposals represent, for the most part, a stripping away of some of the contemporary guises of traditional schooling content and forms. This is differentiated schooling characterized by Anglo-conformity and meritocracy. Deemed "excellent" in the reform rhetoric, this mode of schooling has historically restricted both access to education and achievement of ethnic minority and poor children. Well-intentioned, progressive

*From Oakes, Jeannie. "Tracking, Inequality, and the Rhetoric of Reform: Why Schools Don't Change." *Journal of Education*. Vol. 168, No. 1, 1986. Reprinted by permission of Boston University.

reformers have, at times, succeeded in mitigating the injustice inherent in these forms; even so, the current politics of social conservatism, far from inventing new inequities, appear to be largely capitalizing on endemic ones.


## PREVAILING CONCEPTIONS OF EQUALITY AND SCHOOLING

Traditional schooling forms, so clearly symbolized by the practice of tracking, are deeply rooted in assumptions about student differences and the meritocratic nature of schooling. Political and economic trends generate changes in rhetoric without addressing these assumptions or affecting the essential nature of schools as social institutions. Straightforward intents to eliminate inequality have given way to various rationales for inequality. Both are charged with a tangle of myth, unexamined assumptions, good intentions, and accurate and inaccurate beliefs.

Rarely do either those who press for equality or those who see equality as a costly luxury articulate the relationship between equality and schooling that permeates American schools. The following is an attempt to make explicit the prevailing conceptions of equality and schooling.

1. Educational opportunity, not educational results, must be equal in school.
2. Equal educational opportunity means equal opportunity to develop quite fixed individual potential (intelligence and abilities) to its limit through individual effort in school, regardless of such irrelevant background characteristics as race, class, and gender.
3. Providing equal opportunities to develop individual potential has instrumental value to both individuals and society. For individuals, it provides fair access to the world of work by providing fair access to the technical knowledge, the skills, and the attitudes that make possible the production of goods and services. Work is the way to attain the material and nonmaterial resources of society (wealth, prestige, power). For society, equal educational opportunity means that individuals' talents are developed for the benefit of all. These are contributions that could be thwarted under patronage- or inheritance-based systems.
4. Equal educational opportunity does not guarantee equal social and economic benefits to all individuals, because the rewards for various occupations are not equal. Rather, it provides a fair competition for occupations and their accompanying unequal social and economic rewards. Thus, equal educational opportunity is the means for assuring equal economic and social opportunity.

5. Education provides students with the skills, attitudes, and technical knowledge required for participation in the workforce, but of course the requirements of different occupations vary greatly. They call for quite different levels of ability.

6. Equal educational opportunity does not require the same educational experiences for all individuals, but rather an equal opportunity to develop oneself for an appropriate future in the worklife of the community. This may, and usually does, necessitate quite different educational experiences for individuals of varying abilities and future roles. Equal educational opportunity, then, requires the provision of different educational experiences and the proper match of these educations to individual ability and suitability for future work. In that way all are served equally well.

7. Publicly supported schooling is a neutral, fair, and meritocratic place to determine who is best suited for various kinds of technical knowledge and skill, to provide appropriate educational experiences toward those ends, and to certify individuals for work roles. Further, school provides immigrant and minority groups opportunities to learn mainstream attitudes, values, and behaviors that are required for successful participation in American social, political, and economic institutions. School, with the provision of equal educational opportunity, fairly stages the competition for adult positions in the social and economic hierarchy.

## THE CONTENT OF EDUCATIONAL OPPORTUNITY

Equal educational opportunity, as expressed above, has shaped the structure of the contemporary school. This view has also led to the central struggle of contemporary schooling practice—the development of curriculum and instruction suited to the wide range of abilities and future needs of American children. Differentiated schooling is the structure for equalizing opportunity. But increasing evidence points to fundamental inequalities that result.

As a part of *A Study of Schooling*, data was collected about the curricular content, instructional processes, and classroom climates in nearly 300 secondary school English and mathematics classes. Over 200 of these classes were segregated by student ability or achievement levels.[1] Students had been assigned to these classes on the basis of teacher recommendations, test scores, or the advice of their counselors. Most of the students in upper-level classes were designated as academic-track students; most of the students in average or lower-track classes were in general or vocational programs. And, consistent with other studies of tracking, students in the upper tracks were disproportionately white; those in lower tracks were disproportionately minority. The data about these classes provided an unprecedented opportunity to look carefully at the principles of equal educational opportunity as they are played out in the everyday practice of schooling (Oakes, 1985).

There were considerable differences in the kinds of knowledge students in various tracks had access to. These differences did not represent equally valued alternative curricula. They were differences that could have important implications for the futures of the students involved. Students in high-track classes were exposed to "high status" content—literature, expository and thematic writing, library research, and mathematical ideas. Students in low-track classes were not expected to learn those topics and skills. They rarely, if ever, encountered them. They worked in workbooks and kits and practiced language mechanics and computation. The schools made decisions about the appropriateness of various topics and skills and, in doing so, limited sharply what some students would learn. The lower the track, the greater the limits.

Added to the unmistakable differences in the knowledge students had available to them were differences in their classroom learning opportunities. Both in the amount of time students were provided for learning and in the quality of instruction they received, there were significant differences among track levels. High-track students had more time to learn and more exposure to what seemed to be effective teaching than did other groups. These critical features of classrooms were not equally available to all students. Those students who were judged to learn most slowly and with greatest difficulty were provided the least time and the lowest quality of instruction.

Differences in the social milieus of the tracked classes were also found. In the high-track classes, teachers were perceived as more concerned and supportive; peers were often seen as nonthreatening allies. Students in low-track classes more often characterized their teachers as punitive and fellow students as unfriendly; their classes were more often seen as permeated with alienation, distance, and hostility.

What these students experienced in their classrooms shed considerable light on how equality of opportunity is manifested in classrooms. Despite meritocratic justifications and democratic intent, these data show an unequal distribution of learning opportunities in a direction that favors the already privileged. In the name of equal opportunity, track levels in schools, reflective of social and economic groupings in society, are provided with differential access to school opportunities that is likely to maintain or increase, rather than erase, the inequities in the larger social structure.


## THE CONTEXT OF EDUCATIONAL OPPORTUNITY

To understand how schools arrived at this particular refinement of "separate-but-equal" one needs to look at the historical, political, and social context of differentiated students within schools. Shortly after the turn of the

20th century, as universal public secondary schooling was becoming a reality, the notions of equal opportunity and differentiated schooling converged in both the rhetoric and the organization of the urban high school. In 1908, the Boston school superintendent asserted, "Until very recently they [the schools] have offered equal opportunity for all to receive *one* kind of education, but what will make them democratic is to provide opportunity for all to receive such education as will fit them *equally well* for their particular life work" (Lazerson, 1974). Testing, tracking, and vocational education were the practices instituted to provide these equal opportunities. Both the rhetoric and the practices have changed little in this century.

Several related changes shaped the character of turn-of-the century America: a switch from craftsman-based to industrial production, a population shift toward urban centers, a huge influx of poor, unskilled, and non-English-speaking immigrants, and the expansion of secondary schooling. Together they constituted a transformation of the economic, social, and political realities. All played a part in redefining the American conception of a democratic society. A central focus of this redefinition was establishing the prevailing 20th-century version of the relationship between equality and schooling. What resulted were the principles of equal educational opportunity outlined above.

The ideas undergirding these principles did not materialize from thin air. The air was thick with theories about the relationship of schooling to economic production and work, the value of a meritocracy, human evolution and the superiority of Anglo-Saxon cultures, and the unlimited potential of science and industry. A brief review of these ideas provides insight into the content of both turn-of-the-century and current definitions of educational equality.

School and Work

For the first time, students who would not become scholars, professionals, or gentlemen were attending secondary schools. The traditional academic curriculum seemed a mismatch, especially for immigrants who were difficult to keep in school. Yet it seemed important and humane to postpone these children's entry into the grind of factory life. At the same time industrial employers needed immigrants socialized with the work habits and attitudes required to "fit in" as factory workers (proper deportment, punctuality, willingness to be supervised and managed) and, perhaps less important, technical skills. Native-born youth needed a changed conception of work as well. The autonomy and complexity of a craftsman-based workforce were of the past. Work in the factory required respect for the industrial, in part to make the monotony of factory work tolerable. These requirements of industry coincided with the curricular vacuum in schools. Preparation for work became a central mission of secondary schools (Edson, 1982).

## Social Darwinism and Differentiated Education

The misapplication of the theories of Charles Darwin to human society—social Darwinism—provided a *scientific* basis for viewing immigrant and minority groups as of lesser social and moral development than others. Their lives of squalor could be accounted for biologically, just as the disproportionate economic and social power held by men of Anglo stock could be justified by their "fitness." This misapplied social Darwinism, too, explained the disproportionate school failure and "retardation" rates of immigrant children. They failed because they were incapable, biologically unfit for an academic curriculum. The provision of different school content for these children—namely, industrial training—seemed not only democratic, but humane. Tracking into vocational or academic programs clearly provided equal opportunities for students with such inherently different capabilities (Hall, 1905).

## Americanization and Anglo-Conformity

Not surprisingly, given social Darwinism, the languages and habits of the southern and eastern European immigrants were threatening to native-born Americans. They were numerous, strikingly different, and poor. There emerged a great concern about preserving the dominant WASP culture, eliminating the immigrants' "depraved" life style, and making the cities safe. It seemed absolutely necessary to bring the foreign-born into the American cultural mainstream by teaching them the Protestant American values of hard work, frugality, modesty, cleanliness, truthfulness, and purity of thought and action. The program to do so, closely aligned with preparation for work, was termed Americanization and located in the public schools. The rhetoric was one of an American melting pot, but in reality only certain people were to be melted. Americanization was driven both by a belief in the goodness of Anglo ways and by fear of the immigrants. Along with industrialism, Americanization provided much of the content of educational opportunities that were provided the children of the poor (Cremin, 1964).

## Scientific Management

The concept of industrial efficiency shaped the *form* schooling would take to provide different but equal educations. The country had fallen in love with the idea of the factory busily engaged in a neatly standardized and controlled process of mass production. In went raw materials and, through the application of scientifically determined "best" methods and tools, out came ready-made goods and machinery—all designed to improve the quality of American life. The essence of the factory was efficiency. Human energies were controlled, coordinated, and channeled into machine-like parts, with little waste of material or duplication of effort. The "Taylor System" of scientific management made possible a system of production based on top-down decision making, a rigid division of labor, elaborate rules and regulations, and an attitude of impersonality toward the individual (Nelson, 1980). Schoolmen welcomed and often spearheaded the incorporation of "scientific management" into schools. Compared with the factory, schools seemed to be inefficient and unsuccessful. In an era of specifiable and measurable outcomes, what better way to manage the diversity of children's abilities and provide different educational opportunities than through the infusion of division of labor, standardization, specialization, and a division of labor into the schools?

Meritocracy

Fundamental to American conceptions of democracy is the principle that, while material rewards need not be distributed equally among citizens, the contest for these rewards must be fair. The American view of a "fair" contest is that it be won by effort and ability rather than by inherited status and privilege. Because of the central role of schools in preparing for work, educational opportunities determined by merit were seen as the fair and neutral means of providing access to economic rewards. The development of intelligence testing lent a "scientific objectivity" to the assignment of students to different curricula. Predictions about the appropriate futures of students could be made on the basis of their scores and then the requisite training could be provided.[2] It was clear from the beginning that the different educational opportunities were not equally valued. After all, they led to quite different social and economic outcomes. That poor and immigrant children consistently demonstrated the least merit and were consistently placed in the least-valued programs was not troublesome given belief in the link between race, inherited social and economic status, and ability.

THE STRUGGLE FOR EQUALITY

Even with meritocratic selection, the consistent and obvious disproportionate placement of poor and minority students in inferior school programs required justification consistent with liberal and democratic intents. By mid-century biological explanations of group differences in capability gave way to environmental ones. Cultural deficits explained the gaps in achievement between minority and white student achievement. Poor and minority family life was disorganized, noncompetitive, and anti-intellectual; it provided little motivation for learning. The admission of environmental causes of inequities led, by the '60s, to efforts to use the regulatory power of government to "equalize" the competition by ameliorating these race and class barriers. Importantly, however, neither the neutrality of schools nor the concept of equal opportunity was questioned in these "compensatory" education efforts. School failure resided in the characteristics of the students, and it was these characteristics that must be altered. The influence of Darwinism had largely disappeared, but blaming the victim remained intact (Ryan, 1976). If disadvantaged children could begin school with a "head start," or be permitted to "catch up," equal results for children of various backgrounds would surely follow.

When equal results did not follow, political and social pressure led to the provision of more and more educational resources to poor and minority education. Generous funding was given to those programs that did not upset (a) the control of education, (b) the content or organization of schooling, (c) the pattern of distribution of educational resources, or (d) eventual social and economic payoff for differing educational credentials.

Some reform did question the *principles* of equality of opportunity. This questioning led to demands for educational interventions into previously protected areas. Affirmative action threatened "equal" competition for access; multicultural and bilingual education threatened the Anglo-conformity content and process of schooling (Banks, 1981; Cheng, Brizendine, & Oakes, 1979; Grant, 1977); and minority community control of schools, as in Ocean Hill-Brownsville, threatened elite power over education. Distributing educational resources on the basis of distributive justice threatened the concept of meritocracy (Bell, 1973). The push for reforms to enhance collective good, rather than individual gain (Cagan, 1978), threatened the very heart of society, i.e., individual competition for unequal economic benefits. And in fact those programs that called for significant restructuring to benefit poor and minority children were generally ignored, aborted, or only superficially implemented. What implementation did take place was accompanied by very little enthusiasm, great suspicion, and the closest of scrutiny (looking primarily for failures). For most people in decision-making positions, the only acceptable means of "equalizing" educational opportunities was to allocate additional resources to overcome deficits—to change individual students rather than to change the conduct of schooling or to examine its underlying assumptions.

What deserves our attention is not the evidence of a mid-century move toward greater equality. Far more striking is the evidence of the resilience of the ideology of opportunity and the intransigence of the essential structural properties of schooling. Even in a period of abundant educational spending and generosity toward poor and minority children, differentiated schooling remained essentially unchanged; its justification with notions of individual and cultural differences and democratic opportunity remained virtually un-challenged.


## THE SPECTRE OF SCARCITY

Seeing the mid-century push for better schooling for poor and minorities not as an *equalization* of education, but as an *extension* of educational op-portunity permitted by a period of affluence and global supremacy, permits a clearer understanding of the retrenchment that quickly followed it. The 25 years following World War II were marked by unprecedented economic growth and material abundance. While this growth did not eliminate poverty, there was widespread optimism about prosperity trickling down to the poor. While inequalities and relative deprivation might still exist, in a period of abundance absolute deprivation could be alleviated.

The education enterprise experienced parallel surges in the amount of education and in the number of children served by the system of public schools. Demands for increased education were voiced by poor and ethnic minorities since schooling was seen as the means for commanding a greater share of the expanding wealth. The special needs and demands of poor and minority children in public schools were met by providing these children with additional educational resources, nearly always in the form of extra programs designed to ameliorate their background deficiencies and the dif-ficulties they experienced in regular school programs. The add-on approach to enhancing educational opportunities and providing "equality" in schools was perfectly compatible with an expanding economy and abundant re-sources. In these times of seeming unlimited prosperity, society could provide Head Start lunches, job training, and the like. Society could afford to be generous, even charitable, with the underprivileged. While these educational opportunities did begin to narrow the gap in educational attainment between the rich and the poor, they did not lead to any significant redistribution of economic, political, social, or educational power.

The 1970s, however, brought a set of social, political, and economic events that called this approach into serious question. For the first time, the pros-pects for unlimited economic growth and material abundance were called into question. The American economy reeled, first from the inflationary legacy of the Vietnam war and then from a dramatic rise in energy prices as Third World oil producers flexed their collective muscles. The second half of the decade of the '70s was plagued with inflation, recession, and unem-ployment.

Two quite different responses to the ecological and economic crises were voiced by scientists, politicians, and economists. One stressed the acceptance of the reality of shrinking world resources and encouraged the development of a cooperative human society in harmony with nature toward a no-growth end (see, e.g., Boulding, 1973; Commoner, 1977; Heilbroner, 1974; Schumacher, 1973). The second denied the doomsday prediction and condemned the limited vision of its spokespersons (see, e.g., Kahn, Brown, & Martel, 1976; Lipset, 1979; Macrae, 1972).

With the defeat of Jimmy Carter and the election of Ronald Reagan, the American public turned over political power to the champions of this second response. Government tinkering with the free play of the marketplace and excessive spending on social programs were blamed for inhibiting expansion, suppressing productivity, providing an easy life on the public dole, and leading to the current economic woes. "Social tinkering" had had a destructive effect on the healing and generating forces of economic growth, i.e., personal incentive, thrift, and hard work.[3] Economic recovery required a return to the values and approaches—hard work, free enterprise, and American ingenuity—that had earlier accompanied growth and prosperity. Government action must be limited to two goals: (a) eliminating controls and restrictions on the marketplace and (b) providing incentives to those with the talent, skills, and resources to spearhead the new technological advances. Gains to all would result from the "trickling down" of economic benefits. Needless to say, this approach has had ramifications for the schools.

TRICKLE-DOWN EXCELLENCE

Schools, as Seymour Sarason has so insightfully commented, serve as both scapegoats and sources of salvation (Sarason, 1983). That, of course, is the most salient message of current reforms. Although there have been hundreds of reports and state reform initiatives during the past two years, the tenor of reform is still best articulated in the 1983 round of commission reports. Their tone and substance have become recurrent themes in the educational pronouncements of politicians. Most states have followed their recommendations quite consistently in their efforts to upgrade their schools.

As the reports make plain, the current reform movement both blames schools for our current post-industrial economic woes and places on them the hope for recovery. We are all by now quite familiar with the warning in *A Nation at Risk* that "the educational foundations of our society are presently being eroded by a rising tide of mediocrity that threatens our very future as a Nation and as a people" (NCEE, 1983, p. 5). The reassertion of American dominance of a world of diminishing resources, voiced in terms of keeping and improving the "slim competitive edge we still retain in world markets," (p. 5) will result from re-establishing educational excellence in schools. "Knowledge, learning, information, and skilled intelligence are the new raw materials of international commerce and are today spreading throughout the world as vigorously as miracle drugs, synthetic fertilizers, and blue jeans did earlier" (p. 7). Given this conception of education itself as the medium of economic exchange it is not surprising that the report *Action for Excellence* claims, "Our future success as a nation—our national defense, our social stability and well-being and our national prosperity—will depend on our ability to improve education and training" (TFEEG, 1983, p. 14).

Equality issues are central to both the diagnoses of current educational troubles and the prescriptions for educational reform. The theme consistent in the diagnoses and prescriptions is that we have made a grave error in trying to be all things to all people. We have "squandered the gains in student achievement made in the wake of the Sputnik challenge" (NCEE, 1983, p. 5). After noting that efforts during the '60s and '70s to improve educational opportunities resulted in increased achievement for black students, *Action for Excellence* continues with an indictment of that era: "The fact remains, however, that overall performance in higher-order skills . . . declined in the seventies. . . . This suggests that we may be regressing from the standard of literacy which was considered adequate 15 years ago" (TFEEG, 1983, p. 24). The clear implication is that the price of extending educational opportunities was a decline in educational quality. Furthermore, providing resources to improve achievement exacted a social and economic price greater than the benefits received. *Making the Grade* is blatant in this regard: "Its [the federal government's] emphasis on promoting equality of opportunity in the public schools has meant a slighting of its commitment to educational quality" (TCF, 1983, p. 6).

The thrust of educational reform, then, is toward economic recovery through increased productivity and technological growth. Schools are to provide salvation from the crises of the '70s. The road to this salvation is clearly reflective of these crises and the lingering spectre of scarcity—even in the face of optimistic presidential promises for the future. It is clear that the central problem viewed by the makers of the reform reports is not an educational one. Educational issues have meaning only as they bear upon the issues of "real life": jobs, security, stability, defense, prosperity, and so on. And equality is given even less concern; it is tolerable as a goal only to the degree it is not perceived to stand in the way of these more important issues. And since the "real life" issues are so inextricably tied to perceptions of scarcity and abundance, education itself has meaning largely in the context of its contributions to the "good (economic) life"—Sarason's "salvation." Conversely, to the degree that prosperity, economic well-being, and so on are found wanting, all of education is suspect—Sarason's "scapegoat." If education is primarily a means to the goal of material well-being, it is not surprising that equality in education would receive little attention—no one has proven how to make equality pay. Still further, if equality is perceived as operating *against* life's real purposes (abundance) then it is all the easier to lay equality to rest with the claims that (a) we can't afford it, (b) it's bad for excellence, or (c) we solved the problem in the '60s.

It is in this context that current school reforms must be understood. Energy and resources for education are viewed as scarce. They must be expended judiciously and selectively with an eye toward maximizing economic returns. *Action for Excellence* seeks "more money *selectively invested* in efforts that promote quality" (TFEEG, 1983, p. 36). *Making the Grade* calls for public "report cards" assessing the effectiveness of funded programs (TCF, 1983, p. 18). Selective investment translates into extraordinary attention to preparing students for careers in scientific and technological fields and inattention to the worsening economic plight of the poor. This selectivity results in a reduced willingness to devote educational resources to poor and ethnic minority children. It is on those at the top that economic hopes, and therefore educational resources, are pinned.

It is in this regard that the College Board's report *Academic Preparation for College* (College Board, 1983) is of interest. The report focuses exclusively on the educational needs of the college-bound and is grounded in the view that improving college preparation is the first step toward educational reform. It is striking that a report so focused (and generated by an organization whose self-interest rests in the sale of SAT examinations) has assumed the status of a national report.[4] It symbolizes the current nearly exclusive attention on education for those students who can fulfill the hope for economic supremacy. In the current prevailing view, the provision of special opportunities or extra resources to those perceived as providing limited social and economic returns is a luxury permitted only in times of abundance. For these less promising students, financial stringency prohibits spending anything beyond what is required for preventing social disorganization (dropping out) and providing the minimum levels of competency required for low-level employment.

Still, those at the bottom are seen as benefiting educationally from this current emphasis. A more rigorously academic program at the top will create better programs for all students, it is claimed. Expanded course requirements and numbers of days and hours in school will benefit all—regardless of the differences that may exist inside their schools and classrooms. In this concentration of attention and resources on the best students there is clearly an expression of a "trickle-down" approach to educational excellence that parallels the prevailing mode of providing economic benefits. Emphasis on quality for those at the top will result in an enhanced quality of education for students throughout the system. This mood is made explicit by The College Board:

> Better preparation for the college-bound will spill over and improve the schooling of those who are not college-bound. . . . Just as the Advanced Placement Program has "rubbed off" on other teaching and learning in the schools, so better college preparation will strengthen the education of those who go directly

from high school into the world of work or into the military. (Bailey, 1983, p. 25)

In all of this, little has really changed. The reform proposals are clearly shaped by the public response to scarcity. But the neglect of equality cannot be entirely explained as a response to the current economic crises. It must be viewed also in light of a neo-conservative reassertion of the turn-of-the-century values and beliefs considered earlier, beliefs that emerge virtually unaltered in the proposals for reform. The current crises have led to the stripping away of added-on programs that for a few years masked, but did not change, the fundamentally unequal structure of schooling.

Like the early 20th-century educational advocates, none of the current reformers state that equality should be sacrificed in the quest for excellence in schools. They even purport to uphold equality. But the view of equality presented—mostly by omission—is one firmly lodged in (a) a presumption of the neutrality of schools, (b) an Anglo-conformist perspective on educational excellence, and (c) faith in objective, quantifiable specifications of educational standards. From these proceeds a narrowly meritocratic allocation of educational opportunities and rewards. All of the above are simply variations on earlier themes—themes laid bare in times of crisis.

## The Neutrality of Schools (Social Darwinism Revisited)

In their general indictment of schools, the authors of the reform reports do not attach particular importance to the fact that schools fail to serve all students equally well. Consequently, they do not consider as targets for reform the school content and processes that limit school achievement for poor and minority students. Schools are seen as essentially neutral, and the reforms are presented as color-blind and affluence-blind. The failure of disadvantaged children (especially if they have had the additional benefits of remediation, free lunches, or other "compensatory" help) becomes a matter of their own deficiencies—social, economic, educational, or linguistic—and not of the schools' inadequate response to them. Social and economic inequalities are not seen as affecting students' access to high educational expectations or excellent treatment in school. All children are seen as entrants in an equal, fair, and neutral competition.

Current reform efforts do not address the unequal quality of school facilities, programs, materials, counseling, expectations, and instruction. No interest is shown, for example, in the unequal distribution of competent teachers. Neither do they address school organizational changes likely to equalize access to high-quality educational contexts—desegregation, the elimination of tracking, and reconceptualizing vocational education programs, for example. Even as an issue is made emphatically of increasing the skills and knowledge of teachers, the assumption is that teachers simply need to get better at what they've always done. There is little or no mention of the need for teachers to be more knowledgeable about how poverty, racism, and limited expectations affect the educational treatment of poor and minority children. The omission of these concerns makes clear the prevailing conviction that schools, *as they are now*, are neutral places. While many faults are found with schools, unfairness is not one.

Special resources are seen as necessary to provide separate and different schooling for those children with deficits that prevent them from succeeding in the neutral process of schooling. The assumption that poor and minority children are *unable* to learn lurks close to the surface of these recommendations. It certainly lies behind the assertion in *A Nation at Risk* that disadvantaged children (along with other "special needs" children—gifted and learning disabled) constitute a "thin-Market area" in education. They are a group of students for whom *regular* instructional approaches are not suited. That these regular approaches themselves might be a source of disadvantage is unthinkable, given the assumption of school neutrality. And given this inattention to the race and class bias of schooling, *A Nation at Risk's* final admonition to students becomes a sad and painful message to the poor and nonwhite:

> In the end it is *your* work that determines how much and how well you learn. When you work to your full capacity, you can hope to attain the knowledge and skills that will enable you to create your future and control your destiny. If you do not, you will have your future thrust upon you by others. Take hold of your life, apply your gifts and talents, work with dedication and self-discipline. Have high expectations for yourself and convert every challenge into an opportunity. (NCEE, 1983, pp. 35–36)

## A Single Standard of Excellence
## (Return to Anglo-Conformity)

The elements proposed as the content and processes of excellent schooling are clearly reflective of Anglo-conformist values. Definitions of quality and standards are those that have historically served to discriminate against youngsters who are poor or members of ethnic minorities. There is nothing pluralistic or democratic about the educational content and processes that currently define "excellence." Perhaps *Making the Grade* is most straightforward in this regard. In a major section entitled "The Primacy of English," the report recommends that bilingual programs be replaced with programs "to teach non-English-speaking children how to speak, read, and write English" and calls the failure of bilingual programs to assert the primacy of English "a grave error" (TCF, 1983, p. 12). There is no recognition of the unique contributions of different cultures or of the special problems that

arise from a history of discrimination and racism. There is not even a recognition that cultural differences are legitimate and can contribute to a broad
general education for all American students.

Provisions of compensatory education are not to be interpreted as provisions for pluralism or, in the words of *Making the Grade*, "abandoning a
single standard of excellence. There cannot be a white standard or black
standard or a Hispanic standard when measuring educational performance"
(TCF, 1983, p. 22). This statement ignores the fact that there is a single
standard posed in the reports, and that standard is undeniably white and
middle-class.

Listen also to Secretary of Education William Bennett's response to a
Latino teacher who had pleaded for a multicultural, multi-ethnic perspective
in California schools. Bennett asserted, "I don't think it's the job of the
public schools to introduce you to your grandparents" ("Bennett Says,"
1985). Set next to Bennett's call for a reemphasis on the history and thought
of Western Civilization in undergraduate collegiate education, the point
becomes clear. Being introduced to your grandparents is an irrelevant educational matter—unless your grandparents represent the dominant cultural
tradition. The current move in the Department of Education to dismantle
bilingual education is a logical outgrowth of this perspective. Pluralism is
seen as an intolerable shift from current dominance of Anglo values and
interests.

At the same time, it is clear that what is valued for students with little
academic promise is a quite different version of Anglo-conformity than that
for the best students. The current system of differentiated curricula through
tracking and ability grouping is clearly meant to be continued. The same
subjects, the same "five new basics" of *A Nation at Risk*, are to be learned by
everyone. But whereas the favored students will be helped to develop an
*understanding* of science, mathematics, technology, and foreign language, a
very different and "minimum-competency" education is envisioned for the rest
who will be needed to fill low-status service jobs in a post-industrial economy.
The emphasis for disadvantaged students is much as it has been, an emphasis
on low-level basic literacy and computation skills (Oakes, 1985). There is no
presumption that high-status knowledge is equally appropriate for all.

The Commodification of Educational Opportunity
(Scientific Management Intensified)

In the current push for productivity, education is increasingly treated as a
commodity, measurable by objective tests. Like the scientific managers early
in the century, current reformers appear to consider notions such as learning,
knowledge, and experience to be soft and airy words unless they can be
translated into numbers. Quantification, as expressed in the reports, is used

as a quality-control check against the educational "factory worker" who might otherwise certify as "safe" high-risk minorities and poor. This emphasis on quantitative measures, in fact, signals a lack of trust in the responsibility of educators and their professional judgment (see Sirotnik & Goodlad, 1985). A disturbing result is that quantitative determinations of quality have a disproportionately negative effect on poor and minority children (Gould, 1981; Wigdu, 1982). Witness the disproportionate placement of black males in classes for the educable mentally retarded based on standardized ability tests (Heller, Holtzman, & Messick, 1983).

A Narrowed Meritocracy ("Opportunity . . . as will fit them equally well for their particular life work")

As a marketable commodity, education is increasingly subject to the same individualistic, competitive, acquisitive norms as are material goods (Slaughter, 1985). These norms are all grounded in the presumption of inequality. And in a period of perceived scarcity, there is likely to be a shift in how the poor are provided for. In fact, the meager level of concern in the reports for those on the bottom of the schooling hierarchy clearly indicates "stinginess" in the distribution of educational goods. It is painfully clear that the least promising students are expected to do least well. Staying in school, passing an eighth-grade proficiency test, getting a job, not being a criminal, staying off welfare become "success" indicators. No report advocates substantive reforms to keep larger number of poor and minority students in schools or improve the quality of what they experience there. The expectations for poor and minority students, in other words, are far lower than in the reform proposals of a more abundant time.

The conception of school as a meritocracy is clearly reflective of the belief that some students can learn and others cannot or will not. In current reforms, promotion, assignment to various programs, graduation, and the kind of diploma received are all to be governed by merit in terms of objective measures of student learning. The fact that retention and low-track placement do not lead to increased student learning is irrelevant (see Larabee, 1984). As part of a meritocratic system, retention and low-track placement serve primarily to deny advancement in the educational system of those *not worthy*. "Student progress should be measured through periodic tests of general achievement and specific skills; promotion from grade to grade should be based on mastery, not age" (TFEE, p. 11).

Separate educations based on meritocratic selection within schools (tracking) or at different schools are recommended in several of the reports for students who do well or poorly on tests. *A Nation at Risk* suggests "placement and grouping . . . should be guided by the academic progress of students" (NCEE, 1983, p. 30) and proposes "alternative classrooms, programs, and schools" for those students who don't conform to expected standards of behavior (p. 29). *Making the Grade* calls for federal stipends to allow those "unable to learn in public schools" to attend "small-scale academies." "Such an experiment . . . would free up the substantial resources now being spent on remediation with so little to show for it" (p. 20).

Little attention is paid to rethinking classroom instruction or school organization in such a way as to promote the achievement of poor children. The only concern raised about the race/class consequences of tracking or testing criteria as standards of excellence is in a footnote of *Making the Grade* (TCF, 1983, p. 20). No concern is evidenced regarding the "dead-end" educational experiences of segregated groups of poor students with curricula aimed at passing minimum competency exams (see Darling-Hammond & Wise, 1985, for a review of this literature). Providing different curricula for different students, as at the turn of the century, is seen as the appropriate way of meeting "individual needs." These are individual needs seen in terms of intellectual limits, not as means of enabling students to develop higher-order knowledge and skills. One commission member contributing to *Making the Grade* asserts, "I believe the mixing in the same class of students with vastly differing abilities in the name of equality has been a retrogressive step" (TCF, 1983, p. 21). Funding for children with special needs—poverty or handicaps—is to be used to support separate programs. No provisions for special access to the best educational programs—such as open admission to enriched programs, cultural criteria for placement in special programs for the gifted and talented, or affirmative action programs—are suggested.

The retreat to this narrowly meritocratic approach to the allocation of school opportunities and rewards is justified in part by the perceived successes of prior equality efforts. Both *A Nation at Risk* and *Action for Excellence* laud the gains in opportunity and achievement over the last 30 years. It is as if past wrongs have been redressed and it is now fair to return to the real purpose of education: excellence.

## REFORM AND EQUALITY

Of course, all of the current reform proposals acknowledge educational equity as a national interest. *Educating Americans for the 21st Century*, the report of the National Science Board (NSB, 1983), has equity as a major theme. But little in the current discussion suggests an interest in reaching beyond turn-of-the-century conceptions of social Darwinism and meritocracy to equality in access to knowledge, skills, and educational experiences. Where the reports call for equality as well as excellence, they seem to lack conviction, and they provide no strategies toward this end. As with the emergence in the '80s of economic policies of a much earlier era, the school reforms exhibit a retrenchment into the values of an earlier time. Priorities are set according to prevailing economic interests—which value most highly the kind of human capital development likely to lead to the biggest payoff in the current economic crisis. At the same time, these priorities are also consistent with the interests of the professional elite that dominates educational institutions. It would be a mistake to doubt the sincerity of most educational reformers. It is clearly too crass to suggest that they are setting out deliberately to perpetuate privilege. If overt, villainous intent were the culprit, these problems would be more easily solved. It is harder to engage the well-intended in the critical scrutiny of prevailing assumptions than to oust rascals from positions of influence.

Given the educational "reforms" of the '60s and early '70s (which may have been of considerable benefit to many minority and poor individuals, but did little to change their relative educational or economic position), we may conclude that in times of prosperity a good bit of money may be spent in efforts to create illusions of the fairest possible meritocracy. To the extent that disadvantaged individuals can be helped without jeopardizing the overall structure or control of society, so much the better. (In fact, whatever their motivation, such programs can and do change lives; they deserve a hard fight to retain even if the ground in which they are sown is so infertile as to produce only marginal yields.) In times of scarcity, however, the costs of these "equalizing" programs are deemed intolerable. Recipients of special help are perceived as responsible for the decline of not only their own well-being, but the well-being of the socio-economic classes they supposedly aspire to join.

Only three years have passed since the nation's interest turned to educational reform, and it is too early for a full assessment. But reform has become national policy and the themes of the 1983 reports are sounded repeatedly in the statements of both the President and the Secretary of Education. Several states and hundreds of local school districts have rushed to implement reforms, and a number of scholars have assessed their likely effects. And, of course, many of the specific reforms were well underway at the time of the 1983 reports. In many respects the commissions only heralded and reiterated changes conceived in the economic crises and tax revolts of the 1970s.

Time adds conviction to the suspicion that the reforms will work largely to the advantage of those who are already well-off. Through differentiated schooling experiences, attention will be turned from the difficulties of those served less well by schools. Highly motivated, able students will be offered every opportunity to achieve in ways that will strengthen the US quest for technological, economic, and military supremacy. That the distribution of school achievement has racial and socio-economic dimensions is regrettable, but, as a consequence, there is little expectation that poor and minority children will contribute greatly to the national self-interest. While our humane and democratic ideology requires extending educational resources and opportunity to poor and minority children, the most pressing need at present is to cultivate those children with superior abilities, since they are seen as most likely to provide some relief from our national troubles.

All indications are that the current reform movement will produce success defined in its own terms: Children will spend more hours and days in school, more coursework will be taken in mathematics, science, and technology, and mean achievement test scores will probably rise. But beyond indicators of movement toward "excellence" (higher numbers) lies evidence of an ominous side of reform. We can already see a declining college attendance rate for minorities, increased underrepresentation of minorities in postgraduate and professional education, limited access of minority students to computers in schools and to instruction in programming, disproportionately large enroll-ment of minority students in low-track classes and high enrollment of whites in programs for the gifted, and disproportionately high failure rates on minimum competency tests for minority students.

The lack of evidence of advantages having "trickled-down" is not unique to education. While those at the top have declared the recovery to be in full swing, those at the bottom of the economic hierarchy experience a different reality. Today 20 million Americans—two thirds of whom are children—are estimated to be hungry, a dramatic shift from the "virtual elimination" of hunger in the 1970s (Physicians Task Force on Hunger, 1985). In current policies, social justice programs are seen as harmful to economic growth, just as equitable schooling policies are seen as destructive to educational excellence. For tangible benefits in either sphere, children who are poor and nonwhite must continue to wait.

## NOTES

1. A Study of Schooling was a comprehensive inquiry into a national sample of schools. Results of the study are reported in Goodlad (1984).
2. As an aside, it should be noted that "scientifically" normed intelligence tests spearheaded the rationale for *all* testing even to the point of schoolwide testing and grade-level testing—even into the classroom. So, much of the "real work" of intelligence testing quickly passed down to schools and teachers, where poorer performance on tests, "scientific" or otherwise, justified the daily reinforcement of merit.
3. See Kuttner (1984) for a fascinating counter-argument to the negative influence of social justice programs on economic health.
4. It needs to be noted, however, that the College Board's Equality Project, from which the report came, pays far more attention to the provision of both opportunities and improved educational treatment for minority students than do most current proposals. See, for example, the report *Equality and Excellence: The Educational Status of Black Americans* (College Board, 1985).

## REFERENCES

Bailey, A. Y. (1983). The educational equality project: Focus on results. *Kappan, 65* (September), 22–25.

Banks, J. R. (Ed.). (1981). *Education in the '80s: Multiethnic education.* Washington, DC: National Education Association.

Bell, D. (1973). *The coming of post-industry society.* New York: Basic Books.

Bennett says he is "consumer advocate." (1985). *Los Angeles Times,* March 3, p. 1.

Boulding, K. E. (1973). The shadow of a stationary state. *Daedalus,* 102, 93.

Cagan, E. (1978). Individualism, collectivism, and radical educational reform. *Harvard Educational Review, 48,* 227–266.

Cheng, C. W., Brizendine, E., & Oakes, J. (1979). What is an "equal chance" for minority children. *Journal of Negro Education, 48,* 267–287.

College Board. (1983). *Academic preparation for college: What students need to know and be able to do.* New York: College Board.

College Board. (1985). *Equality and excellence: The education status of black Americans.* New York: College Board.

Commoner, B. (1977). *The Poverty of Power.* New York: Bantam.

Cremin, L. A. (1964). *The Transformation of the school.* New York: Random House.

Darling-Hammond, L., & Wise, A. (1985). Beyond standardization: State standards and school improvement. *Elementary School Journal, 85,* 315–336.

Edson, C. H. (1982). Schooling for work and working at school: Perspectives on immigrant and working-class education in urban America, 1880–1920. In R. B. Everhart, (Ed.), *The public school monopoly.* Cambridge, MA: Ballinger.

Goodlad, J. I. (1984). *A place called school.* New York: McGraw-Hill.

Gould, S. J. (1981). *The mismeasure of man.* New York: W. W. Norton.

Grant, C. (Ed.). (1977). *Multicultural education: Commitments, issues, and applications.* Washington, DC: ASCD.

Hall, G. S. (1905). *Adolescence: Its psychology and its relations to physiology, anthropology, sociology, sex, crime, religion, and education.* New York: D. Appleton.

Heilbroner, R. L. (1974). *An inquiry into the human prospect.* New York: W. W. Norton.

Heller, K., Holtzman, W., & Messick, S. (Eds.). (1983). *Placing children in special education: Strategies for equity.* Washington, DC: National Academy Press.

Kahn, H., Brown, W., & Martel, L. (1976). *The next 200 years: A scenario for America and the world.* New York: Morrow.

Kuttner, R. (1984). *The economic illusion: False choices between prosperity and social justice.* Boston: Houghton-Mifflin.

Larabee, D. F. (1984). Setting the standard: Alternative policies for student promotion. *Harvard Educational Review, 54,* 67–87.

Lazerson, M. (1974). *Origins of the urban school.* Cambridge: Harvard University Press.

Lipset, S. M. (1978). Growth, affluence, and the limits of futurology. In *From abundance to scarcity: Implications for the American tradition.* Columbus: Ohio State University Press.

Macrae, N. (1972). The future of international business. *Economist, 22* (January), 5–7.

NCEE (National Commission on Excellence in Education). (1983). *A nation at risk: The imperative for educational reform.* Washington, DC: Government Printing Office.

NSB (National Science Board Commission on Precollege Education in Mathematics, Science, and Technology). (1983). *Educating Americans for the 21st century.* Washington, DC: National Science Foundation.

Nelson, D. (1980). *Fredrick W. Taylor and the rise of scientific management.* Madison: University of Wisconsin Press.

Oakes, J. (1985). *Keeping track: How schools structure inequality.* New Haven: Yale University Press.

*Physicians Task Force on Hunger Report.* (1985). Cambridge, MA: Harvard University Press.

Ryan, W. (1976). *Blaming the victim.* New York: Vintage Books.

Sarason, S. B. (1983). *Schooling in America: Scapegoat and salvation.* New York: The Free Press.

Schumacher, E. F. (1973). *Small is beautiful.* New York: Harper & Row.

Sirotnik, K. A., & Goodlad, J. I. (1985). The quest for reason amidst the rhetoric of reform: Improving instead of testing our schools. In W. J. Johnson (Ed.), *Education on trial: A midterm report.* San Francisco: Institute for Contemporary Studies.

Slaughter, S. (1985). *The pedagogy of profit: National commission reports on education.* Unpublished manuscript, State University of New York, Buffalo.

TCF (Twentieth Century Fund). (1983). *Making the grade: Report of the task force on federal elementary and secondary education policy.* New York: Twentieth Century Fund.

TFEEG (Task Force on Education and Economic Growth). (1983). *Action for excellence.* Washington, DC: Economic Commission of the States.

Wigder, S. (1982). *Ability-testing, uses and consequences.* Washington, DC: National Academy Press.

# 8
▼▼▼▼▼▼▼

# Money, Schools, & Courts*

Stan Karp

For the past 25 years battles over inequities in school funding have been clogging the nation's courts. Ever since 1973 when the U.S. Supreme Court declared in *Rodriguez v. San Antonio* that education was not a fundamental right protected by the U.S. Constitution, equity advocates and public interest lawyers have fought a state-by-state battle against the "savage inequalities" of school finance systems which provide qualitatively different levels of education to students from different class, race, and community backgrounds.

Typically, these inequities have been traced to wide gaps in per pupil spending among districts and to finance systems that rely heavily on unequal property tax bases as the source of funds for education. They also include bizarre funding formulas that dispense state aid in ways that perpetuate inequality; state and federal tax policies that disinvest from public services like education while preserving pockets of privilege; a general retreat from civil rights era concerns for equity, desegregation, and racial justice; and the growing economic stratification in society at large. Indeed, in many ways the funding mechanisms that deliver drastically different experiences to kids in different classrooms simply mirror the inequality that exists all around us.

Given such deep roots, it's not surprising that, despite the growing number of high-profile legal cases, funding equity has been hard to come by. Since the early 1970s, over 30 state Supreme Court decisions have been issued in school finance cases. Just under half have declared existing funding systems illegal and/or inadequate and mandated a variety of corrective measures. In

*From: Karp, Stan. "Money, Schools, & Courts: State by State Battles Against Inequality." From *Z Magazine*. December 1995 (pp. 25–29). Publisher: Institute for Social and Cultural Communications. Reprinted by permission.

the remaining cases, Courts have rejected the challenges or refrained from intervening, acknowledging inequities, but contending that the issue is a legislative not judicial matter, or more narrowly reading the state's obligation to provide equal education to all.

Even where Courts have declared funding systems illegal, equitable solutions have been far from certain. As New Jersey's Education Law Center, which has battled the state's funding system for over two decades, put it, "Law books are filled with wonderful paper victories which have never been implemented." NJ's finance system has been declared legally inadequate by the Supreme Court in various ways no less than nine times since the early 1970s, yet the state is still struggling to devise an equitable funding formula to meet the next Court deadline, September 1996. Other states have similar histories.

Court decisions, in themselves, have been insufficient to assure equity for several reasons. While glaring disparities in school funding have occasionally persuaded Courts to order reform, it has been almost impossible to prevent Governors and state legislators from evading or limiting the impact of the court orders. Restrained by separation-of-powers concerns and the prevailing conservative political climate, Courts have generally given states wide latitude to proceed with half-measures and "good faith" efforts, sometimes promising further review if they prove inadequate.

In some states, tentative steps toward equity made under Court pressure have been thwarted by the rising tide of anti-tax populism. California is a prime example. The state's Serrano decision in the early 1970s was one of the first requiring a state to correct massive inequities among districts in educational services. Some efforts were made to equalize spending by revising aid formulas and transferring some property tax revenues from wealthier to poorer districts. But these efforts were derailed by Proposition 13, a 1978 ballot initiative that capped property taxes in one of the opening rounds in the "tax revolt" that came to shape local, state, and federal tax policy in the 1980s and 1990s. (Which despite its promise of relief to hard-pressed taxpayers has succeeded primarily in swelling the federal deficit, starving public services, and redirecting wealth upward.)

As a result of Proposition 13, the state was forced to assume a greater share of local school spending which did lead to a degree of greater "equity" among districts. But there was also a dramatic decline in spending on California schools relative to other states. In the 1960s, California was 5th in per pupil spending, by the 1990s it was 42nd. Class size is now the largest in the nation. Because of Proposition 13 and it's offspring, support for California schools has tended toward "equalization" at a level that keeps them in a state of perpetual budgetary crisis. (At the same time, a variety of loopholes and privatizing trends, such as the establishment of private educational foundations to subsidize schools in wealthy districts, has meant that pockets of elite spending persist even in the midst of this "equalization.")

## BUDGET-CUTTERS AND EQUITY ADVOCATES

The balance sheet, then, on 25 years of state litigation for funding equity is, at best, mixed. The legal basis for more equitable funding is clearly stronger in many places than it was in the past. In states where court challenges have been successful, some of the grossest inequities in per pupil district expenditures have been reduced, if not eliminated. School finance reform has become a high priority issue across the nation and an unusually broad consensus has been formed around the proposition that a better system of funding schools needs to be created.

But many of the groups that have come to that consensus have arrived there with decidedly different agendas. On the one hand are those with essentially a budget-cutting agenda who want to restrain spending on schools, cut property taxes, and eliminate "waste" which, depending on the source, can mean everything from bloated administrative bureaucracy to desperately needed reforms, new facilities, and reductions in class size. On the other hand are those with an equity agenda who see school finance reform as an essential ingredient in an effort to revitalize failing, ineffective school districts while also compensating as much as possible for the devastating effects of poverty, race, and class injustice on the lives of children. These competing perspectives rise to the surface whenever the issue turns to specifics. In the end, they may prove that the apparent consensus on the need for fundamental reform of school finances is illusory.

With Courts usually limiting themselves to generalized orders for reform, the focus is turning to legislative and public debates about what alternatives exist to systems based on property taxes and about how educational equity should be defined.

The property tax issue is both a root problem and, in some ways, a diversion from the core issue of equity. Local property taxes still supply 40–50 percent of all school funds. States provide on average 47 percent. The federal government's share of education spending, which peaked at about 9 percent in the 1970s, has dropped to under 7 percent. Given the grossly unequal distribution of property in the U.S. and the intense segregation of communities by race and class, it's inevitable that schools heavily dependent on property taxes will be unequal. In fact, with over 16,000 separate school districts, the reliance on property taxes functions as a sorting mechanism for class and race privilege, and allows pockets of "elite schooling" to exist within the public system. Any real chance of increasing and redistributing education resources requires fundamentally changing the connection between school spending and local property taxes.

Historically, it's been argued that schools rely on local property taxes because of the strong U.S. tradition of local control of schools. But one issue that has been clarified in the state-by-state litigation over funding inequities is that it is the state, not the local district, that has the constitutional responsibility to fund the schools. States may allow education funding to be based on local property taxes, but this is not the result of any immutable standing or compelling interest of local districts. Rather it's a product of state decisions about its funding policies and about the taxing power it does or does not make available to local entities like school boards and city councils, and it provides no legal grounds for permitting inequality to exist. Likewise, the state has the power to remake the funding system in any way it sees fit, retaining or modifying district authority in any given area of school policy or oversight. In other words preserving local control (or even radically extending it, for example, to individual school site councils,) does not depend on retaining the link between school funding and local property taxes.

To sever this link, however, will require a political, rather than a strictly legal, strategy to overturn several obstacles. One of these is that the existing system of funding education through local property taxes, in many respects, serves the agenda of the budget cutters and conservative forces who currently dominate state and local government. When local communities must assume growing fiscal burdens for schools by more heavily taxing local residential and commercial property, it creates a strong budgetary pressure for austerity. When local school budgets are presented like sacrificial lambs to hard-pressed local taxpayers, (who never get to vote on tax abatements for real estate developers or whether the Defense Dept. should build another aircraft carrier), the budget process for schools becomes driven not by what schools and children need, but by how to keep the tax rate flat. Add to this the fact that only a fraction of the local population generally has children in the schools and an even smaller fraction (about 15 percent) usually votes in school elections, and you have a system that works well to undercut, not sustain, quality education. In short, the system of property tax funding for schools works at one level to create inequality in the first place, and at another level, as a vice to squeeze local budgets.

Nevertheless, there remains a growing effort to consider alternatives to funding based on property taxes, fed by Court orders, heavy local tax burdens, and the ongoing national debate about education reform. One set of fiscal reforms is designed to "recapture" or redistribute property tax revenues from richer districts to poorer ones. Another seeks to replace property taxes with other taxes, usually sales taxes, and have the state assume a larger fraction of overall school spending. Still another set of proposals involves redefining state aid formulas so that fewer funds go to districts as "flat grants" regardless of need or local wealth, and more through "foundation formulas" which guarantee a base level of funding for each student and are calculated in ways that promote greater equalization.

The problem is that no particular financial mechanism, in itself, guarantees either equity or quality in education. It's true that relying on some taxes, like property and sales taxes, tends to be regressive, while progressive income taxes are more fair ways to raise revenues. But choosing a particular funding mechanism does not assure that adequate funds will be available.

In fact one danger in the move to reform existing funding systems, is that new ones will be adopted which will continue to deliver inadequate or inequitable levels of education. New formulas promising better, more secure funding, have been adopted in NJ, Michigan, Kentucky, New York, and elsewhere, only to be cut or modified once the costs became clear. If the controlling motivation is a desire to cut property taxes or hold down educational spending, rather than promote quality and equity, it may not matter what fiscal mechanism is chosen to do the job.

These experiences reflect some of the underlying limitations of a state-by-state process which, even where it succeeds, generally produces a Court call for greater equity which is then turned over to a state government unrepresentative of the urban and rural poor who are on the short end of the school spending yardstick. While important progress has been made in the past two decades in narrowing some educational inequities and raising key issues, continued and more substantial progress may depend on finding new strategies to promote funding equity.

## CAMPAIGNING FOR FISCAL EQUITY

The Campaign for Fiscal Equity (CFE), a legal advocacy group representing community school boards, parents, and education groups in New York, proposes what it calls a "dialogic remedy." Based on a study of funding reform in ten states, the CFE concluded that a successful challenge to inequitable school funding systems needs to include "an extensive effort to develop a comprehensive remedial strategy" before going to Court. The failure of equity advocates to "establish clear goals and priorities" and propose "workable mechanisms to implement those goals and priorities," the CFE argues, discourages Courts from intervening and leaves room for legislative deal-making which undermines equity goals.

The CFE proposes a public, coalition-building process, to complement any legal strategy, that could generate broad political support and the concrete outlines of an equitable solution: "Because the standard legislative process cannot provide the balanced compromises that are necessary to devise substantive solutions in this complex, politically-charged area, what is needed now is a new 'dialogic process' characterized by broad-based participation and informed, principled interchanges . . . [that] can lead to agreement on the fiscal, educational, and underlying value issues involved in equity reform."

The CFE recognizes that the various positions that "must be reconciled often reflect deep ideological, class, racial, or ethnic interests." But it contends that the "ideal of education" and "concern for the welfare of the nation's children" provide a basis for achieving some level of consensus. It cites a number of education reform processes and commission studies which drew together disparate community, professional, and business interests to produce progressive reform plans. What's needed, the CFE argues, is to build on these experiences, "but to overcome their limitations by expanding the deliberative process to include active participation by a much larger range of individuals and groups from all affected interests, including those strongly opposed to reform. . . . The hard value conflicts involved in fiscal equity issues are not intractable. Some combination of better use of available resources, increased funding, and qualitative educational reforms that improve the level of learning for all students can provide a solution. If a principled solution with broad public support is achieved . . . its main features can then be incorporated into a court decree and its details fully enacted into law."

There is ample reason to have doubts about the level of consensus that can be achieved between the "budget-cutters" and the "equity advocates." But there is still much about the CFE's strategy that makes sense. Funding equity will not be won by narrow legal or legislative lobbying strategies. Aggressive public organizing that clarifies issues and debates proposed solutions is critical to building the coalitions and political pressure needed to force action. Even where it suffers setbacks, a strategy of public coalition building is more likely to promote grassroots activism and coalesce a progressive constituency for school change on funding and other issues.

At the same time, over the long term, it will be necessary to open up other fronts in the campaign for funding equity that reach beyond state borders. To really make good on promises of educational equity and excellence will take tens of billions of dollars over many years, the kinds of sums that have been poured into the military for decades. Several years ago, the Committee for Education Funding, an umbrella group of education lobbies, documented a need for $25 billion in construction and renovation of K–12 facilities alone (and such capital costs, while far greater in poorer areas, are often not even included in the per pupil expenditures that are generally the focus of equalizing efforts.) Only a national effort can generate that kind of funds.

Yet the U.S. continues to trail other western industrial societies in educational investment. 1990 figures from the Economic Policy Institute placed the U.S. 9th of 16 industrialized nations in per pupil K–12 spending. A 1992 report from the Organization for Economic Cooperation and Development, showed the U.S. was ranked 13th in the percentage of GNP spent on education. Federal funds for local schools dropped to their lowest post World War II levels in the 1980s, and have risen only slightly since.

SEPARATE AND UNEQUAL

Moreover, the willingness of the federal government to support national commitments to equality growing out of civil rights-era legislation has been waning. Increasingly federal courts are ruling that the existence of "separate and unequal" educational programs, in themselves, are not illegal, unless conscious, deliberate "intent to discriminate" can be proved. Combined with persistent inequalities in school finance, this legal doctrine nourishes the existence of a dual school system, in which students of color systematically attend schools with less funding in segregated settings. This is prompting some legal experts to consider a new equity challenge in the federal courts.

"Of all developed countries, only two systematically have spent less money educating poor children than wealthy children," notes Paul Tractenberg, a founder of NJ's Education law center and chief counsel in the state's major funding suits. "One is South Africa, the other is the United Sates." Tractenberg argues that taken together, racial segregation coupled with systematic funding inequities amount to a degree of inequality that wouldn't even satisfy the standards of Plessy v. Ferguson, the historic 1896 Supreme Court decision that set a standard of "separate but equal" until 1954 when it was overturned by the Brown decision mandating school integration. "In the federal courts," argues Tractenberg, "now it's clear that de facto segregation alone doesn't violate the federal constitution. And it's clear that unequal funding by itself is not a federal constitutional violation. But if you put the two together, aren't you creating a situation which wouldn't have even satisfied the standards of Plessy against Fergusson? So how could it satisfy a body of contemporary law that is presumably more demanding in these terms than Plessy was? The question is whether the federal courts might be made to view this issue differently they did in the past."

New legal pressure on the federal courts to make the federal government give tangible substance to promises of equality through greater investment in schools could eventually open up the federal treasury to equity advocates. But like state legal strategies, such success will also likely depend on broader public campaigns to reorder the nation's social priorities. That, after all, is what equity in school funding is ultimately all about.

# 9
▼▼▼▼▼▼▼

# What Should We Call People?
# Race, Class, and the Census for 2000*

Harold L. Hodgkinson

The impending debate over the definition of race to be used in the U.S. Census for the year 2000 could be the most divisive debate over racial issues since the 1960s. Moreover, the subject is of great importance to education at all levels. In this article I will attempt to explain the problem, review its history, and examine the options for the future.

## WHO DEFINES RACE?

In the U.S. the answer to this question is crystal clear: the Office of Management and Budget (OMB), reporting to the House Committee on Post Office and Civil Service, Subcommittee on Census, Statistics, and Postal Personnel. While this subcommittee does not represent the most desirable political plum in the Congress, it has been at the center of a swirling debate on the nature of racial designations, as seen in hearings that began in 1993 and continued into 1994, though they were virtually ignored by the news media. Since 1977 the racial/ethnic categories that can be used on all federal forms have come from OMB Statistical Directive 15, which allows only four racial groups, designated by the following headings: American Indian/Alaskan Native; Asian/Pacific Islander; Black; and White. Ethnicity is broken down into Hispanic and non-Hispanic.[1]

These are the categories that are used on application forms for jobs, on school enrollment forms, on mortgage applications, and on college scholar-

*From: Hodgkinson, Harold. "What Should We Call People? Race, Class, and the Census for 2000." From *Phi Delta Kappan*, October 1995, pp. 173–179.

ship and loan applications. They are also the boxes we must check (choosing only one) on the U.S. Census form. The government does not gather information of this kind just out of idle curiosity: these categories are used by federal agencies to search for job discrimination and segregated schools and to give out large chunks of federal aid. There could be other ramifications as well. For example, it was clear that the suggestion in late 1993 that Hawaiians be classified not as Asian/Pacific Islanders but as Native Americans was made at least in part to allow Hawaiians to operate gambling casinos, a right currently reserved only for Native Americans.

## A SHORT HISTORY OF RACIAL CLASSIFICATION IN THE U.S.

The Constitution requires that a census be conducted every 10 years in order to revise the structure of the House of Representatives so that it reflects the real population—one of the more radical political ideas ever implemented. Since the original U.S. Census of 1790, which was supervised by Thomas Jefferson, virtually every Census has defined race differently. The first one allowed for free white males, free white females, other persons (including free blacks and "taxable Indians"), and slaves.[2] Even in 1790 it was clear that many slaves had lighter skins than their masters, making a division between black and mulatto seem logical. But mulattos were needed in the slave pool.

In order to increase the size of the slave population, the "one drop of blood" rule appeared. That is, even one drop of "black blood" defined a person as black and meant that any child of a slave and a slaveowner would be considered eligible for slavery. Over time, this rule enlarged the slave pool considerably. (The issue of whether one drop of white blood defined you as white apparently never came up.) The "one drop" rule has never been applied to Asians or Hispanics, but it was affirmed as the law of the land by the U.S. Supreme Court as late as 1986.[3]

In our time, the 1960 Census allowed only two categories: white or nonwhite. In 1970 we could be white, black, or "other," but by 1990 we had the four racial/ethnic categories established by OMB Statistical Directive 15, with 13 choices within the "Asian" group, ranging from Chinese to Thai, and with ethnicity broken into Hispanic subcategories for Mexican, Puerto Rican, Cuban, and other. Through most of our history, we believed that "black blood" was a reality, although today we know that there are four major human blood types—A, B, O, and AB—that are distributed across all racial categories. If you are a black person with type O blood, your blood is more like that of other people with type O blood, regardless of their "race," than it is like the blood of black people who do not have type O blood. If you need a blood transfusion, you need the blood of a person of your blood type regardless of that person's "race."

## SKIN COLOR AND RACE

The notion that there are three racial groups—Caucasoid, Mongoloid, and Negroid—has been thoroughly discredited for half a century. There is more variation within each such racial category than across them. Yet the notion persists. Although we think of people as white, red, yellow, brown, and black, in fact a single protein colors the skin of all humans. It is called melanin, and it is brown.

The best way to think about these issues is to assume that skin color exists on a single continuum, from very light to very dark, and that as people have become more mobile, the original function of skin pigment and the original functions of many other so-called racial characteristics have largely disappeared. The word *African* can be used to describe both the world's tallest and its shortest human societies. That should give us pause.

## RACE VERSUS CITIZENSHIP

Indeed, the very idea of race did not appear in any language until the 14th century. The ancient Greeks and Romans defined people by their citizenship: to be a member of the *polis* was to be fully human, regardless of the shape of one's nose or the color of one's skin, both of which were considered accidents of birth.[4] Of course, when the Athenians went to the agora to vote or speak, each citizen left a dozen or so slaves at home. Thus the first Western democracy was a slave-owning society, though their slaves were white and came from the areas we now call Slavic, a fact that gives us the derivation of the word *slave*. The ancient Greeks also referred to a person who was not a citizen as, roughly translated, a subhuman idiot. The Greeks could treat these noncitizens in barbaric ways with no qualms of conscience whatsoever, much as slaves were once treated in the U.S.

But the early Greeks and Romans might be appalled at our willingness to make very complex and subtle distinctions with regard to nose shape, lip shape, and skin color and use these as measures of an individual's innate worth. It might be said that race/ethnicity has displaced citizenship as a badge of identity in our time. We are trained to make exquisitely fine distinctions between people according to their physical characteristics for one reason: these distinctions allow us to make quick judgments about people. What's more, we are trained to develop this expertise from birth.

## SCIENCE OR SUBJECTIVITY?

Different nations define ethnicity in very different ways. In Canada ethnicity means ancestry, while religion, language, and caste are distinguishing characteristics in Malaysia, India, and Indonesia. Recognition by the group defines ethnicity for most American Indian tribes, for native Hawaiians, and for indigenous Malaysians. Race and ethnicity are in the eye of the beholder.

Moreover, if you are defined by the U.S. Census as black, you are 100% black. Thus the "one drop of blood" rule applies to all categories; you are not allowed to be "a little" of any category, just as you can't be a little bit pregnant. But to liken the biological certainties of pregnancy to these ephemeral judgments of "race" is comedic. Earlier in our history, Census-takers had diagrams of nose and lip shape, eye configurations, and so on from which to determine what "race" a given interviewee was. That caused such confusion that the decision was made to allow the respondent to choose the racial/ethnic category he or she belonged in (as long as it was one of the "approved" categories).

Yet in reality, especially if you go back four generations, most of us are a "little bit" Chinese or a little bit something else. Even though OMB Statistical Directive 15 was developed by a federal interagency committee on which I once served, the first caution it contained was: "The racial and ethnic categories set forth in the standard should not be interpreted as being scientific or anthropological in nature."[5] Yet that is precisely how the categories have been treated. When we read that 18% of a state's population is black, Hispanic, Asian, or Native American, we have to assume that everyone in the category belongs completely in that box. The fact is that, on direct measurement, the darkest quarter of the white population is darker than the lightest quarter of the black population. Although racial data sound very scientific (Michigan is 23.5% black), the reality is that the categories are entirely subjective. Even some trained anthropologists have argued that there are three "races," while others have argued for 37 races. Stephen Thernstrom calls this "the figment of the pigment."[6]

Even if we grant that the intention of the OMB was simply to offer neutral, nonscientific statistical descriptions for use in the Census, not to create or define "race," that is precisely what Directive 15 has done for most Americans. The fact that "Hispanic" has become widely used only in the last 20 years is due in large part to the fact that the term entered the Census lexicon in 1970. (When the Census form mentioned "South Americans" as a category, over a million residents of Alabama, Mississippi, and other southern states said that they were South Americans.) Every time "Hispanic" is used in any Census table, a proviso is added that "Hispanics can be of any race." Even language is not a common factor, since more than 10% of California residents with Spanish surnames do not speak Spanish. Moreover, Brazilians, from the largest nation in Latin America, speak Portuguese, not Spanish.

## 'HISPANIC'—A CONCEPTUAL NIGHTMARE

If "Hispanic" is used to define a race in the Census for 2000, which seems likely, horrendous difficulties will arise. First, there are a minimum of three million black Hispanics in the U.S. (If you are from the Caribbean, have dark skin, and speak Spanish, you are, by default, a black Hispanic.) To refer to black Hispanics as African Americans might just add to the confusion. Then, too, Argentines are primarily of white European ancestry. Because of the pervasiveness of mestizo influences, most Mexicans could be counted as American Indian if they were born in the U.S. Today, a mestizo blood line is a primary background factor among Hispanics, most Native Americans, and most people from South and Central America.

This conceptual quagmire is the reason that the Census employed Hispanic or non-Hispanic as the only category of "ethnic group," given that no one knows what an ethnic group is. Now it appears that the Census for 2000 may well say that "Hispanic," having been an "ethnic group," will become a "race"—an idea that resembles science fiction far more than science. Given that the racial/ethnic categories in the Census are a scientific and anthropological joke, why do we keep the categories at all? The answer is a deeply American irony: we need the categories in order to eliminate them.

Without knowing who our oppressed minorities are, how can we develop remedies so that they will no longer be oppressed? Thus many people can benefit from checking off Native American, because special scholarships are available. In fact, the 1990 Census count of more than two million Native Americans is a demographically impossible increase over the 1980 numbers. Clearly, some people decided to change categories. (And almost five million respondents in 1990 said that they had Native American "heritage," even though they were not Native American. It is certainly possible that two million of these five million will seek to reclaim that heritage in the 2000 Census, doubling the number of Native Americans with no increase in births.) Whatever this is, it isn't science.

## IS A 'MULTIRACIAL' CATEGORY THE SOLUTION?

If a box labeled "multiracial"—meaning any racial/ethnic mixing back four or more generations—were added to the next Census, estimates are that 80% of blacks and a majority of Americans in general would check the box.[7] Thus the current black population of 30 million could decline in 2000 to a Census count of three million. At that point, there would probably be no federal aid to the 114 "traditionally black colleges." Asian Americans, most of whom are now marrying non-Asians, and Native Americans, who are producing more children in mixed marriages than in marriages involving two Indian parents, could virtually disappear from the demographic land-scape. Hispanics could either become the largest racial minority or they could disappear, depending on how many of them think their ancestry is mixed and on how the notions of "Hispanic race" and "mixed" are defined.[8]

Consider some of the mind-boggling possibilities. If a Chinese American marries a Mexican American, is that marriage "mixed" in the same sense as if a black person marries a white person? What if the Chinese American marries a Japanese American? And most important, what if the Brazilian American who does not speak Spanish marries the Mexican American who does? What if your great-grandmother entered into a multiracial marriage? Does that mixing still count today? And do we want to force the children of mixed marriages to choose between their mother's ancestry and their father's? With what results?

It is painfully clear that our use of racial/ethnic categories as official data for the federal government needs a major overhaul, as the information these categories provide has become a political reality with virtually no scientific or intellectual validity. Millions of dollars hang in the balance, of course. Black, Hispanic, and Native American tribal colleges could close. Students could lose scholarships. Affirmative action programs might be dealt a death blow. Even departments of African American studies and other minority studies programs and departments could be at risk. Native Americans' rights to run gambling casinos might be reviewed. If we really want children to be judged by the content of their character rather than the color of their skin, as Martin Luther King, Jr. proposed, how do we make that happen? Still, the irony of arguing that we need racial categories in order to eliminate them is akin to the irony of the statement from the Vietnam era, "We had to destroy the village in order to save it."

We are also using combined (often hyphenated) forms more frequently, by which we can give our national origin but not say much about "race." Saying that someone is a Brazilian American and someone else is a Korean American does not help if the one marries the other. Indeed, with about 240 nations in the world—almost all having some residents in the U.S.—this system could get very complex very fast. (When Jim Henson was alive, he recommended that Kermit the Frog apply for citizenship as an "Amphibian American.")

## A MODEST PROPOSAL: SUBSTITUTE POVERTY FOR RACE

When *Brown v. Board of Education* was decided by the Supreme Court more than 40 years ago, virtually all black children in the public schools of Topeka were poor. Today, approximately 40% of black households in the U.S. are in the middle-income range, and, as of 1995, one-quarter of black households have higher incomes than the average white household. Similar changes have taken place with regard to Hispanics and to Asians[9]—if you assume that access to the suburbs is roughly equivalent to middle-income status. While it is good news that the American mobility machine is still in high gear, it would be very dangerous to let down our guard. The concentration of income in the top one-half of 1% of Americans is greater than that in any other nation, and, at the other end of the scale, a higher percentage of America's children are below the poverty line today than in the previous 30 years. The size of the middle-income group is declining, and we now find more very rich individuals and more very poor ones.

While race has always been at least partly a marker variable for poverty, it may be time to go directly to poverty and see about desegregating it. To a large degree, the Kentucky State Supreme Court decision overturning the school finance system was just such a move. The state was spending as much as $20 on some students and as little as $2 on others, and *that* was what was deemed unconstitutional in a state that guaranteed all children a thorough and efficient education. Race is seldom mentioned in the decision, which is clearly an attempt to desegregate the state economically by raising the spending floor in poor districts and (perhaps) lowering the spending ceiling in others (although some Kentucky districts are allowed to raise their own funds to increase ceiling levels). This view of economic desegregation is a strategy of narrowing the spending range between districts to increase equity in the system and to come closer to the ideal of spending an "equitable" amount on every child. (It is well to remember that *equitable* need not mean *identical*. For example, a handicapped child might require a higher spending level than other children in order to be treated equitably.)

The real legal test of the criterion of fiscal equity has yet to occur, and that test must be at the school building level. Differences in spending levels across districts within a state are easier to deal with than the problem of having children from wealthy, well-educated parents going to the same school with children of poor parents who are not well-educated. Rich and poor students almost never live in the same block or neighborhood. Economic desegregation (like racial desegregation) would inevitably mean moving some children out of their neighborhoods, as virtually all neighborhoods are economically segregated, whatever their racial makeup. I am frequently asked, "Are there places in the U.S. where blacks, Hispanics, Asians, whites, and Native Americans can live together in peace and harmony?" My answer is, "Of course. Such places abound. Shaker Heights, Ohio, to name but one." But there are virtually no poor people in Shaker Heights. Next question: "Are there places in the U.S. where rich people and poor people can live together on the same block in peace and harmony?" My answer is, "I have never seen such a place anywhere in the U.S."

THE BEST PREDICTOR OF SCHOOL FAILURE:
POVERTY

If there is one universal finding from educational research, it is that poverty
is at the core of most school failures. And this is as true for white children
from Appalachia as for black and Hispanic children from inner-city slums.
(Most children in poverty in the U.S. are white.) Black children whose parents
are college graduates and who live in the suburbs are not by definition
candidates for "affirmative action." Given that 40% of black households are
solidly middle class and that the number of minorities living in suburbs (a
rough indicator of middle-class status) has increased,[10] it may be time to
make a more complex, as well as more useful, statement on the relationship
between race and class.

Research from the National Educational Longitudinal Survey (NELS)
shows clearly that the wealthiest one-fourth of white, black, Hispanic, and
Asian eighth-graders do at least twice as well in math as the poorest quarter
of their racial/ethnic group—and sometimes three or four times as well.
Wealthy black children do better at math than poor Asian children do. If
you know the educational level of the parents, which correlates well with
household income, you have a better predictor of educational success than
scores on the SAT I. Since the 1930s, research has shown that, while schools
allow a certain amount of social movement, they also reflect and support
the class structure of the communities they serve.

Seemingly, we have been far more successful at leveling the racial "playing
field" than at leveling economic differences. While 20% of black households
are now above the average income level for white households, which represents
significant economic progress for minorities, the data early in 1995 indicated
that some six million children in the U.S. under age 6 were still living below
the poverty line. (There has been no economic progress for these children,
regardless of their racial or ethnic backgrounds.) Thirty years ago, 40% of the
poor were elderly and 10% were children. Today the numbers are almost
exactly reversed. Yet my point remains: the furor some whites showed when
informed that their children would have to go to school with minority children
is mild compared to the reaction of upper- and middle-income parents (of *any*
race or ethnic background) when told that their children will have to go to
school with poor children (of *any* race or ethnic background).

Consider the issue of relative deprivation. Is a child with dark skin more
likely to be disadvantaged in terms of life chances than a child born into
poverty? Today, the answer is clearly no; poverty is a more pervasive index
of social disadvantage than is minority status.

This emphatically does *not* mean that we can ignore poor minority children: it means that a successful strategy will have to lift the largest number
of children out of poverty, regardless of their race. If there are particular

programs that are of unusually high effectiveness for blacks but *not* for Hispanics, let us say, then we would have a good argument for not having the "mixed ancestry" box on the Census form, as we would need to be able to locate the individuals for whom these programs were effective. It is my view that programs that improve family stability, that increase the earning power of parents, that provide adequate nutrition for children who cannot be sure of it through the best efforts of their families, that allow preschoolers to develop self-confidence and learning skills, and that provide mentors and role models when most needed will be successful for *all* children, with but minor fine-tuning for children of some groups. Such programs should be made available to all children whose low household income makes them eligible.

There is clear evidence from the U.S. Government Accounting Office and from other sources that a number of social programs are effective in mitigating the effects of poverty. Head Start, WIC (Women, Infants, and Children feeding program), AFDC (Aid to Families with Dependent Children), and Upward Bound are programs that reduce the effects of poverty and help reduce the number of America's youngsters who remain in poverty. In addition, the prevention agenda—ensuring that bad things do not happen to young children—is "color blind" in its effectiveness for all poor children. We have at our disposal a set of proven programs for reducing poverty for *all* children, from birth to age 18. Why is this agenda not fully implemented?

## WHO CARES ABOUT AMERICA'S CHILDREN

The answer is: an astonishingly small percentage of the U.S. adult population. The demographic reasons are clear: only about one household in four has a child of school age. My conservative guess is that at least one-third of the U.S. adult population has no daily contact with a child under age 18, and the fraction could be far higher. As the median age of Americans continues to rise and as children become an even smaller percentage of the population—down from 34% in 1970 to 25% projected for 2000—the situation is likely to get even worse. People tend to vote their self-interest, and, as fewer adults have contact with children in their daily lives, there will be even less political support for programs benefiting poor children, most of whom live in central cities and rural areas while most adults live in suburbs.

Even the national leadership of groups that style themselves "pro-life" or "pro-choice" has demonstrated scant concern for the lives of the children who are *already* born. It was 30 January 1995 when the news was released that six million U.S. children under age 6 were living in poverty (up one million between 1987 and 1992) and that three-fourths of these poor children had working parents. None of the six newspapers that I checked carried the story on the front page, and two didn't even mention it. Apparently, the fact that 26% of the nation's future students, workers, voters, parents, and taxpayers have been born into the most debilitating condition of all was not deemed newsworthy. Given such a general lack of interest, it seems unlikely that there will be an increase in concern about or action in response to the amazing facts regarding poverty among America's youth.

Clearly, racial and ethnic categories in the U.S. Census are whimsical, changeable, and unscientific. It is also clear that distinguishing such physical characteristics as skin color or nose and eye shape is "taught" to Americans at an early age as a way of judging other people and that those distinctions have been used by our government since the first Census in 1790. As more of us marry across racial and ethnic lines, such differences will become even more blurred and less useful. And this leads to questions as to why they should continue to be used by the Census, even though a large amount of money is involved in the administration of these categories.

It is also clear that desegregation efforts have not been successful in reducing childhood poverty in the U.S. Of course that was not their focus. To some extent race diverted our attention from the most urgent issue: *poverty reduces the quality of the lives of all children, regardless of race or ethnicity.* Had we spent the 40 years since the *Brown* decision systematically seeking to lower the poverty level for *all* American children, we would be in a different, and probably better, condition today. As racial and ethnic characteristics blur over the coming decades, poverty will become an even more obvious problem than it has been.

While attempting to mix rich and poor families in each block seems utopian (one reason people move to the suburbs is to get away from the poor), there are many ways of improving the lot of poor children where they live. As the prevalence of drugs, violence, and guns increases and as juvenile death rates rise in the suburbs as well as in the slums, questions must be raised as to what suburbs and cities owe one another. For example, today "successful" people almost always live in the suburbs. Can't we provide people with safety, comfortable housing, and good schools wherever they choose to live? In most European cities, the best housing is in the middle of the city.

We have more effectively segregated people by wealth than we ever did by race: 37% of America's wealth is owned by only 1.5% of the people, yet one-quarter of our youngest children live in poverty. More rich people and more poor people will necessarily mean fewer people in the middle, and having the largest middle class has long been one key to America's greatness. Questions of income redistribution are usually political suicide for politicians, but, when youth poverty rates are destroying the future of the entire society, one must wonder whether there can be any long-term winners. Kentucky may have hit upon the key strategy: make sure that all children have a minimum "floor" of services that are sufficient to allow each child, through effort and achievement, to fulfill his or her potential.

Each of us, as we age, becomes dependent on the generation that follows us to take care of us when we can no longer do it ourselves. With the huge increase in the elderly population just around the corner (the first baby boomers turned 50 in 1996), it is imperative to ensure that every young person becomes a productive member of society. We will soon have a ratio of one dependent adult per dependent child. The "race" of each is irrelevant. If a quarter of our youngest children are poor and have limited hope of growing out of that poverty, who will earn the wages to pay the taxes to take care of the rest of us when these children grow up? It matters not whether this issue appeals to liberals or conservatives, for it must finally appeal to pragmatists.

## NOTES

1. *Federal Register*, 9 June 1994, p. 29834.
2. Lawrence Wright, "One Drop of Blood," *New Yorker*, 25 July 1994, p. 47.
3. Tom Morganthau, "What Color Is Black?," *Newsweek*, 13 February 1995, p. 64.
4. Ivan Hannaford, "The Idiocy of Race," *Wilson Quarterly*, Spring 1994, pp. 12–15.
5. *Federal Register*, op. cit.
6. Stephen Thernstrom, "The Declining Significance of Race," *The American Experience*, Summer 1993, p. 6.
7. Hannaford, p. 47.
8. Juanita Tamayo Lott, "Do United States Racial/Ethnic Categories Still Fit?," *Population Today*, January 1993, p. 6.
9. Harold Hodgkinson and Anita Obarakpor, *Immigration to America: The Asian Experience* (Washington, D.C.: Institute for Educational Leadership, 1994), pp. 14–15.
10. William P. O'Hare and William H. Frey, "Booming, Suburban, and Black," *American Demographics*, September 1992, pp. 30–38.

# 10

▼▼▼▼▼▼▼

# What We Talk About
# When We Talk About Welfare*

Mark J. Stern

Look out. Here comes welfare reform. As the smoke begins to clear from the health-care reform debate, Congress and President Clinton are hungry for an issue that will give them a little moral sustenance. After the initial, idealistic appeal of a call for universal coverage, the health-care debate quickly fell into arcane discussions of the potential cost-benefit ratios of various plans and the seamy push-and-shove of interest group politics. In contrast, welfare reform promises our public servants a chance to strike a blow for hard work, good family life, and efficient government. Virtue, they might reason, has its rewards.

Unfortunately, the administration and Congress will still have to deal with the reality of the fourteen million Americans on welfare. The tension between the reality of these women and children and the public's desire for simple standards of virtue for work, family, and government will frame the coming debate over welfare reform. As politicians and policy analysts look for formulas that will appeal to Americans' sense of morality, they must also make sense of the millions of lives they will affect through their actions.

One way to do this, of course, is to simplify the reality. If welfare is not really about five million families with five million different stories, but about "the underclass" or "teen mothers," then the reality isn't so complex. Symbols like these help us take a manageable portion of reality and connect it to our vision of the moral order. Although people inevitably categorize and label to get a handle on complex social reality, when the symbols our elected officials and policy-makers use to frame public debate are too simplistic, the

---

*Reprinted from TIKKUN MAGAZINE, A BI-MONTHLY JEWISH CRITIQUE OF POLITICS, CULTURE, AND SOCIETY. TIKKUN, 251 West 100th Street, 5th floor, New York, NY 10025.

results may be distortive, and the consequences for policy-making can be disastrous.

Take the recently enacted crime bill. Americans really want to feel safer, but the symbols we've used to simplify the problem—whether the death penalty or gun control—don't affect the reality of our streets. Yet these symbols virtually dominated the congressional debate on the President's crime legislation. Allocations in the bill for preventive programs were derided as "pork," and the public was treated to the spectacle of New York Senator Alfonse D'Amato chanting nursery rhymes to his colleagues rather than a serious discussion of the causes of crime and possible solutions. When the gap between our symbols and our reality gets too great, we sow the seeds for widespread political alienation.

## A TALE OF TWO STUDIES

The current welfare debate gives us a chance to watch how social reality and moral order mix in American politics. During the past decade, two divergent portraits of the reality of welfare emerged from the social science literature. The differences between these images and their impact on social policy show how those within the political process resolved the tension between morality and reality.

In the mid-1980s, sociologists Greg Duncan and James Morgan of the University of Michigan concluded that most poor people are not permanently poor; a lot of people live in poverty for several years and then move above the poverty line. Furthermore, a vast majority of welfare recipients collect benefits for only a year or two. The policy implications of their work was clear; poverty and welfare recipiency were not limited to a small group. Over the course of a decade, a very large slice of the population could find itself in need of help. Therefore, we needed a welfare system that was generous and helpful, not penurious and punitive.

Using the same data, David Ellwood and Mary Jo Bane, then public-policy professors at Harvard's Kennedy School, asserted that the small minority who stay on welfare for a long time are more likely to be African American, poorly educated, and unmarried. They were likely to stay on welfare much longer than the average recipient and consume a large proportion of welfare spending. Ellwood and Bane proposed a complex set of policies—a higher earned income tax credit, more job training and education, stricter child support, and a two-year limit on welfare—to deal with the complexity of factors leading to long-term welfare dependency. They hoped that by focusing on the problems of long-term recipients and by proposing solutions that were both compassionate and tough, they could get the federal government to enact a program that would benefit both the long- and short-term recipients.

Ellwood and Bane's work caught the attention of then-presidential candidate Bill Clinton. After pledging to "end welfare as we know it" during the campaign, the newly elected President brought Ellwood and Bane to Washington to craft his welfare-reform proposals. The administration proposal that was released in June preserves the scholars' proposals for a two-year time limit on welfare, but it has jettisoned many of their ideas for expanded services and support for recipients.

Ellwood and Bane had hoped that focusing on long-term recipients would bring a program that benefited short-term recipients as well, but they misjudged the role of symbols in the political process. As the welfare debate began to focus only on the long-term recipients, a population that purportedly needed the discipline of time limits and work requirements to behave properly, this image dominated the discussion. For rhetorical purposes, the other 75 percent of the welfare population that stay on welfare for a short time became invisible. After all, the symbol of the chronic welfare recipient is powerful; it simplifies and compresses reality and by doing so, it obliterates the reality of the majority. Thus, once that 75 percent had disappeared from the discussion—once the welfare problem was framed in terms of young, Black, single mothers who stay on welfare forever—the discussion of welfare "reform" turned more and more punitive. If liberals thought welfare recipients needed more discipline and a time limit on benefits, then conservatives felt free to propose eliminating welfare altogether and a holy war against illegitimacy.

It is discouraging—and extremely short-sighted—that neither the President nor any of his principal advisers on social policy seized the debate to focus national attention on the question essential to true welfare reform: What would a program designed to help the majority of people on welfare—the three-in-four women who stay on public assistance for a short time—look like? These people are more likely to be older and better educated than the long-term recipients. They are likely to have suffered a disruption of their work life due to unemployment or sickness or a breakdown of their marriage.

Women in this situation enter a kind of economic and emotional free-fall. They lose their homes, their social networks, and other resources until they hit bottom. They need support, both financial and emotional. They need the resources and the time to put their lives back together.

In fairness, it should be pointed out that the Clinton welfare-reform proposal includes some features that will help the majority. It calls for increases in the incentives for states to get poor women training and education. It provides more funding for child-support enforcement. Finally, it seeks to assure that recipients who find a job will keep their health care and child care while they make the transition to the labor force, something that the 1988 welfare reform promised but failed to deliver.

But the other features of the plan—those that have precipitated the most heated partisan debate and have generated most of the media attention—are intended to punish the 25 percent who are chronic welfare recipients. The plan includes the two-year cut-off, with those who fail to find work then moving into minimum-wage jobs. In addition, the proposals give states great latitude in adopting even harsher sanctions for women who have additional children while on welfare.

The reform proposals do nothing to raise the national minimum benefit for a family. In fact, the adequacy of welfare has almost disappeared as an issue. Yet, because of the steep decline in the value of benefits over the past fifteen years, single mothers who work escape poverty less often today than they did in 1980. In the absence of benefit increases and labor-market reforms, the Clinton plan will trade poor women on welfare for poor women in the labor force.

Ironically, at the same time that the Clinton administration has urged Congress to embrace a national standard of adequate health care for all Americans, it has ignored the issue of adequate welfare benefits. The reasons that adequacy of benefits has vanished as an issue from the welfare debate are many and complex. As some writers in TIKKUN have suggested, liberals' ability to craft an assertive social agenda suffers from their inability to challenge conservatives' dominance of "values" issues.

At the same time, the neglect of the adequacy of benefits reflects a structural crisis of liberalism. The welfare reform efforts of the 1970s foundered on the shoals of low-wage work. If we were to preserve the principle that the lowest paid worker should earn more than welfare recipients, we either had to supplement the wages of the working poor or keep welfare benefits inadequate. Because Congress was unwilling to do what was necessary to raise the earnings of low-wage workers, reformers had to resign themselves to inadequate welfare payments.

The Clinton plan will only marginally change the lives of poor women and children. A few more women will receive job training and find jobs, a few more will be sanctioned for noncompliance, a few more will receive child support, and a few will get dropped from the welfare rolls. Whether they stay on the rolls, find a job, receive more child support, or reach their time limit, however, the Clinton plan will neither improve the odds of women getting back on their feet nor end welfare as we know it.

## WHAT WE TALK ABOUT WHEN WE TALK ABOUT WELFARE

So why should a set of relatively minor adjustments of the American way of poverty generate such emotions? Because the core of the debate about welfare touches most of us, whatever our economic position or political perspective. We have displaced a whole set of anxieties we have about the new world in which we live onto the welfare debate. We worry about the postindustrial transformation of the economy and its insecurities, and we talk about enforcing the work ethic for welfare recipients. We see our children become sexually active earlier and earlier, our neighbors get divorced, and friends discover they are gay, and we talk about resuscitating the traditional family. We live in neighborhoods that seem less safe, less secure, and less stable than they used to be, and we talk about the need for community development in the inner city.

These are all important topics that deserve our attention, but as a practical matter, we should not use the lives of poor women and children to work them out. There is a host of issues that can advance the discussion of the balance of responsibility, caring, and individualism. Health care, child care, and employers' responsibility toward workers and their families all provide opportunities for us to discuss these issues in concrete ways that touch ordinary people's lives. Welfare—clouded as it is with decades of race- and gender-baiting—somehow leads us toward myths and caricatures, not the difficult choices forced upon women and men. The poor have enough problems without serving as a stand-in for the anxieties of the middle class.

Just as important, although we may rail against the Clinton administration's pandering to conservatives, liberals' ambivalence about the unpredictable nature of family and community makes a common "progressive" position on welfare reform unattainable. The recent vogue for communitarian ideas among liberals speaks to a profound uneasiness about the instability that a stress on individual happiness and consensual relationships will inevitably breed.

I suspect that what Lillian Rubin concluded about the working-class in a recent issue of this magazine (" 'People Don't Know Right From Wrong Anymore'," TIKKUN, January/February 1994) is true for other social strata as well: We are in a kind of cultural lag, unable to reconcile our values around family and community with the real choices about commitment and happiness that we make. And when we see the specter of the teen mother—stereotypically sexually promiscuous, hedonistic, and unashamed—many of us are uncomfortable with what may be the logical extrapolation of our own life decisions.

Americans have always overestimated the gap between the well-off and the poor. It is social context, not social values, that creates a chasm between the poor and the mainstream. Poor women, like women in other social classes, no longer accept unhappy marriages as their fate; they want to get out of them. But whereas the wife of a lawyer or computer technician will think twice about leaving because of the probable decline in her standard of living, poor women are less likely to face these consequences.

In fact, Black women's occupational revolution—not the myth of over-generous welfare checks—has provided the greatest economic incentive for these women to get out of bad marriages, or not to marry at all. Three decades ago, Black women, who in most parts of the country could find work only as maids, needed a husband to make ends meet. Now that African-American women have more occupational choices, the wage gap between Black women and men has almost disappeared.

African Americans are the first group in the United States to experiment with economic equality in marriages. For poor couples who are committed to their relationships, the increased earnings of women have allowed most low-wage, dual-earner families to escape poverty. Among women in intolerable relationships, however, these new opportunities have removed the financial penalty they suffer from leaving a relationship, or not entering one in the first place.

Of course, these changes—especially the rises in the number of single-parent families and teen mothers—should worry us, but we need to see that there is more going on than "irresponsibility." Unless we are willing to turn back the clock on this occupational revolution, we are going to have to live with more family instability, no matter how uncomfortable it makes us.

One way of addressing this uneasiness is to take the position (one familiar to TIKKUN's readers) that the irresponsibility of some welfare recipients toward their families and communities is as unacceptable as that of corporations that turn their backs on their communities, or of the well-off who neglect their children's need for guidance and caring. Certainly, some early supporters of Clinton's welfare-reform effort, including Ellwood and Bane, hoped that if liberals accepted work requirements and time limits, we could demand that government and business hold up their responsibility to provide jobs, adequate training, and services. But after a year of conservative sniping and budget constraints, the plan puts few demands on those in power.

Perhaps most distressing of all its shortcomings, the Clinton proposal reinforces the myth that a huge gap separates welfare recipients from the mainstream. We can ask the poor to take any job offered them, make sure their children don't skip school, and limit their fertility, without raising questions about the well-being of families and communities in other social classes. But can we demand that the poor live by a standard of selflessness that we are not prepared to meet? To the extent that the Clinton welfare plan constructs a kind of moral apartheid—if you're not on welfare you can run your personal life as you want, but if you want welfare you have to conform to mainstream values around work and family—it represents an intolerable hypocrisy.

# III
▼▼▼▼▼▼▼▼▼

# MARGINALITY AND DIFFERENCE:
# THE FRACTURED COMMUNITY

*Every migrant knows in his heart of hearts, that it is impossible to return. Even if he is physically able to return, he does not truly return, because he himself has been so deeply changed by his emigration. . . . Today, as soon as very early childhood is over, the home can never again be home, as it was in other epochs. This century, for all its wealth and with all its communication systems, is the century of banishment.[1]*

Berger's powerful words take us into the unifying theme of the third part of this book—a theme now of immense significance in the United States. For Berger and others, spiritual homelessness, or alienation, is the defining condition of humankind in the late 20th century. Men and women feel estranged from their own labors and worlds, that are unattached in any significant way, to where they live, work, or as we see in this part, go to school. From this perspective, one sees a world deeply scarred by what has been called "the poison of separation." Our lives and our cultures are pervaded by fragmentation. Too little do we connect our creative selves to our labor, our private lives to the public world, or the traditionally masculine activities of production and mastery to the typically feminine tasks of reproduction and nurturance. We find ourselves in a world that excludes, sometimes brutally, whole categories of people from any real participation in the collective making of the material or cultural conditions of their lives. Groups of people cast into the role of "surplus populations" find their lives, experiences, values, and ways of life demeaned and invalidated by those who are, or see themselves as, the central players in society. Ultimately, this world of separation places human beings on a path of fatal dissonance with the very context of our existence—the earth and our physical environment. The phenomenon of alienation crosses national boundaries and various forms of political and social life. In the United States, alienation and freedom are opposite sides of the same coin. *Freedom* in this country has always meant a freedom "from." It has meant bourgeois or liberal freedom in which obligation, duty, and responsibility to the state or the community are minimal. Individuals are expected to become self-sufficient beings, unconstrained in their geographical and social mobility by the ties that bind them to others. *Individuality, autonomy,* and *independence* are the watchwords of the American ideology—the heart of the promise of American life. This promise has been enormously appealing to generations of immigrants from lands in which lives were stunted or thwarted by repressive traditions, state coercion, or economic scarcity. Yet, we have paid a heavy price for this type of freedom, founded as it is on separation. Our society denigrates common bonds and collective ties. However much we might wax nostalgic or sentimental about such social connections, the price for entry into the relative security of middle-class life is the dissolution of these ties. Success or achievement is attained primarily through the heartless, competitive, and egoistic drives demanded by the economic marketplace.

Success in America means abandonment of those communal ties that limit the headlong rush for personal achievement. It means shredding the traditions of language, attitudes, beliefs, and values that stand in the way of conforming to the White, male, Christian, heterosexual, middle-class standards that constitute American normalcy. For many, winning one's place in the American mainstream means submission to a brutal process of alienation. One must, in the first place, forfeit those ethnically, linguistically, and racially mediated cultures that are eschewed by the dominant culture. In other words, one must dissolve those historically constituted ties through which whole groups of human beings learned to locate themselves in the world. Doing so, one must not simply abandon social ties, but also eliminate important aspects of one's identity. One must give up parts of oneself. The price of some minimal degree of economic well-being or security is frequently denial, shame, and inauthenticity.

This insistence on cultural homogenization has been accompanied, historically, by a process in which dominant groups rationalize their positions of privilege through myths about their superiority and the purported inferiority of those they oppress. Yet, as our readings make clear, the process of homogenization is neither smooth nor conflict-free. Individually and collectively, human beings often resist the Faustian bargain in which the price of economic survival is a denial of one's community. In education, for example, students and parents often fought to preserve social identities over which schools frequently ride roughshod. At times, these struggles have borne fruit in the form of educational policies that recognize and attempt to assist racial, linguistic, ethnic, or other minorities in the preservation of their communal forms and cultures. Still, such instances do not characterize American education. More often, what we witness is a system that falls far short of respecting human and cultural differences. Indeed, as these readings show, we have only begun to see how the prevailing logic of educational practice—even where it is intended to be ameliorative—confirms and reproduces the traditional structures of hierarchy, reward, and prejudice. More generally, we refuse to confront the way in which educational policies reflect questions of power—cultural, economic, and political. Exploring the enduring and pervasive forms of personal and collective alienation inside, as well as outside the school means recognizing how educational institutions discount the voices of, and exclude from meaningful participation, too many of their students.

In the aftermath of the Los Angeles uprising, Henry Giroux (chap. 11) takes issue with a liberal multiculturalism that merely acknowledges differences and analyzes stereotypes. A "critical multiculturalism," says Giroux, "means understanding, engaging, and transforming the diverse histories, cultural narratives, representations and institutions that produce racism and other forms of discrimination" (p. 183). Multicultural education must mean more than fiestas and sampling diverse foods. It demands an exploration of the forms of political and ethical decisions that create and sustain enormous inequities of wealth, power, and opportunity in American society. It means looking at the way race overlaps with access to health care, produces job discrimination, intersects with the inequities of the justice system, and so on. It also means understanding how education is complicit in a process of producing and reproducing social inequality; how, for example, testing, promoting choice, the development of a national curriculum, and a uniform standard of literacy are injurious to children of color. For Giroux, the project of a critical multiculturalism is closely connected to the struggle for a democratic education in which schools become public spaces deeply committed to challenging all those inequalities that disfigure this society. In such spaces, students learn to both value the diversity of our histories and ethnicities while seeking commonalities of concern with other communities around issues of citizenship and public policy.

Jane Roland Martin begins chapter 12 with the saga of Richard Rodriguez and the human price that must sometimes be paid to achieve educational success—alienation from one's most intimate roots and the feelings and emotions that are nourished through them. In place of the self-congratulatory images of assimilation and acceptance of immigrants to America is the story of human lives lived at the edge of a strange, forbidding, and always foreign culture. Such alienation, Martin argues, is built into our very idea of the educated person. Our ideal splits reason from emotion, mind from body, and thought from action. Rodriguez, Martin says, developed the capacity for "reasoned deliberation rather than spontaneous reaction, dispassionate inquiry rather than emotional response" (p. 200). Such attributes are a preparation for the public world—the place of productive processes. This world—a masculinized realm—excludes feeling, emotion, intimacy, and connection. Instead, Martin says, analysis, critical thinking, and self-sufficiency are valued. The educational ideal, she says, excludes the female-oriented, reproductive processes of society, which involve care, concern, connectedness, and nurturance—capacities that we need not only in the family, but also increasingly to sustain our communities and the earth itself.

James Sears (chap. 13) looks at the question of sexual difference and its implications for education. He argues that the fear of homosexuality and the threat that same-sex relations pose to a male-dominated culture are reflected in our reluctance to include this issue in the school curriculum. As he notes, "blurring gender roles and challenging sexual norms rock the very foundations of a society rooted in male privilege and misogynistic attitudes" (p. 213). Like Giroux, Sears asserts that public education needs to provide spaces that encourage and develop the attitudes and values of a critical democracy. Within such spaces, students can begin to explore how gendered roles and desires are socially constructed; why it is that sex education stresses the dangers and hydraulics of human sexuality, not questions of pleasure; the prohibitions on forms of sexual expression that are not heterosexual, and so on. Sears calls for a critically based sexuality curriculum that challenges the heterosexual agenda in schools and society. It calls on educators to examine their own personal feelings about sexuality to reveal their fears and prejudices. It provides a counterforce to the "plague of sexual ignorance and fear" in this country and teaches students to recognize the diversity of human sexuality. In this way, students would be prepared for participation in our pluralistic, if contentious, culture and would be effective and responsible citizens of a complex democracy.

Svi Shapiro (chap. 14) considers the dilemma between our ethical commitment to particular communities of meaning and history and to furthering the larger sense of solidarity and connectedness among diverse communities. Starting with his own struggle concerning the education of his daughter, he reflects on what is at stake in the decision to send her to a Jewish, parochial school or to a public school. On the one hand, he is aware of the difficulty of transmitting his own minority culture in a society in which the everyday assumptions are steeped in Christianity. Although the opening to a more multicultural and pluralistic awareness in education is applauded, it can be, he says, no substitute for the powerful existential, spiritual, and ethical experience of a Jewish education. Such schooling is rich in the sense of memory and tradition that are so missing in the larger, shallow, and transient American culture. Yet, Shapiro is also deeply concerned with the evisceration in America of the public space and public ideals—a space, however inadequate, that has been embodied by public education. This is a time, he says, when more and more, those public spaces and concerns are being condemned and shortchanged by a political culture that seeks to persuade us that private interests and the marketplace are the only valid moral and institutional forms of social interaction. Offering no easy answers, Shapiro considers the difficult task of balancing specific communal identities with the need to reaffirm our membership in broader, more universal forms of association.

Turning to another, frequently denigrated, segment of society, Rebecca Blomgren (chap. 15) describes the indignities suffered by those labeled as handicapped in our schools. The best intentions of special educators notwithstanding, those students are helped through a medical-scientific model of diagnosis, prescription, assessment, and remediation that views individuals as "to a greater or lesser degree, impaired and thus in need of fixing" (p. 242). Within the framework of educational practice, Blomgren says, the unfixed, unproductive individual is quickly blamed for his or her lack of success. She notes that neither the conventional model of educational reform nor the process of critical pedagogy (which requires rational and expressive skills that many handicapped people lack) provides an adequate model for special education. We need another starting point altogether, one in which help is not in any sense prescriptive, but rather a matter of facing those who come before us in our classrooms as "valued and cherished human beings." Our work, says Blomgren, must be conceived, not as an act of fixing or shaping, but of affirming the dignity and sanctity of human life.

Finally, Donaldo Macedo (chap. 16) returns to the question of education and democracy in a multicultural, multilingual society. Authentic bilingual education, he argues, is about much more than acquiring a particular set of language competencies. It is a primary means by which students come to value their own existential, cultural, and historical realities. It is a crucial aspect of how individuals come to value and respect their own experience and to know their own voices. In this sense, monolingual education is part of the way that schools produce a debilitating sense of the present and future for minority students, denying them the elementary capacity to express and produce significant meaning. In insisting on particular, and often alien, language forms for these students, teachers delegitimize the language experiences that students bring with them into the classroom. School negates (rather than making meaningful) the cultural experiences of subordinate linguistic groups. For Macedo, the movement to deny bilingual education is part of a larger antidemocratic conservatism that seeks to thwart the full social and economic enfranchisement of poor and working class minorities.

It seeks to deny the potential for radical change that an education that affirms the voices of such people can encourage in the United States.

All the writings in this part reflect an important shift in our view of cultures and human behaviors that do not conform to what has been considered normal. In place of the widely held assumption that these other kinds of people are deficient or abnormal, we begin to use a language of "difference" that seeks to treat all human beings with dignity and equal value. No human practices, values, or beliefs can set themselves up as the standard by which everyone should be judged or measured. Through the work of postmodern critics, such as Michel Foucault, we see how claims about what is normal always cloaks the power of one group or another to impose its views about the proper way to live, speak, think, feel, or value. It becomes increasingly apparent how the discourse of normality masks the power to control others who are different because of race, nationality, gender, sexual preference, language, class, physical appearance, and mental or physical ability. From the perspective of difference, a socially just world is impossible without a radically deepened appreciation—and affirmation—of the cultural worth and dignity of all people.

## NOTES

1. John Berger, *And Our Faces, My Heart, Brief as Photos* (New York: Pantheon, 1984), pp. 65–67.

# 11
▼▼▼▼▼▼▼

# The Politics of Insurgent Multiculturalism in the Era of the Los Angeles Uprising*

Henry A. Giroux

## NAMING WHITE SUPREMACY

I want to begin by quoting two teachers, both of whom harbor strong feelings and passions about the issue of multiculturalism and race. The first quote is by the late James Baldwin, the renowned Afro-American writer. The second quote recently appeared in *The Chronicle of Higher Education* and is by Melvin E. Bradford, a former speechwriter for George Wallace and more recently an editorial writer working on behalf of Patrick Buchanan.

> If . . . one managed to change the curriculum in all the schools so that [Afro-Americans] learned more about themselves and their real contributions to this culture, you would be liberating not only [Afro-Americans], you'd be liberating white people who know nothing about their own history. And the reason is that if you are compelled to lie about one aspect of anybody's history, you must lie about it all. If you have to lie about my real role here, if you have to pretend that I hoed all that cotton just because I loved you, then you have done something to yourself. You are mad.[1]

> I am not a scientific racist. . . . But blacks as a group have been here a long time and, for some reason, making them full members of our society has proven almost impossible. They remain outside. The more privileges black Americans have had, the worse they seem to do. At the core of it is black private life—those things we can't legislate and can't control. . . . I have a deep suspicion that in matters

---

*From: CRITICAL MULTICULTURALISM. Kanpol & McLaren (Eds.). Copyright © 1995 by Barry Kanpol and Peter McLaren. Reproduced with permission of GREENWOOD PUBLISHING GROUP, INC., Westport, CT.

**181**

that affect the course of their lives, blacks habitually shoot themselves in the foot.[2]

What these quotes suggest in the most benign sense is that issues concerning multiculturalism are fundamentally about questions of race and identity. A less sanguine analysis reveals what both of these quotes share, but only what Baldwin is willing to name: that multiculturalism is not only about the discourse of alleged others but is also fundamentally about the issue of whiteness as a mark of racial and gender privilege. For example, Baldwin argues that multiculturalism cannot be reduced to an exclusive otherness that references Afro-Americans, Hispanics, Latinos, or other suppressed minorities, as either a problem to be resolved through the call for benevolent assimilation or as a threat to be policed and eliminated. For Baldwin, multiculturalism is primarily about whiteness and its claims to a self-definition that excludes itself from the messy relations of race, ethnicity, power, and identity.

On the other hand, Bradford exemplifies a dominant approach to multiculturalism that serves as a coded legitimation for equating racial, cultural, and ethnic diversity with social chaos, the lowering of standards, and the emergence of an alleged new tribalism that threatens the boundaries of a common culture or national identity. What both of these positions highlight is how differences in power and privilege mediate who speaks, under what conditions, and for whom. In this sense, multiculturalism raises the question of whether people are speaking within or outside a privileged space, and whether such spaces provide the conditions for different groups to listen to each other differently in order to address how the racial economies of privilege and power work in this society.

I want to argue that in the aftermath of the spring 1992 Los Angeles uprising (which occurred after the LA police brutally beat Rodney King during a routine arrest), educators need to rethink the politics of multiculturalism as part of a broader attempt to understand how issues regarding national identity, culture, and ethnicity can be rewritten in order to enable dominant groups to examine, acknowledge, and unlearn their own privilege. In part this demands an approach to multiculturalism that not only addresses "the context of massive black unemployment, overcrowded schools, a lack of recreational facilities, dilapidated housing and racist policing,"[3] but a concerted attempt "to view most racism in this country not as an issue of black lawlessness but primarily as an expression of white 'supremacy.' "[4] More specifically, a critical multiculturalism must shift attention away from an exclusive focus on subordinate groups, especially since such an approach tends to highlight their deficits, to one that examines how racism in its various forms is produced historically, semiotically, and institutionally at various levels of society. This is not meant to suggest that blacks and other subordinate groups do not face problems that need to be addressed. On the contrary, it means that a critical analysis of race must move beyond the discourse of pathology in which whites "confine discussions about race in America to the 'problems' black pose for whites."[5] As Cornel West points out, viewing black people in this manner reveals not only white supremacy as the discursive and institutional face of racism, but it also presents us with the challenge of addressing racial issues not as a dilemma of black people but as a problem endemic to the legacy of internal colonialism rooted in "historical inequalities and longstanding cultural stereotypes."[6]

In opposition to a quaint liberalism, a critical multiculturalism means more than simply acknowledging differences and analyzing stereotypes; more fundamentally, it means understanding, engaging, and transforming the diverse histories, cultural narratives, representations, and institutions that produce racism and other forms of discrimination. As bell hooks points out, for too long white people have imagined that they are invisible to black people. Not only does whiteness in this formulation cease to mark the locations of its own privileges, it reinforces relations in which blacks become invisible in terms of how they name, see, experience, and bear the pain and terror of whiteness. hooks puts it succinctly:

> In white supremacist society, white people can "safely" imagine that they are invisible to black people since the power they have historically asserted, and even now collectively assert over black people, accorded them the right to control the black gaze. . . . [And yet] to name that whiteness in the black imagination is often a representation of terror. One must face written histories that erase and deny, that reinvent the past to make the present vision of racial harmony and pluralism more plausible. To bear the burden of memory one must willingly journey to places long uninhabited, searching the debris of history for traces of the unforgettable, all knowledge of which has been suppressed.[7]

It is worth noting that in the aftermath of the recent Los Angeles uprising, many educational commentators have ruled out any discussion about the relationship between race and class and how they are manifested within networks of hierarchy and subordination both in and out of the schools. This particular silence, when coupled with the popular perception that the L.A. uprising can be explained by pointing to those involved as simply thugs, looters, and criminals, makes it clear why the multicultural peril is often seen as a black threat; it also suggests what such a belief shares with the traditionalists' view of the Other as a disruptive outsider. In this scenario, multiculturalism becomes the source of the problem.

In what follows, I want to address the necessity of creating an insurgent multiculturalism as a basis for a new language of educational leadership, one that allows students and others to move between cultures, to travel within zones of cultural difference. At stake here is the need to develop a language that challenges the boundaries of cultural and racial difference as sites of exclusion and discrimination while simultaneously rewriting the script of cultural difference as part of a broader attempt to provide new spaces for expanding and deepening the imperatives of a multicultural and multiracial democracy. In short, I want to address what it means to treat schools and other public sites as border institutions in which teachers, students, and others learn to think and imagine otherwise in order to act otherwise.[8] For it is within such institutions, engaged in daily acts of cultural translation and negotiation, that students and teachers are offered the opportunity to become border crossers, to recognize that schooling is really an introduction to how culture is organized, a demonstration of who is authorized to speak about particular forms of culture, what culture is considered worthy of valorization, and what forms of culture are considered invalid and unworthy of public esteem. Drawing in part upon Homi Bhabha, I want to argue that schools, in part, need to be understood as sites engaged in the "strategic activity of 'authority,' agency," of exercising authority in order "to articulate and regulate incommensurable meanings and identities."[9] Within this perspective, leadership is removed from its exclusive emphasis on management, and it is defined as a form of political and ethical address that weighs cultural differences against the implications they have for practices that disclose rather than mystify, democratize culture rather than shut it down, and provide the conditions for all people to believe that they can take risks and change existing power relations.

## WHITE PANIC AND ETHNIC RACE

After the fires went out in Los Angeles, the Bush administration once again reneged on its responsibility to address the problems and demands of democratic public life. In the face of escalating poverty, increasing racism, growing unemployment among minorities, and the failure of an expanding number of Americans to receive adequate health care or education, the Bush administration invoked a wooden morality coupled with a disdain for public life by blaming the nation's ills on the legislation of the Great Society, TV sitcom characters such as Murphy Brown, or the alleged breakdown of family values. Within this scenario, poverty is caused by the poverty of values, racism is seen as a "black" problem (lawlessness), and social decay can be rectified by shoring up the family and the logic and social relations of the alleged free market.

The Bush administration's response to the Los Angeles uprising exemplifies the failure of leadership that was characteristic of the Reagan/Bush eras. Abandoning its responsibility for political and moral leadership, the federal government has reduced its intervention in public life to waging war against

Iraq, using taxpayers' money to bail out corrupt bankers, and slashing legislation that would benefit the poor, the homeless, and the disadvantaged. There is a tragic irony at work when a government can raise $500 billion to bail out corrupt bankers and $50 billion to fight a war in Iraq (put in perspective, the combined costs of these adventures exceed the cost of World War II including veterans benefits), while at the same time the same government cuts back food stamp and school lunch programs in a country in which nearly one out of every four children under six live in poverty. But there is more at stake here than simply the failure of moral and political leadership. The breadth and depth of democratic relations are being rolled back at all levels of national and daily life. For example, this is seen in the growing disparity between the rich and poor, the ongoing attacks by the government and courts on civil rights and the welfare system, and the proliferating incidents of racist harassment and violence on college and public school sites.

The retreat from democracy is also evident in the absence of serious talk about how as a nation we might educate existing and future generations of students in the language and practice of moral compassion, critical agency, and public service. The discourse of leadership appears trapped in a terminology in which the estimate of a good society is expressed in indexes that measure profit margins and the Dow Jones average. Missing in this vocabulary is a way of nourishing and sustaining a popular perception of democracy as something that needs to be constantly struggled for in public arenas such as the schools, churches, and other sites that embody the promise of a multiracial and multicultural democracy.

This current assault on democratic public life has taken a new turn in the last few years. At one level, American conservatives have initiated a long-term project of discrediting and dismantling those institutions, ideologies, and practices that are judged incompatible with the basic ideology of the marketplace. In this instance, a diverse alliance of conservatives and neoliberals has launched a full-fledged and unswervering commitment to the principles of individualism, choice, and the competitive ethic. Accompanying this attempt has been a parallel effort to reprivatize and deregulate schools, health care, the welfare system, and other public services and institutions. The extent to which conservatives have gone to promote this project, one that Stuart Hall has rightly called "regressive modernization,"[10] can be seen in former President Bush's suggestion that Los Angeles sells its international airport to private investors in order to use some of the revenue to rebuild South Central L.A.[11] It is quite remarkable that as the fires were burning in this long-suffering city, the nation's highest elected public official refused to address the smoldering social, economic, and cultural conditions that fueled the uprising. In this discourse, the imperatives of privatization and the profit margin become more important than issues of human suffering and social justice. Of course, this should not be surprising given the radical assaults on all aspects of the public sphere that have been waged during the last decade.

Part of the attempt to rewrite the terms of discourse regarding the meaning and value of public life can be seen in the emergence of a new breed of intellectuals, largely backed by conservative think tanks such as the Madison Group, the Hoover Institute, the Heritage Foundation, and a host of other conservative foundations.[12] With access to enormous cultural resources infused by massive financial backing from the Olin, Scaife, and Smith Richardson foundations, right-wing think tanks have begun to mount mammoth public campaigns to promote their cultural revolution. Many of the major right-wing intellectuals who have helped to shape popular discourse about educational reform in the last decade have received extensive aid from the conservative foundations. These include intellectuals such as Diane Ravitch, Chester Finn, Dinish D'Souza, William Bennett, and Allan Bloom, all of whom have targeted public schools and higher education as two principal spheres of struggle over issues of content, privatization, choice, and difference.[13] In order to understand the model of leadership that these intellectuals provide, it is important to examine how some of their underlying ideological concerns relate to the broader issues of democracy, race, and public accountability.[14]

## THE CONSERVATIVE ASSAULT ON DEMOCRACY

For many conservatives, the utopian possibility of cultural democracy has become dangerous at the current historical conjuncture for a number of reasons. First, it encourages a language of critique for understanding and transforming those relations that trap people in networks of hierarchy and exploitation. That is, it provides a normative referent for recognizing and assessing competing political vocabularies, the visions of the future they presuppose, and the social identities and practices they both produce and legitimate. By subordinating the language of management and efficiency to moral and ethical considerations, a critical discourse of democracy keeps alive the importance of democratic values and how they can be institutionalized into practices that animate rather than restrict the discourse of justice, equality, and community. Clearly such a position poses a challenge to right-wing educators whose celebration of choice and the logic of the marketplace abstract freedom from equality and the imperatives of citizenship from its historical grounding in the public institutions of modern society.

In fact, many conservatives such as Lynn Cheney, William Bennett, Herbert Whittle, and Diane Ravitch have been quite aggressive in rewriting the discourse of citizenship *not* as the practice of social responsibility but as a privatized act of altruism, self-help, or philanthropy. It is crucial to recognize that within this language of privatization, the disquieting, disrupting, interrupting difficulties of sexism, crime, youth unemployment, AIDS, and other social problems, and how they bear down on schools, are either ignored or summarily dismissed as individual problems caused, in part, by the people who are victimized by them. Of course, not only does this position ignore the necessity for social criticism in a democratic society, it also erases the moral and political obligation of institutions to both recognize their complicity in creating such problems and in eradicating them. In this scenario, we end up with a vision of leadership in which individuals act in comparative isolation and without any sense of public accountability. This is why many right-wing educators praise the virtues of the competition and choice but rarely talk about how money and power, when unevenly distributed, influence "whether people have the means or the capacity" to make or act on choices that inform their daily lives.[15]

Jonathan Kozol is instructive here in recounting the story of how President Bush told a group of parents in a desperately poor school district in New Jersey that " 'A society that worships money is a society in Peril.' [Kozol responds by asking] Why didn't he say that to the folks in Bloomfield Hills, Michigan or in Great Neck, Long Island? What is the message?"[16] The message, of course, is that power, wealth, and privilege have no bearing on the choices that different groups make, especially if those groups are rich and powerful. Choice in this case serves to rewrite the discourse of freedom within a limited conception of individual needs and desires. What disappears from this view of leadership is the willingness to recognize that the fundamental issues of citizenship, democracy, and public life can neither be understood nor addressed solely within the restricted language of the marketplace or choice. Choice and the market are not the sole conditions of freedom, nor are they adequate to constituting political subjects within the broader discourses of justice, equality, and community. In fact, no understanding of community, citizenship, or public culture is possible without a shared conception of social justice, and yet it is precisely the notion of social justice that is missing in mainstream school reforms. Robert Bellah and his associates have also argued that Americans need a new vocabulary for talking about the problem and future of schooling. They write: "Money and power are necessary as means, but they are not the proper measures of a good society and a good world. We need to talk about our problems and our future with a richer vocabulary than the indices that measure markets and defense systems alone."[17]

It is worth noting that we live at a time when:

a Black person in the U.S. is 7.4 times more likely to be imprisoned than a white person, when there are more Black men aged 20–29 who are under control of the criminal justice system than there are black men in college, and

one out of every four Black men will go to prison at some point in his life.
. . . Furthermore, it costs about $20,000 a year to send a person to prison,
about what it would cost to send that person to Harvard.[18]

Additionally, 45 percent of all minority children live in poverty while the
dropout rate among minority students has attained truly alarming proportions, reaching as high as 70 percent in some major urban areas. These
problems are compounded by an unemployment rate among black youth
that is currently 38.4 percent. In the face of these problems, conservatives
are aggressively attempting to enact choice legislation that would divert funds
away from the public schools to private schools. Against these efforts, it is
worth noting, as Peter Dreier, points out, that

> since 1980 the federal government has slashed successful urban programs—
> public works, economic development, health and nutrition, schools, housing,
> and job training—by more than 70 per cent. . . . In 1980, Federal dollars
> accounted for 14.3 per cent of city budgets; today, the Federal share is less
> than 5 per cent. . . . To avert fiscal collapse, many cities have been closing
> schools, hospitals, police and fire stations; laying off essential employees; re-
> ducing such basic services as maintenance of parks and roads; neglecting
> housing and health codes, and postponing or canceling capital improvements.[19]

Claiming that these problems can be solved by raising test scores, promoting choice, developing a national curriculum, and creating a uniform
standard of national literacy is both cruel and mean-spirited. But, of course,
this is where the discourse of critical democracy becomes subversive; it makes
visible the political and normative considerations that frame such reforms.
It also analyzes how the language of excessive individualism and competitiveness serves to make social inequality invisible, and promotes an indifference to human misery, exploitation, and suffering. Moreover, it suggests that
the language of excellence and individualism, when abstracted from considerations of equality and social justice, serves to restrict rather than animate
the possibilities of democratic public life.

It is becoming increasingly clear that democracy has become a subversive
category to those who would subordinate public institutions to the laws of
the marketplace and treat cultural difference as the enemy of Western civilization. In part this is exemplified in a recent article in *Education Week* in
which Chester Finn attempts to provide a rationale for the privatization of
schools and other public institutions by arguing that the concept of the public
no longer merits either the attention or the support of the American people.
Couched in the bad versus good rhetoric of simplistic binarisms, Finn dismisses public education by arguing that all institutions that attempt to serve
the public as a matter of service rather than profit are doomed to fail (i.e.,
public transportation, public bathrooms, public health, etc.). Like his con-

servative colleague Allan Bloom, Finn argues that he would rather have "'you' send your kid to Princeton."[20] Of course, the ubiquitous "you" in this sentence speaks for everyone while failing to mark its own location of privilege. What kind of politics and notion of choice inform the assumption that all parents occupy an equal ground in being able to send their kids to an Ivy League school? More is revealed here than an offensive elitism (not to mention racism). Lacking any sense of specificity, refusing to address how money and power provide the very conditions for exercising choice, Finn uses choice as a code word to suggest that those who are suffering the most in this society simply lack either the intelligence, character, individual initiative, or competitive spirit to pick themselves up and make a successful go of their lives. These are strange words coming from intellectuals who receive massive financial funding from some of the most aggressive, ideologically conservative foundations in the United States.

The second reason that democracy is so threatening to many conservatives is that it provides a rationale for constructing public spheres in which different groups can reclaim their identities and histories as part of an attempt to exercise power and control over their lives, while simultaneously attempting to take part in the political system as true participants rather than as mere consumers.[21] In this context, democracy foretells how cultural difference can be addressed in relation to wider questions of politics, power, membership, participation, and social responsibility.

Most importantly, numerous groups that have been profoundly underrepresented in the social and cultural narratives of the dominant culture have begun to redefine the relationship between culture and politics in order to deepen and extend the basis for a radical democratic society. In this sense, the promise of a critical democracy has mobilized subordinate groups to question how cultural identity and representation are being defined within existing social, cultural, and political institutions. Central to such concerns are questions regarding how the schools and other institutions are actually responding to the changing conditions of a society that will no longer have a white majority by the year 2010.

It is difficult to imagine what is either unpatriotic or threatening about subordinate groups attempting to raise questions such as: "Whose experiences, histories, knowledge, and arts are represented in our educational and cultural institutions? How fully, on whose terms, and with what degree of ongoing, institutionalized participation and power?"[22] Nor in a democratic society should subordinate groups attempting to fashion a pedagogy and politics of inclusion and cultural democracy be derisively labeled as particularistic because they have raised serious questions regarding either how the public school curriculum works to secure particular forms of cultural authority, or how the dynamics of cultural power work to silence and marginalize specific groups of students. This emerging critique of schools and other

cultural institutions is based on the assumption that cultural differences are
not the enemy of democracy, as E. D. Hirsch and others have argued, but
intolerance, structured inequality, and social injustice.[23]

Rather than engage the growing insistence on the part of more and more
groups in this country to define themselves around the specificity of class,
gender, race, ethnicity, or sexual orientation, conservatives have committed
themselves to simply resisting these developments. While conservatives
rightly recognize that the struggle over the form and context of public school
curriculum is fueled, in part, over anxiety about the issue of national identity,
they engage this issue from a largely defensive posture and in doing so lack
any understanding of how the curriculum itself is implicated in producing
relations of inequality, domination, and oppression. When critical multicul-
turalists criticize how the curriculum through a process of exclusion and
inclusion privileges some groups over others, such critics are summarily
dismissed as being political, partisan, and radically anti-American.[24]

Central to the traditionalist view of multiculturalism is a steadfast refusal
to rethink the source of "moral truth" in light of the expansion of social,
cultural, and political diversity that has come to characterize American life.
As new antagonisms have emerged over the purpose and meaning of schooling, curriculum, and the nature of American democracy, conservatives have
reasserted their allegiance to a foundation of moral truth based on an
orthodoxy that, according to James Davison Hunter, represents:

> a commitment on the part of [its] adherents to an external, definable, and
> transcendent authority. Such an objective and transcendent authority defines,
> at least in the abstract, a consistent, unchangeable measure of value, purpose,
> goodness, and identity, both personal and collective. It tells us what is good,
> what is true, and how we should live, and who we are. It is an authority that
> is sufficient for all time.[25]

In treating national history in fixed and narrow terms, conservatives
relinquish one of the most important defining principles of any democracy—
that is, they ignore the necessity of a democratic society to rejuvenate itself
by constantly reexamining the strengths and limits of its traditions. In the
absence of a critical encounter with the past and a recognition of the importance of cultural diversity, multiculturalism becomes acceptable only if it is
reduced to a pedagogy of reverence and transmission rather than a pedagogical practice that puts people in dialogue with each other as part of a
broader attempt to fashion a renewed interest in cultural democracy and the
creation of engaged and critical citizens.[26] Bhikhu Parekh rightly argues that
such a stance defines what he calls demagogic multiculturalism. For Parekh,
the traditionalists' refusal of cultural hybridity and differences and the fixity
of identity and culture promotes a dangerous type of fundamentalism. He
writes:

When a group feels besieged and afraid of losing its past in exchange for a nebulous future, it lacks the courage to critically reinterpret its fundamental principles, lest it opens the door to "excessive" reinterpretation. It then turns its fundamentals into fundamentalism, it declares them inviolate and reduces them to a neat and easily enforceable package of beliefs and rituals.[27]

Parekh's fear of demagogic multiculturalism represents a pedagogical problem as much as it does a political one. The political issue is exemplified in the conservative view that critical multiculturalism with its assertion of multiple identities and diverse cultural traditions represents a threat to democracy. The fatal political transgression committed here lies in the suggestion that social criticism itself is fundamentally at odds with democratic life. Indeed, this is more than mere rhetoric, it is a challenge to the very basic principles that inform a democratic society. Pedagogically, demagogic multiculturalism renders any debate about the relationship between democracy and cultural difference moot. By operating out of a suffocating binarism that pits "us" against "them," conservatives annul the possibility for dialogue, education, understanding, and negotiation. In other words, such a position offers no language for contending with cultures whose boundaries cross over into diverse spheres that are both fluid and saturated with power. How this type of fundamentalism will specifically impact on the schools can be seen in the increased calls for censorship in the schools as well as in the bleaching of the curriculum to exclude or underrepresent the voices and histories of various subordinate groups.

It should be noted that what is at stake here is not simply the balkanization of history and national identity, but the attempt to critically recover the various narratives of struggle and possibility that have for better or worse defined this country's engagement with democracy. Central to the ongoing debates over multiculturalism and the curriculum is the recognition that curriculum has been increasingly linked to an emerging politics of cultural difference, which has raised a number of serious questions about the conditions and forms of authority produced and secured within public schools. More specifically, issues concerning the canon and curriculum have become a contested terrain around questions of representation and the related battle over self-definition and identity.

In spite of the dismissal of multiculturalism and the politics of cultural difference, the conflict over the curriculum cannot be understood merely as an educational problem in the narrow sense of the term, nor can it be dismissed as the ranting of discontented minorities and radical educators. On the contrary, what is at stake in the debate over multiculturalism and curriculum are crucial issues regarding the meaning and purpose of public life, national identity, and cultural democracy. Renato Rosaldo is quite on target in arguing that "these days questions of culture seem to touch a nerve because they quite quickly become anguished questions of identity."[28] Two issues are often overlooked in current public discussions of multiculturalism. On one hand there are the systemic, economic, political, and social conditions that contribute to the domination of many subordinate groups. On the other hand, too little attention is paid to the sundry struggles subordinate groups undertake through the development of counternarratives that make them the subject rather than the object of history.

Instead of responding to the increasing diversity of histories, ethnicities, and cultures complexly layered over time, dominant institutions and discourses appear increasingly indifferent to the alarming poverty, shameful school dropout rate, escalating unemployment, and a host of other problems that accentuate the alienation, inequality, and racial segregation that fuel the sense of depression, hopelessness, and disempowerment felt by many minorities in this country.

In the aftermath of the Los Angeles uprising, it appears both morally careless and politically irresponsible to define multiculturalism as exclusively disruptive and antithetical to the most fundamental aspects of American democracy. Such a position both fails to explore the potential that multiculturalism has as a critical referent for linking diversity and cultural democracy while simultaneously serving to ignore the social, economic, and political conditions that have spurned the current insurgency among minorities and others around the issue of multiculturalism.

This is not meant to suggest that multiculturalism can be defined in essentialist terms; in fact, in contrast to the notion that multiculturalism is simply dangerous to American society and its public schools, as some traditionalists contend, I would argue that multiculturalism is a complex term that can be defined through a variety of ideological constructs.[29] In fact, I believe that educators need a definition of multiculturalism that offers the possibility for schools to become places where students and teachers can become border crossers engaged in critical and ethical reflection about what it means to bring a wider variety of cultures into dialogue with each other. But if the concept of multiculturalism is to become useful as a pedagogical concept, educators need to redefine it outside of a sectarian traditionalism. They also need to reject any form of multiculturalism in which differences are registered and equally affirmed but at the expense of understanding how such differences both emerge and are related to networks and hierarchies of power, privilege, and domination.

Moreover, in opposition to the liberal emphasis on individual diversity, an insurgent multiculturalism must also address issues regarding group differences and how power relations function to structure racial and ethnic identities. Furthermore, cultural differences cannot be merely affirmed in order to be assimilated into a common culture or policed through economic, political, and social spheres that restrict full citizenship to dominant groups. If multiculturalism is to be linked to a renewed interest in expanding the principles of democracy to wider spheres of application, it must be defined in pedagogical and political terms that embrace it as a referent and practice for civic courage, critical citizenship, and democratic struggle. Bhikhu Parekh offers a definition that appears to avoid both a superficial pluralism and a notion of multiculturalism that is structured in dominance:

> Multiculturalism doesn't simply mean numerical plurality of different cultures, but rather a community which is creating, guaranteeing, encouraging spaces within which different communities are able to grow at their own pace. At the same time it means creating a public space in which these communities are able to interact, enrich the existing culture and create a new consensual culture in which they recognize reflections of their own identity.[30]

Multiculturalism, like any other articulating term, is multiaccentual and it takes on a different meaning when situated in a mcre critical perspective. I believe that an insurgent multiculturalism represents an ideology and a set of pedagogical practices that offer a powerful critique and challenge to the racist, patriarchal, and sexist principles embedded in American society and schooling. Within this discourse, the curriculum is viewed as a hierarchical and representational system that selectively produces knowledge, identities, desires, and values. The notion that curriculum represents knowledge that is objective, value-free, and beneficial to all students is forcefully challenged as it becomes clear that those who benefit from public schooling are generally white, middle-class students whose histories, experiences, language, and knowledge largely conform to dominant cultural codes and practices. More, an insurgent multiculturalism performs a theoretical service by addressing curriculum as a form of cultural politics that demands linking the production and legitimation of classroom knowledge, social identities, and values to considerations of power.

In what follows, I want to suggest some general elements that might inform an insurgent multicultural curriculum. First, a multicultural curriculum must be informed by a new language in which issues of diversity and cultural difference become central to educating students to live in a democratic society. That is, we need a language of politics and pedagogy that is able to speak to cultural differences not as something to be tolerated but as essential to expanding the discourse and practice of democratic life. It is important to note that multiculturalism is not merely an ideological construct, it also refers to the fact that by the year 2010, people of color will be the numerical majority in the United States. This suggests that educators need to develop language, vision, and curriculum in which multiculturalism and democracy become mutually reinforcing categories. Manning Marable has spoken eloquently to this issue and his definition of a multicultural democracy offers important insights for reworking democracy as a pedagogical and cultural practice necessary for what John Dewey once called the creation of an articulate public. Marable is worth quoting at length on this issue:

> Multicultural political democracy means that this country was not built by and for only one group—Western Europeans; that our country does not have only one language—English; or only one religion—Christianity; or only one economic philosophy—corporate capitalism. Multicultural democracy means that the leadership within our society should reflect the richness, colors and diversity expressed in the lives of all of our people. Multicultural democracy demands new types of power-sharing and the re-allocation of resources necessary to great economic and social development for those who have been systematically excluded and denied.[31]

Second, as part of an attempt to develop a multicultural and multiracial society consistent with the principles of a democratic society, educators must take account of the fact that men and women of color are disproportionately underrepresented in the cultural and public institutions of this country. Pedagogically this suggests that a multicultural curriculum must provide students with the skills to analyze how various audio, visual, and print texts fashion social identities over time, and how these representations serve to reinforce, challenge, or rewrite dominant moral and political vocabularies that promote stereotypes that degrade people by depriving them of their history, culture, and identity.[32]

This should not suggest that such a pedagogy should solely concentrate on how meanings produce particular stereotypes and the uses to which they are put. Nor should a multicultural politics of representation focus exclusively on recovering and reconstituting the history of subordinate groups. While such approaches are essential to giving up the quest for a pure historical tradition, it is imperative that a multicultural curriculum also focus on dominant, white institutions and histories in order to interrogate them in terms of both their injustices and their contributions for humanity.

Of course, more is at stake here than avoiding the romanticizing of minority voices, or the inclusion of Western traditions in the curriculum. Multiculturalism in this sense is about making whiteness visible as a racial category; that is, it points to the necessity of providing white students with the cultural memories that enable them to recognize the historically and socially constructed nature of their own identities. In part, this approach to multiculturalism as a cultural politics provides white students with self-definitions upon which they can recognize whether they are speaking from within or outside privileged spaces and how power works within and across differences to legitimate some voices and dismantle others.

Bob Suzuki further extends the pedagogical importance of making whiteness visible as an ethnic category. In teaching a course on racism to college students, he discovered that for many white students their ethnic experiences and histories had been erased. By helping them to recover and interrogate their own histories, he found that the white students "could relate more empathetically to the problems of people of color and become more open to understanding their experiences and perspectives."[33] I would further extend Suzuki's important point by arguing that as crucial as it is to get white students to listen emphatically to students of color, it is also crucial that they come to understand that multiculturalism is also about understanding how dominant institutions provide the context of massive black unemployment, segregated schools, racist violence, and run-down housing. An insurgent multicultural curriculum must shift attention away from an exclusive focus on subordinate groups, especially since such an approach tends to highlight their deficits, to one that examines how racism in its various forms is produced historically, semiotically, and institutionally in various levels of dominant, white culture. Multiculturalism means analyzing not just stereotypes but also how institutions produce racism and other forms of discrimination.

Third, a multicultural curriculum must address how to articulate a relationship between unity and difference that moves beyond simplistic binarisms. That is, rather than defining multiculturalism against unity or simply for difference, it is crucial for educators to develop a unity-in-difference position in which new forms of democratic representation, participation, and citizenship provide a forum for creating unity without denying the particular, the multiple, and the specific. In this instance the interrelationship of different cultures and identities becomes a borderland, a site of crossing, negotiation, translation, and dialogue. At stake here is the production of a notion of border pedagogy in which the intersection of culture and identity produces self-definitions that enable teachers and students to authorize a sense of critical agency. Border pedagogy points to a self/other relationship in which identity is fixed as neither Other nor the same; instead it is both and, hence, defined within multiple literacies that become a referent, critique, and practice of cultural translation, a recognition of no possibility of fixed, final, or monologically authoritative meaning that exists outside of history, power, and ideology. Within this pedagogical cartography, teachers must be given the opportunity to cross ideological and political borders as a way of clarifying their own moral vision, as a way of enabling counterdiscourses, and, as Roger Simon points out, as a way of getting students "beyond the world they already know in order to challenge and provoke their inquiry and challenge of their existing views of the way things are and should be."[34]

Border literacy calls for pedagogical conditions in which "differences are recognized, exchanged and mixed in identities that break down but are not lost, that connect but remain diverse."[35] A border pedagogy suggests a literacy forged in the practices of imagination, narrative, and performance; a literacy that insists on an open-endedness, an incompleteness, and an uncertainty about the politics of one's own location. This is not a literacy that pretends to be amorphous or merely self-reflexive, but one that engages the important question of how to deal with the fact of reflexivity, how to strategize about it in the interests of diverse theoretical and pedagogical projects dedicated to creating a multicultural and multiracial democracy.

Underlying this notion of border pedagogy and literacy is neither the logic of assimilation (the melting pot), nor the imperative to create cultural hierarchies, but the attempt to expand the possibilities for different groups to enter into dialogue in order to further understand the richness of their differences and the value of what they share in common. Jeffrey Weeks speaks to this issue well:

> We may not be able to find, indeed we should not seek, a single way of life that would satisfy us all. That does not mean we cannot agree on common political ends: the construction of what can best be described as "a community of communities," to achieve a maximum political unity without denying differences.[36]

Fourth, an insurgent multiculturalism must challenge the task of merely representing cultural differences in the curriculum; it must also educate students to the necessity for linking a justice of multiplicity to struggles over real material conditions that structure everyday life. In part, this means understanding how structural imbalances in power produce real limits on the capacity of subordinate groups to exercise a sense of agency and struggle. It also means analyzing specific class, race, gender, and other issues as social problems rooted in real material and institutional factors that produce specific forms of inequality and oppression. This would necessitate a multicultural curriculum that produces a language that deals with social problems in historical and relational terms, and uncovers how the dynamics of power work to promote domination within both the school and the wider society.

Finally, a multicultural curriculum must not simply be imposed on a community and school. It is imperative that as a power-sensitive discourse a multicultural curriculum refigures relations between the school, teachers, students, and the wider community. In this case, schools must be willing to draw upon the resources of the community, include members of the community in making fundamental decisions about what is taught, who is hired, and how the school can become an integral part of the society it serves. Teachers need to be educated to be border crossers, to explore zones of cultural difference by moving in and out of the resources, histories, and narratives that provide different students with a sense of identity, place, and possibility.[37] This does not suggest that educators become tourists traveling to exotic lands; on the contrary, it points to the need for them to enter into negotiation and dialogue around issues of nationality, difference, and identity so as to be able to fashion a more ethical and democratic set of pedagogical relations between themselves and their students while simultaneously allowing students to speak, listen, and learn differently within pedagogical spaces that are safe, affirming, questioning, and enabling. In this instance, a curriculum for a multicultural and multiracial society provides the conditions for students to think and act otherwise, to imagine beyond the given, and to critically embrace their identities as a source of agency and possibility.

## NOTES

1. James Baldwin, "A Talk to Teachers," in Rick Simonson and Scott Walker (eds.), *Multicultural Literacy: Opening the American Mind* (St. Paul: Graywolf Press, 1988), p. 8.
2. Melvin E. Bradford quoted in Katherine S. Mangan, "6th Generation Texan Takes on 'Trendy Nonsense,' " *The Chronicle of Higher Education*, July 8, 1992, p. A5.
3. Alan O'Connor, "Just Plain Home Cookin," *Borderlines*, 20/21 (Winter 1991): 58.
4. Marcia Tucker, " 'Who's on First?' Issues of Cultural Equity in Today's Museums," in Carol Becker et al., *Different Voices* (New York: Association of Art Museum Directors, 1992), p. 11.
5. Cornel West, "Learning to Talk about Race," *The New York Times Magazine*, Section 6 (August 2, 1992), p. 24.
6. Ibid.
7. bell hooks, *Black Looks: Race and Representation* (Boston: South End Press, 1992), pp. 168, 172.
8. The notion of imagining otherwise in order to act otherwise is taken from Richard Kearney, *The Wake of Imagination* (Minneapolis: University of Minnesota Press, 1988), p. 370.
9. "The Postcolonial Critics: Homi Bhabha," interviewed by David Bennett and Terry Collits, *Arena*, No. 96 (1991): 50–51.
10. Stuart Hall, "And Not a Shot Fired," *Marxism Today*, December 1991, p. 10.
11. Larry D. Hatfield and Dexter Waugh, "Right Wing's Smart Bombs," *San Francisco Examiner*, May 24, 1992, p. A10.
12. For a brief but informative view of right-wing think tanks, see Lawrence Soley, "Right Thinking Conservative Think Tanks," *Dissent*, Summer 1991, pp. 418–420. For a history of these groups, see Russ Bellant, *Old Nazis, the New Right, and the Republican Party* (Boston: South End Press, 1991).
13. For the connection between right-wing foundations and a number of prominent educators such as Diane Ravitch, Chester Finn, Charlotte Crabtree, Allan Bloom, and others, see Dexter Waugh and Larry Hatfield, "Rightest Groups Pushing School Reforms," *San Francisco Examiner*, May 28, 1992, p. A18.
14. Joan Scott has argued that the right-wing attack on multiculturalism is primarily about the attempt to "neutralize the space of ideological and cultural nonconformity by discrediting it." (Joan W. Scott, "Multiculturalism and the Politics of Identity," *October*, 61 [Summer 1992]:13.) While this is certainly true, it is not the whole story. The conservative attack is not new, it is deeply rooted in a long tradition of anti-Catholic, antiethnic, and antiimmigration rhetoric that saw the "multicultural" problem as largely a racial issue. It is precisely this historical context that exposes the racist character of recent arguments against multiculturalism made by Arthur Schlesinger, Jr., Gary Sykes, Richard Brookshiser, and others. For an attempt to insert the history of racism back into the multicultural debate, see Stanley Fish, "Bad Company," *Transitions*, 56 (1992): 60–67.
15. Stuart Hall and David Held, "Citizens and Citizenship," in Stuart Hall and Martin Jacques (eds.), *New Times: Changing Face of Politics in the 1990's* (London: Verso, 1990), p. 178.

16. Jonathan Kozol, "If We Want to Change Our Schools," unpublished speech given to the Commonwealth Club in San Francisco, 1992, pp. 1–2.

17. Robert Bellah et al., "Breaking the Tyranny of the Market," *Tikkun*, 6(4) (1991): 90.

18. Steve Whitman, "The Crime of Black Imprisonment," *Z Magazine*, May 1992, pp. 69, 71.

19. Peter Dreier, "Bush to Cities: Drop Dead," *The Progressive*, (July 1992), p. 22.

20. Chester E. Finn, Jr., "Does Public Mean Good?" *Education Week*, 11(21) (February 12, 1992): 30.

21. On the relationship between democracy and cultural difference, see Henry A. Giroux: *Border Crossings: Cultural Workers and the Politics of Education* (New York: Routledge, 1992), and *Living Dangerously: Multiculturalism and the Politics of Difference* (New York: Peter Lang, 1993).

22. James Clifford, "Museums in the Border Lands," in Becker, et al., *Different Voices*, p. 119.

23. E. D. Hirsch, Jr., *Cultural Literacy: What Every American Needs to Know* (Boston: Houghton Mifflin, 1987).

24. Such pronouncements have become commonplace among traditionalists such as Lynn V. Cheney, John Silber, William J. Bennett, Chester E. Finn, and Allan Bloom. See, for example, Carolyn J. Mooney, "Scholars Decry Campus Hostility to Western Culture at a Time When More Nations Embrace Its Values," *The Chronicle of Higher Education*, January 30, 1991, pp. A15–A16.

25. James Davison Hunter, *Culture Wars: The Struggle to Define America* (New York: Basic Books, 1991), p. 44.

26. I have paraphrased this insight from Gregory Jay, "The End of American Literature: Toward a Multicultural Practice," *College English*, March 1991, p. 266.

27. Bhikhu Parekh, "Identities on Parade: A Conversation," *Marxism Today*, June 1989, p. 3.

28. Renato Rosaldo, *Culture and Truth* (Boston: Beacon Press, 1989).

29. For an analysis of the history and varied meanings of multicultural education, see Christine E. Sleeter (ed.), *Empowerment Through Multicultural Education* (Albany: State University of New York Press, 1991); Cameron McCarthy, *Race and Curriculum* (Philadelphia: Falmer Press, 1990). Also see Peter Erickson, "What Multiculturalism Means," *Transition* No. 55 (1992): 105–114.

30. Parekh, "Identities on Parade," p. 4.

31. Manning Marable, *Black America: Multicultural Democracy in the Age of Clarence Thomas and David Duke* (Westfield, NJ: Open Media, 1992), p. 13.

32. On this issue, see ibid.

33. Bob Suzuki, "Unity with Diversity: Easier Said than Done," *Liberal Education*, February 1991, p. 34.

34. Roger Simon, *Teaching Against the Grain* (Westport, CT: Bergin & Garvey, 1994), p. 47.

35. Iain Chambers, *Border Dialogues* (New York: Routledge, 1990), p. 114.

36. Jeffrey Weeks, "The Value of Difference," in Jonathan Rutherford (ed.), *Identity, Community, Culture, Difference* (London: Lawrence and Wishart, 1990), p. 98.

37. The issue of border pedagogy and border crossings is taken up in Giroux, *Border Crossings*.

# 12

▼▼▼▼▼▼▼

# Becoming Educated:
# A Journey of Alienation
# or Integration?*

Jane Roland Martin

In his educational autobiography *Hunger of Memory*, Richard Rodriguez (1982) tells of growing up in Sacramento, California, the third of four children in a Spanish-speaking family. Upon entering first grade he could understand perhaps 50 English words. Within the year his teachers convinced his parents to speak only English at home and Rodriguez soon became fluent in the language. By the time he graduated from elementary school with citations galore and entered high school, he had read hundreds of books. He went on to attend Stanford University and, 20 years after his parents' decision to abandon their native tongue, he sat in the British Museum writing a PhD dissertation in English literature.

Rodriguez learned to speak English and went on to acquire a liberal education. History, literature, science, mathematics, philosophy: these he studied and made his own. Rodriguez's story is of the cultural assimilation of a Mexican-American, but it is more than this, for by no means do all assimilated Americans conform to our image of a well-educated person. Rodriguez does because, to use the terms the philosopher R. S. Peters (1966, 1972) employs in his analysis of the concept of the educated man, he did not simply acquire knowledge and skill. He acquired conceptual schemes to raise his knowledge beyond the level of a collection of disjointed facts and to enable him to understand the "reason why" of things. Moreover, the knowledge he acquired is not "inert": It characterizes the way he looks at the world and it involves the kind of commitment to the standards of evidence and canons of proof of the various disciplines that comes from "getting on the inside of a form of thought and awareness" (Peters, 1961, p. 9).

---

*From: Martin, Jane Roland. "Becoming Educated." From *Journal of Education*. Vol. 167, No. 3, 1985. Reprinted by permission of Boston University.

Quite a success story, yet *Hunger of Memory* is notable primarily as a narrative of loss. In becoming an educated person Rodriguez loses his fluency in Spanish, but that is the least of it. As soon as English becomes the language of the Rodriguez family, the special feeling of closeness at home is diminished. Furthermore, as his days are increasingly devoted to understanding the meaning of words, it becomes difficult for Rodriguez to hear intimate family voices. When it is Spanish-speaking, his home is a noisy, playful, warm, emotionally charged environment; with the advent of English the atmosphere becomes quiet and restrained. There is no acrimony. The family remains loving. But the experience of "feeling individualized" by family members is now rare, and occasions for intimacy are infrequent.

Rodriguez tells a story of alienation: from his parents, for whom he soon has no names; from the Spanish language, in which he loses his childhood fluency; from his Mexican roots, in which he shows no interest; from his own feelings and emotions, which all but disappear as he learns to control them; from his body itself, as he discovers when he takes a construction job after his senior year in college.

John Dewey spent his life trying to combat the tendency of educators to divorce mind from body and reason from emotion. Rodriguez's educational autobiography documents these divorces, and another one Dewey deplored, that of self from other. Above all *Hunger of Memory* depicts a journey from intimacy to isolation. Close ties with family members are dissolved as public anonymity replaces private attention. Rodriguez becomes a spectator in his own home as noise gives way to silence and connection to distance. School, says Rodriguez, bade him trust "lonely" reason primarily. And there is enough time and "silence," he adds, "to think about ideas (big ideas)" (p. 47).

What is the significance of this narrative of loss? Not every American has Rodriguez's good fortune of being born into a loving home filled with the warm sounds of intimacy, yet the separation and distance he ultimately experienced are not unique to him. On the contrary, they represent the natural end point of the educational journey Rodriguez took.

Dewey repeatedly pointed out that the distinction educators draw between liberal and vocational education represents a separation of mind from body, head from hand, thought from action. Since we define an educated person as one who has had and has profited from a liberal education, these splits are built into our ideal of the educated person. Since most definitions of excellence in education derive from that ideal, these splits are built into them as well. A split between reason and emotion is built into our definitions of excellence too, for we take the aim of a liberal education to be the development not of mind as a whole, but of rational mind. We define this in terms of the acquisition of knowledge and understanding, construed narrowly (Martin, 1981b). It is not surprising that Rodriguez acquires habits of quiet reflection rather than noisy activity, reasoned deliberation rather than spon-

taneous reaction, dispassionate inquiry rather than emotional response, abstract analytic theorizing rather than concrete storytelling. These are integral to the ideal of the educated person that has come down to us from Plato.

Upon completion of his educational journey Rodriguez bears a remarkable resemblance to the guardians of the Just State that Plato constructs in the *Republic*. Those worthies are to acquire through their education a wide range of theoretical knowledge, highly developed powers of reasoning, and the qualities of objectivity and emotional distance. To be sure, not one of Plato's guardians will be the "disembodied mind" Rodriguez becomes, for Plato believed that a strong mind requires a strong body. But Plato designed for his guardians an education of heads, not hands. (Presumably the artisans of the Just State would serve as their hands.) Moreover, considering the passions to be unruly and untrustworthy, Plato held up for the guardians an ideal of self-discipline and self-government in which reason keeps feeling and emotion under tight control. As a consequence, although he wanted the guardians of the Just State to be so connected to one another that they would feel each other's pains and pleasures, the educational ideal he developed emphasizes "inner" harmony at the expense of "outward" connection. If his guardians do not begin their lives in intimacy, as Rodriguez did, their education, like his, is intended to confirm in them a sense of self in isolation from others.

Do the separations bequeathed to us by Plato matter? The great irony of the liberal education that comes down to us from Plato and still today as the mark of an educated person is that it is neither tolerant nor generous (Martin, 1981b). As Richard Rodriguez discovered, there is no place in it for education of the body, and since most action involves bodily movement, this means there is little room in it for education of action. Nor is there room for education of other-regarding feelings and emotions. The liberally educated person will be provided with knowledge about others, but will not be taught to care about their welfare or to act kindly toward them. That person will be given some understanding of society, but will not be taught to feel its injustices or even to be concerned over its fate. The liberally educated person will be an ivory tower person—one who can reason but has no desire to solve real problems in the real world—or else a technical person who likes to solve real problems but does not care about the solutions' consequences for real people and for the earth itself.

The case of Rodriguez illuminates several unhappy aspects of our Platonic heritage, while concealing another. No one who has seen Frederick Wiseman's film *High School* can forget the woman who reads to the assembled students a letter she has received from a pupil now in Vietnam. But for a few teachers who cared, she tells her audience, Bob Walters, a sub-average student academically, "might have been a nobody." Instead, while awaiting a plane that is to drop him behind the DMZ, he has written her to say that he has made the school the beneficiary of his life insurance policy. "I am a

little jittery right now," she reads. She is not to worry about him, however, because "I am only a body doing a job." Measuring his worth as a human being by his provision for the school, she overlooks the fact that Bob Walters was not merely participating in a war of dubious morality but was taking pride in being an automaton.

*High School* was made in 1968, but Bob Walters's words were echoed many times over by 18- and 19-year-old Marine recruits in the days immediately following the Grenada invasion. Readers of *Hunger of Memory* will not be surprised. The underside of a liberal education devoted to the development of "disembodied minds" is a vocational education whose business is the production of "mindless bodies." In Plato's Just State, where, because of their rational powers, the specially educated few will rule the many, a young man's image of himself as "only a body doing a job" is the desired one. That the educational theory and practice of a democracy derives from Plato's explicitly undemocratic philosophical vision is disturbing. We are not supposed to have two classes of people, those who think and those who do not. We are not supposed to have two kinds of people, those who rule and those who obey.

The Council for Basic Education has long recommended, and some people concerned with excellence in education now suggest, that a liberal education at least through high school be extended to all. For the sake of argument let us suppose that this program can be carried out without making more acute the inequities it is meant to erase. We would then presumably have a world in which no one thinks of him- or herself as simply a body doing a job. We would, however, have a world filled with unconnected, uncaring, emotionally impoverished people. Even if it were egalitarian, it would be a sorry place in which to live. Nor would the world be better if somehow we combined Rodriguez's liberal education with a vocational one. For assuming it to be peopled by individuals who joined head and hand, reason would still be divorced from feeling and emotion, and each individual cut off from others.

The world we live in is just such a place. It is a world of child abuse and family violence (Breines & Gordon, 1983), a world in which one out of every four women will be raped at some time in her life (Johnson, 1980; Lott, Reilly, & Howard, 1982). Our world is on the brink of nuclear and/or ecological disaster. Efforts to overcome these problems, as well as the related ones of poverty and economic scarcity, flounder today under the direction of people who try hard to be rational, objective, autonomous agents but, like Plato's guardians, do not know how to sustain human relationships or respond directly to human needs. Indeed, they do not even see the value of trying to do so. Of course, it is a mistake to suppose that education alone can solve this world's problems. Yet if there is to be hope of the continuation of life on earth, let alone of a good life for all, as educators we must strive to do more than join mind and body, head and hand, thought and action.

REDEFINING EDUCATION

For Rodriguez, the English language is a metaphor. In the literal sense of the term he had to learn English to become an educated *American*, yet, in his narrative the learning of English represents the acquisition not so much of a new natural language as of new ways of thinking, acting, and being that he associates with the public world. Rodriguez makes it clear that the transition from Spanish to English represented for him the transition almost every child in our society makes from the "private world" of home to the "public world" of business, politics, and culture. He realizes that Spanish is not intrinsically a private language and English a public one, although his own experiences made it seem this way. He knows that the larger significance of his story lies in the fact that education inducts one into new activities and processes.

In my research on the place of women in educational thought (1982, 1985), I have invoked a distinction between the productive and the reproductive processes of society and have argued that both historians of educational thought and contemporary philosophers of education define the educational realm in relation to society's productive processes only. Briefly, the reproductive processes include not simply the biological reproduction of the species, but the rearing of children to maturity and the related activities of keeping house, managing a household, and serving the needs and purposes of family members. In turn, the productive processes include political, social, and cultural activities as well as economic ones. This distinction is related to the one Rodriguez repeatedly draws between public and private worlds, for in our society reproductive processes are for the most part carried on in the private world of the home and domesticity, and productive processes in the public world of politics and work. Rodriguez's autobiography reveals that the definition of education as preparation solely for carrying on the productive processes of society is not a figment of the academic imagination.

Needless to say, the liberal education Rodriguez received did not fit him to carry on all productive processes of society. Aiming at the development of rational mind, his liberal education prepared him to be a consumer and creator of ideas, not an auto mechanic or factory worker. A vocational education, had he received one, would have prepared him to work with his hands and use procedures designed by others. They are very different kinds of education, yet both are designed to fit students to carry on productive, not reproductive, societal processes.

Why do I stress the connection between the definition of education and the productive processes of society? *Hunger of Memory* contains a wonderful account of Rodriguez's grandmother telling him stories of her life. He is moved by the sounds she makes and by the message of intimacy her person transmits. The words themselves are not important to him, for he perceives the private world in which she moves—the world of childrearing and homemaking—to be one of feeling and emotion, intimacy and connection, and hence a realm of the nonrational. In contrast, he sees the public world—the world of productive processes for which his education fit him—as the realm of the rational. Feeling and emotion have no place in it, and neither do intimacy and connection. Instead, analysis, critical thinking, and self-sufficiency are the dominant values.

Rodriguez's assumption that feeling and emotion, intimacy and connection are naturally related to the home and society's reproductive processes and that these qualities are irrelevant to carrying on the productive processes is commonly accepted. But then, it is to be expected that their development is ignored by education in general and by liberal education in particular. Since education is supposed to equip people for carrying on productive societal processes, from a practical standpoint would it not be foolhardy for liberal or vocational studies to foster these traits?

Only in light of the fact that education turns its back on the reproductive processes of society and the private world of the home can Rodriguez's story of alienation be understood. His alienation from his body will reoccur so long as we equate being an educated person with having a liberal education. His journey of isolation and divorce from his emotions will be repeated so long as we define education exclusively in relation to the productive processes of society. But the assumption of inevitability underlying *Hunger of Memory* is mistaken. Education need not separate mind from body and thought from action, for it need not draw a sharp line between liberal and vocational education. More to the point, it need not separate reason from emotion and self from other. The reproductive processes *can* be brought into the educational realm thereby overriding the theoretical and practical grounds for ignoring feeling and emotion, intimacy and connection.

If we define education in relation to *both* kinds of societal processes and act upon our redefinition, future generations will not have to experience Rodriguez's pain. He never questions the fundamental dichotomies upon which his education rests. We must question them so that we can effect the reconciliation of reason and emotion, self and other, that Dewey sought. There are, moreover, two overwhelming reasons for favoring such a redefinition, both of which take us beyond Dewey.

All of us—male and female—participate in the reproductive processes of society. In the past, many have thought that education for carrying them on was not necessary: These processes were assumed to be the responsibility of women and it was supposed that by instinct a woman would automatically acquire the traits or qualities associated with them. The contemporary statistics on child abuse are enough by themselves to put to rest the doctrine of maternal instinct. Furthermore, both sexes have responsibility for making the reproductive processes of society work well. Family living and childrearing are not today, if they ever were, solely in the hands of women. Nor should they be. Thus, both sexes need to learn to carry on the reproductive processes of society just as in the 1980s both sexes needed to learn to carry on the productive ones.

The reproductive processes are of central importance to society, yet it would be a terrible mistake to suppose that the traits and qualities traditionally associated with these processes have no relevance beyond them. Jonathan Schell (1982, p. 175) has said "The nuclear peril makes all of us, whether we happen to have children of our own or not, the parents of all future generations" and that the will we must have to save the human species is a form of love resembling "the generative love of parents." He is speaking of what Nancy Chodorow (1978) calls nurturing capacities and Carol Gilligan (1982) calls an "ethics of care." Schell is right. The fate of the earth depends on all of us possessing these qualities. Thus, although these qualities are associated in our minds with the reproductive processes of society, they have the broadest moral, social, and political significance. Care, concern, connectedness, nurturance are as important for carrying on society's economic, political, and social processes as its reproductive ones. If education is to help us acquire them, it must be redefined.

## THE WORKINGS OF GENDER

It is no accident that in *Hunger of Memory* the person who embodies nurturing capacities and an ethics of care is a woman—Rodriguez's grandmother. The two kinds of societal processes are gender-related and so are the traits our culture associates with them. According to our cultural stereotypes, males are objective, analytical, rational, interested in ideas and things. They have no interpersonal orientation; they are not nurturant or supportive, empathetic or sensitive. Women, on the other hand, possess the traits men lack (Kaplan & Bean, 1976; Kaplan & Sedney, 1980).

Education is also gender-related. Our definition of its function makes it so. For if education is viewed as preparation for carrying on processes historically associated with males, it will inculcate traits the culture considers masculine. If the concept of education is tied by definition to the productive processes of society, our ideal of the educated person will coincide with the cultural stereotype of a male human being, and our definitions of excellence in education will embody "masculine" traits.

Of course, it is possible for members of one sex to acquire personal traits or qualities our cultural stereotypes attribute to the other. Thus females can and do acquire traits incorporated in our educational ideal. However, it must be understood that these traits are *genderized*; that is, they are appraised differentially when they are possessed by males and females (Beardsley, 1977; Martin, 1981a, 1985). For example, whereas a male will be admired for his rational powers, a woman who is analytical and critical will be derided or shunned or will be told that she thinks like a man. Even if this latter is intended as a compliment, since we take masculinity and femininity to lie at opposite ends of a single continuum, she will thereby be judged as lacking in femininity and, as a consequence, judged abnormal or unnatural. Elizabeth Janeway (1971, p. 96) has said, and I am afraid she is right, that "unnatural" and "abnormal" are the equivalent for our age of what "damned" meant to our ancestors.

Because his hands were soft Rodriguez worried that his education was making him effeminate.[1] Imagine his anxieties on that score if he had been educated in those supposedly feminine virtues of caring and concern and had been taught to sustain intimate relationships and value connection. To be sure, had his education fostered these qualities, Rodriguez would not have had to travel a road from intimacy to isolation. I do not mean to suggest that there would have been no alienation at all; his is a complex case involving class, ethnicity, and color. But an education in which reason was joined to feeling and emotion and self to other would have yielded a very different life story. Had his education fostered these qualities, however, Rodriguez would have experienced another kind of hardship.

The pain Rodriguez suffers is a consequence of the loss of intimacy and the stunting of emotional growth that are themselves consequences of education. Now it is possible that Rodriguez's experience is more representative of males than of females. But if it be the case that females tend to maintain emotional growth and intimate connections better than males do, one thing is certain: educated girls are penalized for what Rodriguez considers his *gains*. If they become analytic, objective thinkers and autonomous agents, they are judged less feminine than they should be. Thus, for them the essential myth of childhood is every bit as painful as it was for Rodriguez, for they are alienated from their own identity as females.

When education is defined so as to give the reproductive processes of society their due, and the virtues of nurturance and care associated with those processes are fostered in both males and females, educated men can expect to suffer for possessing traits genderized in favor of females as educated women now do for possessing traits genderized in favor of males. This is not to say that males will be placed in the double bind educated females find themselves in now, for males will acquire traits genderized in their own favor as well as ones genderized in favor of females, whereas the traits educated females must acquire today are *all* genderized in favor of males. On the other hand, since traits genderized in favor of females are considered lesser virtues, if virtues at all (Blum, 1980), and the societal processes with which they are associated are thought to be relatively unimportant, males will be placed in the position of having to acquire traits both they and their society consider inferior.

One of the most important findings of contemporary scholarship is that our culture embraces a hierarchy of values that places the productive processes of society and their associated traits above society's reproductive processes and the associated traits of care and nurturance. There is nothing new about this. We are the inheritors of a tradition of Western thought according to which the functions, tasks, and traits associated with females are deemed less valuable than those associated with males. In view of these findings, the difficulties facing those of us who would transform Rodriguez's educational journey from one of alienation to one of the integration of reason and emotion, of self and other, become apparent.

It is important to understand the magnitude of the changes to be wrought by an education that takes the integration of reason and emotion, self and other, seriously. Granted, when girls today embark on Rodriguez's journey they acquire traits genderized in favor of the "opposite" sex; but if on account of trait genderization they experience hardships Rodriguez did not, they can at least console themselves that their newly acquired traits, along with the societal processes to which the traits are attached, are considered valuable. Were we to attempt to change the nature of our educational ideal without also changing our value hierarchy, boys and men would have no such consolation. Without this consolation, however, we can be quite sure that the change we desire would not come to pass.

## TOWARD AN INTEGRATED CURRICULUM

Just as the value structure I have been describing is reflected in our ideal of the educated person, so too it is reflected in the curriculum such a person is supposed to study. A large body of scholarship documents the extent to which the academic fields constituting the subjects of the liberal curriculum exclude women's lives, works, and experiences from their subject matter or else distort them by projecting the cultural stereotype of a female onto the evidence.[2] History, philosophy, politics; art and music; the social and behavioral sciences; even the biological and physical sciences give pride of place to male experience and achievements and to the societal processes thought to belong to men.

The research to which I refer reveals the place of women—or rather the absence thereof—in the theories, interpretations, and narratives constituting the disciplines of knowledge. Since the subject matter of the liberal curriculum is drawn from these disciplines, that curriculum gives pride of place to male experience and achievements and to the societal processes associated with men. In so doing, it is the bearer of bad news about women and the reproductive processes of society. Can it be doubted that when the works of women are excluded from the subject matter of the fields into which they are being initiated, students of both sexes will come to believe, or else will have their existing belief reinforced, that males are superior and females are inferior human beings? Can it be doubted that when in the course of this initiation the lives and experiences of women are scarcely mentioned, males and females will come to believe, or else believe more strongly than ever, that the ways in which women have lived and the things women have done throughout history have no value?

At campuses across the country projects are underway to incorporate the growing body of new scholarship on women into the liberal curriculum. Such efforts must be undertaken at all levels of schooling, not simply because women comprise one half the world's population, but because the exclusion of women from the subject matter of the "curriculum proper" constitutes a hidden curriculum in the validation of one gender, its associated tasks, traits, and functions, and the denigration of the other. Supporting our culture's genderized hierarchy of value even as it reflects it, this hidden curriculum must be raised to consciousness and counteracted (Martin, 1976). Introduction of the new scholarship on women into the liberal curriculum proper—and for that matter into the vocational curriculum too—makes this possible, on the one hand because it allows students to understand the workings of gender and, on the other, because it provides them with the opportunity to appreciate women's traditional tasks, traits, and functions.

In a curriculum encompassing the experience of one sex, not two, questions of gender are automatically eliminated. For the value hierarchy under discussion to be understood, as it must be if it is to be abolished, its genderized roots must be exposed. Furthermore, if intimacy and connection are to be valued as highly as independence and distance, and if emotion and feeling are to be viewed as positive rather than untrustworthy elements of personality, women must no longer be viewed as different and alien—as the Other, to use Simone de Beauvoir's expression (1961).

Thus, we need to incorporate the study of women into curricula so that females—their lives, experiences, works, and attributes—are devalued by neither sex. But simply incorporating the new scholarship on women in the curriculum does not address the alienation and loss Rodriguez describes so well. To overcome these we must seek not only a transformation of the content of curriculum proper, but an expansion of the educational realm to include the reproductive processes of society and a corresponding redefinition of what it means to become educated.

The expansion of the educational realm I propose does not entail an extension of a skill-oriented home economics education to males. Although it is important for both sexes to learn to cook and sew, I have in mind something different when I say that education must give the reproductive processes of society their due. The traits associated with women as wives and mothers—nurturance, care, compassion, connection, sensitivity to others, a willingness to put aside one's own projects, a desire to build and maintain relationships—need to be incorporated into our ideal. This does not mean that we should fill up the curriculum with courses in the three C's of caring, concern, and connection. Given a redefinition of education, Compassion 101a need no more be listed in a school's course offerings than Objectivity 101a is now. Just as the productive processes of society have given us the general curricular goals of rationality and individual autonomy, so too the reproductive processes yield general goals. And just as rationality and autonomy are posited as goals of particular subjects, e.g., science, as well as of the curriculum as a whole, so nurturance and connection can be understood as overarching educational goals and also as the goals of particular subjects.

But now a puzzling question arises. Given that the standard subjects of the curriculum derive from the productive processes of society, must we not insert cooking and sewing and perhaps childrearing into the curriculum if we want caring, concern, and connection to be educational objectives? Science, math, history, literature, auto mechanics, refrigeration, typing: these are the subjects of the curriculum now and these derive from productive processes. If for subjects deriving from productive processes we set educational goals whose source is the reproductive processes of society, do we not distort these subjects beyond recognition? But then, ought we not to opt instead for a divided curriculum with two sets of subjects? One set might be derived from the productive processes of society and foster traits associated with those, with the other set derived from the reproductive processes of society and fostering their associated traits. Is this the only way to do justice to both sets of traits?

If possible, a replication within the curriculum of the split between the productive and reproductive processes of society is to be avoided. So long as education insists on linking nurturing capacities and the three C's to subjects arising out of the reproductive processes, we will lose sight of their *general* moral, social, and political significance. Moreover, so long as rationality and autonomous judgment are considered to belong exclusively to the productive processes of society, the reproductive ones will continue to be devalued. Thus, unless it is essential to divide up curricular goal according to the classification of a subject as productive or reproductive, we ought not to do so. That it is not essential becomes clear once we give up our stereotypical pictures of the two kinds of societal process.

Readers of June Goodfield's *An Imagined World* (1981) will know that feeling and emotion, intimacy and connection can be an integral part of the processes of scientific discovery.[3] Goodfield recorded the day-to-day activities of Anna, a Portuguese scientist studying lymphocytes in a cancer laboratory in New York. Anna's relationship to her colleagues *and* to the cells she studied provides quite a contrast to the rationalistic, atomistic vision of scientists and scientific discovery most of us have. To be sure, some years ago James Watson (1969) made it clear that scientists are human. But Watson portrayed scientific discovery as a race between ambitious, aggressive, highly competitive contestants while Goodfield's Anna calls it "a kind of birth." Fear, urgency, intense joy; loneliness, intimacy, and a desire to share: these are some of the emotions that motivate and shape Anna's thought even as her reasoned analysis and her objective scrutiny of evidence engender passion. Moreover, she is bound closely to her colleagues in the lab by feeling, as well as by scientific need, and she empathizes with the lymphocytes she studies as well as with the sick people she hopes will one day benefit from her work.

If scientific activity can flourish in an atmosphere of cooperation and connection, and important scientific discoveries can take place when passionate feeling motivates and shapes thought, then surely it is not necessary for science education to be directed solely toward rationalistic, atomistic goals. And if nurturant capacities and the three C's of caring, concern, and connection can become goals of science teaching without that subject being betrayed or abandoned, surely they can become the goals of *any* subject.

By the same token, if rational thought and independent judgment are components of successful childrearing and family living, it is not necessary to design education in subjects deriving from the reproductive processes of society solely around "affective" goals. That they can and should be part and parcel of these activities was argued long ago, and very convincingly, by both Mary Wollstonecraft and Catharine Beecher (Martin, 1985) and is a basic tenet of the home economics profession today.

Thus, just as nurturance and concern can be goals of any subject, rationality and independent judgment can also be. The temptation to institute a sharp separation of goals within an expanded educational realm corresponding to a sharp separation of subjects must, then, be resisted so that the general significance of the very real virtues we associate with women and the reproductive processes of society is understood and these virtues themselves are fostered in everyone.

## CONCLUSION

In becoming educated one does not have to travel Rodriguez's road from intimacy to isolation. His journey of alienation is a function of a definition of education, a particular ideal of the educated person, and a particular definition of excellence—all of which can be rejected. Becoming educated can be a journey of integration, not alienation. The detailed task of restructuring an ideal of the educated person to guide this new journey I leave for another occasion. The general problem to be solved is that of uniting thought and action, reason and emotion, self and other. This was the problem Dewey addressed, but his failure to understand the workings of gender made it impossible for him to solve it.

I leave the task of mapping the precise contours of a transformed curriculum for another occasion too. The general problem to be solved here is that of giving the reproductive processes of society—and the females who have traditionally been assigned responsibility for carrying them on—their due. Only then will feeling and emotion, intimacy and connection be perceived as valuable qualities so that a journey of integration is possible.

Loss, pain, isolation: It is a tragedy that these should be the results of becoming educated, the consequences of excellence. An alternative journey to Rodriguez's requires fundamental changes in both educational theory and practice. Since these changes will make it possible to diffuse throughout the population the nurturant capacities and the ethics of care that are absolutely essential to the survival of society itself, indeed, to the survival of life on earth, they should ultimately be welcomed even by those who would claim that the loss, pain, and isolation Rodriguez experienced in becoming educated did him no harm.

## NOTES

1. Quite clearly, Rodriguez's class background is a factor in this judgment. Notice, however, that the form his fear takes relates to gender.
2. This scholarship cannot possibly be cited here. For reviews of the literature in the various academic disciplines see past issues of *Signs: Journal of Women in Culture and Society*.
3. See also Keller (1983).

## REFERENCES

Beardsley, E. (1977). Traits and genderization. In M. Vetterling-Braggin, F. A. Elliston, & J. English (Eds.), *Feminism and philosophy* (pp. 117–123). Totowa, NJ: Littlefield.
Blum, L. (1980). *Friendship, altruism, and morality*. London: Routledge & Kegan Paul.
Breines, W., & Gordon, L. (1983). The new scholarship on family violence. *Signs, 8*(3), 493–507.
de Beauvoir, S. (1961). *The second sex*. New York: Bantam.
Chodorow, N. (1978). *The reproduction of mothering*. Berkeley: University of California Press.
Galligan, C. (1982). *In a different voice*. Cambridge: Harvard University Press.
Goodfield, J. (1981). *An imagined world*. New York: Harper & Row.
Janeway, E. (1971). *Man's world, woman's place*. New York: Morrow.
Johnson, A. G. (1980). On the prevalence of rape in the United States. *Signs, 6*(1), 136–146.
Kaplan, A. G., & Bean, J. P. (Eds.). (1976). *Beyond sex-role stereotypes*. Boston: Little, Brown.
Kaplan, A. G., & Sedney, M. A. (1980). *Psychology and sex roles*. Boston: Little, Brown.
Keller, E. F. (1983). *A feeling for the organism*. San Francisco: W. H. Freeman.
Lott, B., Reilly, M. E., & Howard, D. R. (1982). Sexual assault and harassment: A campus community case study. *Signs, 8*(2), 296–319.

Martin, J. R. (1976). What should we do with a hidden curriculum when we find one? *Curriculum Inquiry, 6*(2), 135–151.
Martin, J. R. (1981a). The ideal of the educated person. *Educational Theory, 3*(2), 97–109.
Martin, J. R. (1981b). Needed: A new paradigm for liberal education. In J. F. Soltis (Ed.), *Philosophy and education* (pp. 37–59). Chicago: University of Chicago Press.
Martin, J. R. (1982). Excluding women from the educational realm. *Harvard Educational Review, 52*(2), 133–148.
Martin, J. R. (1985). *Reclaiming a conversation: The ideal of the educated woman.* New Haven: Yale University Press.
Peters, R. S. (1972). Education and the educated man. In R. F. Dearden, P. H. Hirst, & R. S. Peters (Eds.), *A critique of current educational aims.* London: Routledge & Kegan Paul.
Peters, R. S. (1966). *Ethics and education.* London: Allen & Unwin.
Rodriguez, R. (1982). *Hunger of memory.* Boston: David R. Godine.
Schell, J. (1982). *The fate of the earth.* New York: Avon.
Watson, J. D. (1969). *The double helix.* New York: New American Library.

# 13
▼▼▼▼▼▼▼

# The Impact of Culture and Ideology on the Construction of Gender and Sexual Identities: Developing a Critically Based Sexuality Curriculum*

James T. Sears

Homosexuality is one of the most controversial areas in sexuality education (Forrest & Silverman, 1989). Some states and school districts have banned the discussion of this topic within the formal curriculum. For example, South Carolina legislators barred discussion of homosexuality in the curriculum except in the context of discussing AIDS, and the principal of a Wisconsin public school banned the publication of an issue of a student newspaper that included anonymous interviews with lesbian and gay students. Homosexuality and homosexual students are therefore useful points from which to explore the limits and possibilities of sexuality education for the American adolescent of the 1990s.

As I will illustrate in this chapter, the fear of homosexuality and the reluctance to include this topic in the school curriculum are due, in part, to the social threat that same-sex relations pose to a male-dominated culture. Blurring gender roles and challenging sexual norms rock the very foundation of a society rooted in male privilege and misogynistic attitudes. The fear of a boy acting as a girl and the disgust at a male submitting to the passionate caress of another man are reactions that reflect the challenge to male privilege; the social indifference to a girl engaging in boy-like behavior and a man's pleasure in watching two women engage in sexual intimacies reflect the undercurrent of misogyny hidden by the ideology of heterosexuality.

The first part of this chapter explores the concepts of gender to illuminate issues of social control, ideology, and culture. In the second part of this chapter, I discuss the curricular implications of these ideas by noting the

---

*Reprinted by permission of the publisher from Sears, J. T., SEXUALITY AND THE CURRICULUM (New York: Teachers College Press, © 1992 by Teachers College, Columbia University. All rights reserved.), pp. 139–156.

213

limitations of conventional sexuality education programs and outlining a critically based sexuality curriculum that teaches for sexual diversity and challenges categorical thinking.


CONSTRUCTING GENDER

At a very early age, children in the United States learn gender appropriate behaviors through the assignment of household tasks and childhood toys, adult expectations for their dress and demeanor, and so forth (e.g., White & Brinkerhoff, 1981). Despite this early, prolonged, and extensive socialization process, some children, like Everetta and Isaiah,[1] fail to comply with gender-role norms. Whether refusing to jump rope or play football, there are consequences suffered by these gender nonconformists (Sears, 1989; Sears, 1991).

"The boys like to pick on me for some reason. I wouldn't let them. I would fight back. Most of the other girls, you know, they were just too femme," said Everetta. During recess, Everetta generally would be found roughhousing with the boys while her female classmates jumped rope, played on the swings, or talked quietly on the school steps. Seldom would a school day go by in which Everetta, wearing heavy-rimmed black glasses bandaged together with tape, did not return home without soiled or torn clothes. Her parents, though, didn't seem too concerned with Everetta's tomboyish behavior. "It was like, 'You'll outgrow it,' so I wasn't really given a hard time about being a tomboy at that age." As Everetta entered womanhood, her parents and teachers, like Ms. Peagler, became less understanding. "Ms. Peagler would say, 'That's not right, Everetta. You don't need to be . . . walking like a boy, talking like a boy, and acting like one.' . . . Then she sat me down and told me how a young woman should and should not act and what a young lady should and should not wear."

"I did not fit into the patterns that I was supposed to," explained Isaiah. He did not want to play football; he preferred to play with girls and was labeled "sissy" in elementary school. "That was something that they [the other children] could recognize. I was a whole lot less guarded about how I acted back then." By the time Isaiah entered middle school, however: "I was acting the way other people expected me to act. I just had to learn how to act other people's way."

Conventional studies of gender socialization fail to explain the issue of gender identity and its relationship, if any, to sexual identity. Michele Barrett (1980) observes: "Few of these studies systematically engage with the question of sexual practice, or erotic behaviour, and how this does or does not relate to socially acquired gender identity. This absence . . . reflects the marginality of sexuality in the conventional socialization approach" (p. 63).

Boys and girls have distinctive gendered, sexual scripts, and as they mature into adolescence, there is increased pressure to read from them. Undergirding parental concern and peer harassment over cross-gender behavior among boys is its association with homosexuality, while, for girls, the underlying concern over this behavior is their physical appeal to males.[2] For both, sexual concerns underlie considerations of gender nonconformity—concerns rooted in a belief system that reifies gender and sexuality. This belief system is integrally connected with cultural values, ideology, and social control.

Barrett (1980) goes on to point out the importance of the distinction between gender and sexuality and the relationship of these concepts to the social structure. For example, though substantial scholarship has been devoted to sissiness, "defeminization," and homosexuality, little research has been done on tomboyism, "demasculinization," and lesbianism. This reflects not only the comparatively little stigmatization associated with childhood tomboy behavior but also the centrality of the male in our society. "Defeminization" innocuously suggests that a boy's adoption of "female" traits, not adult misogyny, is the problem; the outward repudiation of male dress and demeanor is a visible rejection of male power and prestige.

## The Impact of Culture

Being born male or female, exhibiting masculinity or femininity, and desiring men or women are three human components that can be arranged in several distinct combinations reflected in terms such as *hermaphrodite, transvestite, bisexual, sissy boy, transsexual,* and *homosexual.* While biological sex is established at conception,[3] gender identity (personal conviction about being male or female) is thought to develop between 18 months and 4 years; the internalization of cultural expectations for gender roles is believed to be established between 3 and 7 years of age (Gramick, 1984; Van Wyk & Geist, 1984; Vance & Green, 1984).

Anthropologists report a wide variety of human gender arrangements (e.g., Davenport, 1965; Mead, 1935). Their findings portray a rich tapestry of male behavior and suggest that this great elasticity in gender roles and traits is culturally ordered, not divinely ordained. In New Guinea, for example, the interests of men in the Tchambuli tribe include art, gossip, and shopping, while women adopt what we might consider masculine roles. On the Trobriand Islands, both husband and wife nurture and care for their children. In northern Madagascar, Yegale men assume their wive's surnames, perform domestic duties, and obediently comply with female demands. These and other studies are discussed in Ann Oakley's (1972) influential work. She concludes:

Quite often one finds these examples of masculinity and femininity in other societies dismissed as eccentric, deviant, peculiar, and irrelevant to the mainstream of human development. This is an absurdly ethnocentric view. . . . The chief importance of biological sex in determining social roles is in providing a universal and obvious division around which other distinctions can be organised. In deciding which activities are to fall on each side of the boundary, the important factor is culture. (pp. 58, 156)

Even within cultures known for relatively rigid codes of male and female behavior, there are acceptable forms of cross-gender behavior for males (Talamini, 1982). Womanless weddings are routinely held in churches within rural communities of the South as fund-raising events. In Japan we find the centuries-honored Kabuki tradition in which men assume theatrical roles as women. In Africa, Masai boys wear women's clothing for several months following circumcision. In Holland, on the island of Marken, boys are dressed as girls until they reach the age of 7. In the United States, even the society pages consider Halloween and Mardi Gras appropriate occasions for such cross-dressing.

While the concept of maleness varies from culture to culture, no society has ignored the temptation to extend physical differences between "males" and "females" into its language, social structure, or ideology. This "sexing of the world," notes British anthropologist Allen Abramson (1984), occurs when "objects and roles tend to become imaginatively annexed to either the male or the female in a way that, conjunctually, may appear to be 'natural' and eternal" (p. 196). As these objects and roles become reified, those who deviate from them are often ostracized. But to claim that such behavior is "unnatural" is to ignore the spectrum of human diversity and to divide the world simplistically and artificially into gendered halves.

Even in those societies in which gender-role divisions are similar to our own, the cultural responses to cross-gender behavior differs markedly. For example, Kenneth Clark (1956), in his classic study *The Nude*, noted that mockery of male "queens" at gymnasia can be found depicted on Greek vases; and Kent Gerard and Gert Hekma's *The Pursuit of Sodomy: Male Homosexuality in Renaissance and Enlightenment Europe* (1989) is filled with accounts of effeminacy used as evidence in sexual prosecutions of the period. In contrast, within 19th-century American Indian cultures, males who did not conform to masculine behavior or dress often assumed special ceremonial roles as healers, shamans, and seers.

Parents of a PaPago Indian son, for example, who suspected that he might be different would "build a small bush enclosure. Inside the enclosure they place a man's bows and arrows, and also a woman's basket. At the appointed time, the boy is brought to the enclosure as the adults watch from the outside" (Williams, 1986, p. 24). After the boy enters the enclosure it is set afire. If the boy takes the basket in hand as he flees, he is recognized by the tribe as a *berdache*—a position of respect and economic status within his community.

Despite the fact that it occurs routinely in other species, across time, and among other contemporary cultures, female gender-role reversal is less documented and, possibly, less prevalent than male gender-role reversal (Goldstein, 1982). For example, the female *berdache* was a relatively rare phenomenon in Native American culture. Anthropologist Harriet Whitehead (1981) posits an explanation:

> The phenomena of adult reproductive processes added to and underscored an image of femininity that could weaken and be counterbalanced by masculine occupations only if the physiological processes themselves were held to be eliminable. Throughout most of North America, they were not so held, at least not for that period of a woman's life when she was realistically capable of taking up the hunter-warrior way of life. Becoming a member of the opposite sex was, therefore, predominantly a male game. (p. 93)

## The Impact of Ideology

Society provides the collective cultural history, social scripts, and language that form the foundation for these gendered identities. Further, the personal meanings of our regional, social class, racial, gender, and sexual identities are inextricably woven into a culture in which being upper class or working class, black or white, male or female, homosexual or heterosexual have social significance. While the intersections of social class, race, gender, and sexuality vary for each person, their existence and importance within our culture are social facts with negative social consequences for those who do not share memberships in the dominant groups.

Scholars from a variety of academic disciplines have argued that categorizing human beings according to their role in the biological process is central in the reproduction of their culture. Sociologist Kenneth Plummer (1981), feminist Mary Daly (1973), anthropologist Claude Levi-Strauss (1969), and social theorist Michel Foucault (1978) have all explored the ideological aspect of the construction of gender and sexuality. These and other scholars convincingly argue that "appropriate and inappropriate" gender behaviors are culturally based and that sexual biographies are integrally related to issues of ideology and social control. As Farganis (1986) states:

> What it means to be a woman, or gendered, is neither fixed nor indeterminably variable, but that interaction between how one defines oneself and the historical circumstances which encase the act of selfhood. The rooting of a "feminine character" in time and place allows us to see it as political, as subject to the social arrangement of the particular society. (p. 80)

In the United States, the social construction of gender and sexuality (i.e., the transference of biological divisions of maleness and femaleness into social categories), the delegation of human roles and traits according to conceptions of femininity and masculinity, and the proscription of certain sexual activities rationalize a particular way of organizing society—patriarchy.

Patriarchy is a system of social arrangements in which the female is economically, politically, and psychologically dependent upon the male (Lerner, 1986). This dependency extends from her roles in the private sphere (housewife, mother) to her status in the public arena (worker, consumer). It is reflected in her comparatively weak control over her economic and reproductive destiny (Zaretzky, 1976) and may be manifested in sexual harassment—a reflection of this lack of power. Through patriarchy the body politic is ideologically reproduced by distinguishing "male" and "female"; and by creating division of opportunities and rewards, traits and interests, privileges and responsibilities in favor of men (Chodorow, 1978).

This social arrangement, while reflected in the products conceived and marketed in big city boardrooms, is rooted in small town bedrooms and classrooms. Legislators may prop up forms of patriarchy (e.g., divorce law, marital rape), but it is legitimized by hundreds of thousands of ideological cops who define the significance of gender and delimit meanings of sexuality.

## Challenging Culture and Ideology

From this perspective, children like Everetta who continue to flaunt their deviant gender behaviors challenge more than social sensibilities; they challenge the foundation of our social system. The ability to define and delimit appropriate gender behaviors and expressions of sexuality is nothing less than the power to shape society; those who threaten to defy these roles thus challenge the hegemony of patriarchy. Self-identified lesbians, bisexuals, and gay men who challenge gender roles are the cultural bandits of the New Age.

The emergence of this New Age of public and private relationships signals the crumbling of a worldview spanning 2 millennia of everyday social discourse. The fear of a social Armageddon lies at the root of misogynist attitudes, sodomy statutes, and heterosexist curricula. A 13-year-old tomboy or a 17-year-old drag queen does more than threaten persons with insecure gender identities; they threaten the social order. For this reason, understanding and reducing homophobia among educators cannot be addressed at the individual level of bigotry or psychopathology; educators' homophobic attitudes and feelings must be understood within a societal context in which ideological beliefs and cultural values prop up existing relations of power and control within society.

*Becoming* a homosexual, despite contrary claims of the Radical Right, poses no social threat; *being* sexual by discarding and challenging gender and sexual norms challenges the very foundations of our society. For example, if lesbians and gay men merely reverse sex roles and bifurcate relationships into roles such as "butch/femme" or "dominant/submissive," then the opportunity to publicly challenge sexual and gender categories is lost.

Choosing same-sex partners does little to end heterosexist society. The greatest dangers are privatizing homosexual relationships, characterizing lesbians and gay men as basically the same as heterosexual women and men, reducing homosexuality to only a small part of what constitutes a human being, and asserting that homosexuality poses no threat to either heterosexuality or the larger social and political structures. Kitzinger (1987) declares:

> Our "inner selves"—the way we think and feel and how we define ourselves— are connected in an active and reciprocal way with the larger social and political structures and processes in the context of which they are constructed. It is for this reason that, as many radical and revolutionary movements of oppressed peoples have argued, "the personal is the political." (p. 62)

Sexuality education is more than sexual hydraulics and sexual hygiene or the cant of the "just say no" *Sex Respect* curriculum. But it is also more than accepting one's sexuality and exercising prudence in sexual activity. By virtue of the genuine interest of adolescents in sexuality, sexuality education can pose questions and provide knowledge that challenge students' everyday concepts of gender and sexuality. More important, sexuality education can help bridge the gap between the personal and political by exploring the ideological bases for gender and sexual identities. Finally, sexuality education can convey the multiple forms of sexual expression and the plasticity of sexual identity to adolescents and, in the process, explore questions about power and ideology in society.

## A CRITICALLY BASED SEXUALITY CURRICULUM

Sex, as many a high school student will freely admit, is an integral part of school life. Though some are reluctant to formally integrate this topic into school subjects, covert sexual instruction comprises a large part of the hidden curriculum: the exchange of lustful looks in the hallway or romantic notes in the classroom; half-glances in the locker-room shower or erotic day dreams in study hall; the homoerotic camaraderie of sports teams; and the sexual energy pulsating in even the most boring of classes. From every vantage point, there are couples: couples holding hands as they enter school; couples dissolving into an endless wet kiss between school bells; couples exchanging rings with ephemeral vows of devotion and love.

The culture of the school mirrors the larger society; schools socialize boys and girls into their presumed heterosexual destiny. On any given day in any particular high school these feelings span the sexual continuum, yet only those feelings at the heterosexual end are publicly acknowledged and peer approved. Unfortunately, when sexuality education is formally discussed in health or biology class, heterosexual mechanics is most often presented (leave it to schools to make even the most interesting subject emotionally dry, moralistically rigid, and intellectually sterile).

Developing critical-thinking skills is a stated priority in many school districts, yet few school districts extend these skills across the curriculum. Sexuality education is a case in point. Sexual values are taught, not explored; sexual danger is stressed while sexual pleasure is minimized; and heterosexual intercourse is placed at the apex of the pyramid of sexual desire. Never asked, never encouraged, never addressed are questions such as:

How does *being* male or female define one's sexual options?

How do sexual options and values vary across time and culture?

Why is masturbation considered less desirable than sexual intercourse?

Who is "gay"? Who is "straight"? How is it that such arbitrary distinctions exist?

There is a great need for a healthy, frank, and honest depiction of the fluidity of sexual behavior and the arbitrariness of sexual identities. Yet, too many educators are partners in a conspiracy of sexual silence in which sexual knowledge is what is salvaged after the scissors-and-paste philosophy of some religious zealots or homosexual activists is applied. This is not the time to accede to the interests of self-created minorities. The fluidity of human sexual response and the capacity of people to create and recreate their sexual identities are integral components of a critical sexuality curriculum.

Teaching for Sexual Diversity

One way to begin developing a critically based sexuality curriculum is to challenge the heterosexual agenda in school and society, first by asking educators to examine their personal feelings about sexuality and thoughts about education.[4] This involves asking personal questions, such as:

How do I feel when talking about sexuality?

During my childhood, how was the subject of homosexuality treated?

Did I have any friends who later identified themselves as bisexual, gay, or lesbian?

How comfortable am I in expressing feelings toward members of my own gender?

This also involves addressing political questions, such as:

In a democratic society, what should schools teach?

Can schools instill knowledge about the world without encouraging self-knowledge?

Are democratic attitudes, values of tolerance and respect for diversity, and the development of critical thinking fostered in the school curriculum?

Within an effective learning environment, what relationships should exist between educators and students?

Public schools in a democratic society are a marketplace for ideas. "Access to ideas," as Justice Brennan wrote, "prepares students for active and effective participation in the pluralistic, often contentious society in which they will soon be adult members" (quoted in Dutile, 1986, p. 37). But spreading ominously across America is a virulent plague of sexual ignorance and fear. Too many schoolchildren remain ignorant of the diversity of human sexuality, and too many teachers and students fear discussing sexuality beyond whispered conversations, cruel jokes, or sexual innuendo (Sears, in press). This plague, so toxic to compassion and common sense, is spread by purveyors of a supposedly moral agenda. But I find the concern of these religious True Believers hardly moral. They do not want to eradicate ignorance and fear; rather they want schools to propagate their skewed concept of morality and sexual orthodoxy. Because they accept the axiom that sexual knowledge may lead to sexual activity, no Tree of Knowledge is welcomed in the Eden of the True Believer.

The educator has an important role in a democratic society: to encourage intellectual flexibility, to foster analytical thought, and to expand tolerance. Sadly, many public schools incubate a narrow set of moral and religious beliefs: A page from a *teacher's* textbook on health science is ordered removed by the board of education for its discussion of birth control; books with references to homosexuality are removed from the shelves of a high school library; teachers are threatened with dismissal and criminal liability for discussing homosexuality. Schools, held hostage to Bible-thumping fundamentalists and right-wing ideologues, are painful places for students who experience same-sex erotic feelings to learn, and they are breeding grounds of intolerance and social bigotry for those repressing these feelings. A healthy understanding of the panorama of human sexual experience must be integrated into our schools as well as our society. Frank discussions and accurate information can replace schoolyard banter and sexual myths. Traditionally, a watered-down version of this task has been ghettoized in the school's sexuality education curriculum.

As documented elsewhere in this book, the quality of sexuality education curricula is poor across the nation. This curriculum primarily consists of sexual hydraulics and social relations skills. Homosexuality is the topic least mentioned by respondents and bisexuality is not even an option open for debate. Even in those states where there are no penalties for deviating from the heterosexual agenda, many school districts forbid discussion of such controversial topics, or teachers, take it upon themselves to avoid them.

The public hysteria associated with AIDS; the anti-human-rights legislation such as Britain's infamous Section 28 prohibiting local governments, schools, and other public agencies from "promoting homosexuality or its acceptability"; the adverse court ruling such as the *Bowers v. Hardwick* (1986) decision reaffirming state homosexuality sodomy laws; and the unabated initiatives of the Religious Right to discredit and discontinue the few supportive counseling programs, such as Project 10 in Los Angeles, for homosexual-identified students—all call for concerted effort by education and allied professions to counteract the heterosexual agenda of most sexuality education efforts. Specific strategies and materials that foster an awareness of homosexuality and homosexual persons already have been proposed (e.g., DeVito, 1981; Powell, 1987; Sears, 1983; Wilson, 1984). Educators have been admonished by scholars and activists alike to sit down and talk with bisexual, lesbian, and gay adults to learn firsthand about the special problems they faced in school; the importance of lesbian and gay educators as role models for homosexual students has been stressed, as has the need for public school systems to follow the lead of communities such as Berkeley and Cambridge in adopting anti-slur policies and nonharassment guidelines (e.g., Chism, Cano, & Pruitt, 1989; Hetrick & Martin, 1987; Martin & Hetrick, 1988; Ross-Reynolds & Hardy, 1985; Sears, 1987; Slater, 1988). In some schools, antihomophobia workshops with students and educators have been advocated and conducted (e.g., Dillon, 1986; Schneider & Tremble, 1986).[5] Professional educators as well as lesbian and gay activists ask, at the very least, for the construction of a nonjudgmental atmosphere in which homosexual-identified students can come to terms with their sexuality (e.g., Benvenuti, 1986; Sears, 1988), the acquisition by school libraries of biographical books where students can discover the homosexuality of some famous people, and the integration of references to homosexual men and women as well as the topic of homosexuality into the high school curriculum (Hipple, Yarbrough, & Kaplan, 1984; Jenkins, 1990; Sears, 1983).

The claim of scholars and activists that the homosexual experience has been expurgated from the high school curriculum has merit. In English, for example, students can read Whitman's a "Song of Myself" in *Leaves of Grass* or McCuller's *The Ballad of the Sad Cafe* without gleaning a hint of these authors' physical love for persons of their own sex; in the classics, they can translate the drama of Sophocles and the philosophy of Socrates without ever exploring ancient Greek homosexual practices; in history, they can study the military genius of Alexander the Great without ever learning the importance of male lovers for him and other members of his army; in mathematics, students can marvel at the genius of computer founder Alan Turing yet remain ignorant of his sexual struggles; in physical education, students can exchange "fag" jokes while admiring sports stars such as Martina Navratilova and David Kopay; music and drama students play from the works of Bessie Smith or Oscar Wilde without knowing to whom some of their art was dedicated.

Given recent resolutions by professional associations such as the National Educational Association (1988) and the Association for Supervision and Curriculum Development (1990) on the necessity for schools to meet the needs of homosexual students, some teachers have begun to write about the academic difficulties confronting such students.

> During an autobiography unit a student who has lesbian parents fails to turn in an entry about how his family is unique, claiming that he can't think of anything to write about. . . . At the middle school and high school level where I teach, the peer group reigns supreme. . . . For students attempting to hide their identity, the writing classroom is both scary and frustrating. (Smith, 1989, pp. 2–4)

But the writing classroom, as Brunner aptly demonstrates, can be a promising place for adolescents to explore sexuality. Teachers are now exploring ways to provide gay, lesbian, and bisexual students a voice on paper and seeking ways for others to acknowledge sexual diversity (Hart, 1989; Hewett, 1989), and the Dallas-based National Gay Alliance for Young Adults now sponsors a nationwide writing contest, with cash awards, for 10th- through 12th-grade students on the theme "What is it like being gay or lesbian in America today?"

## Challenging Categorical Thinking

While some may argue that these advocates want to replace the heterosexual curriculum with a homosexual one, it is more fair to say that they seek to redress the imbalance currently found within the schools. Unquestionably, such imbalance exists. For example, in reviews of representations of homosexuality in high school and college health texts, researchers have found few references to the subject, and many of those references are blatantly homophobic (McDonald, 1981; Newton, 1982; Whitlock & DiLapi, 1983). And those few texts that treat homosexuality in at least a neutral manner tend to ghettoize it by discussing the topic in a condensed section or by switching from a personalized "you" voice to a detached "they." "This treatment," note health care specialists Katherine Whitlock and Elena DiLapi (1983), "implies that homosexuality is less significant than or inferior to heterosexuality—an auxiliary form of sexuality, if you will, and somehow just not 'the real thing' " (p. 20).

Redressing the heterosexual imbalance by adopting the strategies cited above, however, will not challenge the heterosexual agenda. Rather, it reifies sexuality, splitting it into unequal heterosexual and homosexual categories. This strategy reaffirms a sexual caste structure in which the vast majority are (genetically fortunate?) heterosexual persons and a minority (the infamous 10%?) are homosexually oriented. Same-sex fantasies or behaviors by the majority can simply be written off as childhood exploits or evidence of middle-age crises; heteroerotic feelings and experiences by the minority can simply be rationalized as existential escapes from biological destiny or political duty. Women and men who affirm their bisexuality become the untouchables in this system of sexual castes.

Incorporating the homosexual experience into the school curriculum, hiring homosexual-identified educators, and adopting anti-slur policies will not adequately address the sexuality needs and interest of our children. Discussing the homoerotic poetry of Sappho or Dickinson is not the same as exploring the homoerotic imagery that all of us experience. Highlighting the achievements of Alexander the Great or David Kopay while failing to discuss the homoerotic component of men in combat—whether on the battleground or the gridiron—does not illuminate how many of our social institutions are built over a river of subterranean same-sex feelings. Integrating one or two openly lesbian or gay educators into a teaching staff of 50 does little to dispel the belief that only a minority engage in homosexual behavior or share intimate same-sex feelings.

A central objective of a critical sexuality curriculum is to challenge students' (and educators') categorical thinking. For example, a critical examination of sex roles could elucidate questions such as: "Where do these roles come from?" "How are we socialized to them?" "How are they enforced?" "How do 'masculinity' and 'femininity' fit with maleness and femaleness?" (MacDonald, 1974, p. 179). In the process, students may come to understand both the social construction and the absurdity of such either/or concepts.

Categorical thinking can also be challenged by integrating discussions of sexuality throughout the curriculum. Conventional sexuality education, taught as a separate unit or integrated into biology or health science, communicates that sexuality can be appropriately separated from the mainstream of school life. Just as healthy sexuality can be expressed in a variety of ways and cannot be segregated to one aspect of a person's life, so, too, must it be discussed freely and openly in a wide range of courses, from literature to social sciences to the natural and applied sciences. Carlson's suggestion of developing an undergraduate course in cultural studies rooted in a thorough exploration of sexuality is one strategy appropriate in higher education. There are other higher education examples that I will briefly review.

Fonow and Marty describe how they challenge conventional thinking about sexual identity from a feminist perspective in a basic women's studies survey undergraduate course at Ohio State. Using role-playing exercises, oral histories, simulations, coming-out stories, films, and lesbian and heterosexual panels, they "help students confront and challenge the naturalness of human arrangements" as they ask, "How do we ground a sexual politics that deconstructs sexual identity?"

Richard Mohr (1989) teaches philosophy at the University of Illinois, Urbana. Advocating a philosophical basis for gay men's studies, he argues that the women's studies model and its emphasis on theory is essential for confronting homosexual stereotypes as "norm-laden ideology." Assigning social history and the natural sciences to a "subordinate role," he believes that ethics and moral education ought to be the intellectual foundation for the study and teaching of homosexuality. He writes, "Gay studies is the study of gays as a minority—the normative study of the social circumstances and treatment of gays. . . . As a moral project which criticizes and prescribes social forms . . . [gay studies] need[s] to be critically and philosophically informed" (p. 130).

Kay Williamson and Jacqueline Williams (1990), teaching at the University of Massachusetts, prepare undergraduate students to teach physical education. A course on equity awareness encourages college juniors to reflect on problems of sexism, racism, motor elitism, and homophobia. By encouraging students to critically examine personal experiences and school observations through the use of biographical activities, noncompetitive games, films, and discussions, these teachers couple the personal and social worlds. "The undergraduates reflected on many questions: 'As teachers, would they collude in prejudice and ridicule homosexual persons?' 'How would they feel and act if one of their own children were gay?' 'What is their position on employment of gay and lesbian teachers?' " (p. 121).

Anthony D'Augelli teaches an undergraduate course on human development at the Pennsylvania State University. Operating from a human development model whose propositions reflect a constructionist orientation (e.g., affectional interests are a lifelong developmental process; human sexual behavior is malleable; an individual's development is unique). D'Augelli (1991) applies a Freirian teaching model to assist students in making connections between their personal sexual histories and the dialectical impact of culture, history, and ideology. As his students explore their personal feelings and beliefs about aging, families, and friendship, he draws upon the social and behavioral sciences to bridge their feelings and beliefs with a critical understanding of culture, history, and society.

Although these authors teach in different intellectual disciplines, all agree on the necessity of a critically based sexuality curriculum.

## CONCLUSION

For the first time in recent history, the media and the schools are publicly discussing the long taboo topic of sexuality. The renewed emphasis on sexuality education, fueled by the AIDS crisis and the efforts of the former U.S. surgeon general, has legitimized the discussion of topics, such as condoms and homosexuality, in some school districts that only a few years ago would have self-righteously ignored them. From public service announcements promoting abstinence and safer sex to evening news reports on issues affecting lesbian and gay communities, the veil of sexual science is lifting. While this issue now is at the public forefront, we must work for a healthy, frank, and honest depiction of the fluidity of sexual behavior and a critical examination of the arbitrariness of gender and sexual identities.

## NOTES

1. All names are pseudonyms. Interviews were conducted between July 1986 and February 1988. For a discussion of the methodology employed, see Sears, 1991, pp. 431–464.
2. For example, Green and Money (1966) noted the interrelationships between effeminacy, role-taking, and stage-acting among a small sample of effeminate males during childhood. However, on both logical and empirical grounds the etiological linkage of homosexuality to social sex roles is questionable (Ross, 1983).
3. There are case studies of individuals whose genetic and anatomic characteristics do not match at birth. These children, raised male or female according to their physical characteristics, fail to develop gender-appropriate secondary sex characteristics during puberty and thus face a conflict between their gender and biological identities (e.g., Money, Devore, & Norman, 1986).
4. Other sources of ideas for educational strategies in working with homosexual students or addressing homosexuality within the school curriculum include: Jenkins, 1990; Morey, 1984; Sears, 1983.
5. Researchers also have reported on the positive impact that seminars, lectures, guest speakers, films, debate, and dialogue have had on reducing prejudice against lesbians and gay men (e.g., MacLaury, 1982; Rudolph, 1988). Those courses that demanded active involvement by students, such as role-playing, appeared the most promising in effecting and sustaining attitudinal change (Watter, 1987).

## REFERENCES

Abramson, A. (1984). *Sarah: A sexual biography*. Albany, SUNY Press.
Association for Supervision and Curriculum Development. (1990, July). *ASCD adopts resolution on student orientation* [press release].

Barrett, M. (1980). *Women's oppression today: Problems in Marxist feminist analysis.* London: Verson.

Benvenuti, A. (1986). *Assessing and addressing the special challenge of gay and lesbian students for high school counseling programs.* Paper presented at the annual meeting of the California Educational Research Association. (ERIC Reproduction No. ED 279 958)

Bowers v. Hardwick, 478 U.S. 186, 106 S.Ct. 2841, 92L.Ed.2d 140 (1986).

Chism, N., Cano, J., & Pruitt, A. (1989). Teaching in a diverse environment: Knowledge and skills needed by TAs. In J. Nyquist, R. Abbot, & D. Wulff (Eds.), *Teaching assistant training in the 1990s* (pp. 23–36). San Francisco: Jossey-Bass.

Chodorow, N. (1978). *The reproduction of mothering: Psychoanalysis and the sociology of gender.* Berkeley: University of California Press.

Clark, K. (1956). *The nude: A study of ideal art.* Princeton, NJ: Princeton University Press.

Daly, M. (1973). *Beyond God the father: Toward a philosophy of women's liberation.* Boston: Beacon.

D'Augelli, A. (1991). Teaching lesbian and gay development: A pedagogy of the oppressed. In W. Tierney (Ed.), *Culture and ideology in higher education: Advancing a critical agenda* (pp. 213–233). New York: Praeger.

Davenport, W. (1965). Sexual patterns and their regulation in a society of the Southwest Pacific. In F. Beach (Ed.), *Sex and behavior* (pp. 164–207). New York: Wiley.

DeVito, J. (1981). Educational responsibilities to gay male and lesbian students. In J. Chesbro (Ed.), *Gayspeak: Gay male and lesbian communication* (pp. 197–207). New York: Pilgrim.

Dillon, C. (1986). Preparing college health professionals to deliver gay-affirmative services. *Journal of American College Health, 35*(1), 36–40.

Dutile, F. (1986). *Sex, schools and the law.* Springfield, IL: Thomas.

Farganis, S. (1986). *Social reconstruction of the feminine character.* Totowa, NJ: Rowman & Littlefield.

Forrest, J., & Silverman, J. (1989). What public school teachers teach about preventing pregnancy, AIDS and sexually transmitted diseases. *Family Planning Perspectives, 21*(2), 65–72.

Foucault, M. (1978). *The history of sexuality: Vol. 1. An introduction.* New York: Pantheon.

Gerard, K., & Hekma, G. (1989). *The pursuit of sodomy: Male homosexuality in Renaissance and Enlightenment Europe.* New York: Harrington Park.

Goldstein, M. (1982). Some tolerant attitudes toward female homosexuality throughout history. *Journal of Psychohistory, 9*(4), 437–460.

Gramick, J. (1984). Developing a lesbian identity. In T. Darty & S. Potter (Eds.), *Women-identified women* (pp. 31–44). Palo Alto, CA: Mayfield.

Green, R., & Money, J. (1966). Stage-acting, role-taking, and effeminate impersonation during boyhood. *Archives of General Psychiatry, 15*(11), 535–538.

Hart, E. (1989). *Literacy and the empowerment of lesbian and gay students.* Paper presented at the annual meeting of the Conference on College Composition and Communication. (ERIC Reproduction No. ED 304 662)

Hetrick, E., & Martin, A. D. (1987). Developmental issues and their resolution for gay and lesbian adolescents. *Journal of Homosexuality, 14*(1/2), 25–43.

Hewett, G. (1989). A rhetoric of androgyny: The composition, teaching and ethics of gender (Doctoral dissertation, State University of New York at Albany, 1989). *Dissertation Abstracts International, 50,* 2476A.

Hipple, T., Yarbrough, J., & Kaplan, J. (1984). Twenty adolescent novels (and more) that counselors should know about. *School Counselor, 32*(2), 142–148.

Jenkins, C. (1990, September 1). Being gay: Gay/lesbian characters and concerns in young adult books. *Booklist,* pp. 39–41.

Kitzinger, C. (1987). *The social construction of lesbianism.* London: Sage.

Lerner, G. (1986). *The creation of patriarchy.* New York: Oxford University Press.

Levi-Strauss, C. (1969). *The elementary structures of kinship*. Boston: Beacon.

MacDonald, A. (1974). The importance of sex-role to gay liberation. *Homosexual Counseling Journal, 1*(4), 169–180.

MacLaury, S. (1982). *A comparison of three methods of teaching about human sexuality to determine their effectiveness in positively modifying attitudes about homosexuality*. Unpublished doctoral dissertation, New York University, New York.

Martin, A. D., & Hetrick, E. (1988). The stigmatization of gay and lesbian adolescents. *Journal of Homosexuality, 15*(1–2), 163–185.

McDonald, G. (1981). Misrepresentation, liberalism, and heterosexual bias in introductory psychology textbooks. *Journal of Homosexuality, 6*(3), 45–59.

Mead, M. (1935). *Sex and temperament in three primitive societies*. New York: Morrow.

Mohr, R. (1989). Gay studies as moral vision. *Educational Theory, 39*(2), 121–132.

Money, J., Devore, H., & Norman, B. (1986). Gender identity and gender transposition: Longitudinal study of 32 male hermaphrodites assigned as girls. *Journal of Sex and Marital Therapy, 12*(3), 165–181.

Morey, R. (1984). *Demystifying homosexuality: A teaching guide about lesbians and gay men*. New York: Irvington.

National Educational Association. (1988, July). *NEA urges special attention to gay/lesbian students* [press release].

Newton, D. (1982). A note on the treatment of homosexuality in sex education classes in the secondary school. *Journal of Homosexuality, 8*(1), 97–99.

Oakley, A. (1972). *Sex, gender and society*. New York: Harper & Row.

Plummer, K. (1981). *The making of the modern homosexual*. London: Hutchinson.

Powell, R. (1987). Homosexual behavior and the school counselor. *School Counselor, 34*(3), 202–208.

Ross, M. (1983). Homosexuality and social sex roles: A re-evaluation. *Journal of Homosexuality, 9*(1), 1–6.

Ross-Reynolds, G., & Hardy, B. (1985). Crisis counseling for disparate adolescent sexual dilemmas: Pregnancy and homosexuality. *School Psychology Review, 14*(3), 300–312.

Rudolph, J. (1988). The effects of a multimodal seminar on mental practitioners' attitudes toward homosexuality, authoritarianism, and counseling effectiveness (Doctoral dissertation, Lehigh University, 1988). *Dissertation Abstracts International, 49*, 2873B.

Schneider, M., & Tremble, B. (1986). Training service providers to work with gay or lesbian adolescents: A workshop. *Journal of Counseling and Development, 65*(2), 98–99.

Sears, J. (1983). Sexuality: Taking off the masks. *Changing Schools, 11*, 12–13.

Sears, J. (1987). Peering into the well of loneliness: The responsibility of educators to gay and lesbian youth. In A. Molnar (Ed.), *Social issues and education: Challenge and responsibility* (pp. 79–100). Alexandria, VA: Association for Supervision & Curriculum Development.

Sears, J. (1988). Growing up gay: Is anyone there to listen? *American School Counselor Association Newsletter, 26*, 8–9.

Sears, J. (1989). The impact of gender and race on growing up lesbian and gay in the South. *NWSA Journal, 1*(3), 422–457.

Sears, J. (1991). *Growing up gay in the South: Race, gender, and journeys of the spirit*. New York: Haworth.

Sears, J. (in press). Educators, homosexuality, and homosexual students: Are personal feelings related to professional beliefs? *Journal of Homosexuality*.

Slater, B. (1988). Essential issues in working with lesbian and gay male youths. *Professional Psychology: Research and Practice, 19*(2), 226–235.

Smith, L. (1989). *Writers who are gay and lesbian adolescents: The impact of social context*. Paper presented at the annual meeting of the Conference on College Composition and Communication. (ERIC Document No. ED 304 695)

Talamini, J. (1982). *Boys will be girls: The hidden world of the heterosexual male transvestite.* Landham, MD: University Press of America.

Vance, B., & Green, V. (1984). Lesbian identities. *Psychology of Women Quarterly, 8*(3), 293–307.

Van Wyke, P., & Geist, C. (1984). Psychosocial development of heterosexual, bisexual, and homosexual behavior. *Archives of Sexual Behavior, 13*(6), 505–544.

Watter, D. (1987). Teaching about homosexuality: A review of the literature. *Journal of Sex Education and Therapy, 13*(2), 63–66.

White, L., & Brinkerhoff, D. (1981). The sexual division of labor: Evidence from childhood. *Social Forces, 60*(1), 170–181.

Whitehead, H. (1981). The bow and the burden strap: A new look at institutionalized homosexuality in native North Americans. In S. Ortner, & H. Whitehead (Eds.), *Sexual meanings: The cultural construction of gender and sexuality* (pp. 80–115). Cambridge, MA: Cambridge University Press.

Whitlock, K., & DiLapi, E. (1983). "Friendly fire": Homophobia in sex education literature. *Interracial Books for Children Bulletin, 14*(3/4), 20–23.

Williams, W. (1986). *The spirit and the flesh.* Boston: Beacon.

Williamson, K., & Williams, J. (1990). Promoting equity awareness in the preparation of physical education students. *Teaching Education, 3*(1), 117–123.

Wilson, D. (1984). The open library. *English Journal, 43*(7), 60–63.

Zaretzky, E. (1976). *Capitalism, the family and personal life.* New York: Harper.

# 14
▼▼▼▼▼▼▼

# A Parent's Dilemma:
# Public vs. Jewish Education*

Svi Shapiro

The time for decision always seemed to be far off. It would be six years from the beginning of kindergarten before my daughter would complete her elementary schooling—a seemingly endless period of time during which I would surely find the clarity of thinking to decide on the future course of her education. Yet fifth grade at B'nai Shalom Day School had arrived far more rapidly than I wanted. I would now have to seriously confront my own commitments to public education, and to Jewish education—to say nothing of my ambivalence about private schooling and the privileges of class, the rootlessness of a postmodern America, and the comforts of parochial communities.

For leftist academics, there is always the danger of allowing the particularities of one person's life to become lost in the much grander narratives of moral, ideological, and political considerations. This is, after all, a decision about where my eleven-year-old daughter Sarah is to spend her sixth grade. Nor, as I have reminded myself many times, can I hold her needs hostage to my own heavily worked concerns about the course of social justice and identity in this country.

We live in Greensboro, North Carolina. This is not New York or Philadelphia. The Jewish community (well established and comfortable as it is) exists as a very small island in an overwhelmingly dominant Christian milieu. This is what is sometimes referred to as the New South—middle class, moderately conservative. Greensboro is a city of several colleges and universities; we recycle garbage; our mayor is a woman and an environmentalist.

*Reprinted from TIKKUN MAGAZINE, A BI-MONTHLY JEWISH CRITIQUE OF POLITICS, CULTURE, AND SOCIETY. TIKKUN, 251 West 100th Street, 5th floor, New York, NY 10025.

Despite a notorious 1979 shoot-out involving the Ku Klux Klan, this is not Klan country.

To grow up Jewish here is certainly a minority experience. But it is far from the culturally marginalizing and politely silent experience I had growing up Jewish in England in the 1950s. Here, Jewish holidays are visibly and positively commented on in the local media, the television stations wish their viewers a happy Chanukah, and the downtown Christmas decorations are referred to as the "Festival of Lights." Even our supermarkets consult with our Conservative rabbi on Jewish dietary laws and culinary tastes.

The Jewish day school my daughter attends is a quite beautiful institution. Its enrollment is about 190 students—fairly remarkable in a city of about 1,200 Jewish families. Recently celebrating its twenty-fifth anniversary, the school provides a warm, very *haimish* Jewish environment, where holidays and Shabbat are richly celebrated, and the Hebrew language ubiquitous. Its religiosity is traditional though non-dogmatic, and it affirms the notions of *tikkun olam*. While I find the pedagogy too conventional, my daughter has found the place to be nurturant and loving. She has, for the most part, found delight in being there—a place where schooling has sustained her, not opposed her life.

What was at stake in my choice of Sarah's schooling was no abstract pedagogic exercise. I want my daughter's heart and soul to be shaped and nurtured by a *Yiddishkeyt* that would ensure her allegiance to a Jewish identity. As spiritually or historically compelling as this might be, I make no claim that this is not, at root, a selfish act. Such an education would ensure my continuing ability to recognize my own self in my daughter's being—the natural, if not entirely laudable, desire of most parents. Until now, my decision has been richly repaid; she has indeed absorbed not only some of the knowledge and culture of Jewish life, but more significantly its texture and feel. She senses its importance and its uniqueness. The joys and significance of this belong not only to the private sphere of family life, but also for her to the sphere of communal participation. Jewish life exists not merely in home or synagogue, but richly and vibrantly in the everyday, Monday-through-Friday world from which, for most of us, it is abstracted.

The mobilization of support for a politics that eviscerates public institutions is bound up with the widely felt hostility in modern societies toward the state, with all of its impersonality, inefficiency, and waste. It is precisely this perception that has fueled the relentless drive of the Right to gut almost everything that has the word "public" in it.

At the heart of this assault is an ideology that lionizes the marketplace and scorns society's attempts to ameliorate social injustice. In this view, the marketplace and market forces are regarded as the only legitimate means to allocate resources and to assign economic or cultural values. The resultant push for smaller government and a balanced budget has the effect of drastically reducing the scope and scale of the social safety net. It means ever more drastic cutbacks in society's supports to the elderly, children, the unemployed, the poor, and the sick.

So, our culture continues to foster self-interest and a lack of concern for the common good. Where the marketplace alone is to be arbiter of economic investment and social values, attempts are made to eliminate or reduce publicly financed education and culture. Prisons become one of the few areas of public investment. And where public policy collides with the imperatives of the market, as in environmental and consumer regulation, then the latter need be scaled back if not eradicated.

The political discourse that has sought to achieve these ends is not without its own conflicts and contradictions. It is clear, for example, that many people subscribe to the notion of smaller, less wasteful government, but also support a state that lessens the hazards and dangers of the free market. In this sense the state is, paradoxically, both the focus of much popular anger and re- pository of much of our needs and aspirations as a community. It irks us with its demands and intrusiveness, but it also instantiates our collective responsibilities and obligations. For all of its flaws, the state embodies some notion of a shared purpose; its ultimate client purports to be the public good, not simply the desirous ego.

The irony is that those conservatives who have often been the loudest in their condemnation of the decline of community and an ethic of responsibility have pursued a politics that has sought to allow the standards and ethics of the market to exert ever more freedom and dominance in our social, eco- nomic, and cultural lives. In working to ensure a world in which private interests and profits are less and less hindered by broad public responsibilities, and where the public arena is endlessly demeaned and savagely attacked, these free-marketeers have helped create a society that more and more resembles a predatory jungle. The violence of the Oklahoma bombing and the shut-down of the federal government, with its callous layoffs of workers and undelivered unemployment checks, are the most recent visible evidence of a discourse which has effectively trashed the public domain.

Sadly, it is often only when cuts in services and benefits are directly felt that individuals become more critical of what is happening on a broader level. Until then, the politics of racism and division succeed in legitimating the Right's social policies. A bunker mentality spreads, which calls for a social ethic of each for him or herself; individualism, separateness and isolation frame our disposition toward the rest of the world. All of this has been given added impetus by corporate behavior in the 1980s and '90s, replete with lay-offs, downsizing, closings, and relocations. It is a world that mocks any notions of obligation or commitment to workers, consumers, or community. Nothing really counts except the hunt for immediate profitability. Public accountability is a barrier to be subverted by whatever means necessary.

Yet in spite of all of this, there is still a deep hunger for communal life and the public good in America. Despite the shift to the Right, large majorities continue to affirm the importance of protecting our environment, maintaining investments in public libraries and cultural resources, and ensuring the availability of health care. Sometimes it becomes crystallized in ways that seem narrow or even repressive (protecting "our" flag). Yet behind these can be heard a cry for a society in which our collective concerns, not just our private interests, are honored, and where there is a strong sense of the public good instantiated in our civic world and in our social institutions.

Perhaps nowhere has this struggle been more focused than around the institutions of public education. Indeed, all of our societal schizophrenia around questions of public and private, marketplace and equity, democracy and capitalism, are in evidence there. In its most ideal rendering, public schooling represents a space where all of our children may be educated; a place where the rights of citizenship take precedence over the privileges or disadvantages of social and economic life. Understood in this way, public education becomes a crucial element in the making of a democratic civil society. It is an indispensable site for the nurturing of a new generation in those attitudes and values that ensure the possibility of meaningful democratic life.

Public school brings together in one setting children who, regardless of their class, race, gender or ethnicity, may acquire the capacity for critical intelligence, the sense of community, and the cultural literacy that are requisites for democracy. As many political commentators have pointed out, the current crisis of democracy in the United States is closely related to the decline of meaningful public spaces where citizens can engage in a thoughtful and critical consideration of our society's pressing issues and concerns. In a world where commercial malls and presidential debates simulate real public interaction and involvement, there is a growing urgency to preserve those places where notions of equity, community, citizenship, and the public good still have validity.

Sadly, the reality of public schools has always been a long way from its democratic promise. The fundamental ideal of a place where the offspring of all citizens might meet and come together as a community has always been upset by the harsh realities of privilege, inequity, and racism. The historic struggles to eradicate the effects of a racially segregated system of public education are well known. Less obvious have been the continuing pernicious effects of class and race in maintaining schools vastly different in their resources, funding, expectations of students, and educational climate. Jonathan Kozol, among others, vividly documented the horrendous conditions that beset schools in poor and underfunded districts, producing debilitating and demoralizing third-world environments for kids in many of this nation's cities.

This public sphere mirrors the increasing polarization of wealth and opportunity found in the wider society. Urban schools with their violence, high drop-out rates, low achievement, and poor morale exist as altogether different institutions from those in suburban areas that function as conduits to good colleges and economic well-being.

Far from equalizing opportunities for diverse groups of students, education typically reinforces the already existing advantages and disadvantages found in the larger culture. The bitter irony of the process is that it occurs under the apparently well-meaning rhetoric of educational theories that promise to teach to the intellectual and emotional differences among students. Yet, in practice, the effect is usually to rationalize racism and classism. The ubiquitous grouping and tracking of students becomes little more than a way of affirming the "cultural capital" of some individuals and invalidating that of others. It takes only a cursory look at many schools to see how education dignifies the knowledge and experiences of some young people and silence and marginalizes that of others.

Typically, schooling represents a process of mindless absorption of knowledge separated from any notion of existential or social meaning. Successful learning comes to be seen as a regurgitation of bits and pieces of knowledge abstracted from a context that might provide them with relevance to the lives, hopes, interests and dreams of kids' lives. And the "hidden curriculum" of schooling is such that the emphasis on achievement, individual success and competition undermines efforts to build communities of respect and care. Indeed, where the latter are taken seriously, they must confront the contradictions not only of school culture but that of the larger social milieu. The daily grind of public school life with its boredom, alienation and bureaucratic regimentation are the resonant features of contemporary, adolescent popular culture.

In my struggle to decide the fate of my fifth-grade daughter, I am mindful of the desperate need to sustain the promise of public life in this country. The withdrawal of the middle class from public institutions is the certain vehicle for their demoralization and decline. Not only in this country but in other places such as the United Kingdom, the turn toward more individualistic lifestyles and privatized institutions, promoted by conservative governments, has turned the public space into one of neglect and decay. Whether in health care, housing, or in education, the story is one of double standards—where publicly provided institutions or systems are synonymous with the poor, and where standards are increasingly inferior as compared to those found in the private domain.

In wrestling with whether to send my daughter to a public school, I feel compelled to weigh my own moral responsibility as to whether I am to be part of the flight from our public world into the safety and privileges of a private institution. A commitment to progressive politics would seem to demand commitment to those public institutions where we may share, to some degree, our lives with those who inhabit economic, cultural or racial worlds quite different from our own.

Among all these concerns, one is of particular significance to me. How do we reconcile a commitment to public education with the need to recognize and affirm cultural, religious, or other differences? For many on the Left, this validation of difference has been central to the contemporary struggle to deepen the meaning of democratic life. It has been seen as a critical feature of democracy in a "postmodern" world. The struggle to recognize the multiplicity of voices and the diversity of histories and experiences of those who inhabit our nation and world has been a key focus of progressive educators.

And there has been increasing recognition of the ways that education has for so long denied the contributions and presence of many kinds of people. Whether because of class or race or ethnicity or gender or religion or nationality, it has become clear just how much we have ignored or invalidated the knowledge and traditions of others—those who fall outside the constructed norms of the culture. As educators, we have come to see how this process demeans and silences our students as the classroom becomes a place that is quite foreign to their homes, neighborhood, or communities.

In this regard, the emergence of a "multicultural" awareness in our schools is an important and liberating phenomenon. It is certainly a mark of progress that children are being taught to question the notion that "Columbus discovered America" with all its ethnocentric and racist assumptions about civilization; or that history, social studies, and English are beginning to be taught in more expansive and inclusive ways. Even where there are good-faith efforts, multiculturalism too often becomes trivialized—a matter of food, fiestas, and dressing up. It offers a very superficial appreciation indeed of what difference has meant to communities often denigrated or despised by those in the mainstream of society. Whatever its limitations, these efforts represent real cracks in the wall of cultural assumptions that have confronted generations of young people, shutting out or silencing those whose language, history, beliefs, and culture have been made to seem peripheral to the society.

Yet even where difference is valued and the plural nature of cultures in America is celebrated, the texture of the particular cultures recognized by our public schools is likely to be "thin." For my daughter, no multicultural environment can offer the judaically rich, evocative and full experience that would be available to her in a Jewish day school. Only in that environment does Jewishness become a form of life that colors moral expression, joyful celebration, the moments of soulful reflection and sadness, and the days and seasons of the calendar. Jewishness becomes more than an abstract focus of intellectual discussion: the living vehicle through which my daughter can construct her identity and articulate her ethical and spiritual commitments.

Such a voice is a matter of both the heart and the mind, and only a pedagogic environment that is flooded with the resonance of Jewish memory and experience can nurture it. Nor is a deep sense of value about Jewish life easily available outside of a context which integrates it into a community's daily practice—one that draws in some way from the moral and spiritual meanings of our people's historical wisdom. The "thick" texture of Jewish life—the pervasive sounds of Hebrew, the smell of challah, the *niggunim* and Israeli songs, the benching after meals—are the resources upon which are built an identity that contains an enduring commitment to Jewish life and continuity.

The intensity of this experience, however, holds the potential danger of nurturing parochial or arrogant attitudes. Such schooling may produce a *shtetl* consciousness that shuns or disparages anything foreign—one that later fuels the intolerance of "*goyim*-bashing," or the self-righteousness that underlays so much of the American-Jewish support for chauvinistic, right-wing Israeli politics.

While at B'nai Shalom, much hard work goes toward developing a sense of social responsibility and celebrating the values of human community and global connectedness, the school my daughter attends is nevertheless a sheltered, limited community that is separated from much that other children must confront and deal with in their lives. Certainly its ambiance is too competitive, oriented to the goals of individual success and achievements. Its selectivity as a Jewish and predominantly middle- and upper-middle-class institution ensures that it is the kind of secure and cohesive community so appealing to parents. Yet in this sense it also provides a powerful, if disturbing, answer to some of the dilemmas of a postmodern world.

In their observations of postmodern society, there is a surprising convergence among both left- and right-wing critics. At the center is the belief that the world we have entered is one in which barriers—spatial, moral, political, intellectual, and aesthetic—have collapsed. Even the boundaries of gender appear permeable in an age in which sexual borders are easily crossed and labile. Our age is one of unfixity, uncertainty, and flux.

There is much to celebrate in all of this. The unfixing of boundaries, verities, and distinctions has given us the promise of a world that is more fluid, open, and free. Yet there is a price to pay—one, I believe, that has traumatic consequences for the young. And in this the conservative critique finds a powerful resonance in the anguish of many parents, by no means all of whom can be dismissed as simply and predictably right wing.

It is quite clear that the desire for discipline and structure in the raising of the young now hits a powerful chord across a wide range of parents. This desire emanates from the increasing recognition of a world in which a moral and spiritual homelessness is the prevailing sensibility. More and more there is the sense of being uprooted from the stabilities of place, family, and normative communities. The postmodern world is one in which individuals increasingly feel as if they are in exile—existentially and morally adrift in a world that constantly disrupts and dissolves any sense of situatedness in an enduring web of meaning and community. Indeed, far from acknowledging the pain of so much alienation, we are urged by Madison Avenue as well as the hipper cultural critics to enjoy the tumultuous ride.

In ways that distort the broad concern for the disintegration of ethical life and the erosion of the sense of social responsibility, talk of tradition, values, and discipline is mistakenly understood as only a discourse of the Right. Yet a world in which all that is solid melts—moral commitment, identity, community, social connection—is a matter that confronts all of us. And nowhere is this more painfully so than in regard to the upbringing of our own children. Daily, all of us, especially parents, are forced to confront the fall-out from the postmodern condition—the self-destructiveness of adolescent suicide, drugs, alcoholism and compulsive dieting, widespread depression and generalized rage, and a cynical detachment from social institutions. However manipulative or distorting, conservative discourse succeeds because it speaks to the widespread anguish of an older generation.

In this context of disintegration, rootlessness, and the culture of images, Jewish schooling offers a sense of possibility not easily found elsewhere. Here there is the hope of nurturing an identity grounded in the Jewish people's long history—a history rich with the struggles for a world of justice and freedom. Here, too, is the real possibility of transmitting what it means to be a "stranger in the land"—developing personalities empathic to the pain of exclusion and human indignity.

Jewish 'memory' roots us in a temporal community of unbelievable human tragedies, celebrations, suffering, courage, and the will for physical and spiritual survival. And such history makes powerful claims on the living—an insistence on the vision of *tikkun olam*; to act as if we ourselves had experienced the bondage of Egypt. Far from the Disney World theme park of historical images, Jewish pedagogy can offer a deep sense of historic and communal identification. Such identification is one of connectedness to an enduring moral and spiritual vision.

The religious sensibility forged in this history is one that continually demands that we create and recognize boundaries—distinctions within our world between ways of living that express the sacred and those that are profane. Judaism is a religion of everyday life that constantly seeks to make sacred the so-called ordinary, taken-for-granted acts of daily existence. Those of us who grew up in Orthodox homes know the rigidity and frequently stultifying nature of halakhic Judaism. Yet, at the same time, one can find here a powerful rejoinder to the dehumanization and degradation of our common world—one that insists that we seek to make holy human life and behavior, as well as the whole environment that makes life possible.

Certainly Judaism, like all religions, can become dogmatic and reified; a series of mindless rituals and practices. Yet I have reason to believe that B'nai Shalom offers my daughter the beginning of a deeper set of meanings that points to the limits and boundaries that structure our relationship to the world as one of respect, consciousness of the needs of others, and responsibility toward them. In this school's Judaism there is, too, a sense of celebration and festivity—one that seeks to teach the young something about experiencing lives of joy, wonder and appreciation. It is, I believe, in this synthesis of social responsibility and joyful mindfulness that we can find the beginnings of a meaningful response to the rampant cynicism and nihilism of our culture.

It is true that the school offers an environment that is only very cautiously questioning or critical of the injustices of our world. And I am concerned lest it limit the importance of developing the critical mind and spirit—the lifeblood of a democratic culture. But beyond the need for our young to be educated to enable them to challenge their world, there is a need for the sense of hope and possibility that the world can be changed and transformed. And this, I believe, happens best in an environment where we feel a deeply shared, and inspiring, sense of connected fate. For Jews, there is our long history of struggle in a harsh world of brutality and oppression, and the will to maintain our hope for a better world.

Without this communal rootedness and affirmation of a way of life there is, I think, little emotional capacity to act in the world—at least not where acting means trying to transform the moral character of our lives and the political shape of our society. There is only disconnected apathy and cynicism—the world of the young so well reflected in the recent popular movies, *Slacker* and *Clueless*.

The Right is correct to argue that without an internalized discipline the self becomes passive, unable to act in the world. Yet the discipline that empowers is not that of the obedient drone but the structure that comes from participation and responsibility in the life of a meaningful and enduring community.

These are not easy times. Such communities are not easy to find. All of us must somehow find the capacity for commitment in a world where all beliefs seem uncertain, visions uncertain, and social relations fragile or broken. Yet the need to find a place in which our commitments are shared and our identities confirmed is the necessary ground of our being as moral agents in the world.

Let me be clear that my real interest is not in what is referred to today as "Jewish continuity." The continuation of a set of practices and rituals is of no particular significance to me. The ultimate value of Jewish education is not found in my daughter's capacity to read or speak Hebrew, or her knowledge of Judaica, but in whether she will become a human being deeply concerned for the worth and dignity of all the lives that share our world. My hope is that her Jewish education will be a powerful vehicle for developing such a way of being. The particular here, I hope, will provide a gateway to the universal.

Yet I worry that my desire for this education will also boost the arguments of those who favor "school choice." These are often no more than thinly veiled attempts to promote educational policies that are elitist, racially separatist, or religiously fundamentalist, and have little to do with creating a more compassionate or respectful civic culture. As I wrestle with my daughter's future, I feel the strong and inescapable claims of the particular in a world that more and more demands a recognition of our universal connectedness and responsibilities.

## GLOSSARY

| | |
|---|---|
| Yiddishkeyt | Jewishness |
| Goyim | Non-Jews |
| Challah | Sweet-tasting bread eaten on the Jewish Sabbath |
| Niggunim | Traditional melodies |
| Tikkun Olam | To heal and repair the world |
| Heimish | Familiar and inviting enviroment |
| Benching | Grace said after meals |
| Shtetl | Small town in Eastern Europe with vibrant Jewish community |
| Halakhic Judaism | Religious practice followed by orthodox Jews |

# 15

▼▼▼▼▼▼▼

# Special Education and the Quest for Human Dignity

Rebecca Blomgren

Within the context of education, we occasionally ponder the purpose of our actions and the direction in which those actions and resulting choices turn us. As special educators, many of these reflections and methodological choices revolve around issues of help, remediation and compensation. How do we envision our help and what are the realities within which we practice these concerns? How do we regard those who come before us in their various stages and states of disability? What do we do to them and with them in the name of help? What are the discrepancies between our desire to help and the voices with which we have chosen to express this assistance? Where does this leave us educationally? personally? and collectively? What does this say about our humanity or inhumanity?

This chapter, while situated within the arena of special education, will attempt to delve into the dilemmas we all face when we attempt to understand the purpose of school, the meaning of help and the hope we hold for education. As we strive to couple our democratic ideals of equality, freedom and inclusion with productivity, competition and education within the process of education, the tensions of this structure begin to emerge. The tensions become increasingly painful and horrifying as they are filtered through the lives, realities and experiences of the handicapped. Special education offers an intense focusing point in which the tensions, dilemmas, and paradoxes are illuminated and magnified.

In reflecting upon the issues that press upon special educators, the message of Martin Buber offers an opportunity to seriously consider how we prepare ourselves to encounter the challenges that teaching presents.

He [the modern educator] enters the school room for the first time, he sees them crouching at the desks, indiscriminately flung together, the misshapen and the well-proportioned, animal faces, empty faces and noble faces in indiscriminate confusion, like the presence of the created universe; the glance of the educator accepts and receives them all. (Buber, 1965, p. 94)

Buber's image addresses the dignity of the noble acts of teaching and further sparks the vision that many of us, as educators, initially held.

It is my impression, as an educator, that most of us enter into the varying fields of educational practice with some degree of concern for and awareness of an underlying impulse for care and a compassion for humanity. Those of us in special education, at least initially, seem to be very sensitive to and aware of this helping impulse. However, ironically, special educators frequently find themselves knowingly and obliviously performing the most inhumane deeds, ranging from obvious acts of violence as manifest in severe behavior modification programs that are justified by assertive discipline plans to the more subtle abuses of person as witnessed in the detrimental effects of assessment and labeling that are the prerequisites for special education placement and intervention.

The discrepancy between our initial concern for helping and the reality of our practices in the classroom surfaces as we ponder over just how we meet those who appear before us. How do we respond to the "animal faces," the "misshapen," the "noble faces" and the "empty ones"? Our current and for the most part unexamined response becomes one of efficiently and thoroughly categorizing, tracking and controlling those who come before us year after year. Our educational efforts center upon being absolutely certain that we can label and identify the "animal faces" and the "empty ones" so that we may direct and divert those students into more appropriate programs, where we deceive ourselves, our students and their parents into believing that this special education process will enable these "animal faces" to fulfill their potential and be the most they can be.

We seek to identify and repair these "misshapen ones" and we respond to them with an understanding gained from the medical, scientific models of help. Our desire to help is expressed in terms of diagnosis, prescription, assessment and remediation. The implication of such medical language results in our viewing these individuals as being, to a greater or lesser degree, impaired and thus in need of fixing. As educators, it becomes our responsibility to perform our teaching tasks in the roles of diagnosticians and technicians. It is our job to meet those who come before us prepared to prescribe a task analysis, an Individual Education Program (IEP) and behavioral objectives that will enable these students to acquire techniques and skills that will fix them or at least help them compensate for their problems. As teachers, we attempt to prescribe an education program that will guide them to conformity so they can be as "normal" as possible. As Kliebard suggests, in his critique of Tyler's transmission models of education, "our teaching responsibility becomes one of turning out as useful and as finished a product as possible" (Gress & Purpel, 1978, p. 266).

Helping as diagnosis, teaching as prescription and learning as remediation and production turns very quickly into an educational dilemma in which the unfixed, unproductive, non-useful individual is blamed for his or her lack of success. We rapidly degenerate into blaming the victim for his or her learning disability, educable mental retardation or emotional handicap. When our best prescriptive attempts to remediate an individual fail, we begin to accuse the individual for his or her inability to become a useful product. With the hope that success resides in some elusive technique or method, we quicken our pace as we search for a better task analysis or a more comprehensive behavior contract. All the while, we continue to blame ourselves and our students for the failure. We delude ourselves into thinking that this is being done in the best interest of the student and in the name of help.

Only upon a deeper look or an examination of our taken-for-granted assumptions regarding help and teaching can we begin to penetrate the destructive cycle of blaming the victim. Whose interest is being served as we meet one another for the purpose of categorizing and prescribing? How might we reconstruct our perception of help? Who is being uplifted by our diagnostic procedures in education? As Camus so poignantly writes, "The evil that is in the world always comes of ignorance, and good intentions may do as much harm as malevolence, if they lack understanding" (Camus, 1972, p. 124). As educators responding to an impulse to help through an unexamined practice which encompasses prescription, remediation, assessment and competitive productivity, we might, as Camus suggests, be ushering in evil through our unexamined good intentions.

In considering resistance as an analytical construct, Giroux provides a vehicle for revealing and examining the painful paradoxes that surface as the tensions between special education, help and productivity are seriously examined. Resistance critique enables us to question our good intentions and to articulate our concerns regarding interest by looking at those who resist conformity and standardization, regardless of the obvious reasons as indicated by the various labels we have placed upon them. The learning disabled, the mentally retarded and the emotionally disturbed who are unable to produce and compete efficiently and who consequently do not fit into our existing educational picture are those who resist the propulsion of our transmission-productivity paradigm. They are the ones who slow down the general productivity in the classroom by seeking explanations for assignments, by requiring additional assistance in order to complete a project or by interrupting the class routine because they are unable to keep pace with the others. They are often cast out, dismissed or viewed as problems by today's educators. These are the students who present us with nondeliberate and frequently unintended pictures of resistance. Although unintended, their resistance serves as a focusing point for analytical critique.

Giroux points out, however, "not all oppositional behavior has 'radical significance,' nor is all oppositional behavior rooted in a reaction to authority and domination" (Giroux, 1983, p. 103). Further, he points out that all behaviors do not automatically "speak for themselves; to call them resistance is to turn the concept into a term that has no analytical preciseness" (p. 109).

However, when resistance, as an analytical tool, is reframed and placed into the dimension of criticism, we are able to examine our "good intentions." Oppositional behaviors and school failures are moved into the political arena in which the questions of interest surface. Functional explanations and understandings based upon educational psychology that tend to contribute to the phenomenon of blaming the victim no longer provide the educational solutions. Rather than being viewed as the result of individual psychology and learned helplessness, oppositional behavior is regarded as having to do with moral and political indignation. Resistance, when understood from this perspective, contains "an expressed hope, an element of transcendence, for radical transformation" (Giroux, 1983, p. 108).

When resistance critique is used to examine our good educational intentions, the actual voices of those who have not fit into the production, transmission models of traditional educational practice begin to be heard. Resistance critique offers a personal and powerful tool for examining our good intentions and for revealing the political dimensions of culture and knowledge. It calls into focus the actual, lived experiences of those who have been denied access or who have felt anguished by the production, transmission pulse of most educational practice. It is through these voices that we may begin to glimpse an insight into the truly alienating conditions of our human existence as manifest through the unexamined, taken-for-granted and good intended practices in education that we call "help" and "teaching."

The voices of Dee and Kay articulate two such stories of resistance that begin to point to the depth of alienation created by our unexamined educational good intentions. Their stories provide us with an opportunity to give voice to the experience of many who have been traditionally dismissed and unheard. Even so, it is difficult to hear the extent of their hegemony, to attend to the depths of their despair and to admit the degree to that they have been prevented from engaging in the process of inquiry. However, Dee and Kay only touch upon the beginnings of voicing the anguish that must be the experience of the excluded handicapped. The vast majority of severely and profoundly handicapped persons in our society remain inarticulate, without language, non-communicative and voiceless. They are placed in the precarious care of those who must speak for them! What about those stories that we may never hear? What can these people reveal to us regarding our good intentions? What are our responsibilities in light of such reflection?

As I began these interviews I did so with a concern for human affirmation, feeling that labeling and special education, although well intended, perpetuated more harm than good. Initially, I felt that I would hear these young women express evidence of poor self-concepts and reveal injured self-esteem; however, their pain was much deeper and their anguish was directed toward the frustration and despair of having been denied their human dignity. These women revealed stories that spoke directly to the issues of exclusion and marginality and of the struggle to be recognized as being human!

*Dee*

Dee, a 21-year-old interior design student had been labeled as having a learning disability and was placed in a special program when she was in the third grade. She remained in special education programs through the eighth grade. As she reflects upon her special education experience in a resource room, she focuses upon the extensive evaluation and continual assessment that seemed to dominate her school life. Most of these evaluations were not explained, leaving her with a sense of alienation. She recalls feeling extremely frustrated with a third-grade standardized test: "I remember barely being able to read everything that was on there, because most of it was too hard. . . . I felt stupid and frustrated." She goes on to describe a hearing test she was administered in the third grade:

> *At one point . . . they even tested me for hearing because they thought I couldn't hear. . . . You had to put those ear, headphones on. I was so nervous all I could do was hear my heart beat. So, they told my parents I couldn't hear.*

At the conclusion of this interview, I asked Dee if there was anything else she would like to mention and she stated further her feelings with regard to testing:

> *I feel like an IQ's more the experiences you have instead of all of your book learning. I think people are intelligent in different areas and you can't be perfect in everything. I guess the tests are for society's perfect persons. I don't know. . . . I just don't think the whole testing thing is fair. I mean that's something that's sort of circumstantial. I mean, everything that's been going on in your life, whether you're stressed or not, has a great deal to do with how you do, how well you do, and how you feel that day.*

Although she has experienced the injustice of testing and has a sense of the discomfort it caused, she does not question the validity of the function of testing and has internalized the value for the necessity of tests designed to determine whether or not one has learned the important facts considered to be knowledge. Throughout the interview, she blames herself for her lack of success and her academic problems. She says, "If I was older and had more experience, I'm sure I could apply it, but I didn't." She goes on to say, "I was just slower and didn't put forth the effort that I really should have, in study."

She is unclear as to whether or not the resource center was helpful in providing her with assistance in remediating her reading and spelling problems, but she did feel that it offered her a pleasant escape from the regular classroom. "I felt relieved because the resource teacher was so much nicer and I really liked doing that, getting away from my [classroom] teacher." She goes on to say, however, with regard to the effectiveness of the resource center, "I don't know, I feel if I had had a private tutor early on, I would have been OK." Although she had had tutors from fourth through ninth grades, after school and during the summer, Dee felt that maybe she would not have had as many difficulties in school if tutoring had begun at an earlier point. The significance lies in the fact that Dee perceived herself as not being OK and that the cure required assistance from an external authority.

Dee goes on to describe herself: "I wasn't as smart as the average student. . . . I think I was as smart as the other students, I was just slower and I didn't put forth the effort that I really should have, in study, I mean, I did my homework." She is ambiguous about her own ability and once again partially sees her difficulties as being her own fault. She blames herself for her problems and for her inability to solve them. Dee was unsure about the actual label that she had been given in elementary school but remembered it as having been associated with being slow. "I was labeled, I've forgotten, they had two different labels. One meant you were just a little bit slow and the other one meant you were a little bit retarded . . . and I was the one that was a little bit slow."

In describing the actual resource center experience she commented, "I'd go down [the hall] and we'd have to have hall passes and all that stuff. I've had hall passes all my life!" The labeling process brought with it tickets of admission and identification. The "hall pass" indicated that permission was required for entrance and if denied permission, one might face the existential dilemma of remaining in the hall, therefore not being allowed to participate and at the same time wondering why. Essentially, she was being placed into a position, with the hall pass, which potentially denied her admission to the conditions that enable one to construct meaning within the competitive framework existing in our schools. Those who carry hall passes are designated as marginal; they may or may not be granted permission to compete.

Feelings of being different permeate Dee's experiences and relationships. She felt most intensely alienated from the teachers for whom she perceived herself as being a structural problem in terms of causing an interruption.

*I think they [teachers] were hostile because they wanted everyone to do this, this and this, [to] be very structured. I messed up the structure because I was slower and went to the resource room, more from being slower.*

She perceived herself as an interruption to the routine because she needed to have things explained and therefore she caused a problem for the efficient functioning of the classroom.

Dee felt also that the expectations of the teachers were lowered as a result of her being placed in the resource center.

*I remember Mrs. B [a sixth-grade teacher] not letting me be on my level of math because I did go to the resource room. . . . She was telling me that I needed to do this and finally I convinced her to let me be in there, it was a little bit above average, and I did fine. . . . Her expectation was a lot lower; it was back to the math I did in second grade, just addition and subtraction of single digits.*

Generally her memories of teachers were unpleasant, remembering teachers as being impatient and herself as being an interruption.

With regard to feelings about herself, she recalls that throughout elementary school and junior high school she felt she was slower than other students and that she needed more time. She felt different and stressed. She says she is still insecure about spelling and reading aloud. She also expressed insecurity with regard to encountering new situations and leaving familiar settings. She recalls the time of high school graduation as being an especially frightening period:

*When I graduated from high school, I didn't know what I would do because I felt so stupid. I had a very good GPA and I still have one, but I didn't think I could go to college because I wasn't smart enough to do the work.*

Self-doubt and a feeling of inadequacy continue to be a part of her living experience. She comments that during her studies in interior design she still experiences moments of uncertainty:

*I'm very cautious to look up words, sometimes every single word, especially when I'm stressed. [Sometimes I'll] have somebody proofread my work before I hand it in. . . . I think I could do it in the real world, [but] before I would hand anything to a client, I would not have it written in my scribbly writing. I think that would be uncalled for.*

In referring to the insights gathered from Giroux, Freire and other critical theorists, my interpretations of Dee's view of school is one that is shaped by a consideration of alienation and resistance.

It seems that Dee's view of school, as shaped by her experiences, revolves around the idea that school is a place of much testing and that this testing transformed her into an object to be labeled and manipulated. She felt victimized by the whims of teachers who decided how she was to be grouped, what she was taught and where she was to go. She also victimized herself by feeling that the problems were her fault and that if she tried harder, put forth more effort, had had tutoring earlier, she would have been "OK." She viewed herself as being a bureaucratic problem. She was an interruption to the schedule and class routine, and she interfered with the efficiency of the educational process. She has had "hall passes all her life"; she is different, alienated and removed.

She requires a "pass" in order to gain entrance into the educational game. She lives her life with the fear that the admission may be denied at any point along the way, that she may be designated to remain in the hall and that if that happens it would somehow be her own fault.

## Kay

The second young woman, Kay, a 17-year-old high school junior, had also been labeled as having a learning disability and had been placed in a special education resource program while in the first grade and was dismissed from special programs upon completion of fifth grade. Kay's school activities include various school clubs, honor society, track team and theatre. She has a part-time job and engages in an assortment of physical activities ranging from biking to weight lifting.

Kay's school memories are also filled with recollections of extensive and unexplained testing, leaving her feeling like a specimen.

> *I can't remember anyone ever talking to me about the tests. They probably talked to my parents, but I don't know. . . . I sort of felt like a specimen. I just felt like a guinea pig when it came to those books. You know you look at the books or something and you say what is it. And then, not knowing whether it is right or wrong and nobody tells you. . . . I feel like they are deciding. When it comes to the things that I have to do every day, I do feel like everyone is deciding if, you know, what kind of person I am or if. . . . I'm smart. . . . I've been tested so much. I remember those big books. You look at them all the time. The teachers won't tell you if you've done them right or wrong. You're just sitting there all the time.*

Tests are a tremendous source of anxiety for Kay and evoke waves of feelings of self-doubt. She recalls the competency testing in high school as causing her a great deal of fear. She was afraid because she didn't know what to expect, and she wondered whether or not she should hire a tutor in order to do as well as the other students who would be taking the competency test. She also didn't know how to fill out the information section on the test: "I have those little decisions, should I say that I'm this special person or should I go on and act normal?" She was uncertain as to whether or not she should check the learning disabilities box. In retrospect she describes the test as having been as "easy as pie" and she is aggravated with herself for having been so nervous about it. But she says,

> *So, it scares me when I don't know my results on tests and that goes back to learning disabilities. Because when I had LD, I didn't know the results. It's not like it is today, you know your results, PSAT, SAT, and competency. Then I didn't know how I was doing at all.*

With regard to resource class experiences, Kay doesn't remember exactly how she got into it, but does remember it as "not being that bad." Basically, she just feels that she has been through "a lot of schooling."

*They put me in a resource room and then I started improving. I don't know exactly how I got in there. I might have been tested. . . . I just remember being in there and that I had to go. No one told me why I had to go. I don't remember. I don't remember when I think back to school. I've been through so much school. When I think back, I remember going to the classroom and having different special classes and I feel I've had a lot of schooling.*

She recalls that being in a resource program did make her feel different and insecure.

*I remember being in class and working and I remember one day sitting in there and it was time for me to go to the resource room and everyone asking, "Where are you going?" I felt weird because no one else had to go, except a few other people. I didn't want to go; I wanted to stay in that class. I felt dumb that I had to go to special class. I didn't want anyone to know, or to miss out on something in class and have to catch up.*

In retrospect Kay considers the resource experience as having been a positive event in her life. She says, "Then it was bad, but now it's good." This is because the resource program provided her with a condition that she wanted to get away from. When she got out of the resource program, she considered it as having been the accomplishment of a goal that has given her confidence that she might not otherwise have had.

*See, I was in there but that gave me, I mean, everyone has a goal in their life, and you see, I've already accomplished one goal. You see, a lot of people haven't done that yet and they're 17, and that was a big goal. And so, like if anyone ever asked me, "What goal have you ever accomplished?" You know, just wondering. They [might] say, "Oh well. . . . I tried out for and made the theatre." I'd say, "I made the theatre, too, and made the track team, too, and I did everything you did, and I also did one more thing that you didn't do. . . . I got out of the resource room!"*

Getting out of the resource room was an achievement and a source of confidence for Kay. She says, "It was an achievement. . . . It was a big responsibility on a little mind, that's exactly what it was. But I'm glad I'm not in it now. Even though I've got my mind now, I'm glad I'm not in there." Part of Kay's "getting her mind" seems to be in being able to fully participate in the educational game. She seems to have fully accepted the necessity for and consequences of the hierarchical competitive structure of school. Although the evaluations inherent in competition are a source of fear and anxiety for her, she tenaciously hangs on to the unquestionable necessity for and legitimacy of competition. She has earned the right to play the game and to act "normal."

Kay was very clear about her label as that of being learning disabled and recalls,

> *It was a great excuse. . . . I could say, "Well, I have a learning disability, leave me alone! I'll pick it up in a minute. You might pick it up, but I'll pick it up, maybe longer." I was relieved. I was still scared that I wasn't going to do my best, but not as scared.*

She views the label as providing her with a sense of relief. Before she had been labeled learning disabled, she couldn't understand what was happening to her or why she couldn't learn in the prescribed way. "I just remember that I couldn't do anything and that I just felt dumb." The learning disability label provided Kay with a reason for her difficulties and a sense that something could be done about them. However, even though it gave her hope, it also carried with it the fear that if she didn't try hard enough, she couldn't be successful. So, in some removed way, it was still somehow her fault but not completely; she was still scared but not as scared.

Interestingly enough, although Kay considers getting out of the resource room as being one of her major life accomplishments, her actual removal from the resource room seems to have been a vague, mysterious process. She recalls, "I was getting tired of it; I didn't want to go anymore. I didn't want to be different. I was ready to get out and I got out." She remembers forgetting to attend her resource classes and the teacher deciding that she probably didn't need to come anymore. She doesn't remember any specific tests or conferences. She just remembers being told that she didn't need resource anymore. She honestly recalls that she forgot about it and then she was told she didn't have to go. So, her achievement was accomplished through an act of passive resistance of which she is not actually conscious.

Basically, Kay regarded her peers as being smarter than she and was fearful that they would think she was dumb. She describes herself as having been friendly with other students, while at the same time feeling removed from them and different. She felt that they thought she was different, but she was even more fearful that others would get the labels confused and think even worse of her.

> *I was afraid people would get confused. I don't think slow learner is as bad as mentally retarded. If they thought I was mentally retarded, I'd probably freak. I wonder what thought they'd think . . . that I was weird, strange, or different? I think they thought I was different, not strange or weird.*

Kay felt alienated from her regular classroom teachers, describing them as "impatient, old bats. I felt like some teachers were angry with me because it would take [them] longer to explain it to me." Consequently, Kay also felt that she caused a disruption of the daily school and class routine. She felt removed from the flow of the class because she was slower and needed explanations.

Kay's learning disability was considered to be a "family thing" in the sense that the other family members helped Kay. Her mother and sister also participated in local community activities that were aimed at working with the handicapped. Kay recalls that when she went to summer school her mother and sister went with her. She described her mother as being "another tutor who drilled stuff into my head." Generally she felt good about her family involvement and support. The only major conflict that Kay had with her family was concerned with Kay's attending a summer school tutorial program the summer following her dismissal from the resource program. Kay had always resented attending this program and was extremely upset with the idea of having to continue in that program after having been removed from the resource room. Kay sensitively realized that her mother was anxious about whether or not she could succeed without the additional assistance, but Kay recalls, "I was scared, scared enough for both of us."

Feelings of being different and of being fearful permeate Kay's memories regarding herself at the time of placement in a resource room. However, she now perceives herself as being confident, more determined and responsible as a result of her past experiences. She is not concerned with whether others know that she was in a resource program because she feels that most would not believe that she had actually been in the program. She says, "It's fine with me. It makes me feel good that they can't believe I was in there." Kay feels that she has her learning disability "under control" and is determined to keep it from resurfacing. She regards herself as being an example to other learning disabled individuals. "I think I'm an example, not an exception. I don't know anyone like me, but I know there are other people about like me." In a sense, she objectifies herself and places herself on display for others to note. She has committed herself to the rigors of competition and at this moment she is winning. However, I feel that in some ways this activity is displayed for the purpose of proving that she is "normal" or OK. Without being conscious of it, I feel that Kay senses that she is in a period of remission and that there is always an underlying fear that she might experience a relapse that would cause her disability to surface. I view her frantic achievement-oriented actions as being an attempt to construct a "buffer" in order to ward off the potential reoccurrence of the disease.

In general Kay's view of school is that of being a place that is to be approached with suspicion—a place where there is a lot of testing and where people are deciding about you and keeping the results hidden. School is a place where one is examined impersonally and made to feel like a specimen. She felt objectified by the testing process and alienated from herself and others as a result of that process. Decisions were being made about her in which she had no participation or awareness. She was labeled and officially recognized as being different. She sensed that she was somehow to blame for her problems and felt that if she tried hard enough to "act normal" that she would be OK. School is a place where Kay has learned well the lesson of winners and losers. She has absorbed that lesson into her very soul. She views her determined acts as being the safeguards that will hopefully enable her to remain on the winning side. She senses, but does not give voice to, the possibility that this game of "acting normal" could collapse and she would once again find herself disabled.

The evolving worldview of these two women, as having been shaped by their school experiences as a result of having been labeled and placed in special educational programs, seems to be one that is interpenetrated with themes of alienation and resistance. Their alienation from self and others is manifest in the fear and suspicion they experience in various concrete and abstract situations. Their fears are concretely recognized in testing situations and classroom settings in which the circumstances for success or failure are more or less clearly established. Voiced fears of general failure, time limitations and testing seem to be consciously recognized, but their expressions are not the consciously recognized voices of resistance!

The more subtle forms of alienation seem to be more abstractly formulated in feelings of anxiety. There is a vague sense of discomfort that seems to haunt both of these young women as they move through their lives wondering where, when, or if their existing reality is going to collapse, leaving their disabilities exposed. They walk on the borderline, "acting normal" but always carrying their "hall passes." They are extremely vulnerable to the possibility of being "found out" and consequently being denied access to commonly agreed upon conditions of completion in which meaning is constructed in our schools and our greater society. They live with an unvoiced anxiety that accompanies them in the form of doubt.

They are alienated from themselves in the sense that they doubt their authenticity and are constantly seeking validation from external sources. The ever present nagging doubt has damaged their sense of self-worth; their dignity has been diminished by doubt. They are alienated from others as a result of not being able to name themselves; they are officially recognized as being different. In Tillich's (1952) sense of the "courage to be," they have been denied the dignity which would have allowed them to construct the meaning that would have enabled them to "be as oneself." In so doing, they are denied the possibility of constructing meaning as "being as oneself" in community. They are robbed of dignity and ultimately alienated from self and others. They have been objectified and denied the opportunity of reciprocally engaging in relationships in which there is the possibility of dynamic interchange between subjects.

The theme of resistance, manifest as an attempt to hold on to one's dignity and to affirm oneself as a human being with the right to name oneself, is apparent in the few but persistent acts of not accepting the prescribed labels and placements. Although not so apparent to themselves or others, both women resisted attempts by authorities to completely determine their fate. Passively forgetting to attend the resource program, not fully recognizing the label that had been prescribed and actively confronting teachers about academic groupings are examples of acts of resistance. In spite of these few acts, it seems that a worldview dominated by a sense of alienation prevails. The anguish of this alienation is made more painful as one recognizes that neither Kay nor Dee is able to name her condition.

Their worldview is one in which the hegemony, transmission-productivity, educational paradigm is reflected. Dee and Kay have been perceived by others and themselves as being on the margin and, in wishing and hoping to be admitted, have not questioned seriously the existing flaws in the dominant structure as reflected in the educational system. They have not examined the value of the conditions that enable one to construct meaning or that allow one to be received into the school hierarchy. They have internalized the ethic of competition and abide by the rules of evaluation which determine one's worth. The diagnostic-prescriptive educational view has contributed to their further oppression as they perceive their own problems and difficulties within a psychological framework. They are unable to place themselves within the social context by constructing a history that is sociologically framed. They are the victims of the productivity-transmission rationality, and they have internalized the consciousness of their oppressors. Dee and Kay are alienated in their isolation. Their acts of resistance have been precarious efforts to become a part of the dignity-denying, oppressive structure that further intensifies their anxiety and insecurity.

These stories reach far beyond our typical educational concerns regarding positive self-esteem to much more serious and wrenching problems of marginality, exclusion and alienation. The voices of Dee and Kay call into our consciousness the responsibility we have as educators for responding to and embracing those who come before us, the animal faces, the empty faces and the noble ones alike. Their stories cause us to confront the inconsistencies in our educational practices in which we purposefully seek to exclude and avoid the misshapen and empty ones. The voices of these two women point out that our good intentions and our focus upon productivity and competition are handicapping evils that we can no longer afford to avoid. Camus cautions us regarding the consequences of such a lack of scrutiny:

On the whole, men are more good than bad; that however isn't the real point; but they are more or less ignorant, and it is this that we call vice or virtue; the most incorrigible vice being that of ignorance that fancies it knows everything and therefore claims for itself the right to kill. The soul of the murderer is blind; and there can be no true goodness nor true love without the utmost clear-sightedness. (Camus, 1972, p. 124)

We must examine our taken-for-granted practice of meeting those who come before us. Our good intention as expressed in our educational desire to help has degenerated into the practice of sorting, labeling and tracking special education students so that we can provide them with what we refer to, from an unexamined position, as being the most appropriate and specialized instruction. This must be revealed as the dignity-denying and alienating process it is. In assuming that we know everything, we have claimed the right to kill, we dismiss the already disenfranchised and we blame them for their disempowerment. We must look more closely at our medical model of help and reappraise our notion of successful education as it is currently understood in terms of utility, productivity and competition. Evaluation and competition, the prized elements of today's educational practice, need to be exposed for the roles they play in establishing and maintaining the educational hierarchy, a hierarchy that systematically excludes and dismisses vast numbers of our students and prevents them from obtaining the promised "keys to the kingdom" as they participate in the educational obstacle course.

As we listen to the voices of the handicapped expressing their moral outrage at being labeled and excluded, the taken-for-granted assumptions that this process is the "lesser of evils" or in the "best interest" of those being identified begins to turn on itself. The unexamined acceptance of competition and productivity also begins to surface as we listen to the outrage of those who have been denied access to success as a result of an inability to compete and/or produce. In hearing the stories of Dee and Kay, we take a second look at our good intentions and the ways in which we respond to those who come before us. Currently, who you are and how far you go on the educational hierarchy depends upon how much you can produce and what you can do. In special education, no matter how much we talk about enabling one to aspire to his/her full potential, the current framework for success, specifically competition and productivity, ultimately requires that some of us will be more highly prized and valued in this system than others. Some of us have more worth and greater potential as competitors and producers than others and therefore will be the recipients of the educational rewards and benefits at the cost of those who have been excluded.

The voices of the labeled, when contemplated critically and when examined with clear-sightedness, affirm the insights of Maria Montessori as she discusses the rewards and punishments of educational competition and productivity:

> . . . in school there is only one prize for all those of good will who enter the race, a fact that generates pride, envy and rivalries instead of that thrill coming from effort, humility and love which all can experience. In this way we create conflict not simply between school and social progress but also between the school and religion. One day a child will ask himself if the prizes won at school were not rather obstacles on the way to eternal life, or if the punishments with which he was humiliated when he was in no position to defend himself did not make him one of those "hungering" and thirsting after justice. . . . (Montessori, 1976, pp. 13 and 14)

The stories of our handicapped, the misshapen, the empty faces and the animal faces, poignantly reveal the injustice that is manifest in our current educational practice grounded in competition and production, which serve exclusive ends.

The critical consciousness of emancipatory praxis, which has given us the "clear-sightedness" to examine our "good intentions," has also provided us with the tools to begin to rethink the educational values of productivity and competition. Thus the anguish of the handicapped is felt as we recognize that the vehicles of educational success are denied them. The handicapped personify the greater failings of the transmission, productivity ethic in educational practice. Regardless of how well we sort, track and label, many of our handicapped will remain unable to participate in the educational game. As educators, many of us avoid a deeper examination of the failing of the handicapped because it highlights the more profound alienation of our general educational practices. Namely, the handicapped point out the inadequacy of remediation and the futility of help when help and remediation are placed within a context of evaluation, competition and utility.

To become clear-sighted so that we as educators do not sustain a fundamentally evil practice seems to be the message illuminated by the anguish, hegemony and confusion of Dee and Kay. The process of becoming clear-sighted appropriately addresses the educational needs of many of our labeled students who are disproportionately represented in our underclasses by racial and ethnic minorities and are frequently the victims of poverty.

The educational response would be one of engaging in dialogue for the purpose of facilitating the conversation out of which students could acquire more language with which to begin to name themselves and their experiences. Finding one's voice and naming oneself as oppressed and outraged rather than slow, strange, weird or different offers the opportunity to criticize the existing educational hierarchy and to move beyond the defeating cycle of blaming the victim for failure. As Freire points out,

> Only when the people of a dependent society break out of the culture of silence and with their right to speak—only, that is when radical structural changes transform the dependent society—can such a society as a whole cease to be silent toward the director society. (Freire, 1985, p. 73)

This is a liberating pedagogy based upon finding one's voice while engaging in critical dialogue about one's actions and experiences and which can result in sustained critical reflection, examined practice and empowerment.

It seems that fostering a critical consciousness is truly a noble educational ideal and one toward which the acts of teaching ought to be directed. After all, it is Dewey who writes, "We are free to the degree in which we act knowing what we are about" (Dewey, 1929, p. 250). Further, Dewey reminds us,

> Genuine freedom, in short is intellectual; it rests in the trained power of thought, an ability to "turn things over" to look at matters deliberately, to judge the amount and kind of evidence requisite for decision is at hand, and if not, to tell where and how to seek such evidence. (Dewey, 1934, p. 67)

For many teachers and students alike, educational aims grounded in dialogue and critical consciousness offer the hope of freedom and empowerment.

However, just as many handicapped individuals are alienated by their inability to produce and compete, so too are they excluded by the empowerment process that requires rational, critical, logical and expressive skills that many handicapped people lack. Consequently, they may remain in the precarious care of the emancipated who may or may not view them affectionately. The vulnerable population of the handicapped, who lack the intellectual and emotional capacities necessary to participate in the empowering relationship and emancipating dialogue, remain excluded and voiceless.

As John Merrick, the Elephant Man, screams, "I am a human being!" and as the mentally retarded adolescent boy coloring a Thanksgiving picture asks, "Am I a people?" while the aide taunts him by saying, "Turkey, color yourself! Turkey!", one becomes painfully aware that the anguish expressed here comes from a much more fundamental exclusion. It is an exclusion that has resulted not in a damaged self-concept or a lowered self-esteem but in the denial of one's human dignity. The outrage and pain expressed by the handicapped as they come up against the competitive, productive sorting practice of our educational structure are a response to their objectification and a resistance to their being denied the relationship within which they can be affirmed.

In reexamining our good intentions in light of the exclusion of the handicapped that takes place not only as a result of the production-transmission-competition values of traditional educational practice but also occurs within the empowering thrust of critical pedagogy, one begins to rethink the purpose of teaching and the composition of help. If the fundamental starting point, as the Elephant Man suggests, is the recognition of our humanity, then the character of help changes radically. The task of facing those who come before us is one of recognizing and beholding them as valued and cherished human beings. Help becomes not an act of fixing, imposing or shaping but instead one of love, commitment and responsibility. This is not to be trivialized or sentimentalized but to be gravely contemplated.

We are humbled and sobered by the words of Abraham Heschel as he addresses a class of graduating nursing students. Although he recognizes the nobility of all "helping" professions and affirms those who choose to do such work, he seriously reminds us of the sacredness and weight of genuine help when he says, "We must never forget that when we truly wish to help our fellow human beings we must remove our shoes, for the ground we walk upon, when we seek to help, is sacred ground."

Help is not prescriptive; we do not know nor can we determine how someone else should be; however, within a partnership we might foster the care and compassion with which to affirm each other's dignity. The teaching-helping act is a calling to participate in the partnership in such a way that we do not diminish our capacity to confirm or be confirmed. The educational mission and calling require action that passionately propels us to engage in the mystery. Such engagement leaves us with awe and wonder, enabling us to become aware of the mystery but never resulting in our comprehension of it. Heschel writes,

> Awe is an intuition for the dignity of all things, a realization that things not only are what they are but also stand, however remotely, for something supreme. Awe is a sense for the transcendence, for the reference everywhere to mystery beyond all things . . . what we cannot comprehend by analysis, we become aware of in awe. (Heschel, 1965, pp. 88–89)

"With an intuition for the dignity of all things," we must face those who come before us, recognizing the wonder and the mystery. The alienation of Dee and Kay, the anguish of the Elephant Man and the confusion of the young man inquiring into his humanity direct us to the fundamental ground upon which the acts of teaching rest. The voices and the faces of the handicapped require us to center ourselves as educators within the caring acts of love that illuminate the questions that deal with who we are and what we are about. We must be prepared to meet and receive those who come before us, the empty, the misshapen and the noble, not to make them less misshapen or more noble but so that we may each gain a deeper understanding of what it means to be here or at least to be able to wonder why.

This wondering process and its significance are poetically and simply illustrated by Albert in Alice Walker's *The Color Purple*. As Albert grapples with the dilemma of why we suffer, why we are men or women he concludes that "it don't mean nothing if you don't ask why you here, period." He goes on to say,

> I think us here to wonder, myself. To wonder. To ast. And that in wondering bout the big things and asting bout the big things, you learn about the little ones, almost by accident. But you never know nothing more about the big things than you start out with. The more I wonder, he say, the more I love. (Walker, 1982, p. 247)

In our more reflective moments, the examination of the exclusion of the handicapped enables us to seriously contemplate educational theories, policies and practices. The recognition of the marginality and the hegemony of these individuals as they deny who they are as they strive for inclusion enables us to wonder. Their existence and their resistance help us to focus upon the big questions, finding the pieces that address the smaller ones in the process. The handicapped challenge us and remind us that we are here to wonder why! Their presence requires us to ponder the tensions and the paradoxes.

So where are we? If educational aims and ideals should be generated from a platform of love and affirmation of human dignity rather than from the existing positivistic, technical, productive, competitive frameworks, then is there not a cry for a different way of conceptualizing and conversing about our educational theory and practice? If we take seriously the voices of Dee and Kay, then do we not have a responsibility for attempting to construct a liberating and empowering pedagogy? Further, if the screams of the Elephant Man and the confusion of the mentally retarded adolescent have any significance, then what is it educationally that we can no longer afford to leave to chance?

We must take clear-sighted action and be willing to accept the responsibility for the risk we take as we turn toward a different discourse and as we turn away from the technical language that frames our existing view of educational practice. As Philip Jackson points out, if we do not examine the serious problems of our current educational practice with an intent to do more than just remediate the symptom, then we may, through our good intentions, be repairing a structure that is moving in the wrong direction:

> After all, it is easier to put oil on squeaky wheels than to ask about where the vehicle is headed in the first place and to ponder the necessity of a change in direction. The danger of course, is that by so doing we may create a smoothly running machine that is moving in the wrong direction or not at all. (Noll, 1987, p. 111)

In light of the dilemmas illuminated while reflecting upon issues of inclusion, affirmation, love and help within the context of special education, it seems apparent that the current technical language, although facilitating a superficially smoothly functioning practice, ultimately highlights a vacuum. Technically framed educational discourse does not have the words for contemplating relationship, compassion or confirmation. It points to an empty, lifeless void, one in which we are inarticulate and illiterate when it comes to dignity-talk, which Donald Vandenberg refers to as "talk of the heart." "It may be that dignity-talk is less intelligible to the intellect than to the heart" (Vandenberg, 1983, p. 31). We can no longer ignore the evil that is being perpetuated by our unexamined good intentions. We must at the risk of appearing "sentimental, fuzzy and pious," thereby repelling many of our readers (Macdonald & Purpel, 1987, p. 186), turn to the religious language that allows us to begin to voice love, relationship and justice.

It becomes apparent that whatever action we take, it entails moral responsibility. We are as responsible for our unexamined good intentions as we are for our clear-sighted ones. We, as educators, must have the courage to move from a naive, unexamined position of neutral, technical, objective, lifeless practice to intellectually and compassionately responsible action framed by spiritual discourse. Such discourse enables us to examine our good intentions and to change our direction.

# REFERENCES

Buber, M. (1965). *Between man and man.* New York: Macmillan Publishing Company.

Camus, A. (1972). *The plague.* New York: Vintage Books.

Dewey, J. (1929). *The quest for certainty: A study of the relation of knowledge and action.* New York: Minton, Balch and Company.

Dewey, J. (1934). *A common faith.* New Haven: Yale University Press.

Freire, P. (1985). *Politics of education.* New York: The Continuum Publishing Company.

Giroux, H. A. (1983). *Theory and resistance in education: A pedagogy for the opposition.* South Hadley, MA: Bergin and Garvey Publishers, Inc.

Gress, J., & Purpel, D. E. (1978). *Curriculum: An introduction to the field.* Berkeley, CA: McCutchan Publishing Corporation.

Heschel, A. J. (1965). *Who is man?* Stanford, CA: Stanford University Press.

Macdonald, J. B., & Purpel, D. E. (1987). Curriculum and planning visions and metaphors. *Journal of Curriculum and Supervision, 2*(2), 178–192.

Montessori, M. (1976). *The discovery of the child.* New York: Ballantine Books.

Noll, J. W. (1987). *Taking sides: Clashing views on controversial educational issues.* Guilford, CT: The Dushkin Publishing Group, Inc.

Tillich, P. (1952). *The courage to be.* New Haven: Yale University Press.

Vandenberg, D. (1983). *Human rights in education.* New York: Philosophical Library, Inc.

Walker, A. (1982). *The color purple.* New York: Washington Square Press.

# 16
▼▼▼▼▼▼▼

# English Only:
# The Tongue-Tying of America*

Donaldo Macedo

During the past decade conservative educators such as ex-secretary of education William Bennett and Diane Ravitch have mounted an unrelenting attack on bilingual and multicultural education. These conservative educators tend to recycle old assumptions about the "melting pot theory" and our "common culture," assumptions designed primarily to maintain the status quo. Maintained is a status quo that functions as a cultural reproduction mechanism which systematically does not allow other cultural subjects, who are considered outside of the mainstream, to be present in history. These cultural subjects who are profiled as the "other" are but palely represented in history within our purportedly democratic society in the form of Black History Month, Puerto Rican Day, and so forth. This historical constriction was elegantly captured by an 11th-grade Vietnamese student in California:

> I was so excited when my history teacher talked about the Vietnam War. Now at last, I thought, now we will study about my country. We didn't really study it. Just for one day, though, my country was real again. (Olsen, 1988, p. 68)

The incessant attack on bilingual education which claims that it serves to tongue-tie students in their native language not only negate the multilingual and multicultural nature of U.S. society, but blindly ignores the empirical evidence that has been amply documented in support of bilingual education. An example of a truly tongue-tied America materialized when the ex-foreign minister of the Soviet Union, Mr. Eduard Shevardnadze, began to deliver a speech in Russian during a recent commencement ceremony at Boston Uni-

---

*Macedo, Donaldo. "English Only: The Tongue-Tying of America." From *Journal of Education*. Vol. 173, No. 2, 1991. Reprinted by permission of Boston University.

versity. The silence that ensued was so overwhelming that one could hear a pin drop. Over 99% of the audience was saved from their monolingualism thanks to the intervention of an interpreter. In fact, the present overdose of monolingualism and Anglocentrism that dominates the current educational debate not only contributes to a type of mind-tied America, but also is incapable of producing educators and leaders who can rethink what it means to prepare students to enter the ever-changing, multilingual, and multicultural world of the 21st century.

It is both academically dishonest and misleading to simply point to some failures of bilingual education without examining the lack of success of linguistic minority students within a larger context of a general failure of public education in major urban centers. Furthermore, the English Only position points to a pedagogy of exclusion that views the learning of English as education itself. English Only advocates fail to question under what conditions English will be taught and by whom. For example, immersing non-English-speaking students in English as a Second Language programs taught by untrained music, art, and social science teachers (as is the case in Massachusetts with the grandfather clause in ESL Certification) will hardly accomplish the avowed goals of the English Only Movement. The proponents of English Only also fail to raise two other fundamental questions. First, if English is the most effective educational language, how can we explain that over 60 million Americans are illiterate or functionally illiterate (Kozol, 1985, p. 4)? Second, if education solely in English can guarantee linguistic minorities a better future, as educators like William Bennett promise, why do the majority of Black Americans, whose ancestors have been speaking English for over 200 years, find themselves still relegated to ghettos?

I want to argue in this paper that the answer lies not in technical questions of whether English is a more viable language of instruction or the repetitive promise that it offers non-English-speaking students "full participation first in their school and later in American society" (Silber, 1991, p. 7). This position assumes that English is in fact a superior language and that we live in a classless, race-blind society. I want to propose that decisions about how to educate non-English-speaking students cannot be reduced to issues of language, but rest in a full understanding of the ideological elements that generate and sustain linguistic, racial, and sex discrimination. That is, educators need to develop, as Henry Giroux has suggested, "a politics and pedagogy around a new language capable of acknowledging the multiple, contradictory, and complex subject positions people occupy within different social, cultural, and economic locations" (1991, p. 27). By shifting the linguistic issue to an ideological terrain we will challenge conservative educators to confront the Berlin Wall of racism, classism, and economic deprivation which characterizes the lived experiences of minorities in U.S. public schools. For example, J. Anthony Lukas succinctly captures the ideological elements that promote racism and segregation in schools in his analysis of desegregation in the Boston

Public Schools. Lukas cites a trip to Charlestown High School, where a group of Black parents experienced firsthand the stark reality their children were destined to endure. Although the headmaster assured them that "violence, intimidation, or racial slurs would not be tolerated," they could not avoid the racial epithets on the walls: "Welcome Niggers," "Niggers Suck," "White Power," "KKK," "Bus is for Zulu," and "Be illiterate, fight busing." As those parents were boarding the bus, "they were met with jeers and catcalls 'go home niggers. Keep going all the way to Africa!' " This racial intolerance led one parent to reflect, "My god, what kind of hell am I sending my children into?" (Lukas, 1985, p. 282). What could her children learn at a school like that except to hate? Even though forced integration of schools in Boston exacerbated the racial tensions in the Boston Public Schools, one should not overlook the deep-seated racism that permeates all levels of the school structure. According to Lukas:

> Even after Elvira "Pixie" Paladino's election to The Boston School Committee [in 1975] she was heard muttering about "jungle bunnies" and "pickaninnies." And John "Bigga" Kerrigan [head of the School Committee] prided himself on the unrestrained invective ("I may be a prick, but at least I'm a consistent prick"), particularly directed at Blacks ("savages") and the liberal media ("mother-fucking maggots") and Lem Tucker, a Black correspondent for ABC News, whom Kerrigan described as "one generation away from swinging in the trees," a remark he illustrated by assuming his hands upwards, and scratching his armpits (Lukas, 1985, p. 282).

Against this landscape of violent racism perpetrated against racial minorities, and also against linguistic minorities, one can understand the reasons for the high dropout rate in the Boston public schools (approximately 50%). Perhaps racism and other ideological elements are part of a school reality which forces a high percentage of students to leave school, only later to be profiled by the very system as dropouts or "poor and unmotivated students." One could argue that the above incidents occurred during a tumultuous time of racial division in Boston's history, but I do not believe that we have learned a great deal from historically dangerous memories to the degree that our leaders continue to invite racial tensions as evidenced in the Willie Horton presidential campaign issue and the present quota for jobs as an invitation once again to racial divisiveness.

It is very curious that this new-found concern of English Only advocates for limited English proficiency students does not interrogate those very ideological elements that psychologically and emotionally harm these students far more than the mere fact that English may present itself as a temporary barrier to an effective education. It would be more socially constructive and beneficial if the zeal that propels the English Only movement were diverted toward social struggles designed to end violent racism and structures of poverty, homelessness, and family breakdown, among other social ills that characterize the lived experiences of minorities in the United States. If these social issues are not dealt with appropriately, it is naive to think that the acquisition of the English language alone will, somehow, magically eclipse the raw and cruel injustices and oppression perpetrated against the dispossessed class of minorities in the United States. According to Peter McLaren, these dispossessed minority students who

> populate urban settings in places such as Howard Beach, Ozone Park, El Barrio, are more likely to be forced to learn about Eastern Europe in ways set forth by neo-conservative multiculturalists than they are to learn about the Harlem Renaissance, Mexico, Africa, the Caribbean, or Aztec or Zulu culture. (McLaren, 1991, p. 7)

While arguing for the use of the students' native language in their educational development, I would like to make it very clear that the bilingual education goal should never be to restrict students to their own vernacular. This linguistic constriction inevitably leads to a linguistic ghetto. Educators must understand fully the broader meaning of the use of students' language as a requisite for their empowerment. That is, empowerment should never be limited to what Stanley Aronowitz describes as "the process of appreciating and loving oneself" (1985). In addition to this process, empowerment should also be a means that enables students "to interrogate and selectively appropriate those aspects of the dominant culture that will provide them with the basis for defining and transforming, rather than merely serving, the wider social order" (Giroux & McLaren, 1986, p. 17). This means that educators should understand the value of mastering the standard English language of the wider society. It is through the full appropriation of the standard English language that linguistic minority students find themselves linguistically empowered to engage in dialogue with various sectors of the wider society. What I must reiterate is that educators should never allow the limited proficient students' native language to be silenced by a distorted legitimation of the standard English language. Linguistic minority students' language should never be sacrified, since it is the only means through which they make sense of their own experience in the world.

Given the importance of the standard English language in the education of linguistic minority students, I must agree with the members of the Institute for Research in English Acquisition and Development when they quote Antonio Gramsci in their brochure:

> Without the mastery of the common standard version of the national language, one is inevitably destined to function only at the periphery of national life and, especially, outside the national and political mainstream. (READ, 1990)

But these English Only advocates fail to tell the other side of Antonio Gramsci's argument, which warns us:

Each time that in one way or another, the question of language comes to the fore, that signifies that a series of other problems is about to emerge, the formation and enlarging of the ruling class, the necessity to establish more "intimate" and sure relations between the ruling groups and the popular masses, that is, the reorganization of cultural hegemony. (Gramsci, 1971, p. 16)

This selective selection of Gramsci's position on language points to the hidden curriculum with which the English Only movement seeks to promote a monolithic ideology. It is also part and parcel of an ongoing attempt at "reorganization of cultural hegemony" as evidenced by the unrelenting attack by conservative educators on multicultural education and curriculum diversity. The ideological force behind the call for a common culture can be measured by the words of syndicated columnist Pat Buchanan, who urged his fellow conservatives "to wage a cultural revolution in the 90's as sweeping as the political revolution of the 80's" (Giroux, 1991, p. 15). In other words, as Henry Giroux has shown, the conservative cultural revolution's

more specific expressions have been manifest on a number of cultural fronts including schools, the art world, and the more blatant attacks aimed at rolling back the benefits constructed of civil rights and social welfare reforms constructed over the last three decades. What is being valorized in the dominant language of the culture industry is an undemocratic approach to social authority and a politically regressive move to reconstruct American life within the script of Eurocentrism, racism, and patriarchy. (Giroux, 1991, p. 15)

Derrick Z. Jackson, in his brilliant article "The End of the Second Reconstruction," lays bare the dominant conservative ideology that informs the present cultural hegemony when he argues that "From 1884 to 1914, more than 3,600 African-Americans were lynched. Lynching is passé today. AIDS, infant mortality, violence out of despair, and gutted public education do the same trick in inner cities neatly redlined by banks" (1991, p. 27). In contrast to the zeal for a common culture and English only, these conservative educators have remained ominously silent about forms of racism, inequality, subjugation, and exploitation that daily serve to wage symbolic and real violence against those children who by virtue of their language, race, ethnicity, class, or gender are not treated in schools with the dignity and respect all children warrant in a democracy. Instead of reconstituting education around an urban and cultural studies approach which takes the social, cultural, political, and economic divisions of education and everyday life as the primary categories for understanding contemporary schooling, conservative educators have recoiled in an attempt to salvage the status quo. That is, they try to keep the present unchanged even though, as Renato Constantino points out:

Within the living present there are imperceptible changes which make the status quo a moving reality. . . . Thus a new policy based on the present as past and not on the present as future is backward for it is premised not on evolving conditions but on conditions that are already dying away. (1978, p. 201)

One such not so imperceptible change is the rapid growth of minority representation in the labor force. As such, the conservative leaders and educators are digging this country's economic grave by their continued failure to educate minorities. As Lew Ferlerger and Jay Mandle convincingly argue, "Unless the educational attainment of minority populations in the United States improves, the country's hopes for resuming high rates of growth and an increasing standard of living look increasingly dubious" (1991, p. 12).

In addition to the real threat to the economic fabric of the United States, the persistent call for English language only in education smacks of backwardness in the present conjuncture of our ever-changing multicultural and multilingual society. Furthermore, these conservative educators base their language policy argument on the premise that English education in this country is highly effective. On the contrary. As Patrick Courts clearly argues in his book *Literacy for Empowerment* (1991), English education is failing even middle-class and upper-class students. He argues that English reading and writing classes are mostly based on workbooks and grammar lessons, lessons which force students to "bark at print" or fill in the blanks. Students engage in grudgingly banal exercises such as practicing correct punctuation and writing sample business letters. Books used in their classes are, Courts points out, too often in the service of commercially prepared ditto sheets and workbooks. Courts's account suggests that most school programs do not take advantage of the language experiences that the majority of students have had before they reach school. These teachers become the victims of their own professional ideology when they delegitimize the language experiences that students bring with them into the classroom.

Courts's study is basically concerned with middle-class and upper-middle-class students unburdened by racial discrimination and poverty, students who have done well in elementary and high school settings and are now populating the university lecture halls and seminar rooms. If schools are failing these students, the situation does not bode well for those students less economically, socially, and politically advantaged. It is toward the linguistic minority students that I would like to turn my discussion now.

## THE ROLE OF LANGUAGE IN THE EDUCATION OF LINGUISTIC MINORITY STUDENTS

Within the last two decades, the issue of bilingual education has taken on a heated importance among educators. Unfortunately, the debate that has emerged tends to recycle old assumptions and values regarding the meaning and usefulness of the students' native language in education. The notion that education of linguistic minority students is a matter of learning the standard English language still informs the vast majority of bilingual programs and manifests its logic in the renewed emphasis on technical reading and writing skills.

I want to reiterate in this paper that the education of linguistic minority students cannot be viewed as simply the development of skills aimed at acquiring the standard English language. English Only proponents seldom discuss the pedagogical structures that will enable these students to access other bodies of knowledge. Nor do they interrogate the quality of ESL instruction provided to the linguistic minority students and the adverse material conditions under which these students learn English. The view that teaching English constitutes education sustains a notion of ideology that systematically negates rather than makes meaningful the cultural experiences of the subordinate linguistic groups who are, by and large, the objects of its policies. For the education of linguistic minority students to become meaningful it has to be situated within a theory of cultural production and viewed as an integral part of the way in which people produce, transform, and reproduce meaning. Bilingual education, in this sense, must be seen as a medium that constitutes and affirms the historical and existential moments of lived culture. Hence, it is an eminently political phenomenon, and it must be analyzed within the context of a theory of power relations and an understanding of social and cultural reproduction and production. By "cultural reproduction" I refer to collective experiences that function in the interest of the dominant groups rather than in the interest of the oppressed groups that are objects of its policies. Bilingual education programs in the United States have been developed and implemented under the cultural reproduction model leading to a de facto neocolonial educational model. I use "cultural production" to refer to specific groups of people producing, mediating, and confirming the mutual ideological elements that merge from and reaffirm their daily lived experiences. In this case, such experiences are rooted in the interest of individual and collective self-determination. It is only through a cultural production model that we can achieve a truly democratic and liberatory educational experience. I will return to this issue later.

While the various debates in the past two decades may differ in their basic assumptions about the education of linguistic minority students, they all share one common feature: they all ignore the role of language as a major force in the construction of human subjectivities. That is, they ignore the way language may either confirm or deny the life histories and experiences of the people who use it.

The pedagogical and political implications in education programs for linguistic minority students are far-reaching and yet largely ignored. These programs, for example, often contradict a fundamental principle of reading, namely that students learn to read faster and with better comprehension when taught in their native tongue. The immediate recognition of familiar words and experiences enhances the development of a positive self-concept in children who are somewhat insecure about the status of their language and culture. For this reason, and to be consistent with the plan to construct a democratic society free from vestiges of oppression, a minority literacy program must be rooted in the cultural capital of subordinate groups and have as its point of departure their own language.

Educators must develop radical pedagogical structures which provide students with the opportunity to use their own reality as a basis of literacy. This includes, obviously, the language they bring to the classroom. To do otherwise is to deny minority students the rights that lie at the core of a democratic education. The failure to base a literacy program on the minority students' language means that oppositional forces can neutralize the efforts of educators and political leaders to achieve decolonization of schooling. It is of tantamount importance that the incorporation of the minority language as the primary language of instruction in education of linguistic minority students be given top priority. It is through their own language that linguistic minority students will be able to reconstruct their history and their culture.

I want to argue that the minority language has to be understood within the theoretical framework that generates it. Put another way, the ultimate meaning and value of the minority language is not to be found by determining how systematic and rule-governed it is. We know that already. Its real meaning has to be understood through the assumptions that govern it, and it has to be understood via the social, political, and ideological relations to which it points. Generally speaking, this issue of effectiveness and validity often hides the true role of language in the maintenance of the values and interests of the dominant class. In other words, the issue of effectiveness and validity becomes a mask that obfuscates questions about the social, political, and ideological order within which the minority language exists.

If an emancipatory and critical education program is to be developed in the United States for linguistic minority students in which they become "subjects" rather than "objects," educators must understand the productive quality of language. James Donald puts it this way:

> I take language to be productive rather than reflective of social reality. This means calling into question the assumption that we, as speaking subjects, simply use language to organize and express our ideas and experiences. On the contrary, language is one of the most important social practices through which we come to experience ourselves as subjects. . . . My point here is that once we get beyond the idea of language as no more than a medium of communication, as a tool equally and neutrally available to all parties in cultural exchanges, then we can begin to examine language both as a practice of signification and also as a site for culture struggle and as a mechanism which produces antagonistic relations between different social groups. (Donald, 1982, p. 44)

It is to the antagonistic relationship between the minority and dominant speakers that I want to turn now. The antagonistic nature of the minority language has never been fully explored. In order to more clearly discuss this issue of antagonism, I will use Donald's distinction between oppressed language and repressed language. Using Donald's categories, the "negative" way of posing the minority language question is to view it in terms of oppression—that is, seeing the minority language as "lacking" the dominant standard features which usually serve as a point of reference for the minority language. By far the most common questions concerning the minority language in the United States are posed from the oppression perspective. The alternative view of the minority language is that it is repressed in the standard dominant language. In this view, minority language as a repressed language could, if spoken, challenge the privileged standard linguistic dominance. Educators have failed to recognize the "positive" promise and antagonistic nature of the minority language. It is precisely on these dimensions that educators must demystify the standard dominant language and the old assumptions about its inherent superiority. Educators must develop liberatory and critical bilingual programs informed by a radical pedagogy so that the minority language will cease to provide its speakers the experience of subordination and, moreover, may be brandished as a weapon of resistance to the dominance of the dominant standard language of the curriculum.

In this sense, the students' language is the only means by which they can develop their own voice, a prerequisite to the development of a positive sense of self-worth. As Giroux elegantly states, the students' voice "is the discursive means to make themselves 'heard' and to define themselves as active authors of their worlds" (Giroux & McLaren, 1986, p. 235). The authorship of one's own world also implies the use of one's own language, and relates to what Mikhail Bakhtin describes as "retelling a story in one's own words" (Giroux & McLaren, 1986, p. 235).

## A DEMOCRATIC AND LIBERATORY EDUCATION FOR LINGUISTIC MINORITY STUDENTS

In maintaining a certain coherence with the educational plan to reconstruct new and more democratic educational programs for linguistic minority students, educators and political leaders need to create a new school grounded in a new educational praxis, expressing different concepts of education consonant with the principles of a democratic, multicultural, and multilingual society. In order for this to happen, the first step is to identify the objectives of the inherent colonial education that informs the majority of bilingual programs in the United States. Next, it is necessary to analyze how colonialist methods used by the dominant schools function, legitimize the Anglocentric values and meaning, and at the same time negate the history, culture, and language practices of the majority of linguistic minority students. The new school, so it is argued, must also be informed by a radical bilingual pedagogy, which would make concrete such values as solidarity, social responsibility, and creativity. In the democratic development of bilingual programs rooted in a liberatory ideology, linguistic minority students become "subjects" rather than mere "objects" to be assimilated blindly into an often hostile dominant "common" culture. A democratic and liberatory education needs to move away from traditional approaches, which emphasize the acquisition of mechanical basic skills while divorcing education from its ideological and historical contexts. In attempting to meet this goal, it purposely must reject the conservative principles embedded in the English Only movement I have discussed earlier. Unfortunately, many bilingual programs sometimes unknowingly reproduce one common feature of the traditional approaches to education by ignoring the important relationship between language and the cultural capital of the students at whom bilingual education is aimed. The result is the development of bilingual programs whose basic assumptions are at odds with the democratic spirit that launched them.

Bilingual program development must be largely based on the notion of a democratic and liberatory education, in which education is viewed "as one of the major vehicles by which 'oppressed' people are able to participate in the sociohistorical transformation of their society" (Walmsley, 1981, p. 74). Bilingual education, in this sense, is grounded in a critical reflection of the cultural capital of the oppressed. It becomes a vehicle by which linguistic minority students are equipped with the necessary tools to reappropriate their history, culture, and language practices. It is, thus, a way to enable the linguistic minority students to reclaim "those historical and existential experiences that are devalued in everyday life by the dominant culture in order to be both validated and critically understood" (Giroux, 1983, p. 226). To do otherwise is to deny these students their very democratic rights. In fact, the criticism that bilingual and multicultural education unwisely question the traditions and values of our so-called "common culture" as suggested by Kenneth T. Jackson (1991) is both antidemocratic and academically dishonest. Multicultural education and curriculum diversity did not create the S & L scandal, the Iran-Contra debacle, or the extortion of minority properties by banks, the stewards of the "common culture," who charged minorities exorbitant loan-sharking interest rates. Multicultural education and curriculum diversity did not force Joachim Maitre, dean of the College of Communication at Boston University, to choose the hypocritical moral high ground to excoriate the popular culture's "bleak moral content," all the while plagiarizing 15 paragraphs of a conservative comrade's text.

The learning of English language skills alone will not enable linguistic minority students to acquire the critical tools "to awaken and liberate them from their mystified and distorted views of themselves and their world" (Giroux, 1983, p. 226). For example, speaking English has not enabled African-Americans to change this society's practice of jailing more Blacks than even South Africa, and this society spending over 7 billion dollars to keep African-American men in jail while spending only 1 billion dollars educating Black males (Black, 1991).

Educators must understand the all-encompassing role the dominant ideology has played in this mystification and distortion of our so-called "common culture" and our "common language." They must also recognize the antagonistic relationship between the "common culture" and those who, by virtue of their race, language, ethnicity, and gender, have been relegated to the margins. Finally, educators must develop bilingual programs based on the theory of cultural production. In other words, linguistic minority students must be provided the opportunity to become actors in the reconstruction of a more democratic and just society. In short, education conducted in English only is alienating to linguistic minority students, since it denies them the fundamental tools for reflection, critical thinking, and social interaction. Without the cultivation of their native language, and robbed of the opportunity for reflection and critical thinking, linguistic minority students find themselves unable to re-create their culture and history. Without the reappropriation of their culture, the valorization of their lived experiences, English Only supporters' vacuous promise that the English language will guarantee students "full participation first in their school and later in American society" (Silber, 1991, p. 7) can hardly be a reality.

## REFERENCES

Aronowitz, S. (1985, May). "Why should Johnny read." *Village Voice Literary Supplement*, p. 13.

Black, C. (1991, January 13). Paying the high price for being the world's no. 1 jailor. *Boston Sunday Globe*, p. 67.

Constantino, R. (1928). *Neocolonial identity and counter consciousness*. London: Merlin Press.

Courts, P. (1991). *Literacy for empowerment*. South Hadley, MA: Bergin & Garvey.

Donald, J. (1982). Language, literacy, and schooling. In *The state and popular culture*. Milton Keynes: Open University Culture Unit.

Ferlerger, L., & Mandle, J. (1991). *African-Americans and the future of the U.S. economy*. Unpublished manuscript.

Giroux, H. A. (1983). *Theory and resistance: A pedagogy for the opposition*. South Hadley, MA: Bergin & Garvey.

Giroux, H. (1991). *Border crossings: Cultural workers and the politics of education*. New York: Routledge.

Giroux, H. A., & McLaren, P. (1986). Teacher education and the politics of engagement: The case for democratic schooling. *Harvard Educational Review, 56*(3), 213–238.

Gramsci, A. (1971). *Selections from Prison Notebooks*, (Ed. and Trans. Quinten Hoare & Geoffrey Smith). New York: International Publishers.

Jackson, D. (1991, December 8). The end of the second Reconstruction. *Boston Globe*, p. 27.

Jackson, K. T. (1991, July 7). Cited in a *Boston Sunday Globe* editorial.

Kozol, J. (1985). *Illiterate America*. New York: Doubleday Anchor.

Lukas, J. A. (1985). *Common ground*. New York: Alfred A. Knopf.

McLaren, P. (1991). Critical pedagogy: Constructing an arch of social dreaming and a doorway to hope. *Journal of Education, 173*(1), 9–34.

Olsen, L. (1988). *Crossing the schoolhouse border: Immigrant students and the California public schools*. San Francisco: California Tomorrow.

Silber, J. (1991, May). *Boston University Commencement Catalogue*.

Walmsley, S. (1981). On the purpose and content of secondary reading programs: Educational and ideological perspectives. *Curriculum Inquiry, 11*, 73–79.

# IV
▼▼▼▼▼▼▼▼

## CURRICULUM AND TEACHING: DANGERS AND DREAMS

This volume has thus far mostly dealt with broad social, cultural, and educational issues and policies that emerge from social theories, economic models, intellectual paradigms, and historical forces. In this part, we extend the theme of the connections between social–cultural forces and educational issues to the classroom and to the issues of curriculum and teaching. We are concerned here with the theories and orientations that inform the most basic of all pedagogical questions: What should we teach?

The field of curriculum studies reflects the major cultural and educational trends of the times. The 1960s and early 1970s were times of important curriculum innovation, although it would be misleading to characterize the era as a radical one for curriculum. In fact, a great deal of the change was directed at revitalizing the traditional school disciplines, particularly science and mathematics, with some significant concern for foreign languages. It came in the aftermath of the American reaction to Sputnik, the first space satellite, interpreted as a sign of Soviet educational superiority. Interestingly, much of this curriculum movement was directed at encouraging student creativity and deep understanding, as represented in the popularity of such terms as *problem solving* and *structures of thought* (a marked contrast to the current emphasis on *mastery* and *minimum competencies*). This curriculum movement was greatly aided by significant funding from the federal government and foundations. In addition, many major universities were deeply involved in these efforts, as prominent academics helped develop curriculum materials. Some of these materials gained wide national distribution and acceptance, in part because they were of a very high academic quality. These packages were often given alphabetic signatures—for example, SMSG (School Mathematics Study Group), PSSC (Physical Science Study Committee), and BSCS (Biological Sciences Curriculum Study)—and often included sophisticated content (e.g., "the new math"), pedagogy (e.g., a stress on experiential and inductive learning), and teaching materials such as films.

At about the same time, there was renewed interest in elementary education, some of it directed at such organizational and structural aspects as team teaching and nongraded instruction. However, there was also considerable interest in imaginative curriculum packages designed for younger children, particularly in science, mathematics, and foreign languages. The most famous innovation in elementary education, however, was an orientation that came to be known as "open education." Never a coherent and definable theory, this orientation nonetheless had a number of identifying themes (e.g., concern for individual rates and modes of learning, experiential learning, stress on learning rather than instruction, concern for student responsibility, fluid structure, etc.).

These interesting and imaginative projects were to become victims of the general cultural and educational backlash of the 1970s and 1980s. However creative these curriculum reforms of the 1950s and 1960s may have been, they never seriously challenged the basic structural dimensions of educational ideology, although they did raise questions about some well-established practices in the existing structure. However, even if we accept these reforms as provocative and challenging, their impact on the schools was very slight. Indeed, their failure to have a major effect on the schools led many curriculum theorists to the bleak land of disenchantment. The development of the curriculum packages of the 1950s and 1960s was, to some extent, the realization of the theorist's fantasy—to bring together bright, knowledgeable, and creative people, a large budget, and a commitment to modern pedagogic insights. The disenchantment emerged from the realization that even with the availability of wonderful curriculum materials, the schools maintained their steady course of conformity and competition. What many educators came to recognize was that what schools teach and what students learn go beyond what is contained in course syllabi and lesson plans. The focus of curriculum research shifted from issues of content and technique to the school's structure, ideology, intent, and values—what is called the *hidden curriculum*.

The reality of the way in which curriculum and teaching are shaped by social forces can be vividly seen in the enormous popularity of the back-to-basics movement of the 1970s and 1980s. This movement—with its renewed emphasis on mastery, achievement, and discipline and with its concern for knowledge retention, cultural transmission, and teacher control—mirrors society's backlash to the cultural stirrings of the 1960s (the antiwar movement, the struggle for civil rights, and the pressures for participatory democracy). Those who saw these activities as destabilizing and threatening included schools on the list of contributing offenders. The mildly interesting educational innovations were seen as promoting permissiveness, if not license; insufficient structure, if not chaos; and laxity, if not sloth.

Simultaneous with the cultural backlash came the severe recession of the 1970s and with it, the end of the consciousness of continuous and boundless economic growth. A new cycle of fear, protectiveness, and resentment culminated in a climate of renewed narcissism, greed, and hyperindividuality. The metaphors of the 1970s shifted from growth to steady state, from making peace and love to simply making it. The language of educational reform correspondingly shifted from such terms as *discovery, structure, self-paced,* and *creativity* to *accountability, competence tests, mastery,* and *excellence.* In a more hostile and economically competitive world, what was needed, according to our leaders, was a leaner, tougher, more skilled workforce not enervated by the seductions of freedom and choice. Life is tough and real, they say in so many words, and there are serious competitors out there willing and eager to work harder, to endure more, and to compete more ruthlessly. These people are succeeding because America has grown soft and flabby, the consequences of a permissive and lazy educational system. Educators thought much less about Deweyan democracy and much more about social Darwinism; they shifted their interests from Bruner's notions of structures of learning to Skinner's ideas about maximizing learning.

For curriculum theorists, this was an era with only two games in town. One involved the dreary, reactionary, and anti-intellectual efforts to improve the technology of instruction, or more precisely, to find ways in which students could do well on tests. The other challenge was the much more intellectually rewarding and productive one of critically analyzing the social and cultural context and meaning of curriculum. A great deal of this work was enormously helpful, insightful, and liberating (as reflected in many of the selections in this collection), but until recently, curriculum critics tended to maintain an analytic posture and to slight the continuously important task of affirming an educational program congruent with a cultural and social vision. One of the exciting portents of hope is the relatively recent emergence of a third body of work, that is, a spate of bold, creative, and affirmative curriculum theorizing (some of which is included in this part).

The selections on curriculum and instruction in this volume are varied in their approach, but share a common view—that the conventional curriculum is, at best, maladaptive and, at worst, a contributor to our social and cultural crises. Dennis Carlson (chap. 17) examines the discourse of the recent urban school reform movement, particularly as it relates to the emphasis on basic skills and accountability. He connects these efforts to a broader agenda as reflected in what he calls "the conservative, bureaucratic state discourse" (p. 280). In this way, Carlson underscores the economic and political dimensions of curriculum making, moving the discussion beyond the artificial and misleading notion that such matters are only educational. His analysis also deals with the effects of the so-called basic skills approach on issues of race, class, gender, and teacher empowerment. Carlson complements his critique of the existing curriculum, grounded in a concern for higher productivity and cultural conformity, with an alternative approach, one directed at promoting and nourishing nonalienated work, personal liberation, and social justice.

Peter McLaren (chap. 18) writes passionately about what he perceives to be the betrayal of the aspirations of a democratic society. He describes our society as being pervaded by consumerism, conformity, and cultural oppression. McLaren calls for a critical pedagogy of "discontent and outrage," with particular attention to the importance of developing a "media literate citizenry." This critical capacity is, in his words, "grounded in the ethical imperative of examining the contradictions in U.S. society between the meaning of freedom, the demands of social justice, and the obligations of citizenship on one hand, and the structured silences that permeate incidents of suffering in everyday life" (p. 297).

Like all the selections in this part, Eugene Provenzo (chap. 19) emphasizes the underlying values that inform the particulars of the content, form, and presentation of the curriculum. He asks us to be especially mindful of the centrality of values as we enter the computer age with so much enthusiasm and excitement. Provenzo is very much aware (as we all are) of the immense power and capacity of computers, but insists that we have a responsibility to probe beyond the magic of the technical and instrumental pyrotechnics of this technology. The questions he raises about the ideological assumptions and the cultural implications of computers are critical not only to the world of computers, but also to education in general and culture as a whole.

The selection by Nel Noddings (chap. 20) deals even more directly with the issue of values. In her chapter, she offers an alternative to the cognitive-developmental and character education approaches to moral education. Writing from a feminist perspective, Noddings proposes a most provocative and imaginative curriculum framework, namely that the schools, without in any way compromising their commitment to academic standards, endeavor to teach children to care and be cared for. She provides us with a philosophical as well as a curricular analysis to support her position that schools should and could be sites of *compassionate dialogue*—educational communities energized by and committed to an ethic of care.

Dwayne Huebner (chap. 21) suggests the possibility of discussing curriculum from a spiritual perspective, that is, using the metaphors, language, and images of religious and spiritual traditions to help us reflect on curriculum questions and other educational matters. To Huebner, education is about the "journey of the soul" and the vocation of the school is to respond to the students' quest for truth (done in the context of the content of the curriculum), justice (as reflected in how the institution responds to conflicting interests), and love (enacted in the relationship between teacher and student). He grounds his own quest in the traditions and images of Christianity, but strongly urges those with differing traditions to enrich the conversations about our varying spiritual journeys.

This part concludes with two chapters on an approach to curriculum called *holistic education*, a movement rooted in the traditions of progressive and humanistic education. In chapter 22, Christine Shea addresses the complex set of ideas contained in the concept of postmodernism, with reference to their implications for education. She also discusses the profoundly important issues of the ecology and the necessity of an education that can transform the current materialistic and consumerist consciousness that so threatens the survival of the planet. Her analysis reveals varying forms of postmodern thought, one strand that is heavily pessimistic, if not nihilistic, tends to engender despair whereas other strands offer hope in the kind of constructive criticism that urges us not only to deconstruct our visions but also to reconstruct them. She then goes on to offer some suggestions for a classroom pedagogy directed at "(re)envisioning ecologically viable postmodern ways of relating to self, community, nature, and the cosmos."

David Purpel's (chap. 23) critique of holistic education focuses on the necessity to ground educational policies in a truly holistic frame, one that includes not only the spiritual and aesthetic, but also involves the moral, political, cultural, economic, and social aspects of our existence. He takes the position that education has been reified to the point that many of us have become blind to the ideological forces that drive educational policy. Within a context of the precarious nature of our society, Purpel affirms the liberating possibility of existing traditions of holistic education, such as its concern for creativity, wholeness, and the inner life, and urges that these emphases be integrated with concerns for a critical pedagogy focused on social justice.

The critiques that emerge from these chapters suggest several important issues for educators. The selections all indicate that considerations of school reform must be seen in systematic terms. Issues of curriculum, educational policy, social priorities, and cultural goals are intertwined and hence, must be addressed as a whole, not compartmentally. Moreover, these chapters reveal a deep dissatisfaction with the quality of the current so-called educational reform movement, which seems for the most part to focus (at best) on short-term amelioration rather than on long-term transformation. Higher pay for teachers (an act of justice by itself) will not improve the quality of teaching if they are forced to submit to a narrowly conceived and control-oriented curriculum. A policy of rigid planning and frequent testing is antithetical to the development of a fundamental shift in the nature of the educational program.

These chapters reflect a rejection of Tylerian thinking, with its emphases on clearly stated goals, resonant techniques, and close testing and measurement. In its place is a concern for the *hidden curriculum*, a concept that signifies a much broader sense of the social, political, and cultural implications of the curriculum. Moreover, this concern reflects a change from the tremendous reliance educators have placed on the social sciences. Instead of the usual psychological and sociological perspectives, we see aesthetic, philosophical, spiritual, and moral viewpoints that provide deeper insight and understanding to the human condition. They also afford us new energy and hope for the possibility of genuine social transformation.

# 17
▼▼▼▼▼▼▼

# Education as a Political Issue (I)*

## Dennis Carlson

If, as Michel Foucault suggests, power and knowledge are inseparable, then curriculum may be studied in terms of the power relations it constitutes and by which it is constituted.[1] Furthermore, since power is always *about* something, that is, always deployed strategically to advance a particular project, the curriculum may be studied as an apparatus of power deployed within educational sites to reconstitute power in some interests rather than others, to advance one social project rather than another. Finally, since curriculum constitutes relations of power, it cannot but artificially be separated from the organization of the schools which structures curriculum use. This all implies that curriculum reform involves much more than merely changing the knowledge that students learn. It also involves changing the way teachers' work is organized and the way schools are organized and operated, and for what purposes.

In what follows I want to examine the discourse and practice of urban school reform over the past several decades—a period Ira Shor has characterized as the "conservative restoration." This examination will focus on the power relations that have shaped the schools and are embedded with the malformation of class, race, and gender oppression.[2] I argue that because reforms have not addressed the roots of crisis in urban schools or countered the inequalities that generate conflict and resistance among various groups, "basic skills" reforms are undermined by their own set of contradictions and crisis tendencies. Finally, such a perspective on the curriculum and urban school crisis directs our attention to the role the schools *might* play in

*Carlson, Dennis. "Education as a Political Issue." From *Thirteen Questions: Reframing Education's Conversation*, 2nd ed., New York: Peter Lang, 1995, pp. 281–291. Reprinted by permission.

reconstructing power relations consistent with democratic–progressive movements organized around agendas of "equity," "justice," "community," and
"workplace democratization." In this regard I conclude with a few comments
on the articulation of an alternative, democratic–progressive discourse on
urban school reform.


## THE CONSERVATIVE, BUREAUCRATIC STATE
## DISCOURSE ON URBAN SCHOOL REFORM

Over the past several decades, a conservative, bureaucratic state discourse
has articulated urban school reform around a "basic skills" or "functional
literacy" curriculum, performance and output-based program evaluation and
instructional objectives, minimum competency testing, and the reorganization of urban school consistent with "effective schools" research findings.
Most directly and overtly, the "basic skills" restructuring of urban schools
around standardized testing and a skill-based curriculum has been a response
to the changing character of work in post-industrial America, and it has
participated in the construction of a new post-industrial working class. Prior
to the 1960s, major urban school districts had enrolled a heavily white,
ethnic, working class student population. General education and vocational
programs prepared most of these students for clerical and trade union jobs
in manufacturing that were available upon graduation, and a small college
preparatory program was available for those who aspired to more. The jobs
available to high school graduates in industry were often routine and unre-
warding, but they paid relatively high wages and offered some job security.
Literacy requirements often took a back seat to manual skills in these jobs,
particularly for boys but also for girls. The progressive-era urban school
curriculum participated in the pre-skilling and socializing of this industrial
working class by teaching students how to cooperate and be "good" workers,
and it emphasized manual labor, typing, and home economics skills which
were more manual than mental in their orientation.

The changing character of work in post-industrial America was already
becoming apparent by the 1960s when business and state leaders began to
talk of a growing mismatch between the literacy skills of high school graduates and the literacy requirements of the new jobs in urban areas. Enrollments
in vocational education programs and tracks were still relatively high, but
graduates of these programs found fewer and fewer jobs waiting for them
that required their particular skills.[3] As manufacturing moved to the Second
and Third World, the "good" trade union jobs began to disappear, and they
have been replaced by clerical, data processing, janitorial, and service industry jobs. The new entry-level jobs increasingly require more in the way of
basic reading (word and sentence decoding), comprehension and direction-

following skills.[4] Workers frequently have to refer to sets of standard operating procedures and record data on forms or punch it into a computer. They also need to be able to interact with clients and customers and categorize customer data. Thus they need generalizable literacy skills and competencies of a certain minimal level (generally defined at about the 9th grade reading level) that can be put to use and adapted to a number of diverse work settings. As D. W. Livingstone has observed, education for this new, semi-skilled labor force

> . . . entails instruction in general preparatory skills that are open-ended and can be built upon or refined in a range of work settings. In other words, it means the creation of labor market entrants who will be increasingly technically adaptable and capable of mobility among work settings in response to rapidly changing workplace technologies.[5]

The urban school curriculum, in response to these changes, has been reconceived in terms of the minimal language decoding, comprehension, and processing skills that students "need" to be "effective" workers in the new service industry, maintenance, data processing, and "para-professional" fields. Furthermore, the form of the curriculum, by organizing students' work in terms of direction-following and the routine production of workbook and drillsheet "piecework," orients students to the ways of working that are most typically associated with the new urban working class jobs. Many urban students are enrolled in several remedial basic skills courses to help them pass minimum competency tests, and also are placed in low ability group classes that emphasize basic skills over subject area knowledge.

While the urban school curriculum has been reconstructed by bureaucratic state reform initiatives around "basic skills," urban schools have not, after several decades of reform, been able to achieve even the very limited objective of "certifying" that their students are "functionally literate" by the time they graduate, and they have not been able to keep much more than half of all socioeconomically disadvantaged students in school long enough to graduate. In 1989, it was still possible for the *New York Times* to warn of an "impending U.S. jobs 'disaster'" with a "work force unqualified to work" and with "schools lagging far behind needs of employees."[6] Like the Vietnam War and the "war on poverty," the war on illiteracy and the drop-out problem in urban schools has become bogged down, and it offers no light at the end of the tunnel.

Why is it that corporate and state reform initiatives in urban education have not been more successful in ensuring that socioeconomically disadvantaged students learn the literacy skills they "need" for gainful employment in the new working class? Several factors need to be considered. First, because the basic skills curriculum is highly rationalized and regimented, it contributes to student motivation problems rather than improves them. As more and more students are enrolled in basic skills courses, where instruction is organized around routine drillsheet and workbook, "seatwork" and rounds of standardized pre- and post-testing, teachers may have to lower work demands on students even more in order to reduce conflict and keep students from dropping out. Second, not only is a "basic skills" curriculum lacking in intrinsic motivation, it fails to hold out much for urban students once they leave school. Students are exhorted to stay in school, work hard to pass minimum competency tests, graduate, and then have a chance at one of the new service industry or data processing jobs that are available to urban high school graduates. However, the new working class jobs are low paying with little room for advancement, they offer little in the way of job security or health benefits, and workers may have to work six or more hours a week at various jobs merely to maintain their families above the poverty line. Subsistence on public welfare may seem a better option that works for many who face the prospect of entry into this working world, and for welfare subsidence a high school diploma is not required. Given the growing disparities of wealth and power in America, with fewer "good" jobs available, it may become increasingly difficult to "sell" a "basic skills" education to urban students in the years ahead.

To this point, I have limited my comments to an analysis of the urban school crisis and curriculum reform that relies upon a political economic and class theory of schooling. However, urban school reform also has participated in racial power relations and dynamics in ways that are related to class but have a somewhat independent development. Racial minorities were in the 1960s reclaiming America's inner cities, and traditional white working class and middle class neighborhoods were disappearing at a rapid rate as suburbanization accelerated. To some extent racial minorities were drawn to urban areas by the new service industry and jobs which many working class white males refused (at first) to take. Minorities had been effectively excluded from the trade union movement throughout the 1950s and white working class males continued in the 1960s to enjoy a relatively privileged status, although that status was threatened as the "good" unionized, industrial jobs began to disappear very quickly in the 1970s. The new post-industrial working class thus was initially constituted along heavily racial lines, and many new low-skill and semi-skilled jobs were readily available to minorities in urban areas. Aside from economic considerations, African American and Hispanic people were drawn to America's major urban areas because they were seeking "space" within a highly oppressive society—space to assume control of their own institutions, and thus reclaim those institutions from the control of a repressive white power structure.[7] The hope was that once minority peoples became an electoral majority within a given geographical space, they could use their power to make public institutions serve new emancipatory purposes by empowering minority communities.

The state-sponsored "basic skills" reform movement, in these terms, has had the effect of overriding local control of the schools at a time when poor African American and Hispanic peoples were becoming the numerical majority in urban America. State-mandated minimum competency testing, all of the bureaucratic regulations associated with "aligning" the urban school curriculum with the new basic skills test, the growing financial dependency of urban schools on the state (resulting from chronic fiscal crisis in urban America and particularly in urban schools), and the growing threat of a direct state takeover of "failing" urban school districts have had the effect of countering efforts by African American and Hispanic communities to "reclaim" urban schools. The local school board members, superintendent, and other local school leaders may be minorities, but so long as urban schools have to teach to the state test and adhere to a myriad of state funding guidelines and procedures, local or community control of urban schools is more formal than substantive or real. To challenge these curricular and educational power relations, African American and Hispanic groups will need to move beyond formal democratic control of local school boards to reclaim involvement in substantive rather than merely technical educational decisions, and this implies challenging the "basic skills" model of bureaucratic state control.

Finally, the conservative, bureaucratic state discourse on "basic skills" and urban school reform participates in gender power relations in the school. Most obviously, basic skills curricular reforms have taken for granted a bureaucratic and hierarchical chain of command in urban schools that rigidly subordinates women teachers (particularly elementary teachers) to male administrators. However, it is not merely a case of individual male administrators dominating individual female teachers. Even when women have been "promoted" from the corps of teachers to the ranks of administrators, it has generally been because they have learned how to speak a patriarchal discourse that is taken as the norm—a phenomenon that might be referred to as the "Thatcherising of women administrators."[8] It is this patriarchal discourse that is involved in the construction of the dominant models of school reform. As Michael Apple observes:

> The very program of rationalizing all important social relations in our major institutions is, in fact, pre-eminently a masculine discourse. . . . Such a hierarchical conception is not neutral. It disenfranchises alternative concerns for human relations, connectedness, and care.[9]

In education, the "teacher-proofing" of the curriculum, which has been advanced through "basic skills" reforms, also has been based on the masculine presumptions that teachers are not intelligent or intellectual enough to be seriously involved in important curricular decisions, that they need to be told exactly what to do, and that they prefer leaving important decisions to administrators.[10] Basic skills reforms have also been consistent with a patriarchal structuring of power relations in education because they take for granted a rigid bifurcation of administrative and teaching roles within an asymmetrical power relationship, and because they privilege a technical rather than discursive or dialectic rationality. Consequently, teacher support for "whole language," "cooperative learning," and other progressive approaches to curriculum and instruction that hopefully return power to teachers and students to construct the curriculum through discourse, practice, and self-reflection, represent a threat to continued patriarchal hegemony in the discourse on urban school reform. In the meantime, teachers' lack of support for performance-based "teach to the test" approaches to basic skills instruction undermines the effectiveness of top-down reforms.

I have suggested some of the ways that urban school reform during the basic skills era has served to organize class, race, and gender power relations in urban schools in highly inequitable ways. The increased centralization, bureaucratization, and rationalization of curriculum and instructional decision-making has not, consequently, been a "neutral phenomenon." However, while state officials have been relatively successful in "selling" or legitimating a basic skills reform agenda by appealing to broad public support for high standards and more "accountability" in education, the conservative reform agenda has not solved or even ameliorated the basic problems that beset urban schools.

## TOWARD A DEMOCRATIC-PROGRESSIVE DISCOURSE ON URBAN SCHOOL REFORM

Over the past several decades of the "conservative restoration," progressive opposition to the bureaucratic state reform discourse has remained largely fragmented and politically marginalized. Liberal groups have exerted some influence on policy-thinking, but little on actual policy-making. Liberal discourse has advanced concerns over "equity" and "excellence," supported a curriculum organized around "higher order" literacy skills, a college preparatory curriculum for all students, emphasized the need to professionalize teachers rather than deskill them, personalize instruction rather than regiment it, and called for a decentralization and de-bureaucratization of authority through some form of "site-based management."[11] These have been important concerns, and they provide some basis for struggle in response to concrete reform proposals sponsored by the conservative, bureaucratic state. However, for a number of reasons liberalism has failed to "deliver" fully on its promises, even when liberal politicians have gained control of the state, and this has to do with a failure to take on certain "hard" questions about whose interests are served by the current system of structured inequalities and what it will take to fundamentally change the way power is arranged and distributed in schools.[12] In moving beyond these limitations in liberal discourse, without abandoning its insights, let me briefly suggest several elements of a democratic-progressive discourse in education that help us better address the crisis in urban schools and reconceptualize urban school reform in ways that move beyond the current impasse.

First, while a democratic-progressive discourse would move beyond a "human capital" or economically functional analysis of the curriculum, with its presumption that what is learned in schools must bear a rather direct functional relationship to current economic "needs," it would not completely reject economic or workplace considerations in curriculum decision-making. On the contrary, some relationship *should* exist between school work and work in other important institutional sites in society, since education serves to initiate individuals into the "productive" work of building culture and objectifying experience in useful ways. Marx argued that people make themselves and culture through work: "What they [humans] are, therefore, coincides with their production, both with *what* they produce and with *how* they produce."[13] This suggests the importance of preparing students with the discursive skills and capacities associated with non-alienating, self-enhancing, productive work within the context of the democratization of the workplace.[14]

Second, while the conservative state discourse has organized a discussion of the urban school curriculum around the notion of "functional literacy," and while the liberal discourse has emphasized "higher order" literacy skills (generally corresponding to the higher rungs of Bloom's taxonomy), a democratic-progressive discourse would reconceptualize the curriculum around notions of "critical literacy." This latter notion suggests a capacity for discursive reflection on one's own identity formation with a culture characterized by struggle and change along a number of axes, including class, gender, race, sexuality, etc.[15] In urban schools, students need to learn how to critique the discourses and practices that keep them subordinated and reflect on their own role in the social construction of inequalities. For teachers, critical literacy education implies a reconceptualization of the pedagogic roles. Henry Giroux writes that teachers need "to undertake social criticism not as outsiders but as public intellectuals who address the social and political issues of their neighborhood, their nation, and the wider global world."[16] They must engage themselves, as well, in the struggles of their students to articulate their own voices and construct identities.

Third, beyond a reconceptualization of students' work, and in order to make such a reconceptualization possible, a democratic-progressive discourse would imply a restructuring of teachers' work and the organization of the school consistent with workplace democratization. This would imply drastic changes in the way schools are organized and how educational decisions are made that shifts substantive decision-making power from bureaucratic state officials to local communities, schools, and classrooms. Workplace democratization may be consistent with some aspects of "site-based management." However, it goes beyond most such plans in that it advances a real democratization of decision-making in urban schools and communities rather than merely bureaucratic decentralization of authority within a system that continues to be overwhelmingly under the control of bureaucratic state and central office officials.

Finally, a democratic-progressive discourse would focus our attention on the need to link-up educational theory and practice with social and cultural movements. Social movements involve a collective rearticulation and reappropriation of cultural meanings and values in advancing particular agendas for changing the distribution and use of power in society. They arise out of contradictions within existing power relations and institutional structures and offer a way of moving beyond current crisis tendencies. To ward off crisis, dominant groups in education have become quite adept at crisis management and "muddling through" from one crisis to another. However, should the various groups which have been disempowered by basic skills reforms (in ways that are related to their class, gender, and race) articulate their different concerns as part of a common movement to challenge bureaucratic state discourse and practice in education, it might yet become possible to build a new democratic-progressive "voice" and movement for change that looks beyond crisis management and mismanagement towards crisis resolution.

## NOTES

1. Foucault, M. (1980). *Power/Knowledge: Selected Interviews and Other Writings, 1972–1977.* In Colin Gordon (ed.). New York: Pantheon Books.
2. Shor, I. (1986) *Culture Wars: School and Society in the Conservative Restoration, 1969–1984.* Boston: Routledge & Kegan Paul.
3. Gray, K. (1991, November 6) "Vocational education in high school: A modern phoenix?" *Phi Delta Kappan, 72,* pp. 437–445.
4. Levin, H. & Rumberger, R. (1986) *Educational Requirements for New Technologies.* Palo Alto: Stanford Center for Educational Research.
5. Livingstone, D. W. (1985, January) "Class, educational ideologies, and mass opinion in capitalist crisis." *Sociology of Education, 58,* p. 8.
6. Fiske, E. (1989, September 25) "Impending U.S. jobs 'disaster': work force unqualified to work." *New York Times,* p. 1+.
7. Lefebvre, H. (1979) For Henri Lefebvre, spatial conflict entails the appropriation of space by marginalized groups from its capitalist spatial organization see "Space: social product and use value." In J. W. Freiberg (ed.). *Critical Sociology: European Perspectives,* p. 293. New York: Irvington Publications.
8. Blackmore, J. (1989) "Educational leadership: A feminist critique and reconstruction." In J. Smyth (ed.). *Critical Perspectives in Educational Leadership.* New York: Falmer Press.

9. Apple, M. (1986) *Teachers and Texts: A Political Economy of Class and Gender Relations in Education*, p. 142. New York: Routledge & Kegan Paul.

10. Freedman, S. (1988) "Teaching, gender, and curriculum." In L. Beyer & M. Apple (eds.). *The Curriculum: Problems, Politics, and Possibilities*, pp. 204–218. Albany: SUNY Press.

11. As examples of the liberal discourse in education see:

   The Carnegie Foundation for the Advancement of Teaching Reports (1986) *A Nation Prepared: Teachers for the 21st Century*. New York: Carnegie Forum Task Force on Teaching as a Profession.

   The Carnegie Foundation for the Advancement of Teaching Reports (1988) *An Imperiled Generation: Saving Urban Schools*. Lawrenceville, NJ: Princeton University Press.

   Sizer, T. (1984) *Hoarce's Compromise: The Dilemma of the American High School*. Boston: Houghton-Mifflin.

12. Grubb, W. N. & Lazerson, M. (1988) *Broken Promises: How Americans Fail Their Children*. Chicago: University of Chicago Press. Gintis, H. & Bowles, S. (1988) "Contradiction and reproduction in educational theory." In M. Cole (ed.). *Bowles and Gintis Revisited: Correspondence and Contradiction in Educational Theory*, pp. 16–32. New York: Falmer.

13. Marx, K. & Engels, F. (1974) *The German Ideology, Part One*, p. 42. New York: International Publishers.

14. Davis, E. & Lansbury, R. (1986) "Democracy and control in the workplace: An introduction." In Davis & Lansbury (eds.). *Democracy and Control in the Workplace*, pp. 1–29. Melbourne, Australia: Longman Cheshire. Shuler, T. (1985) *Democracy at Work*. New York: Oxford University Press.

15. McLaren, P. & Lankshear, C. (eds.). (Upcoming) *Critical Literacy*. Albany: SUNY Press.

16. Giroux, H. (1990) "Rethinking the boundaries of educational discourse: Modernism, postmodernism, and feminism." *College Literature, 17* (2/3), p. 42.

# 18
▼▼▼▼▼▼▼

# Education as a Political Issue (II)*

## Peter McLaren

We live at a precarious point in time in which relations of subjection, suffering, dispossession and contempt for human dignity and the sanctity of life remain at the center of our social existence. Emotional dislocation, moral sickness and individual helplessness remain a ubiquitous feature of history. Our much heralded form of democracy has become, unbeknownst to many Americans, subverted by its contradictory relationship to the very object of its address: human freedom, social justice, and a tolerance and respect for difference. In the current historical juncture, discourses of democracy continue to masquerade as disinterested solicitations, and to reveal themselves as incommensurable with the struggle for social equality. The reality and promise of democracy in the United States has recently been invalidated by the ascendency of new postmodern institutionalization of brutality and the proliferation of new and sinister structures of domination. This has been followed by an ever fainter chorus of discontent as the voices of the powerless and the marginalized grow increasingly despondent or else are clubbed into oblivion by the crackling swiftness of police batons.

Although pain and suffering continue to pollute the atmosphere of social justice in the United States in alarming proportion to previous decades, the dream of democracy and the struggle to bring it about has taken on a new intensity, as recent events in Europe and Haiti attest. In its unannounced retreat in the United States over the past decade, democracy has managed to recreate power through the spectacularization of its after-image, that is, through image management and the creation of national myths of identity primarily through the techniques of the mass media.

*McLaren, Peter. "Education As A Political Issue." From *Thirteen Questions: Reframing Education's Conversation*. 2nd ed., New York: Peter Lang, 1995, pp. 266–280. Reprinted by permisssion.

The prevailing referents around which the notion of public citizenry is currently constructed have been steered into the ominous direction of the social logic of production and consumption. Buyers are beginning to culturally merge with their commodities while human agency is becoming absorbed into the social ethics of the marketplace. Social impulses for equality, liberty, and social justice have been flattened out by the mass media until they have become cataleptically rigid while postmodern images threaten to steal what was once known as the "soul."

Given the current condition of end-of-the-century ennui and paranoia, we have arrived at the zero-degree reality of the kind that once only graced the pages of surrealist manifestos or punk fanzines. Andre Breton's "simplest Surrealist act"—firing a pistol into a crowd of strangers—is no longer just a contemporary symbolic disruption of the grudgingly mundane aspects of everyday life or a symbolic dislocation circulating in avant garde broadsheets. It is precisely in this current North American historical conjuncture that people *are* really shooting blindly into crowds: at children in hamburger establishments, at employees and employers in factories, at teachers and classmates in schools, and at female engineering students in university seminar rooms. In some urban settings, children are murdering other children for their status-line foot gear—not to mention the lurid reality at L.A. 'drive-bys'. In New York City, manufacturers of bullet proof vests are starting special fashion lines for toddlers and elementary school children who might accidentally absorb stray bullets from homeboy dealers in pumps, ten dollar gold tooth caps and who carry customized AK 47 assault rifles. The guns are not fashion accessories—yet. But gas masks are. New York celebrity fashion designer, Andre Van Pier, after the Gulf War announced a spring fashion line based on the theme of Desert Storm: the "Gulf War look." Fashion accessories revealed include neon-colored camouflage pattern, canteen purses, and gas masks slung renegade-chic over the shoulder. A major New York manufacturer of baseball cards revealed a new line of Gulf War cards that were supposed to be "educational." Of course, included were photos of the major American military hardware and portraits of the generals but the only item represented from Iraq in this educational collection was a "scud" missile.

Today's social ugliness that makes the bizarre appear normal is no longer just a (white, male) surrealist fantasy or proto-surrealist spin-off, or a Baudrillardean rehearsal for a futureless future. This scenario *is* the present historical moment, one that has arrived in a body bag—unravelled and stomped on by the logic of a steel-toed boot. Serial killer Ted Bundy has donated his multiple texts of identity to our structural unconscious and *we are living them*. A funky nihilism has set in; an aroma of cultural disquiet. There is a yearning for a comfortable apocalypse accompanied by forms of everyday life where salvation is unnecessary because chaos is always sublime and morality is frictionless in the age of MTV. Feelings of despair about the global condition have gone high-tech: We can not eroticize our depression and rearrange and reterritorialize our feelings by plugging our central nervous system in to the electromagnetic spectrum via TV waves and charting out our lives according to designer moods.

The erosion of the American dream has forced today's youth to occupy, if not a dystopian parody of *The Cosby Show*, then paracriminal subcultures of sardonic nihilism focussing on drugs and violence, apotheosized in movies like *Clockwork Orange* and *Colors*. Corporate rock's celebration of the subversion of adult authority gives its youthful listeners the illusion of resistance but not a language of critique or hope. It works to produce a politics of pleasure but simultaneously functions as a form of repression and forgetting—a motivated social amnesia and forced disavowal of the nation's complicitousness in racial demonization and colonialism.

The New Right has used the media effectively (and affectively) not simply to transform gangsters or actors into politicians through the services of high-tech image consultants, but even more impressively, to seduce Americans to retreat into cultural nostalgia and social amnesia as a way out of this postmodern era of retreat and despondency (many students I teach are already feeling a nostalgia for the Persian Gulf War as it was ideologically produced through CNN). At the same time the New Right has, through foreign and domestic policies shaped by the heritage of imperialism, helped the U.S. flex its global muscles in Grenada, Panama, and Iraq, setting the stage for a renewed patriotic zeal and construction of the postmodern national subject. Kellner (1990) notes that, under the control of multinational capital, the media have effectively served as ideological mouthpieces for Reagan/Bush disinformation and have helped to forge a conservative ideological hegemony.

Kellner (1990: 219) writes:

It is a historical irony that the 1980s marked the defeat of democracy by capitalism in the United States and the triumph of democracy over state communism in the Soviet bloc countries. At present, the "free" television media in the United States are probably no more adversarial and no less propagandistic than *Pravda*, or the television stations in the Eastern European countries. Hence the very future of democracy is at stake—and development of a democratic communications system is necessary if democracy is to be realized.

Largely because of the way in which the media function to shape and merchandise morality and to construct certain forms of citizenship and individual and collective identities, our understanding of the meaning and importance of democracy has become impoverished in proportion to its dissolution and retreat from contemporary social life. In the current historical juncture of democratic decline in the United States, ideals and images have become detached from their anchorage in stable and agreed-upon meanings and associations and are now beginning to assume a reality of their own. The world of the media is one that splinters, obliterates, peripheralizes, partitions and segments social space, time knowledge, and subjectivity in order to unify, encompass, entrap, totalize and homogenize them. What is missing from the educational debate is the way in which capitalism is able to achieve this cultural and ideological totalization and homogenization through its ability to insinuate itself into social practices and private perceptions through various forms of media knowledge (see Grossberg, 1988).

Ironically, today's increasingly "disorganized" capitalism has produced a gaudy sideshow that has managed to promote a counterfeit democracy of flags and emblems—one that has managed to harness the affective currency of popular culture such that the average American's investment in being "American" has reached an unparalleled high the likes of which has not been seen since the years surrounding the post WWII McCarthy hearings. The question that needs to be asked is: How are the subjectivities (experiences) and identities of individuals and the production of media knowledges within popular culture mutually articulated?

What isn't being talked about in today's educational debate is the desperate need within our schools for creating a media literate citizenry that can disrupt, contest, and transform media apparatuses so that they no longer have the power to infantilize the population and continue to create passive, fearful, paranoid, and apolitical social subjects (McLaren and Hammer, 1991, 1995).

George Gerbner (1989/90) and others have pointed out that American television viewers are accepting a distorted picture of the real world "more readily than reality itself." Television reality is one in which men outnumber women three to one, where women are usually mothers or lovers, rarely work outside the home, and are natural victims of violence. It is a reality where less than ten per cent of the population hold blue collar jobs, where few elderly people exist, where young Blacks learn to accept their minority status as inevitable and are trained to anticipate their own victimization (they are usually portrayed as the white hero's comic sidekick or else drug addicts, gang members, or killers). It is a world in which 18 acts of violence an hour occur in children's time programs. Violence in television demonstrates the social power of adult white males who are most likely to get involved with violence but most likely to get away with it. It also serves as a mass spectacle reflecting the allocative power of the state. And this is occurring in a country that in 1990 reported the largest number of rapes against women in its history and a prison incarceration rate of Blacks that exceeds that of South Africa. A country where rich Angelenos are hiring private police, where the wealthy neighborhoods display signs warning (Armed Response!) and where security systems and militarization of urban life are refiguring social space along the lines of the postmodern film, *Bladerunner*.

What educators need to realize is that the New World Order of the New Right cannot be realistically achieved without creating a new moral order at home first (and that means in the classrooms and the living rooms of the nation)—one that refuses to challenge the received truths or accepted conventions that have provoked the current crisis of history and identity. So far conservatives have been successful in reproducing a moral order in which young people are able to resist being motivated to enter into any logic of opposition through counterpublic spheres of cultural resistance.

Missing from the debate over public education is a serious examination of the way in which contemporary forms of schooling reproduce national images of citizenship modelled on the John-Wayneing of America and captured in the renumerative cliches, Rocky Balboa's "Go for it!" and Clint Eastwood's "Go ahead. Make my day!" which adorn the discursive fountain head of United States bravado culture. These slogans have become cultural aphorism that reveal a great deal about the structural unconscious of the United States—slogans that constitute a combination of insurance company rationality, the politics of Sunday School charity drives, and the patriarchal, xenophobic and militaristic logic of terror (both Ronald Reagan and George Bush referred to "Go ahead, make my day!" during their time in office). When Clint Eastwood delivered "Go ahead, make my day!" in the movie, *Sudden Impact* (made during the Reagan presidency), he is daring a black man to murder a woman so that he (Dirty Harry) can kill him. As Michael Rogin (1990) has pointed out, Dirty Harry is willing to sacrifice women and people of color in the name of his own courage. Reagan had made women and Blacks his targets by destroying their welfare-state tax benefits—an act he was defending when he dared his detractors to "Make my day!" George Bush made the black criminal and white rapist of *Sudden Impact* into the figure of Willie Horton, as he attempted for the first time to organize American politics around the ominous image of interracial rape (Rogin, 1990). Rogin brilliantly articulates the use of movies such as *Rambo* and *Sudden Impact* as a form of political spectacle which operates as a form of social amnesia (1990, p. 107).

The kind of curriculum focus needed in today's schools is one that actively contests the historical amnesia created by contemporary cultural forms found in the mass media. Students should be invited to explore why they identify with Dirty Harry and Rambo, and begin to historicize such an identification in the context of the larger political and social issues facing the country.

It should come as little surprise that public opinion among those groups most advantaged by wealth and power is more supportive of the public school system and current reform efforts than those disempowered on the basis of race, socioeconomic status or gender. For those very populations that will be increasing in the coming decades—African Americans and Latino youth—the conditions in this country's school systems have appreciably worsened. Groups actively lobbying for minority positions on issues dealing with race, social and welfare concerns, are now being labeled within the conservative agenda by spokespersons such as Diane Ravitch, Roger Kimball, William Bennett, Rush Limbaugh, Lynne V. B. Cheney and others as "ethnocentric" or "separatist." Within this rationality, the call for diversity is sanctioned only when the converging of diverse voices collapses into a depoliticized co-existence based on capitulation to the hidden imperatives of Eurocentrism, logocentrism, and patriarchy. Those educators and students who refuse to genuflect before the Western cultural tradition and regard it glowingly as the apogee of cultural and political achievement are branded as perverse, ignorant and malicious sophists who have "defiled reason" (Kimball, 1990; see also Ravitch, 1990). What this ideological position effectively does is sound an alarm for the impending demise of white culture: "If white people have any pride in their heritage, now is the time to act because your history is under assault!" This clarion call for white authenticity embalms the past for people of color and shrouds their histories in the thinning strands of the moral and social consciousness of a nation plagued by social amnesia. It also shrouds domination in a white sheet of race, class, and gender purity by exiling questions of racism, sexism, homophobia, and class oppression.

On the other side of the educational debate we have a population that has been taught to think so extravagantly about success and power being pushed even closer to the dream of cultural and moral salvation. This dream has taken shape in Allan Bloom's colonial imagination where an "imperialist nostalgia" for the former grandeur of the empires of the center transforms itself into an inveterate fear of the unwashed masses. Bloom's highbrow petulance over *declasse* academics wanting to teach courses on popular culture translates for public schools into educational initiatives towards a national curriculum designed to maintain American "standards" in the world of international market competition (in other words, to maintain a uniform identity defined by Europe's demonization of the darker skinned populations—one that pits the Anglo "I" against the dark, forbidding "Other"). Bloom's reaction against the transdisciplinary character of much of what is occurring in recent literary theory and its capacity to reterritorialize the structure of academic discourse is really a form of pining for the loss of the authority of and consensus on the meaning of Greek and Roman Antiquity and collapse of late-Victorian highbrow academic dilettantism.

In the effete paradise of Bloom (which, of course, consists of Victorian salons and Tudor libraries populated by white bourgeois males and *belles lettristes* from Ivy League schools) the non-Western thinker becomes the debased and inverted image of the hypercivilized metropolitan intellectual.

In other words, both non-Western knowledge and the uncultivated thought of the masses become, for Bloom, a primitive non-knowledge that serves as a conduit to savagery and barbarism—a descent into hell, reason's Negative Other. Bloom's collision of empires of consciousness (the radiantly civilized high culture of hellenism of which Bloom himself is a prime representative and the dark, primitive culture of the mob) occurs in a theatre of the Western mind (whose doors are being forced shut by the incursion of unholy thought into American culture) where a fantasy narrative is played out that is common to many bourgeois male academics and one in which the hegemony of the universalized and eternalized language and tropes of the colonizer makes it easier to script: Euro-American civilization is keeping the grandeur of the savage at bay in the name of Truth, and is morally policing the borders of that dark continent of the psyche where female sensuality remains unmediated by the realm of ideas and where the violence of the "blood-male" remains untempered by reason and the rule of law. For Bloom, both these savage verities of sex and violence must be cruelly trussed rather than cossetted by the Western mind.

What educators like Bloom fail to understand is that our schools are failing large numbers of minority students precisely because too much emphasis is already being placed on trading in on the status of one's cultural capital. Ironically, those students who populate urban settings in places such as New York's Howard Beach, Ozone Park, El Barrio, etc., are likely to learn more about Eastern Europe in contexts designed by *soi-dissant* metropolitan intellectuals than they are about the Harlem Renaissance, Mexico, Africa, the Carribean, or Aztec or Zulu culture. The sad irony is that test scores based on the information filtered from the Western canon and bourgeois cultural capital are used to justify school district and state funding initiatives. The reality of schooling is that U.S. society is comprised of differentially empowered publics and mainstream schooling ensures that those publics already enjoy most of the power and privilege in such a society will continue their advantage for succeeding generations. In this way, intergenerational continuity is ensured: working-class students get working-class jobs; affluent students get the kind of employment that will advantage their life chances and those of their children.

Cultural literacy spokespersons such as E. D. Hirsch have recently reduced literacy to a cultural thesaurus to be memorized by students aspiring to become active, engaged citizens. Yet when culture is despairingly viewed as a storehouse of dead facts, a time capsule of frozen memories detached from historical context, then the concept of difference, when applied to issues of race, class, gender, age, sexual preference, or disability, can be absorbed into what I call "dead pluralism." Dead pluralism is what keeps at bay the need to historicize difference, to recognize the hierarchical production of systems of difference in whose interests such hierarchies serve, and to acknowledge difference as a social construction forged within asymmetrical relations of power, conflicting interests, and a climate of dissent and opposition. The "pluralism" that supposedly already undergirds our so-called multicultural society in the vision of Ravitch and Kimball is one that is based on uncoerced consensus, interracial and intergenerational harmony and zero-degree public unity—a perspective shrouded in the lie of democratic ubiquity. When Ravitch and Kimball call for pluralism over separatism they are really buttressing the status quo against disempowered minorities seeking social justice.

The real danger facing education is not simply the refusal of the general public to recognize its embeddedness in relations of power and privilege at the level of everyday life, but rather the fact that the public prefers to act as if there exists few—or no—such political linkages. The danger is not an apathetic nation, nor a cynical one but rather the ability of the public sphere to exist relatively uncontested. Why? I believe that it has to do with the ability of the larger public sphere to mobilize desire, and secure the passion of the public, and the relative inability of progressive educators to analyze the social, cultural, moral and political implications of such an ability.

Another area of concern that relates to the ability of the schools to create a passive, risk-free citizenry is the ability of schooling to conflate citizenship values based on characteristics of nationhood and Christianity. The question not being asked in the current debate over education in this country is how nationalism and religion work together in debilitating ways to construct racist formations within the wider citizenry. For instance, self-righteous Christians who are making such an issue of curriculum censorship should be confronted by an educational system committed to curricular practices that examine the relationship among religion, nationalism and racism in our schools.

Citing the work of Alan Davies, David Seljak (1991) explores the various ways the figure of Christ has been constructed geopolitically that have had consequences for the way in which certain races have been viewed. For instance, students should be invited to examine The Germanic Christ (a combination of Lutheran pietism, romantic German nationalism and modern pseudo-scientific theories of racial purity and genetic superiority), the Latin Christ of France (a figure that embodies French nationalism, aristocratic resentment against the post-revolutionary bourgeois, classical Catholic anti-Judaism), the Anglo-Saxon Christ of the United Kingdom and Anglo North America (The United States and English Canada) which includes the incarnation of social Darwinism and the Aryan myth, the Afrikaaner Christ (Calvinist categories of double predestination and sphere sovereignty which through distortion came to justify the color dualism and racial segregation of later apartheid ideology). Students should also be invited to examine how the figure of Christ is being reconfigured in Latin America within the theology of liberation as a means of working for the empowerment of oppressed groups. Students should also be invited to examine the role Christianity has placed in the development of homophobia and violence against gays and lesbians (Sears, 1987). Religion plays an important role in the life of Americans and students should be given the opportunity to examine both the enabling and disabling effects of religious ideology in the shaping of future generations.

Needed for the coming decade is a critical pedagogy that is able to provide conditions for students to reject what they experience as a given. A pedagogy that includes a sharpened focus on the relationship among economies of capital investment, political economies, moral economies, economies of 'free' expression, sexual economies, economies of belief and identity formation and the construction of desire and formation of human will. Needed is a pedagogy of discontent and of outrage that is able to contest the hegemony of prevailing definitions of the everyday as the "way things are." A pedagogy that refuses the hidebound distinction between prosaic expression and popular culture, between art and experience, between reason and the imagination. We need a critical pedagogy in our colleges of education that can problematize schooling as a site for the construction of moral, cultural, and national identity, and emphasize the creation of the schooled citizen as a form of emplacement, as a geopolitical construction, as a process in the formation of the geography of cultural desire. Teaching in our schools must be transformed into acts of dissonance and interventions into the ritual inscription of our students into the codes of the dominant culture. It must promote structured refusals to naturalize existing relations of power. And finally, it needs to help create subaltern counterpublics.

Also needed is a curriculum that has as its focus of investigation the study of everyday, informal, and popular culture and how the historical patterns of power that inform such cultures are imbricated in the formation of individual subjectivity and identity. Pedagogy occurs not only in schools but in all cultural sites. The electronic media is perhaps the greatest site of pedagogical production that exists—you could say it is a form of perpetual pedagogy. In addition to understanding literacies applicable to print culture, students need to recognize how their identities are formed and their "mattering maps" produced through an engagement with electronic and other types of media so that they will be able to engage in alternative ways of symbolizing the self and gain a significant purchase on the construction of their own identities and the direction of their desiring. It is in such an investigation that teachers and students become transformed into cultural workers for self and social emancipation. I am calling for a pedagogy of critical media literacy that is linked to what Paul Willis (1990) has referred to a "grounded aesthetics" designed to provide students with the symbolic resources for creative self and social formation in order that they can more critically re-enter the vast, uncharted spaces of common culture.

I am suggesting that students need to make critical judgments about what society might mean, and what is possible or desirable outside existing configurations of power and privilege. Students need to be able to cross over into different zones of cultural diversity and form what Trinh T. Minh-ha (1988) calls hybrid and hyphenated identities in order to rethink the relationship of self to society, of self to other, and for deepening the moral vision of the social order. This raises an important question: How are the categories of race, class, gender, sexual preference shaped within the margins and centers of society, and how can students engage history as a way of reclaiming power and identity? The critical media literacy of which I speak is structured around the notion of a politics of location and identity as border-crossing. It is grounded in the ethical imperative of examining the contradictions in U.S. society between the meaning of freedom, the demands of social justice, and the obligations of citizenship on the one hand, and the structured silence that permeates incidents of suffering in everyday life. The politics of difference that undergirds such a critical literacy is one in which differences rearticulate and shape identity such that students can actively refuse the role of cultural servant and sentinel for the status quo in order to reclaim, reshape, and transform their own historical destiny.

## REFERENCES

Giroux, H. A., & McLaren, P. (1991). "Radical Pedagogy as Cultural Politics", in Donald Morton and Mas'ud Zavarzadeh (Eds.) *Theory/Pedagogy/Politics*, Urbana and Chicago: University of Illinois Press, pp. 152–186.

Gerner, G. (1989/90). "TV vs. Reality", *Adbusters, 1*, p. 12.

Grossberg, L. (1988). *It's A Sin*, Sydney, Australia: Power Publications.

Hammer, R., & McLaren, P. (1991). "Rethinking the Dialectic", *Educational Theory, 41*, pp. 23–46.

Hochschild, A. R. (1983). *The Managed Heart*, Berkeley: University of California Press.

Kellner, D. (1990). *Television and the Crisis of Democracy*, Boulder, San Francisco, Oxford: Westview Press.

Kimball, R. (1991). "Tenured Radicals", *The New Criterion, 9*, pp. 4–13.

Minh-ha, Trinh T. (1988). "Not You/Like You: Post-Colonial Women and the Interlocking Questions of Identity and Difference", *Inscriptions, 3/4*, pp. 71–77.

McLaren, P., Hammer, R., Sholle, D., & Reilly, S. (1995). *Rethinking Media Literacy: A Critical Pedagogy of Representation*, New York: Lang.

Ravitch, D. (1990). "Multiculturalism", *The American Scholar, 59*, pp. 337–354.

Rogin, M. (1990). " 'Make My Day!': Spectacle as Amnesia in Imperial Politics", *Representations, 29*, pp. 99–123.

Sears, J. T. (1987). "Peering into the Well of Loneliness: The Responsibility of Educators to Gay and Lesbian Youth", in Alex Molnar (Ed.) *Social Issues and Education*, Alexandria, Virginia, Association for Supervision and Curriculum Development.

Seljak, D. (1991). "Alan Davies on Racism", *The Ecumenist, 29*, pp. 13–14.

Willis, P. (1990). *Common Culture*, Boulder: Westview Press.

# 19

▼▼▼▼▼▼▼

# Educational Computing as a Value-Laden Technology

Eugene F. Provenzo, Jr.

In his book *Mind and Nature*, Bateson raised the unsettling premise that schooling in Europe and America has a consistent tendency to avoid "crucial issues." In a slightly tongue-in-cheek fashion, he asked why the schools avoid addressing questions related to evolution, "social thinking—to daily life and to the eating of breakfast." According to him, most adults—supposedly educated adults—cannot provide their children with:

> ... a reasonable account of concepts such as entropy, sacrament, syntax, number, quantity, pattern, linear relation, name, class, relevance, energy, redundancy, force, probability, parts, whole, information, tautology, homology, mass (either Newtonian or Christian), explanation, description, rule of dimensions, logical type, metaphor, topology, and so on. What are butterflies? What are starfish? What are beauty and ugliness?[1]

Bateson's argument is well taken. I believe that contemporary education at both the elementary and secondary levels, and to a lesser degree, at the university level, tends to ignore most of the crucial issues facing our culture. This is particularly true in the case of issues related to technology and culture.

In this chapter, I discuss the extent to which we ignore the role of the technology of the computer in shaping our culture and educational system. In doing so, I hope to make clear what I believe are the critical social issues involving computing and contemporary education. My argument is straightforward. Although computing is playing an increasingly important role in understanding (on the part of the people using this technology—i.e., students, teachers, and administrators—and of the values and assumptions underlying its use); its deeper cultural meaning is largely ignored.

This failure to consider the cultural meaning of computing—to consider how computing affects the ecology and dynamics of the classroom and the schools—is part of a larger tendency to ignore how technology in general affects our everyday lives. We avoid questions such as: How has the automobile changed our social relations since the beginning of this century? How has it influenced where we live, where we work, how we shop, and how we interact with our neighbors and families? How has the telephone changed how we communicate? What has its effect been on business, on letter writing, on commercial transactions? How has television affected how we entertain ourselves? How has it had an impact on the social interaction of families and on what children and adults know or do not know?

In the case of computers and education, educational technologists tend to look at the computer strictly as a tool. In doing so, they assume that the machines and the software that runs them are neutral. This is not the case. The educational theorist Bowers, drawing on the work of Idhe and Heiddegger, argued that to assume that the computer is a neutral technology is naïve. Instead, Bowers maintained that it is essential to understand that computers, like all technologies, *"mediates human experience through its selection/amplification and reduction characteristics."*[2]

What this means is that the computer as a technology tends to reinforce or to de-emphasize specific cultural traits or tendencies. In doing so, the technology of the computer transforms our cultural experiences and pushes or directs us (as human beings and as learners) to experience the world in very specific ways. This is true of other technologies as well. Automobiles, for example, make possible suburbs, and in turn, shopping malls. Cars, in turn, shape the way we shop, our social interactions with shop keepers, neighbors, and so on. Such things profoundly affect our lives. Why, as Bateson asked, do we ignore these issues in so much of our education?

An example is seen in video games. Video games, such as Nintendo and Sega, are not given much attention as cutting edge computer technologies—ones that change the way children look at the world around them and that have the capacity to empower them in important new ways. The Nintendo 64 bit game player, for example, is a $200 machine that puts the power of what was a few years ago a $10,000, silicon-graphic, computer workstation in the hands of a child. Using 3-D effects that are described by the industry as "immersive," the effect is so powerful that the user is able to forget that there is a television between them and the world that is created by the machine's Reality Co-Processor chip.[3]

Entering the game world of the Nintendo 64 bit machine is a surreal experience. The graphics and sound are intensely realistic. As an adult using the system, you feel almost as though you are in a dream as the game and its challenges whiz by. Watching children play the game reveals their intense engagement in a surreal cyberscape—one with which they seem to be remarkably at ease. Games such as these are critical entry points for children to the world of computing. As Papert, the developer of the children's programming language Logo, argued:

> Video games are toys—electronic toys, no doubt, but toys—and of course children like toys better than homework. By definition, play is entertaining, homework is not. What some parents may not realize, however, is that video games, being the first example of computer technology applied to toy making, have nonetheless been the entryway for children into the world of computers. These toys, by empowering children to test out ideas about working within prefixed rules and structures in a way few other toys are capable of doing, have proved capable of teaching students about the possibilities and drawbacks of a newly presented system in many ways adults should envy.[4]

The world presented to children in video games is driven by very specific ideologies and value systems. The microworld the child enters when playing a video game was created by someone else. Unlike free play, they have little or no opportunity to shape its content. In interviewing children for my book *Video Kids: Making Sense of Nintendo*, I found 8- and 9-year-old boys wanting to be able to define the characters in the games they played to create the settings and backgrounds for the microworld constructed by the computer.[5]

Basically, video games present children with highly programmed systems of knowledge. As such, they represent very specific social and symbolic constructs. In effect, I believe that video games are powerful teaching machines and instruments of cultural transmission, which both amplify and reduce different aspects of culture.

In the case of women, for example, video games have consistently depicted them as individuals who are acted on rather than as initiators of action. In the most extreme and disturbing manifestation of this phenomenon, they are depicted as victims. This fact not only has important consequences for girls, but also for boys, who may learn to assume from the images and scenarios provided by the games that women are indeed the "weaker sex" and are continually in need of assistance and rescue. Thus, the games not only socialize women to be dependent, but also condition men to assume dominant gender roles.

For *Video Kids: Making Sense of Nintendo*, I looked at the social content of Nintendo games from the early 1990s. Part of my research involved an analysis of the 47 most popular games on the Nintendo system. Of these 47 games a total of 13—or approximately 30%—were based on scenarios in which women were kidnapped or had to be rescued as part of the game. These figures are even more revealing when one realizes that of these 47 games, 11 are based on sports such as car racing, where gender discrimination is not generally an issue. Rescue themes in which men had to be rescued were rare and the rescue was never led by a woman.

Video games are not just limited to teaching children about women as victims and their need to be rescued, but they also teach the acceptance of violence as a norm in our culture. Of the 10 most popular games on the Nintendo system, which included such titles as *Bad Dudes*, *RoboCop*, *Double Dragon* and *Double Dragon II*, all had violence and fighting as their main theme. In fact, of the 47 games analyzed in *Video Kids*, only 7 did not have violence as their main theme. Of the 40 games that emphasize violence, virtually all are based on the principle of an autonomous individual acting on his own. Although the theme of the single individual bound on a quest is not a new theme in Western culture, it is one that has disturbing implications for the establishment of traditions of community and sharing.[6]

Considering video games as a computer-mediated technology can delineate important issues about how computing communicates specific cultural and social messages, as well as providing new ways for children to perceive and understand the world. Stepping beyond the video game into more traditional models of educational computing, we can clearly see how the technology of the computer has begun to change traditional learning in profound ways. For example, the computer makes it possible for the dyslexic child to be able to gain access to information that in the past was largely limited to those who could read well. Speech synthesizers, CD-ROM discs, and related technologies make it possible for students with only limited reading capabilities to have texts read aloud to them. Individuals limited by their ability to spell can now spell perfectly, using a spell check system. Likewise, grammar checking systems can eliminate problems with verb tenses or split infinitives.

The computer contributes to greater equity in educational settings. In the case of the Internet and World Wide Web, for minimal cost (the price of a basic computer and connection to an Internet service provider—as little as $800–$1,000 per year), any school can have access to vast data banks of information—essentially to a world library. Poor schools can circumvent limited library budgets and gain access to vast sources of data.

In doing so, however, schools are also subject to a series of new forces and influences. What happens to an isolated rural school that suddenly has access to information and data on a worldwide basis? Although it can be argued that such access is little different from the type of information access provided by television (another non-neutral technology), it is, in fact, qualitatively different because it is interactive. In other words, the user can request specific types of information rather than being a passive receiver, as is the case with television or radio.

Access to information can have many consequences. A gay student, not out of the closet, living in a conservative rural community can be in touch with other youths or possibly adults with alternative sexual orientations. Information that is not normally accessible is now easily obtained. Depending on the values of the local community, such possibilities can be seen as positive or as highly undesirable.

Putting value judgments aside, the World Wide Web and Internet can change the cultural experience and, in turn, the ecology of the school and community in which it is used. Issues such as these, however, are rarely discussed as part of the training of teachers or in the context of curriculum development in the schools.

In a similar fashion, we consistently fail to discuss how the use of the computer changes the work of teachers. Do bad teachers make maximum use of the computer as an unreflective rote drill and memory device? Is the computer simply used as a means by which students can be kept busy with largely meaningless seatwork? Will a creative and dynamic teacher use a computer to bring a wider range of resources to the student?

How do administrations and bureaucracies make use of computers? Are computers only record keeping devices for them or tools for empowering teachers and students? Are they a means of keeping students and teachers under surveillance and control? Computer instructional programs can be designed to record and evaluate every input and keystroke made by a student. How should such information be used? Who should have access to it? Should such information even be compiled? Should teachers be held accountable for their students' answers?

Educational computing clearly changes both the administration and the content of instruction. As someone who regularly uses computers not only as a tool for preparing classes, but also as an actual tool in classroom settings, I have had to significantly change my role as an instructor because of the new technology. For example, in a graduate course on immigration and education, which I recently taught, I used extensive online resources with students. For several evenings, we went to the computer lab and connected to Web sites on the Internet that I had previously located and that were relevant to the course's lectures and reading and discussion assignments.

Because many of the Web sites I selected were linked to other sites, students had a tendency to wander to new sites and data sources that I had not visited. Sometimes these sites were interesting and relevant to what I was trying to accomplish with the course. Often, however, they proved to be distractions. What was clear was that as an instructor using the Web with my students, I lost part of my control over the texts we were examining. My teaching had to be adjusted accordingly, as an introductory lecture and reading course began to take on many of the characteristics of an advanced research seminar. This was not necessarily bad. Yet, what needed to be understood was that the possibilities offered by the Web and the Internet and how students used it changed how and what I taught.

The point of this is that which Bowers maintained—the use of computers in educational settings selects for the amplification and reduction of different things. This can be a result of the computer program and how it shapes the information that is presented to the learner—i.e., the computer as a programmer of the child can be seen to operate in a number of different ways. An example of the computer as programmer of the child is seen in the use of simulation software. Prior to the introduction of computers to the schools, the use of simulation models was relatively limited as a form of instruction. In large part, this was a result of the difficulty of putting a good simulation together and keeping it running. With computers, however, the use of simulations became much more convenient.

Simulations are inherently limited and contain within them specific ideological perspectives or points of view. Our use of them in classroom settings needs to be careful and considered. A popular simulation used in many middle school and junior high school classrooms demonstrating this point is *Populous*.

In *Populous*, you assume the role of one of two gods who rule a world and its people. One of the gods is evil and the other is good. Each god is assigned a population of people whom they nurture and try to help flourish. As a review of the game explains, "Your task is to make the lives of your people as prosperous as possible, fostering their growth by divinely manipulating their environment."[7]

The perspective provided in *Populous* is of an omniscient god who shapes and directs the lives of the people (called "walkers") on the planet. A review of the game by Firme explained how:

> Skeptics will be surprised at how enjoyable playing a god turns out to be. The walkers, both good and bad, are fascinating to watch as they move about. They really seem to have lives of their own, and your control over their lives gives you an undeniable sense of power. . . . Soon you'll find yourself feeling parental about your followers, nurturing them and watching them grow. You'll be happy to wipe out the evil walkers with volcanoes, swamps and earthquakes should they stand in the way of your chosen people.[8]

What is clearly at work in this simulation are a series of assumptions about the desirability of power and control and about the need of other people to be directed. The viewpoint is that of an all-powerful god who acts on people (walkers) rather than with people (walkers). The world is shaped and defined by a relatively narrow and circumscribed set of forces (volcanoes, earthquakes, and so on).

A simulation such as *Populous* is neither neutral nor without a specific point of view. As Firme noted, "It's amazingly easy to develop delusions of grandeur while playing *Populous*, . . ."[9] Will students playing games such as *Populous* simply assume that this is how the world is run? Will they incorporate such models into their own lives? Does a teacher using such a system in the classroom have any means by which to distinguish good from evil, to delineate variables that may be affecting what is occurring in the simulation? How does the omniscient perspective influence what the players do? Would they act differently if they were one of the walkers?

Concerns about the use of a simulation, such as *Populous*, directly address Bowers' question of "whether the current state of computer technology used in the classroom strengthens those cultural orientations contributing to a technicist social order and weakens others that cannot be integrated into the new emerging order."[10] It should also be noted that as increasingly sophisticated simulations are created using technologies such as virtual reality, the power of these simulations over the user has the potential to become even greater.

I would argue that the very nature of a simulation, and the hardware and software that runs it, tends to encourage the type of model seen in *Populous*. A similar phenomenon is seen in video games such as *Super Mario Bros. 2* or *Street Fighter II*, where the player in an almost godlike manner, manipulates a small figure on the screen, compelling it to act in certain ways.

To what extent models such as these actually influence students is difficult to say. The point is that educators need to be aware of the extent to which specific cultural messages are being communicated or not communicated. In addressing this issue, it is useful to introduce concepts such as the *hidden curriculum* and *null curriculum*. In the case of *hidden curriculum*, computer programs frequently provide much more in the way of specific social instruction than seems to be the case at first. In a simulation, such as *Populous*, students may be taught that the world is controlled—or should be controlled—by master planners and that the little people do not count and are simply pawns to be manipulated. The essentially antidemocratic message of such a model is obvious.

In the case of the *null curriculum* and educational computing, we need to consider what is excluded from the learning process by using the computer. What happens when a student goes on an electronic field trip via the Internet or a CD-ROM to an art museum versus actually visiting a museum in person or using a well-illustrated textbook?

Although most people readily concede that the Internet is a limited learning environment when compared to an actual art museum with its galleries and exhibits, they would not necessarily see it as a less rich environment than a well-illustrated book. Yet, the information provided on a computer screen is far less dense than a printed book. Most high quality art books print with screens at 1,200 dots per inch. The average computer screen has a resolution of only 480 by 640 dots per inch. The intensity of the graphic message, details of the image, and so forth, as a result, are significantly less than those provided through a printed source.

In fact, the computer presents a very different type of information than the traditional book. Books are relatively static documents. They are written by an author, edited, revised, and finally frozen in print. They describe rather than illustrate phenomena. Except for an occasional photograph or drawing, most books are text-based. Individuals using books draw on certain models for processing information. Reading and learning from books favors certain models of learning and behavior. Silent reading for study is a solitary act. When you read from a book, you are largely locked in a single source or way of viewing the world. Although there can be references to other sources, the work you are reading at the time tends to take on a greater authority.

Information presented on the computer by means of a delivery system, such as the Internet, can easily be revised and updated. Multimedia functions, such as sound and motion pictures, can be inserted in the place of more traditional text descriptions. Individuals who learn better in a visual or auditory context rather than a strictly textual context are better served by the computer. A new electronic space for reading and learning is created— one that is significantly different from more traditional print-based books.

An Internet-based text or learning space can connect the reader to multiple texts and sources. Thus, if I go to George Landow's home page at Brown University and enter his *Victorian Web*, which is a World Wide Web research and teaching site on Victorian literature, I do not simply read his analysis, but I can be linked to original documents, critical analysis by authors, as well as to other web sites that are concerned with issues involving Victorian culture and society. Not only can I read Landow's work, but I can leave comments for him or even contribute materials to his web site. Suppose, for example, that I develop an independent Web site on Victorian education. Such materials would almost certainly be of interest to Landow and his students. Through a hyperlink, they could easily be connected at their web site to whatever material I collected. Teaching a course in a university through the Internet now has the potential to become a much more extended process in which courses and materials across universities and distant geographic sites can be connected and linked together.

How does all of this change the fundamental nature of learning, our definitions of literacy, and education in the future? These are critical issues and represent just a few cases of how computers shape cultural assumptions and act as filters for interpreting the world. Each example points to Bowers' argument for the non-neutrality of the computer, and his point that, "Understanding how the educational use of computers influences our pattern of thinking, and thus contributes to changes in the symbolic underpinnings of the culture, should be considered an essential aspect of computer literacy."[11] Current programs in teacher training, as well as workshops and classes for bringing experienced teachers up to speed in using technology in the classroom, consistently fail to look at educational computing in a social and cultural context. Like Bowers, I believe that this is extremely dangerous. As computers are increasingly integrated into the curriculum of the schools, we need to critically understand what they amplify and reduce. Educational computing, although having enormous potential, is ultimately a dangerous thing if the students, teachers, and administrators who use it have no notion of the values and social constructions that underlie it.

What are the ideological assumptions underlying educational computing? What aspects of culture are amplified or reduced through its use? These are significant questions that deserve greater consideration if we are to have a better understanding of the potential of educational computing to shape and define not only our schools and what our children learn, but also our culture.

## NOTES

1. Gregory Bateson, *Mind and Nature: A Necessary Unity* (New York: Bantam Books, 1980), pp. 3–4.
2. C. A. Bowers, *Educating for an Ecologically Sustainable Culture: Rethinking Moral Education, creativity, Intelligence and Other Modern Orthodoxies* (Albany, N.Y.: State University of New York Press, 1995), p. 79. Also see: C. A. Bowers, *The Cultural Dimensions of Educational Computing: Understanding the Non-Neutrality of Technology* (New York: Teachers College Press, 1988).
3. For a discussion of the merging of video games and television into a new interactive media see: Eugene F. Provenzo, Jr., " 'Brave New Video,'. Video Games and the Emergence of Interactive Television for Children," *Taboo: The Journal of Culture and Education*, Vol. 1 #1, Spring 1995, pp. 151–162. Also see: Eugene F. Provenzo, Jr., "Video Games and the Emergence of Interactive Media for Children," in *Kinderculture: Exploring Cults of Childhood*, edited by Shirley R. Steinberg and Joe L. Kincheloe (Denver: Westview Press, in press); and Eugene F. Provenzo, Jr., "Electronically Mediated and Simulated Playscapes," *Play from Birth to Twelve: Contexts, perspectives and Meanings*," Doris Fromberg and Doris Bergen, editors (New York: Garland Press, in press).
4. Seymour Papert, *The Children's Machine: Rethinking School in the Age of the Computer* (New York: Basic Books, 1993), p. 4.
5. Eugene F. Provenzo, Jr., *Video Kids: Making Sense of Nintendo* (Cambridge: Harvard University Press, 1991).
6. *Ibid*, p. 109.
7. Matthew A. Firme, "Populous," *Game Player's PC Strategy Guide*, March/April 1990, p. 91.
8. *Ibid.*
9. *Ibid.*, p. 90.
10. Bowers, *The Cultural Dimensions of Educational Computing*, p. 6.
11. *Ibid*, p. 3.

# 20

▼▼▼▼▼▼▼

# Care and Moral Education*

Nel Noddings

Increased interest in moral education in the past few years has led to vigorous debate among moral educators. In addition to the ongoing dialogue between cognitive-developmentalism and character education,[1] the ethic of care has been introduced as a perspective on moral education.[2] Because the ethic of care has roots in both feminism and pragmatic naturalism, and because moral education is at its very heart, it holds interest for educators as well as philosophers.

## AN ETHIC OF CARE AND ITS SOURCE

Like deontological ethics—ethics of duty and right—the ethic of care speaks of obligation. A sense that *I must* do something arises when others address us. This "I must" is induced in direct encounter, in preparation for response. Sometime we, as carers, attend and respond because we want to; we love the ones who address us, or we have sufficient positive regard for them, or the request is so consonant with ordinary life that no inner conflict occurs. In a similar fashion, the recipients of such care may respond in a way that shows us that our caring has been received. When this happens, we say that the relation, episode, or encounter is one of natural caring. The "I must" expresses a desire or inclination—not a recognition of duty.

At other times, the initial "I must" is met by internal resistance. Simultaneously, we recognize the other's need and we resist; for some reason—the other's unpleasantness, our own fatigue, the magnitude of the need—we do

---

*Reprinted from *Critical Conversations in Philosophy of Education*, edited by Wendy Kohli, 1995, with permission of the publisher, Routledge, NY.

not want to respond as carers. In such instances, we have to draw on ethical caring; we have to ask ourselves how we would behave if this other were pleasant or were a loved one, if we were not tired, if the need were not so great. In doing this, we draw upon an ethical ideal—a set of memories of caring and being cared for that we regard as manifestations of our best selves and relations. We summon what we need to maintain the original "I must."

Now why should we do this? Why, that is, do we recognize an obligation to care? If we were Kantians, we would trace our obligation to reason, to a commitment that logic will not allow us to escape. But in the ethic of care we accept our obligation because we value the relatedness of natural caring. Ethical caring is always aimed at establishing, restoring, or enhancing the kind of relation in which we respond freely because we want to do so.

An ethic of care does not eschew logic and reasoning. When we care, we must employ reasoning to decide what to do and how best to do it. We strive for competence because we want to do our best for those we care for. But reason is not what motivates us. It is feeling with and for the other that motivates us in natural caring. In ethical caring, this feeling is subdued, and so it must be augmented by a feeling for our own ethical selves.

Kant subordinated feeling to reason. He insisted that only acts done out of duty to carefully reasoned principle are morally worthy. Love, feeling, and inclination are all supposed by Kant to be untrustworthy. An ethic of care inverts these priorities. The preferred state is natural caring; ethical caring is invoked to restore it. This inversion of priority is one great difference between Kantian ethics and the ethic of care.

Another difference is anchored in feminist perspectives. An ethic of care is thoroughly relational. It is the *relation* to which we point when we use the adjective "caring." A relation may fail to be one of caring because the carer fails to be attentive or, having attended, rejects the "I must" and refuses to respond. Or, it may fail because the cared-for is unable or unwilling to respond; he or she does not receive the efforts of the carer, and therefore caring is not completed. Or, finally, both carer and cared-for may try to respond appropriately but some condition prevents completion; perhaps there has been too little time for an adequate relation to develop and the carer aims rather wildly at what he or she thinks the cared-for needs. A relational interpretation of caring pushes us to look not only at moral agents but at both the recipients of their acts and the conditions under which the parties interact.

Of course, the adjective "caring" is often used to refer to people who habitually care. There are people who attend and respond to others regularly and who have such a well-developed capacity to care that they can establish caring relations in even the most difficult situations. But, at bottom, the ethic of care should not be thought of as an ethic of virtue. Certainly, people who care in given situations exercise virtues, but if they begin to concentrate on their own character or virtue, the cared-for may feel put off. The cared-for is no longer the focus of attention. Rather, a virtue—being patient, or generous, or cheerful—becomes the focus, and the relation of caring itself becomes at risk.

From this very brief exposition of an ethic of care, we can see that moral education is at its very heart. We learn first how to be cared for, how to respond to loving efforts at care in a way that supports those efforts. An infant learns to smile at its caregiver, and this response so delights the caregiver that he or she seeks greater competence in producing smiles. Caregiver and cared-for enter a mutually satisfying relation. Later, the child learns to care for others—to comfort a crying baby, pet a kitten, pat a sad or tired mother with a murmured, "Poor mommy!"

The source of adult caring is thus two-fold. Because we (lucky ones) have been immersed in relations of care since birth, we often naturally respond as carers to others. When we need to draw on ethical caring, we turn to an ethical ideal constituted from memories of caring and being cared for. Thus the ethic of care may be regarded as a form of pragmatic naturalism. It does not posit a source of moral life beyond actual human interaction. It does not depend on gods, nor eternal verities, nor an essential human nature, nor postulated underlying structures of human consciousness. Even its relational ontology points to something observable in this world—the fact that *I* am defined in relation, that none of us could be an *individual*, or a *person*, or an entity recognizably human if we were not in relation.

It is obvious, then, that if we value relations of care, we must care for our children and teach them how to receive care and to give care. Further, our obligation does not end with the moral education of children. Contrary to Kant, who insisted that each person's moral perfection is his or her own project, we remain at least partly responsible for the moral development of each person we encounter. How I treat you may bring out the best or worst in you. How you behave may provide a model for me to grow and become better than I am. Whether I can become and remain a caring person—one who enters regularly into caring relations—depends in large part on how you respond to me. Further, ethical caring requires reflection and self-understanding. We need to understand our own capacities and how we are likely to react in various situations. We need to understand our own evil and selfish tendencies as well as our good and generous ones. Hence moral education is an essential part of an ethic of care, and much of moral education is devoted to the understanding of self and others.

## THE COMPONENTS OF MORAL EDUCATION

Modeling, the first component of moral education in the care perspective, is important in almost every form of moral education. In the character education tradition, for example, it is central because exemplars constitute the very foundation of moral philosophy.[3] In the care perspective, we have to show in our modeling what it means to care.

There is a danger in putting too much emphasis on the modeling component of caring. When we focus on ourselves as models, we are distracted from the cared-for; the same peculiar distraction occurs, as we have seen, when we concentrate on our own exercise of virtue. Usually, we present the best possible model when we care unselfconsciously, as a way of being in the world. When we do reflect, our attention should be on the relation between us and the cared-for: Is our response adequate? Could we put what we have said better? Has our act helped or hindered? We do not often reflect on our observers and what our behavior conveys to them. And this is as it should be.

But sometimes we must focus on ourselves as models of caring. When we show a small girl how to handle a pet, for example, our attention may be only peripherally on the pet. Our focal attention is on the little girl and whether she is learning from our demonstration. Similarly, as teachers, we often properly divert our attention from a particular student to the whole class of watchers. What does our behavior with this particular student convey to the class about what it means to care? As I said earlier, the shift of focus has its dangers and carried too far, it actually moves us away from caring.

In quiet moments, in the absence of those we must care for, reflection is essential. Not only should we reflect on our competence as carers, but we can now also consider our role as models. If I am, as a teacher, consistently very strict with my students "for their own good," what am I conveying? One teacher may emerge from such reflection satisfied that caring rightly forces cared-fors to do what is best for them. Another may emerge appalled that her efforts at care may suggest to students that caring is properly manifested in coercion. If the two get together to talk, both may be persuaded to modify their behavior, and this observation leads logically to the second component of moral education in this model.

Dialogue is the most fundamental component of the care model. True dialogue is open-ended, as Paulo Freire wrote.[4] The participants do not know at the outset what the conclusions will be. Both speak; both listen. Dialogue is not just conversation. There must be a topic, but the topic may shift, and either party in a dialogue may divert attention from the original topic to one more crucial, or less sensitive, or more fundamental.

The emphasis on dialogue points up the basic phenomenology of caring. A carer must attend to or be engrossed in the cared-for, and the cared-for must receive the carer's efforts at caring. This reception, too, is a form of attention. People in true dialogue within a caring relation do not turn their attention wholly to intellectual objects, although, of course, they may do this for brief intervals. Rather, they attend non-selectively to one another. Simone Weil described the connection this way:

The love of our neighbor in all its fullness simply means being able to say to him: "What are you going through?" It is a recognition that the sufferer exists, not only as a unit in a collection, or a specimen from the social category labeled "unfortunate," but as a man, exactly like us. . . . This way of looking is first of all attentive. The soul empties itself of all its own contents in order to receive into itself the being it is looking at, just as he is, in all his truth.

Only he who is capable of attention can do this.[5]

The other in a dialogue need not be suffering, but carers are always aware of the possibility of suffering. If the topic-at-hand causes pain, a caring participant may change the subject. Dialogue is sprinkled with episodes of interpersonal reasoning as well as the logical reasoning characteristic of intellectual debate.[6] A participant may pause to remind the other of her strengths, to reminisce, to explore, to express concern, to have a good laugh, or otherwise to connect with the other as cared-for. Dialogue, thus, always involves attention to the other participant, not just to the topic under discussion.

Dialogue is central to moral education because it always implies the question: What are you going through? It permits disclosure in a safe setting, and thus makes it possible for a carer to respond appropriately. Dialogue provides information about the participants, supports the relationship, induces further thought and reflection, and contributes to the communicative competence of its participants. As modes of dialogue are internalized, moral agents learn to talk to themselves as they talk to others. Such dialogue is an invitation to ever-deepening self-understanding. What do I really want? What was I trying to do when I acted as I did? What (good or evil) am I capable of? Am I too hard on myself? Am I honest with myself? One important aim of dialogue with others or with self is understanding the "other" with whom one is in dialogue.

Dialogue as described here rejects the "war model" of dialogue. It is not debate, and its purpose is not to win an argument. It may, of course, include intervals of debate, and both participants may enjoy such intervals. But throughout a dialogue, participants are aware of each other; they take turns as carer and cared-for, and no matter how great their ideological differences may be, they reach across the ideological gap to connect with each other.

One organization that has put aside the "war model" of dialogue is a group of women on opposite sides of the abortion issue; they call themselves Common Ground. (Actually, several organizations using this name have sprung up around the country, but the one to which I refer here is in the San Francisco Bay Area.) The purpose of Common Ground is not for each side to argue its own convictions and effect a glorious victory over ignorant or evil opponents. Rather, the explicit primary goal is to "reject the war model of the abortion argument and fully recognize that human beings, not cardboard cut-outs, make up the 'other side'."[7] The women of Common Ground describe themselves as "frustrated and heartsick at what the abortion controversy has done to traditionally female values such as communication, compassion, and empathy." But can an issue like abortion be resolved through communication, compassion, and empathy? That question misses the whole point of the approach being discussed here. The point of coming together in true dialogue is *not* to persuade opponents that our own position is better justified logically and ethically than theirs. The issue may never be resolved. The point is to create or restore relations in which natural caring will guide future discussion and protect participants from inflicting and suffering pain. Many of the women of Common Ground continue their advocacy roles in pro-life or pro-choice organizations because advocacy/adversary roles are the only ones widely accepted in American politics. But their advocacy functions are deepened and softened by the goal of Common Ground—to maintain caring relations across differences. Strategies that participants might once have considered against faceless adversaries are now firmly rejected.

Common Ground may well achieve desirable practical outcomes beyond a cessation of violence and name-calling. Already, women of opposing views on abortion have agreed on other goals: providing aid to existing children who are needy, helping poor mothers, defending women who are deserted or abused. Energies have been diverted from condemning and fighting to accomplishing positive, cooperative goals and, more important, to the establishment of relations that will allow ideological opponents to live constructively with their differences.

Talk, conversation, and debate are used in every form of moral education, but often the focus is on justifying moral decisions. Cognitive programs of moral education concentrate on helping students to develop moral reasoning. In sorting through dilemmas, students learn to justify the positions they take and to judge the strength of other people's arguments. It is certainly worthwhile to exercise and strengthen students' powers of reason, but advocates of the care perspective worry that students may forget the purpose of moral reasoning—to establish and maintain caring relations at both individual and societal levels. Of course, advocates of a cognitive approach to moral education may deny that caring relations are central to moral reasoning. They may argue, instead, that the purpose of moral reasoning is to figure out what is right. This involves an evaluation of principles and selection of the one that should guide moral action. If this were done regularly by everyone, they might argue, we would achieve a just society and reduce individual suffering considerably. But care advocates worry about principles chosen and decisions made in abstract isolation, and we worry, too, about the assumption that what is right can be determined logically, without hearing what others are actually going through.

The theoretical differences between care and justice perspectives are too many and too deep to explore here. However, one point is especially relevant to the present discussion. There is some evidence that students exposed to cognitive approaches often come to believe that almost any decision can be justified, that the strength of their arguments is what really counts.[8] Cognitivist educators are not happy with this result, but to change it, they have to lead students toward concepts that help to anchor their thinking. They usually depend on a procedural mechanism to determine right or wrong. Care theorists more often line up with consequentialists here. In trying to figure out what is right, we have to find out what is good for the people involved. But this does not make us utilitarians, either. We do not posit one stable, abstract, universal good and try to produce that for the greatest number. Rather, we must work to determine what is good for this person or these people and how our proposed action will affect all of those in the network of care. Dialogue is the means through which we learn what the other wants and needs, and it is also the means by which we monitor the effects of our acts. We ask, "What are you going through?" before we act, as we act, and after we act. It is our way of being in relation.

A third component of moral education in the care perspective is practice. One must work at developing the capacity for interpersonal attention. Simone Weil thought that this capacity could be developed through the "right use of school studies"—especially subjects like geometry.[9] But all of us know people who are wonderfully attentive in an intellectual field and almost totally insensitive to people and their needs. To develop the capacity to care, one must engage in caregiving activities.

In almost all cultures, women seem to develop the capacity to care more often and more deeply than men. Most care theorists do not believe that this happens because of something innate or essential in women. Care theorists believe that it happens because girls are expected to care for people, and boys are too often relieved of this expectation. This is an open question, of course, but the hope of moral educators is that both sexes can learn to care. Indeed, most care theorists oppose any position that confines caring to women because it would tend to encourage the exploitation of women and undermine our efforts at moral education. Caring is not just for women, nor is it a way of being reserved only for private life.

What sort of practice should children have? It seems reasonable to suggest that, just as girls should have mathematical and scientific experience, boys should have caregiving experience. Boys, like girls, should attend to the needs of guests, care for smaller children, perform housekeeping chores, and the like. The supposition, from a care perspective, is that the closer we are to the intimate physical needs of life, the more likely we are to understand its fragility and to feel the pangs of the inner "I must"—that stirring of the heart that moves us to respond to one another.

Similarly, in schools, students should be encouraged to work together, to help one another—not just to improve academic performance. Teachers have a special responsibility to convey the moral importance of cooperation to their students. Small-group methods that involve inter-group competition should be monitored closely. Competition can be fun, and insisting that it has no place whatever in cooperative arrangements leads us into unnecessary confrontation. But, if competition induces insensitive interactions, teachers should draw this to the attention of their students and suggest alternative strategies. Such discussions can lead to interesting and fruitful analyses of competition at other levels of society.

Many high schools—more independent than public—have begun to require community service as a means of giving their students practice in caring. But a community service requirement cannot guarantee that students will care, any more than the requirement to "take algebra" can ensure that students will learn algebra in any meaningful way. Community service must be taken seriously as an opportunity to practice caring. Students must be placed in sites congenial to their interests and capacities. The people from whom they are to learn must model caring effectively, and this means that they must be capable of shifting their attention gently and sensitively from those they are caretaking, to those they are teaching. Students should also participate in a regular seminar at which they can engage in dialogue about their practice.

The last component of moral education from the care perspective is confirmation.[10] To confirm others is to bring out the best in them. When someone commits an uncaring act (judged, of course, from our own perspective), we respond—if we are engaging in confirmation—by attributing the best possible motive consonant with reality. By starting this way, we draw the cared-for's attention to his or her better self. We confirm the other by showing that we believe the act in question is not a full reflection of the one who committed it.

Confirmation is very different from the pattern found in many forms of religious education: accusation, confession, forgiveness, and penance. Accusation tends to drive carer and cared-for apart; it may thereby weaken the relation. Confession and forgiveness suggest a relation of authority and subordinate and may prevent transgressors from taking full responsibility for their acts. Further, confession and forgiveness can be ritualized. When this happens, there is no genuine dialogue. What happens does not depend on the relation between carer and cared-for, and the interaction is not aimed at strengthening the relation. Hence it has little effect on the construction of an ethical ideal in either carer or cared-for, since this ideal is composed reflectively from memories of caring and being cared for.

Confirmation is not a ritual act that can be performed for any person by any other person. It requires a relation. Carers have to understand their cared-fors well enough to know what it is they are trying to accomplish. Attributing the best possible motive consonant with reality requires a knowl-

edge of that reality, and cannot be pulled out of thin air. When carers identify
a motive and use it in confirmation, the cared-for should recognize it as his
or her own. "That is what I was trying to do!" It is wonderfully reassuring
to realize that another sees the better self that often struggles for recognition
beneath our lesser acts and poorer selves.

PHILOSOPHICAL ISSUES

The model of moral education discussed here is based on an ethic of care.
That ethic has an element of universality. It begins with the recognition that
all people everywhere want to be cared for. Universality evaporates when
we try to describe exactly what it means to care, for manifestations of caring
relations differ across times, cultures, and even individuals. In roughly similar
settings and situations, one person may recognize a cool form of respect as
caring, whereas another may feel uncared for without a warm hug.

   Because of its beginning in natural attributes and events, caring may
properly be identified with pragmatic naturalism. John Dewey started his
ethical thought with the observation that human beings are social animals and
desire to communicate. The ethic of care begins with the universal desire to be
cared for—to be in positive relation with at least some other beings. We note
that human beings do in fact place a high value on such relations, and so our
most fundamental "ought" arises as instrumental: If we value such relations,
then we ought to act so as to create, maintain, and enhance them.

   As Dewey filled out his moral theory, he moved rapidly to problem
solving—surely one aim of communication. As we fill out an ethic of care,
we concentrate on the needs and responses required to maintain caring
relations. The difference need not be construed as a gender difference, but
it may indeed be the case that the care orientation arises more naturally and
fully from the kind of experience traditionally associated with women. Dewey
himself once remarked that when women started to do philosophy, they
would almost surely "do it differently." This observation in no way implies
that a gender difference must forever divide philosophical thinking. Mutual
influence, critical reciprocity, may produce models that incorporate elements
of both perspectives. However, it may be years before female philosophies
are themselves fully developed. Will we finish up at the same place by a
different route? Or will even the endpoint be different? These are intriguing
questions for contemporary moral philosophy.

   Whereas there is an element of universality in the ethic of care, we cannot
claim universality for the model of moral education. Probably all moral
educators incorporate modeling and practice in their educational programs,
but many would reject confirmation, and some would reject the focus on
dialogue, emphasizing instead commandment and obedience. Proponents of

caring do not regard the lack of universality as a weakness. On the contrary, many of us feel that insistence on universal models is a form of cultural arrogance. Here we differ strongly with Kohlbergians on at least two matters: First, we see no reason to believe that people everywhere must reason or manifest their caring in identical ways; second, although we put great emphasis on intelligent action, we reject a narrow focus on reason itself. It is not just the level and power of reasoning that mark moral agents as well developed but the actual effects of their behavior on the relations of which they are part. Moreover, it is not so much the development of individual moral agents that interests us but the maintenance and growth of moral relations, and this is a very different focus.[11]

Care advocates differ also with certain aspects of character education. Although we share with Aristotelians and others who call themselves "communitarians" the conviction that modern moral philosophy has put far too much emphasis on individual moral agents wrestling in lonely isolation with logically decidable moral problems, we also fear the Aristotelian emphasis on social role or function. This emphasis can lead to hierarchies of virtue and demands for unwavering loyalty to church or state. Different virtues are expected of leaders and followers, men and women, bosses and workers. Further, educational models tend to suppose that communities can arrive at consensus on certain values and/or virtues.

Early in this century, the Character Development League sought to inculcate in all students a long list of virtues including obedience, industry, purity, self-reliance, courage, justice, and patriotism.[12] Probably both Kohlbergians and care advocates would agree that school children should have many opportunities to discuss such virtues and that they should read and hear inspiring stories illustrating the exercise of virtue. But to rely on community consensus is to lean on a wall made of flimsy material and colorful paint. If we all agree that honesty is somehow important, we probably disagree on exactly how it is manifested and how far it should be carried. Whereas Kant would have us never tell a lie and Charles Wesley spoke approvingly of the ancient father's statement "I would not tell a wilful lie to save the souls of the whole world,"[13] most of us would lie readily to save a life, a soul, or even the feelings of someone, if doing so would cause no further harm. Indeed, we might feel morally obligated to do so.

From a care perspective, we might begin with *apparent* consensus but with the frankly acknowledged purpose of uncovering and developing an appreciation for our legitimate differences. The need to do this—to respond to the universal desire for care (for respect, or love, or help, or understanding) underscores the centrality of dialogue. We must talk to one another. Sometimes we are successful at persuading them, sometimes they persuade us, and sometimes we must simply agree to go on caring across great ideological differences. Unless we probe beneath the surface of apparent consensus, we risk silencing divergent and creative voices. We risk also, allowing a core of powerful authorities to establish a fixed set of approved virtues and values.

A central question today in debate over the introduction of values education is exactly the one alluded to above: Whose values? One group would press for its own; another would press for consensus. Care theorists would answer, "Everyone's!" But, with cognitivists, care theorists would subject all values to careful, critical scrutiny and, with character educators, we would insist that the effects of our choices on our communities and the effects of our communities on our choices be treated with appreciation. We would insist that our community—nation, town, classroom, family—stands for something, and we would attempt to socialize our children to the stated standards.[14] But we would do this with a respectful uncertainty, encouraging the question *why*, and recognizing our responsibility to present opposing alternatives as honestly as we can. Despite sometimes irresolvable differences, students should not forget the central aim of moral life—to encounter, attend, and respond to the need for care.

This reminder is well directed at moral educators as well. Although we differ on a host of issues in moral philosophy and psychology, as educators, we have a common aim—to contribute to the continuing moral education of both students and teachers. With that as our aim, we, too, should reject the war model and adopt a mode of constructive and genuine dialogue.

## NOTES

1. See Larry P. Nucci, ed., *Moral Development and Character Education* (Berkeley: McCutchan, 1989).
2. See Nel Noddings, *Caring: A Feminine Perspective on Ethics and Moral Education* (Berkeley and Los Angeles: University of California Press, 1984); also *Women and Evil* (Berkeley and Los Angeles: University of California Press, 1989); and *The Challenge to Care in Schools* (New York: Teachers College Press, 1992).
3. For the foundation of this approach, see Aristotle, *Nicomachean Ethics*, trans. Terence Irwin (Indianapolis: Hackett, 1985).
4. Paulo Freire, *Pedagogy of the Oppressed*, trans. Myra Bergman Ramos (New York: Herder and Herder, 1970).
5. Simone Weil, "Reflections on the Right Use of School Studies with a View to the Love of God," in *Simone Weil Reader*, ed. George A. Panichas (Mt. Kisco, N.Y.: Moyer Bell Limited, 1977), p. 51.
6. See Nel Noddings, "Stories in Dialogue: Caring and Interpersonal Reasoning," in *Stories Lives Tell: Narrative and Dialogue in Education*, ed. Carol Witherell and Nel Noddings (New York: Teachers College Press, 1991), pp. 157–70.
7. Stephanie Salton, "Pro-life + pro-choice = Common Ground," *San Francisco Chronicle*, August 30, 1992, A15.
8. Instructors at the University of Montana, which now requires all undergraduates to take two courses in ethics, have noted this unfortunate result of the dilemma approach.
9. Weil, "Right Use of School Studies."
10. Confirmation is described in Martin Buber, *I and Thou*, trans. Walter Kaufmann (New York: Charles Scribner's Sons, 1970).

11. The relational perspective is described in psychological terms in Carol Gilligan, *In a Different Voice* (Cambridge: Harvard University Press, 1982); see also Mary F. Belenky, Blythe M. Clinchy, Nancy R. Goldberger, and Jill M. Tarule, *Women's Ways of Knowing* (New York: Basic Books, 1986).

12. See James Terry White, *Character Lessons in American Biography for Public Schools and Home Instruction* (New York: The Character Development League, 1909).

13. Quoted in Sissela Bok, *Lying: Moral Choice in Public and Private Life* (New York: Vintage Books, 1979), p. 34.

14. Even Lawrence Kohlberg acknowledged the need to socialize children. See Kohlberg, "Moral Education Reappraised," *The Humanist* 38 (Nov.–Dec., 1978): 13–15. In this article Kohlberg accepts the need to "indoctrinate." I do not think we need to indoctrinate. We socialize but always encourage students to ask *why*.

# 21
▼▼▼▼▼▼▼

# Education and Spirituality*

Dwayne Huebner

How can one talk about the education, specifically, curriculum, and also talk about the spiritual? The problem is one of language and of the images that are both a source and consequence of that language. With what language tools and images (metaphors, ideas) do we describe, envision, and think critically about education? Thanks to Macdonald, Pinar, Apple, and a variety of other curriculum writers who stand on their shoulders, we no longer have the horrendous hegemony of technical language (drawing primarily on learning theory and ends/means structures) usurping discussion of education. Nevertheless, that language orientation is strongly established, embodied in educational architecture, materials, methods, organizations, and teacher education. Breaking out of that language is difficult, however, for the structures and processes which shape education—themselves derivatives of that language—force conversation into that technical mode. Our very locations and practices are framed by the language tools and images we would like to overcome.

We depend upon the language, practices, and materials as if they were the givens with which we have to work. We have forgotten or suppressed that imagination is a foundation of our so-called "givens." Our languages, practices, and resources are merely the embodied or materialized images in which we chose to dwell. Other images, in which we could dwell, are currently unembodied in worldly structures and abandoned. But embodied images are no more a reality than are unembodied images a mere figment of an "unreality." Embodied, or materialized images, and the language patterns associated with them, are more directly related to our sensory systems and our

*Huebner, Dwayne. "Education and Spirituality." From *Journal of Curriculum Theorizing*, Rochester, NY: Corporation for Curriculum Research, 1991, Vol 11: No. 2, 9/95 (pp. 13–34).

relations with powerful people. However, our sensory systems, and our social/political systems, are in touch with but a small part of the reality of the universe. The complicated and expensive technologies of modern physics take us into the strange world of electromagnetic frequencies, matter and anti-matter, particles and waves that several years ago were far beyond our wildest dreams, rooted only in the imaginations of science fiction writers. The mysterious crop circles throughout the globe also indicate the limited contact of our sensory systems, and their congruent language resources, with a larger, more encompassing reality. Religious and meditative communities point to other limitations of our sensory systems, and to alternative social/political structures.[1]

Can education be re-imagined? This does not mean inventing new language, new practice, and new resources, new buildings. It means having a different view of people, of our educational spaces and resources, of what we do and what we say—a view that will enable us to critique the embodied images, see obstacles, and recognize alternatives.

My vocational history indicates how one person became aware of the problem and tried to solve it—a move from secular to religious education. I recall my first year or two of teaching in elementary schools. Piaget had not yet influenced educational language—although the research on concept development was underway. Aware of that beginning research, I wishfully thought that I could do a better job of planning and teaching if I knew what was going on in the heads of my students. I wanted to discover what was going on inside heads, through my own research or that of others. Several years later I began to question the educator's dependency on the research enterprise, and realized the absurdity of my wishful thinking. It had the same quality as the question, "What do you do until a cure is found for the disease that we have?" Do you stop living and working and wait until there is more knowledge? Can action be postponed until more is known? If so, we have an infinite regress of waiting as new problems emerge. Is empirically based knowledge necessary before one can teach? Is there wisdom independent of research, yet open to that research? People have been teaching for centuries without research based knowledge. Obviously, they have not been without wisdom.

What do we do until a cure is discovered? We live and work, talk and play, laugh and cry, love and hate with our friends and neighbors. Our students share with us the human condition. They are our neighbors, if not our friends. The language of teacher/student—specifically the language of teacher/learner—hides that neighborliness, and the student's strangeness. We and our students are part and parcel of the same mysterious universe.

It is a universe in which we know more than we can say, and often say more than we know, to quote Polanyi. It is much fuller, deeper, stranger, more complex, mysterious than I, and I am bold to say we, can ever hope to know. I know that

The world is charged with the grandeur of God.
It will flame out, like shining from shook foil,
It gathers to a greatness like the ooze of oil
Crushed. Why do men then now not reck His rod?
Generations have trod, have trod, have trod;
And all is seared with trade; bleared smeared with toil;
And bears man's smudge, and shares man's smell; the soil
Is bare now, nor can foot feel being shod.
And for all this, nature is never spent;
There lives the dearest freshness deep down things;
And though the last lights from the black west went,
Oh, morning at the brown bring eastward springs -
Because the Holy Ghost over the bent
World broods with warm breast, and wish, ah, bright wings.[2]

We may differ in our choice of words. Hopkins writes from within the Christian tradition, and feels comfortable with the word "God" and the words "Holy Ghost." Others may not or do not, and for me, in this paper, it matters not.

There is more than we know, can know, will ever know. It is a "moreness" that takes us by surprise when we are at the edge and end of our knowing. There is a comfort in that "moreness" that takes over in our weakness, our ignorance, at our limits or end. It is a comfort that cannot be anticipated, a "peace that passeth all understanding." Call it what you will. Hopkins calls it the Holy Ghost. One knows of that presence, that "moreness," when known resources fail and somehow we go beyond what we were and are and become something different, somehow new. There is also judgment in that "moreness," particularly when we smugly assume that we know what "it" is all about and end up in the dark or on our behinds. It is this very "moreness," that can be identified with the "spirit" and the "spiritual." In fact Kovel defines "spirit" as what "happens to us as the boundaries of the self give way."[3] Spirit is that which transcends the known, the expected, even the ego and the self. It is the source of hope. It is manifested through love and the waiting expectation that accompanies love. It overcomes us, as judgment, in our doubts, and in the uncomfortable looks of those with whom we disagree, particularly those with whom we disagree religiously. One whose imagination acknowledges that "moreness" can be said to dwell faithfully in the world.

If one dwells "faithfully" in the world, what images of education, specifically curriculum, are possible? I speak as one who tries to dwell as a Christian, because that is my religious tradition, and because I am more familiar with its many qualities, quirks, and its language than I am that of other traditions. Those in other traditions are invited to attempt the same, thereby enriching the ensuing conversation.

I use the word image in the sense of a view of a landscape. I assume that there is an educational landscape that may be envisioned (or imaged) in many ways. Different images of the same landscape enable us to see different possibilities, different relationships, and perhaps enable us to imagine new phenomena in that educational landscape.

A new image must be articulated or described so others can move within the landscape as they did in the past, but with greater freedom and new awareness of their choices and limitations. The current images of the educational landscape provide the comfort of the already known, even old familiar problems. A different image must not disorient those who feel that comfort. An image of the educational landscape that makes room for, or includes the spiritual, cannot be too alienating. It must welcome the experienced educator and the stranger. An image that lets the spiritual show needs to use most of the current categories of education. However, once inside that image, the educational landscape should appear differently, showing limitations in current educational practices and perhaps opening up new options for action. Traditional curriculum concerns need to be addressed—namely the goal or meaning of education, the social and political structures of education, content, teaching, and evaluation. However, an image of education that permits the spiritual to show will depict these dimensions differently. An image that acknowledges the spiritual shows other problems and tasks more clearly, such as moral and spiritual values, and the need for spiritual or religious disciplines for the teacher.

## THE GOAL OF EDUCATION

The bewitching language of psychology and the behavioral sciences has skewed our view of education. The language of ends and objectives, which guides educational practice and decision making, is used to depict a future state of affairs. The process whereby an individual moves from one state of being to another and develops new capacities or competencies is identified as "learning"—a term so much a part of the coin of the realm that it blocks the imagination. We ask how "learning occurs," thus hiding the fact that we dwell in a near infinite world, that our possibilities are always more than we realize, and that life is movement, change, or journey. "Learning" too quickly explains and simplifies that movement or journey.

The "moreness" in the world, spirit, is a moreness that infuses each human being. Not only do we know more than we say, we "are" more than we "currently are." That is, the human being dwells in the transcendent, or more appropriately, the transcendent dwells in the human being. To use more direct religious imagery, the spirit dwells in us. Our possibilities are always before us. Our life is never a closed book, until death. In the Judeo-Christian tradition, there is no better image than Augustine's "our hearts are restless until they repose in Thee."[4] Kovel defines spirit as "connoting a relation between the person and the universe; while soul is the more self-referential term, connoting the kind of person who undergoes that relation. In a sense, soul cuts even closer home than spirit, because while spirits can be—and are—seen everywhere, soul refers to who we are, and necessarily, to what we make of ourselves. We may define soul, therefore, as the spiritual form taken by the self."[5]

What has this to do with education? The fact that we partake of the transcendent means that we are never complete, until death. We can always be more than we are. Within the Christian tradition, we are always open to a "turning"; to forgiveness, redemption and the new being which results. The future is before us as open and new if we are willing to turn away from what we are and have, if we are willing to let the past in us (the self) die. Life is a journey of constantly encountering the moreness and constantly letting aspects of us die that the new may be born within us. It is not necessarily a comfortable journey, and moments of rest and peace are often more infrequent than we might want.

"Learning" is a trivial way of speaking of the journey of the self. The language of growth and development is a rather mundane way of talking about the mystery of participating in the transcendent, or in uniquely Christian language, the mystery of incarnation, death and resurrection.[6] We do not need "learning theory" or "developmental theory" to explain human change. We need them to explain our fixations and neuroses, our limits, whether imposed by self or others. The question that educators need to ask is not how people learn and develop, but what gets in the way of the great journey—the journey of the self or soul. Education is a way of attending to and caring for that journey.

Educators and students are blinded by social and cultural systems and do not recognize their participation in the transcendent, in their ever open future. The journey of the self is short circuited or derailed by those who define the ends of life and education in less than ultimate terms. We are always caught in our proximate goals (our idols) or in the limitations imposed by others (our enslavements). Infrequently do we look beyond these limits or notice how life has been restricted by the social/cultural context. We are reminded of unrealized possibilities through social criticism, through art that points to other ways of seeing and being, through the stranger in our midst who illustrates that we too could be different, through worship and confession, and perhaps by divine discontent.

Our caughtness in systems that restrict our ultimate journey points to the fact that the journey is never a solitary one. In spite of this culture's bias toward privacy and individualism, we cannot be human beings without others.[7] We journey with others. Some precede us, some accompany us, some follow us. Consequently, we have paths, maps, models, scouts, and co-journeyers. We must be thankful for and wary of these co-journeyers. They show us the way, and lead us astray. Life with others is never a substitute for the individuation required of us. Others cannot take our journey. Yet being with others on the journey is a source of hope, comfort, and love—all manifestations of the transcendent. It is also the source of the ever present possibility of domination. Given this existential fact, it is essential that our image of the educational landscape show the social/political structures of education.

The image of journey also shows the possibility of falling off the trail, deviating from the journey, being caught in byways and dead ends. In the Biblical tradition this is known as sin, a word much distorted in some circles, but which means falling away from God or off the path toward God. This risk in the educational landscape is best noticed when the problems of content come into view.

## THE SOCIAL/POLITICAL STRUCTURE OF EDUCATION

An image of the educational landscape that allows the spiritual to be noticed points to the ultimate goal of education—the journey of the soul. The question that needs answering is why human beings try to derail that journey for their own purposes? Why do we try to shape the journey of others to fit cultural molds—whether of class, race, economic setting? Why do we try to shape the journey of others to maintain the present distribution of power, subjugating some people to the whims and fancies of others? Once we have in view the ultimate aim of education, then the misuses of power in the human world, and in education, are clearly seen. In the social/political context—e.g., the ordinary context of life—the journey of life is predefined for many, severely restricted for others, and the ultimate journey to God encouraged for only a few.

What must the image of the educational landscape contain to enable us to think about the constraints within which we work as teachers and educators? Joel Kovel's *History and Spirit* helps explore this as he renews the language of spirit in this culture, removing it from the restrictions of any one religious tradition.[8] Walter Wink's *Engaging the Powers*,[9] is most helpful in thinking about this problem from within a Christian perspective. In Biblical language, the journey and the corresponding commitment to God, is restrained, redirected, and derailed by the principalities and powers—the forces that no longer serve God, but serve false gods and human beings. The principalities and powers bring us into their spheres of interest, where we serve their ends, rather than the ultimate end. Bob Dylan's "You Gotta Serve Someone," depicts the problem. The pursuit of our journey to God is short-circuited by the pursuit of lesser ends or outcomes, which are manifestations of the principalities and powers. They restrict and impede the religious journey, condition human life to the mundane world, or fixate human life before the journey is completed. Fortunately, educators now have ample depictions of the restrictive forces operating in education,[10] and ideas to think about those restrictions. References to "education as liberation" or "education as self realization" acknowledge and seek to overcome these principalities and powers in the ordinary structures of education. The idea of liberal education, which frees one from the limits of a particular culture and society in order to take on the awesome responsibility of freedom, also acknowledges and seeks to overcome the restrictions of the principalities and powers. However, the articulation of these ideas is often merely another political claim, albeit liberal or progressive, rather than a religious claim, and hence often another effort to restrict the journey.

Wink calls attention to the domination systems of this world, and speaks of a world free from domination, obviously a utopian ideal, but also a central religious image in Christianity and other religious traditions. In the world controlled by domination systems redemption is through violence. Wink calls this the "myth of redemptive violence," which is implicit in almost all of the images of mass media and popular culture (Popeye, Superman, Robocop, etc.), as well as in the military systems that, by the threat of violence, keep peace in the world (and sell their excess arms to nations of the third world). In a domination free world the redemptive myth is that of redemptive love. According to Wink the myth of redemptive violence is deeply ingrained in each of us—we have internalized the principalities and powers, or as Pogo said many years ago, "We have met the enemy, and they are us." Because the myth of redemptive love (in the Christian tradition, the "story" of redemptive love) is not deeply ingrained in our characters (a major failure of religious traditions), our educational system short circuits the journey of the self or leads it to dead ends.

The organization of the school, the selection of content, and teaching itself clearly illustrate this. The school is the one social institution constructed with children and youth in mind, yet they are often alienated in and from that institution. Others dwell in it and make it their own. Schools are a major institution of the principalities and powers, and a major source for teaching the myth of redemptive violence—that the world can be corrected and redeemed through power (including the power of knowledge) and might, but not through love. This criticism has been common enough in educational crises since the sixties, and I need not dwell on it. The influence of the principalities and powers in education is seen more clearly, as problems of curricular content are brought into focus.

## THE CONTENT OF EDUCATION

In current images of the educational landscape teachers and curriculum people ask what is to be taught. The question is asked prematurely, for there is a prior realm of thinking and imagining, which if by-passed, ignores a crucial starting point. Even the prior thinking of epistemology brackets questions of spirituality.[11]

Where do we start to think about the content of education? The religious journey, the process of being educated, is always a consequence of encountering something that is strange and different,[12] something that is not me. That which is "other" and strange can be part of the I. In the infant the "other" is the hands, the sounds made, the feet that move; in childhood it might be feelings; in adolescence sexuality. The internal "otherness" continues throughout life as shadow, as thoughts, dreams, yearnings and desires that frighten, shock or stir us. Usually we think of the "other" as something in the external environment that is unknown, strange, new. Hovering always is the absolute "other," Spirit, that overwhelms us in moments of awe, terror, tragedy, beauty, and peace. Content is the "other." Knowing is the process of being in relationship with that "other." Knowledge is an abstraction from that process.

When the world no longer appears as "other," no longer seems strange, or has no strangeness, education appears to come to an end. Woe is that day, of course, for the power of knowledge has become prejudice, and the power of influence has become ownership, bringing all "otherness" into a relationship of domination. The whole world still seems new and strange to the young child, and education happens easily and naturally. This is curiosity. With age, less and less seems new or strange, and education appears less natural and frequent. Curiosity seems to end. The problem is not that education is just for the young, or that curiosity is a phenomenon of children and youth. The problem is that our controlling tendencies result in the hermetic environment, self or socially constructed, and we fail to recognize, or we forget, our relationship with and indebtedness to the absolute "Other" often manifested through the neighbor and the strange. The cause is not the decay of curiosity. It is idolatry and slavery. Educators, and people still being educated by the otherness of the world, easily slip into conditions of idolatry and slavery. The protection against this, of course, is criticism—calling attention to how our attention and our journey have become fixated or overpowered, a theme addressed later.

This image of the educational landscape helps us notice our traps, our limits, our idols, our slaveries. How does it help us plan? How can we use the image of the "other," the stranger, to design environments that educate? The topic is too vast for this paper, and I can only call attention to a few characteristics. First of all, it is crucial not to reify educational content, the otherness of the world, as if it were merely stuff made by human beings. To forget that knowledge and objects of culture are manifestations of and outcroppings from the creativity of the human species is a disastrous mistake. Priority must be given to human beings and the natural order. Then we can see more clearly how human kind participates in the continual creation of the world. We can also see how the "creations" of human kind sometimes bring us closer to extinction. Hopefully, then, our students can see, more easily, their own journey as a participation in the continual creation (or destruction) of the world.

Content is, first of all, "other" human beings. Others see the world differently, talk differently, act differently. Therefore they are possibilities for me. They point to a different future for me, another state on my journey. I could be like them. By being different they bring my particular self under criticism. What I am, I do not have to be. What they are, I could be. Other people call attention to a future that is not just a continuation of me, but a possible transformation of me. Through the presence of the "other" my participation in the transcendent becomes visible—the future is open if I will give up the self that is the current me and become other than I am. As content, other people are sources of criticism and new possibility.

Beside criticism and possibility, the "other" as content provides an opportunity to listen and speak with a stranger. Not only are the visions of my own journey shifted, perhaps reformed or transformed, but my party of co-journeyers is also enlarged. Strangers become neighbors. I have others to listen me into consciousness of self and the world. I have the gift of other stories of the great journey. Through conversation, I have a chance to refine my way of talking about the world, and to participate in the refinement of theirs. Through the caring act of listening and speaking, I have a chance to participate in the mystery of language. In listening and speaking the transcendent is present as newness comes forth, as forgiveness is given and received, and as the poetic shaping of the world happens.

Whereas I have referred to the "otherness" primarily in terms of human beings, it is crucial to give the same credibility and respect to nature. Our habits do not include thinking about how the possibilities of the natural world intertwine with ours, or how we might carry on "conversations" with non-human "others." Hence the increased destruction of the natural world. The religious response to the ecological crisis, the interest in how other cultures (Native Americans for instance) respect the land and its occupants, and the emerging paradigms of the new physics and other sciences indicate how the world view is gradually shifting to see nature and human beings as part of the same creation. The thinking of educators has not kept pace with these changes, in part because of dominant economic interests that view nature as resource and commodity.

When we shift our focus from the content which is "other" people, to the content which is the outcropping of their creativity and actions—symbols, bodies of knowledge, works of art, institutions, technologies, products, and practices—we face problems too numerous for an essay. The strangeness persists, the "otherness" is still there. These are parts of the world still "other" to the student. How does the presence of this cultural object bring me under criticism? What new possibilities does it offer me? How can my life be different because of it? What new paths, maps, scouts and co-journeyers are before me? What new conversations can I enter? What new stories of the great journey are available? But ownership also exists, in that these outcroppings of human creativity are usually in the possession of other people or other communities. These outcroppings are available as gifts, or they may be stolen or purchased. The teacher should be a gift giver. However, there are segments of the educational community, particularly at the graduate level, where one has to purchase the symbolic "other," perhaps by paying dues for belonging to that community of cultural ownership.

Wink suggests that all human constructions (institutions, structures of knowledge, etc.) have vocations and spiritual dimensions. They serve God. They can also serve Caesar or mammon. They have the possibility to free people for their journey, or to tie them into structures of idolatry or slavery. All content areas of the curriculum need to be looked at with this in view, a task much too complicated for this essay. Phenix does this in some ways in *Realms of Meanings*.[13] Foshay looked at the spiritual in mathematics.[14] Noddings and Shore explore aspects of this in their work on intuition.[15]

From within this image, planning appears different. The question is not what does this "other" mean to the student, for meaning is an operation from within the current self. Rather, the question is how will the student be different because of this "other." For people already captivated by idols, or fixated to other aspects of self and world, the question is, what must be given up, or in Christian language, what part of oneself must die so new life becomes possible? Those familiar with the Christian Gospels, may recall that in Mark the followers of Jesus exclaimed, after an exorcism, "What is this? A new teaching—with authority! He commands even the unclean spirits, and they obey him."[16] Teaching is, in part, a form of exorcism, the casting out of the "unclean spirit" so new vitality and life is possible. But we must be exceedingly careful, for the power to destroy seems easier than the power to give. Too frequently teachers ask "How do we motivate?" or "What threats (such as grades and testing) can we use?" More appropriate questions are— "How can this student see himself or herself anew in this content?" and "How can one be supported while one gives up one's old self to become a new self?" The first question must be answered esthetically, for it requires attention to the presentation of the "other" in a way that "grips" the student. The answer to the second question is of a "pastoral" nature because dying to one's self, giving up a part of one's self or past, entails grief work, and requires a community of life wherein one can die and know that life will not be lost, but found.

The second step in the planning process is that of displaying the fascination and structure of the "other." The student is invited in and begins to recognize new power and pleasure of self. "Playing with" is the image, because play is nonthreatening and gradually introduces one into the rules, habits, and forms of the content. This should be a "playing with" that gradually introduces the student to more complexity, and to the feeling of more power or more pleasure. Many of the achievements of the post Sputnik period with respect to math and science were of this kind—displaying structure as an invitation to "come and play" so the student could feel enhanced. This is not to imply that education is never work. However, the word "work," in school and in society, has come to mean a form of losing self for others, of alienation, not of finding myself, my power, my future and my journey. Similarly, the significance of the word "study" has been destroyed. Students study to do what someone else requires, not for their own transformation, a way of "working" on their own journey, or their struggle with spirit, the otherness beyond them. Just as therapy is work, hard work, but important for the loosening of old bonds and discovering the new self, so too should education as study be seen as a form of that kind of work.

## TEACHING

Teaching has been seen as a set of skills, as particular kinds of action. Teachers are not replaceable cogs in an educational machine, nor is teaching carrying out a set of tactics and strategies owned by others. Teaching does require skills, and hence depends, at times, on reproducible knowledge. However, if teaching is restricted to that image, there are few ways of thinking about the spiritual aspects of teaching and the teacher. Teaching needs to be grounded in a life. It is not a way of making a living, but a way of making a life. The spiritual dimensions of teaching are recognized by acknowledging that teaching is a vocation.[17] When that is acknowledged other dimensions of teaching will also be seen more clearly.

A vocation is a call. In the religious traditions it is a call from God, or a call to serve God. But the religious meaning need not be invoked here. A teacher is called to a particular way of living. Three voices call, or three demands are made on the teacher. Hence the life that is teaching is inherently a conflicted way of living. The teacher is called by the students, by the content and its communities, and by the institution within which the teacher lives. Depending upon the institution, teachers feel this conflict differently. For elementary school teachers the call of the students is probably more dominant. College and university teachers hear the call of content and its communities as primary. Of course, given the institutional binds that teachers feel, few ever feel called by the institution. But it is there, if only fully responded to by those aspiring to administrative posts. Each of these calls place demands or obligations on the one who would live the life of a teacher.

That part of the teaching life that is a response to the call of the student results in the work of love; to the call of content, the work of truth; to the call of the institution, the work of justice. As in all vocations, these works are easily distorted by the principalities and powers. Spiritual warfare is inherent in all vocations.

The work of love is obvious. The teacher listens to the student, and speaks with great care, that the gift of language, jointly shared, may reassure and disclose a world filled with truth and beauty, joy and suffering, mystery and grace. The teacher makes promises to the student. The journey of the student is filled with hope, rather than despair; more life, rather than less. The teacher introduces the student to the "otherness" of the world, to that which is strange, and assures the student that the strangeness will not overpower but empower. If the encounter with the "other" requires that old ways of knowing, relating, feeling, be given up, the teacher assures the student that during the resulting vulnerability no harm will come and that the grief will be shared. If the student is temporally disabled by the loss, the teacher may step in to fill the void. If some dying of the self happens, the past will not be forgotten, but celebrated and integrated as useful memory. If idols are given up, the teacher promises the security of the spirit that is the source of all transcendence. If the security of slavery is thrown overboard, the teacher will help the student find new communities in which power is shared. These positive images, derived in part from the redemptive myth of love, disclose the negative power of the social/political context wherein the life that is teaching is lived.

The work of truth is a work of stewardship. Responding to a particular discipline or content area the teacher is called to keep it truthful and useful. The language and other symbols of the content are easily distorted, tarnished and stained by the principalities and powers. They lose their luminosity— their power to disclose. They hide more than they reveal. They become idolatrous, ends in themselves, and no longer point to the spirit that enlivens human beings. The teacher's work of truth is to keep vitality and signs of transcendence in the language and symbols. The content that makes up the curriculum is part of creation and a source for its continuance. Thus the deadness must be rooted out, and those parts that have become idols, criticized and renewed or placed in the museum of the past—to be beheld as that which once gave and celebrated life. To be called to the work of truth is to recognize that the "other" also has a vocation of honoring spirit and participates in the transcendent. Thus that part of the "other" by which it is criticized, transformed, improved, made more serviceable, must also be available for the student. In science, this is done by making accessible not only the outcroppings of the scientists, the theories and technologies, but also the methods, procedures, and communities through which a science renews itself.

The work of justice is the third call, the call of the institution within which the teaching life is lived. The institution of the schools is the meeting ground of conflicting interests. It is not and cannot be a neutral place. The teacher lives and works in an almost unbearable conflict zone among those competing interests. The present form of the institution is shaped by the balance of interests. To assume that the present order and structure are givens is to yield unthinkingly to the principalities and powers of the past.

The school as an institution also has a vocation. It serves students, the communities with interest in the curriculum content, the teachers, and those who support it economically. Its vocations become tainted when justice does not prevail among these competing interests, and one or more of the interests, or some other power, gets control. Justice, which is never an absolute value, always requires the adjudication of competing claims.

Teaching is a vulnerable form of life, for the teacher works among these competing interests. Teachers often fall away from the vocation of teaching and become mere functionaries as they do the work demanded by others in workbooks, schedules, exams, grading and what have you. It is often easier to deny the vulnerability, the competing interests, and to fall into the form demanded by the principalities and powers, those in control. Teachers lose hope, accept idols and enslavement, and burn out. Teachers give up teaching as part of their own spiritual journey, to pick up the journey at the end of the school day, the beginning of summer, or the end of their career.

The work of justice requires acknowledging the impotency of the isolated individual, and the danger of the closed classroom door. Teachers called to the work of justice need alliances and coalitions of those called to the same vocation. The struggle for justice in schools requires sensitivity to pain and unfairness. Such sensitivity brings under question curriculum materials, teachers' skills, and institutional practices like grading, grouping. The pain of teachers, unable to respond to the call of some students, is often too much, and they seek relief by hardening their hearts.


CRITICISM


The fourth rubric in traditional curriculum planning, after goals, content, and teaching, is evaluation. The process involves stepping back and asking how we are all doing in this educational enterprise. Students and teacher are evaluated, because they are the weakest politically, and most at the mercy of the principalities and powers. Students move on. Teachers can be replaced. Thus they are the scapegoats in the domination system. The school's procedure, materials, and basic organization have longer lives.

An image of the educational landscape that makes room for the spiritual suggests other ways of thinking about evaluation. In *The Protestant Era*[18] Tillich calls attention to the necessity for continuous protest against form. Form gradually loses its vocation, becomes idolatrous, and no longer points to the transcendent. Continual protest against form is necessary for reformation and renewal of vocation. Others speak of the necessary dialectic of creation and criticism. Forms created by human beings soon become idols or enslave others. Criticism calls attention to what is still beautiful, truthful, transparent for God, filled with the possibilities of transcendence and the promise of life. It also calls attention to the breakdown of vocation and the fading of luminosity.

The dialectic of criticism and creation is hidden by the idea of evaluation. Evaluation is the act of those already in power to determine the effectiveness of their power. Some forms of evaluation are used appropriately in the instructional process for diagnostic purposes. This is criticism of instructional materials and techniques, based upon teacher and student sensitivity to their failure to serve students. Such evaluation should result in different materials or procedures, a reforming of method to fit the student.

However, the power of existing evaluation instruments points to the impotency of other participants in the schooling process to criticize and reform education. In some ways, the discipline problems of students are forms of criticism; the lunch room, coffee break, and after school conversations among teachers are forms of criticism; parent complaints can be forms of criticism. However, the possibilities to reform schools and classrooms are not in the hands of those who live there, for a variety of reasons. Hence criticism is removed as part of the creative process and becomes merely carping and blowing off steam. This is a denial of the spirit in those who work in the educational landscape, for criticism is also part of the creative power of the spirit.

## CONCLUSION

I have briefly sketched an alternative image of some of the basic principles of curriculum and instruction, drawing upon sources and images that make room for the spiritual aspects of human life. Much more needs to be done. Two problem areas can be seen more clearly through this image.

First, recent discourse about moral and spiritual values in the classroom is incorrectly focused. That discourse assumes that there is something special that can be identified as moral or spiritual. This assumption is false. Everything that is done in schools, and in preparation for school activity, is already infused with the spiritual. All activity in school has moral consequences. The very highlighting of the need to teach moral and spiritual values in schools implies a breakdown not in the spirituality and morality of the student, but a breakdown in the moral activity and spirituality of the school itself, and of the people in control of the school. Those in control of the schools cover over their own complicity in the domination system by urging the teaching of moral and spiritual values. They do not urge that the moral and spiritual climate of the schools, which they control, be changed. That teachers do not feel the freedom to be critical and creative is a sign of their enslavement to other principalities and powers. The need is not to see moral and spiritual values as something outside the normal curriculum and school activity, but to probe deeper into the educational landscape to reveal how the spiritual and moral is being denied in everything. The problem of the schools is not that kids are not being taught moral and spiritual values, the problem is the schools are not places where the moral and spiritual life is lived with any kind of intentionality.

It is also quite clear to me that it is futile to hope that teachers can be aware of the spiritual in education unless they maintain some form of spiritual discipline. This needs to be of two kinds. Given the inherent conflicts involved in teaching, and the inherent vulnerability of their vocation, teachers need to seek out communities of faith, love, and hope. Teachers can deal with conflict and vulnerability if they are in the presence of others who radiate faith and hope and power. To be in the company of co-journeyers is to be enabled to identify personal and collective idols, to name oppression, and to undergo the continuing transformation necessary in the vocation of teaching. The second discipline is a disciplining of the mind, not in the sense of staying on top of all the educational research and literature, but in the sense of developing an imagination that has room for the spiritual. When teachers examine the educational landscape we should see what is there and hear the call to respond with love, truth and justice. We should also see the principalities and powers, the idols and the spiritual possibilities hidden behind all of the forms and events that are taken for granted. Teachers should be able to see that

> nature is never spent;
> There lives the dearest freshness deep down things;
> And though the last lights from the black west went,
> Oh, morning at the brown brink eastward springs—
> Because the Holy Ghost over the bent
> World broods with warm breast, and with, ah, bright wings.

## NOTES

1. For example in the Christian traditions see Stanley Hauerwas and William H. Willimon, *Resident Aliens* (Nashville: Abingdon Press, 1989) and Dietrich Bonhoeffer, *Life Together*, trans. John W. Doberstein (New York: Harper and Row, 1954).
2. Gerald Manley Hopkins, "The Grandeur of God," in *The Oxford Book of English Mystical Verse* (Oxford: Clarendon Press, 1953).
3. Joel Kovel, *History and Spirit: An Inquiry into the Philosophy of Liberation* (Boston: Beacon Press, 1991).
4. *The Confessions of St. Augustine, Book One*, trans. J. Sheed (New York: Sheed and Ward, 1943).

5. Kovel, *History and Spirit*, p. 33.
6. Other religions have other ways of talking about this mystery. The work of Ken Wilber has been the most helpful in bringing together the multitude of religious and psychological perspectives. See "The Spectrum of Development" in *Transformations of Consciousness*, eds. Ken Wilber, Jack Engler & Daniel Brown (Boston: New Science Library, 1986), pp. 65–106.
7. See John MacMurray, *Persons in Relation* (New York: Harper, 1961).
8. Kovel, *History and Spirit*.
9. Walter Wink, *Engaging the Powers* (Philadelphia: Fortress Press, 1992).
10. See, among others, the works of Michael Apple.
11. I explored this in two previous essays. See Dwayne Huebner, "Spirituality and Knowing," in *Learning and Teaching The Ways of Knowing* (Chicago: National Society for the Study of Education, 1985) pp. 159–173, and "Religious Metaphors in the Language of Education," *Phenomenology & Pedagogy: A Human Science Journal*, Vol. 2, No. 2 (1984), also in *Religious Education*, Vol. 80, No. 3 (Summer, 1985), pp. 460–472.
12. The best psychological analysis of this process is Robert Kegan, *The Evolving Self* (Cambridge: Harvard University Press, 1982).
13. Phillip Phenix, *Realms of Meaning* (New York: McGraw-Hill Book Co., 1964).
14. Arthur W. Foshay, "The Curriculum Matrix: Transcendence and Mathematics," *Journal of Curriculum and Supervision*, Vol. 6, No. 4 (Summer, 1991), pp. 277–293.
15. Nel Noddings and Paul J. Shore, *Awakening the Inner Eye: Intuition in Education* (New York: Teachers College Press, 1984).
16. Mark 1:27
17. See Dwayne Huebner, "Teaching as a Vocation" in *Teacher Renewal: Professional Studies, Personal Choices* (New York: Teachers College Press, 1987). A revised form is available in *The Auburn News*, Fall 1987 (New York: Auburn Theological Seminary).
18. Paul Tillich, *The Protestant Era* (Chicago: University of Chicago Press, 1948).

# 22
▼▼▼▼▼▼▼

# Critical and Constructive Postmodernism: The Transformative Power of Holistic Education*

Christine M. Shea

One of the problems of living in a period of transition comes from the dissonance created by an episodic shift away from older meaning systems and our inability to react with any kind of sensibility or coherence to the fragmentary new symbol systems that strike our bewildered consciousness. If the old order seems too rigid and constraining, the new order offers an equally obscure and incoherent range of unfamiliar fragmented belief systems and attitudes. Advanced industrial societies are deep in the midst of a period of transition. In his book *The Post-Industrial Utopians*, Boris Frankel catalogs some of the terms that have been used to express this epochal break with the modern era: the postmodern era, the post-bourgeois society, the post-economic society, the post-scarcity society, the post-industrial society, the knowledge society, the personal service society, the service class society, and the technetronic era (Frankel, 1987, 2). Taken as a whole, these labels tell us that existing institutions are being dramatically reshaped.

In the "Introduction" to his analysis of postmodern trends in education, Donald Oliver and Kathleen Gershman write of the loss of a sense of belongingness that such paradigm shifts inevitably provoke:

> It is an age in which the unconscious cultural symbols providing our lives with deep meanings are losing their vitality, the passion that drives our love for inventing material things is drying up, and our intimate connection with the natural living world is steadily decreasing. Although awed by the power of our technical achievements, we are nevertheless bewildered by the crassness that increasingly characterizes our personal relationships. (Oliver & Gershman, 1989, 2)

---

*From: "Critical and Constructive Postmodernism: The Transformative Power of Holistic Education." *Holistic Education Review*, 1996, 9(3), 40–50. Reprinted by permission.

Quoting a passage from Walker Percy's book *The Message in the Bottle*, they liken us to people who live ". . . by reason during the day and at night dream bad dreams" (Oliver & Gershman, 1989, 2).

## THE ENLIGHTENMENT DREAM

The Enlightenment dream entered history as a progressive force promising to liberate humans from ignorance and irrationality. The good society, for most of the sons and daughters of the Enlightenment, was the meritocratic ideal where individuals took up their positions in life not because of special privilege resulting from wealth, caste, status, or power, but due to natural talent and virtue. The various inequalities that resulted from caste, class, and privilege had to be overcome in order to allow the true natural talents of human beings to emerge and be rewarded.

This Enlightenment dream became the American dream as well. American educators, likewise, predicted that in the scientific society of tomorrow, a universal system of enlightened education would be created (Dewey, 1929). But, this Enlightenment dream included more than the mere identification and development of natural talent and opportunity. That dream evolved into a process of social selection promising to shape individuals more easily to the ideals of the emerging meritocratic state (Karier, 1973; Shea, 1980). This agenda was most aptly expressed by Edward Ross when he suggested that to educate is ". . . to collect little plastic lumps of human dough from private households and shape them on the social kneadingboard" (Ross, 1912, 168).

Enlightenment social science thereby became a story not of the triumphal emergence of the great "American paideia," but rather, a saga showing how the idea of rationality as social control (i.e., the quest for certainty in the new post-Newtonian world) became the fundamental societal quest (Karier et al., 1973). Thus, while the Enlightenment dream entered history as a progressive force promising to liberate humankind from ignorance and ir-rationality, its nightmarish fulfillment in the concentration camps, Hiroshima, Vietnam, and the Persian Gulf have obliterated any continuing naive commitment to its social ideals. The concept that real social progress will only occur through the continued application of science and technology to solve social problems sounds awkwardly archaic (i.e., politically and morally bankrupt) in this emerging postmodern era.

## WHAT DOES POSTMODERNISM MEAN?

The question of what postmodernism actually means is not an easy one to answer. The term "postmodernism" has been used in a confusing variety of ways, some of them contradictory to others. It has meant different things to different people at different times. In a flood of recent articles, scholars have reviewed some of these endless questions, debates, and schisms in regard to the term, and have posed some probing questions: Is postmodernism primarily an epistemological, artistic, political, scientific, theological, linguistic, or social phenomenon? (Bertens, 1995; Callinicos, 1989; Deleuze, 1988; Giroux, 1991; Jameson, 1991; Lather, 1991; Natoli & Hutcheon, 1993; Rosenau, 1992). Does it promise liberation from outmoded traditions or regression into irrationalism? What are the implications of postmodernism for educational theory and practice? Is it a theoretical movement that will enable us to escape the patriarchal paradigms of Western thought, or is it just more "class privileged, Eurocentric, logo-obsessed white male discourse?" (Lather, 1991, 155). Does it allow us to image what a real emancipatory politics might be?

The variety and complexity of the current postmodernism discourse has led to an extraordinarily rich and playful dialogue as significant players crisscross and interrupt one another in an endless stream of argumentation. Giles Deleuze focuses on the microlevel and the interaction of bodies driven by desire (Deleuze, 1991). For Lash, too, postmodernism is inextricably bound up with a "theory of desire," the equivalent of Nietzsche's will to power (Lash, cited in Bertens, 1995, 218). Hutcheon argues that postmodernism "is a contradictory phenomenon that uses and abuses, installs and subverts, the very concepts it challenges—be it in literature, painting, sculpture, film, video, dance, television, music, philosophy, aesthetic theory, psychoanalysis, linguistics of historiography" (Hutcheon, 1991; reprinted in Natoli & Hutcheon, 1993). Others view postmodernism as a new form of abstract, disengaged radical chic or "nouveau smart" and celebrate its "intellectual vandalism" as a necessary process of erasing the old, harmful intellectual structures of liberal humanism (Norris, cited in Bertens, 1995, 8). Lyotard, too, understands postmodernism as an "incredulity toward metanarratives" and urges the further debunking of the empiricist model of science (Lyotard, cited in Peters, 1989, 99).

Jurgen Habermas condemns postmodernism as a neoconservative reaction against the emancipatory ideals of the Enlightenment (Habermas, 1987). Allan Bloom expresses the conservative view of postmodernism as "the last, predictable, stage in the suppression of reason, and the denial of the possibility of truth" (Bloom, cited in Nicholson, 1989, 197). Conservative scholars, in this vein, tend to bemoan the postmodern fascination with the "degraded landscape" of pop culture, TV series, advertising, late shows, B-grade movies, airport pocketbook novels, freak shows, fantasy sitcoms, and popular biographies. They charge that postmodernism fosters nihilism, relativism, irrationality, anarchy, and political irresponsibility.

Others use the term postmodern in a derogatory sense and see it hopelessly enmeshed with the exhaustion of monopoly capitalism in its final stages, as the inevitable outcome of capitalist decline and decadence (Callinicos, 1989,

10). Frederick Jameson, for example, characterizes postmodernism as resulting from the forces of multinational capitalism, a necessary by-product of its "schizophrenic" attitude toward space and time (Jameson, 1991, 154). Cornell West fears that it is especially dangerous for the marginalized (West, cited in Lather, 1991, 154).


## WHAT ARE SCHOOLS FOR? EDUCATION
## IN/FOR A POSTMODERN ERA

The divergent, even contradictory, expositions of postmodernism underline the need to distinguish among its various orientations. With this in mind, I would like to explore in this essay some of the elements that would help provide a coherent conceptual framework for a new postmodern educational program. The attempts to transcend modernism, I think, has resulted in three very different postmodern agendas: the first, characterized by a more nihilistic deconstructivist agenda; the second, grounded in a more critical poststructuralist discourse; and the third, characterized by a more visionary, constructive postmodern program. It is important to differentiate between the terms "deconstructionism" and "poststructuralism" conceptually. "Deconstructionism" refers to the analytic method of dissecting or tearing apart a "text" in order to reveal its basic contradictions, inconsistencies, or assumptions. Deconstructionists consider everything a "text"—events, situations, experiences, as well as books. The intent of deconstructionism is not to improve, revise, resolve, or offer a better version of a "text," but rather, to disclose tensions, often using a sensational, bombastic style. "Poststructuralism" is a postmodern philosophy that questions the legitimacy of any authoritative metanarrative, social standard, or social structure; it attacks the assumption that societies are made coherent by their underlying form or structures. Poststructuralists reject the notion of universal truth or that the mind has an innate, underlying structure. Instead, they work from the premise that language/discourse constitutes rather than merely reflects reality; "reality" is the by-product of historically and socially constructed ways of making sense of the world (Leistyna et al., 1996, 342). They hold that dominant groups (especially Western European white males) have controlled not only access to social power but also access to the standards by which society determines what is valuable and legitimate. Therefore, they place great emphasis on the presentation of "multiple voices" and "multiple realities" to explain or interpret any event or situation, especially the voices of the less powerful members of the social system—women, minorities, and students.

In the later part of this paper, I would like to explore why I believe that a comprehensive postmodern educational framework might well include a growing alliance between the critical poststructuralist critique and the work of the emerging revisionary constructive postmoderns. Lastly, I would like to discuss the rise of the holistic education movement in the 1990s and to situate it strongly within this new constructive postmodern paradigm.

## VARIETIES OF POSTMODERN CRITIQUE

### Nihilistic Deconstructive Postmodernism

The nihilistic deconstructive postmodern paradigm, popularized by Derrida and Baudillard, offers a pessimistic, negative, gloomy assessment of the human condition by arguing that the postmodern age is one of fragmentation, disintegration, and malaise, absent of any moral commitments. As Rosenau has pointed out in her recent book *Post-Modernism and the Social Sciences* (1992), this paradigm is inspired by the earlier continental European philosophers, especially Heidegger and Nietzsche, and represents the dark side of postmodernism—the postmodernism of despair and nihilism (Rosenau, 1992, 168). This nihilistic strand of postmodernism speaks of the demise of the subject, the impossibility of truth, and the repudiation of representation. When postmodern theorists talk about "the demise of the subject" they do not mean that they wish to become more objective, but rather, they seek to challenge the liberal humanist ideal of the rational, effective, unified subject. Instead, the nihilistic deconstructive postmoderns conceptualize one's subjectivity as multiple, contradictory, and largely irrational—the inevitable result of the renouncement of the subject-object dichotomy. They contend that the subject is "... only a mask, a role, a victim, at worst an ideological construct, at best a nostalgic effigy" (Carravetta, quoted in Rosenau, 1992, 42). In a tonal discourse strangely reminiscent of that in Hobbes's *Leviathan*, these postmodern texts proclaim that all is grim, cruel, alienating, hopeless, mean, nasty, and ambiguous.

In their deconstructivist critiques of objective science, these postmoderns reject even modern chaos theory as ultimately embedded in a positivist paradigm. Instead they view the universe as impossible to understand. In contemplating the universe, Lyotard and Latour write only of "undecidables," "fractors," "catastrophes," and "paradoxes" (cited in Rosenau, 1992, 170). Closely related to their postmodern critique of objective science is their critique of representation. What is really interesting cannot be represented: ideas, symbols, the universe, the absolute, God, the just, or whatever. Like Derrida, they argue that representation is dangerous and basically bad (Derrida, Lyotard; cited in Rosenau, 1992, 170).

The nihilistic postmoderns argue that reality is pure illusion; everything is intertextual, not causal or predictive. Their preferred social critique is introspective interpretation and deconstruction. Relativism and uncertainty characterize their views. They doubt the value of reason and contend it is impossible to establish objective, standard criteria. Many of these nihilistic postmoderns also dismiss democracy as easily as they repudiate representation. As political agnostics, they propose that all political views are mere constructions. Many are pessimistic about changing society; some argue for nonparticipation as the most revolutionary position in the postmodern age; others argue for play; still others recommend terror, suicide, and violence as the only truly authentic political gestures that remain open. Time and space are conceived to be uncontrollable and unpredictable: ". . . time becomes disparate, crisscrossed, layered, and maligned rather than homogeneous, evolutionary, purposive, and regular . . . what the postmoderns refer to as 'pastiche' reigns" (Rosenau, 1992, 171). As time and space dissolve, nothing can be assumed; nothing is worthy of commitment; nothing is foundational; no one is to be trusted.

Critical Poststructuralist Postmodernism

With the increasing politicization of the debate on the postmodernism in the 1980s, the earlier nihilistic, deconstructionist postmodernism rapidly lost its attraction. A new critical deconstructivist program grounded in the emerging poststructuralist approaches derived from Foucault, and, to a much lesser extent, Lacan, gained popularity in America (Turkle, 1979; Poster, 1984). This poststructuralist paradigm is especially designed to critique the power that is inherent in the discourses and in the institutions that support these discourses (i.e., education). It attempts to expose the politics that are at work in our everyday lives, to challenge institutionalized hierarchies, and to work against the hegemony of any single discursive system. Specifically, the poststructuralists choose to see their work within a politically critical framework, as engaged in the necessary process of challenging the outmoded repressive institutions and ideologies of positivist Enlightenment social science.

Much of the earlier critical and revisionist educational research agendas of the 1960s and 1970s generally defined power as a negative force that only worked in the interests of domination. Theories of ideological hegemony and social reproduction were used almost exclusively to show the extent of elite and professional social control and domination of American schools. Questions about how elite power worked focused on debating various theories of social reproduction and hegemonic control.

The work of Michel Foucault began to change the focus of American social theorists, and later, American critical theorists and revisionist historians working in education began to consider the schools as more active, conflictual sites for social class, ethnic, racial, and gender-related intervention and struggle. Foucault, for example, believed that power was both a positive and a negative force, as he wrote:

> If power were never anything but repressive, if it never did anything but to say no, do you really think one would be brought to obey it? What makes power hold good what makes it accepted, is simply the fact that it doesn't only weigh on us as a force that says no, but that it traverses and produces things, it induces pleasure, forms of knowledge, produces discourse. It needs to be considered as a productive network which runs through the whole social body, much more than as a negative instance whose function is repression (Foucault, quoted in Aronowitz & Giroux, 1985, 155).

In repudiating the nihilistic postmodern discourse, the critical poststructuralist agenda called for "a return of the subject." However, this new subject was not a return to the outmoded, instrumental agenda of the Enlightenment citizen in search of mastery and control, but rather, one who struggled against oppression, humiliation, and subjection as a "subject-in-process." These critical poststructuralists were as likely as the nihilists to reject universal truth and dismiss the idea that "truth is out there" waiting to be discovered. However, in contrast to nihilistic postmodernism, the poststructuralist stance argued that while "the real" was mediated through language, it had not disappeared (Lather, 1991, 166). Instead, the critical poststructuralists were concerned with relativizing the language games into specific local, personal, and community forms of social praxis. In rejecting an extreme linguistic relativism, the critical poststructuralists argued that there could be a certain consensus about words and concepts and language games, both scientific and narrative. Certain truths might hold for a certain community at a specific place and time. In rejecting the intellectual hegemony of grand theory, the critical postmoderns relied instead on everchanging, community-based, micronarratives, and geneology to ground social praxis. Instead of repudiating representation per se, these critical poststructuralists talked more about the need for more and better forms of representation.

In the course of the 1980s, this mostly Foucauldian postmodernism had a far-reaching democratizing influence within educational institutions and enabled close links to be established with feminism and multiculturalism, terms that are now generally associated with this critical poststructuralist stance. Those committed to a "postmodernism of resistance" have identified a multitude of critical strategies and commitments in quest of a politics of empowerment. These critical postmoderns support a wide range of political and social alliances and recommend moving back and forth among the various critical discourses—i.e., of the poor Appalachian elderly; urban black teenage males; lesbians; teenage Latino gangs; Native Americans on reservations; the unemployed; the homeless; gays; punk rockers; Black separatists; AIDS victims; rural teenage girls; migrant laborers; prison inmates; the handicapped—in order to interrupt one another, in search of a more spontaneous and dynamic discourse. Here, subjectivity is no longer a search for "essences," but rather, is ". . . multiple, layered, and non-unitary . . . constituted out of oftentimes different and contradictory selves . . . (here) . . . the self is constructed as a terrain of conflict and struggle; as a site of both liberation and subjugation" (Giroux, 1991, 30). Such an approach to social praxis places an examination of one's own and others' oppression at the center of a critical politics of opposition, difference, and cultural struggle, and as a GSU faculty colleague of mine teaches, these "oppressions must be linked" (Spencer, 1966). The recovery, affirmation, and sharing of their "stories of oppression" from these discontiguous and marginalized local groups, it was thought, would result in a social praxis that embodied a kind of struggle and resistance that was nondogmatic, tentative, and nonideological. Giroux put it well:

> I believe that by foregrounding and interrogating the variety of textual forms and voices that inform such narratives, students can deconstruct the master-narratives of racism, sexism, and class domination while simultaneously questioning how these narratives contribute to forms of self-hatred and contempt that surround the identities of blacks, women, and other subordinate groups (Giroux, 1991, 244).

In this way, the poststructuralism praxis nurtures, prods, and honors the emergence of a variety of everchanging alliances amongst these previously marginalized and silenced groups.

## Postmodernism as a Doubled Movement/Doubled Consciousness

The third broad orientation in the postmodern debate is that of the constructive postmodern approach. While the constructive postmoderns do not question the accomplishments of the critical postmoderns, they realize that the critical postmodern paradigm is one of critique, opposition, and emancipation from, rather than one of creation and construction. They perceive, rightly I think, that this model's dominant emphasis on subverting the Enlightenment agenda has rendered both its tonal and textual orientation less sensitive to the power and language of other more transformative, visionary, futuristic agendas, particularly those concerned to help us see our human and natural relationships in more holistic, dynamic, and dialogical frameworks.

Although the critical theorists talk and write about creating "a language of possibility" and "a discourse of hope," in fact, their own critical discourse has failed to move beyond a language of critique, and oftentimes, seems to confuse an authentic transformational program with merely the introduction of a new language of critique (Senese, 1991, 13). In their book *Education Under Seige*, Aronowitz and Giroux (1985) seem dramatically aware of this difficulty: "In our view, most exciting critical accounts of schooling fail to provide forms of analysis that move beyond theories of critique to the more difficult task of laying the theoretical basis for transformative modes of curriculum theory and practice" (p. 154). Peter McLaren similarly pointed out recently that "little in the corpus of poststructural or postmodernist theories has been significantly appropriated for the purposes of educational reform, except by way of critique" (McLaren, 1986; quoted in Nicholson, 1989, 201).

What seems to be lacking is some kind of collaborative praxis/discourse upon which to construct a vision of postmodern education that embodies both the critical discourse needed to emancipate ourselves from the class privileged, Eurocentric, white male discourse embedded in the Enlightenment tradition (in both its classical and Progressive liberal phases) and the more visionary, constructive postmodern discourse needed to situate us meaningfully in the emerging multicultural ecosystem-sensitive global economy of the twenty-first century. However, both orientations are essential to a comprehensive postmodern program. It is in what W. E. B. DuBois and others have called this "doubled movement" of "doubled consciousness," this dizzy dance between subversion and inscription, that rests in the heart of a comprehensive postmodern agenda (Lather, 1991, 154). Thus, a transductional dialectic paradigm that joins the largely contestatory, oppositional work central to the work of critical theorists and revisionist historians with the more futuristic, creative, exploratory, metaphoric visionary work of the constructive postmoderns could form the superstructure for a more authentic, transformational postmodern discourse.

## Constructive Ecological Postmodernism

In his SUNY Series in "Constructive Postmodern Thought," David Ray Griffin, the series editor, describes some of the underlying themes and commitments in the constructive postmodern orientation (Griffin, 1992, preface). This new emerging postmodern paradigm obviously represents a major shift in the context through which we understand ourselves and our relationships to each other and our natural world. Very little before the 1970s prepared us to understand the crisis in ecological sustainability—what Madhu Prakash referred to as ". . . the global race toward an ecological holocaust" (Prakash, 1994, 1). This crisis is unique in its range and scope, including the pollution of freshwater and marine environments; atmospheric pollution; chemical and nuclear wastes; the degradation of our croplands, forests, and grazing lands; desertification; the destruction of wilderness habitats and ecosystems; the extinction of plant and animal species; and the ever-increasing human population growth (Fox, 1990, 3). The magnitude of this ecological crisis, in effect, now confronts us with the challenge to completely reconstitute our guiding ideological and epistemological frameworks.

While the overwhelming task of rethinking our cultural habits, attitudes, and values in terms of their implications for creating ecologically sustainable ecosystems has only just begun, some of the key elements in such an enterprise now seem obvious. In particular, I would like to identify four themes that seem to reveal the deepest underlying commitments in constructive postmodern thought, which might well be employed to help establish a beginning foundation for collaborative praxis between the critical and constructive postmodern paradigms.[1]

*The Environment as the Ultimate Context.*   Constructive postmodernism is about seeing the environment as the ultimate context in which all social and political activism can be viewed. All of us are nourished and nurtured by the earth and without this lifeline of nourishment we would perish. Thus, issues of social justice, equality, economic opportunity, political empowerment all derive from and are enabled by an environment that provides sustenance for people and other living systems. In this way, the environment is the ultimate ground of being. Without clean air, fresh water, and healthy food, survival would be impossible; all other issues become subordinate.

*Beyond the Anthropocentric Self.*   The Enlightenment way of understanding the subjectivity of the individual was predicated on maintaining a series of dualisms (specifically, mind and body, and mind and nature) that led to the calculating pattern of thought essential to scientifically based technological advances. Indeed, the entire Judeo-Christian tradition is based on metanarratives that represent humans as essentially separate from the natural world, and only in the most optimistic of these, humans view themselves merely as "wise stewards" of nature. The Romantics metaphorically diminished the concept of nature even further by reducing it to an inner subjective Self, grounding its view of individual growth, social progress, and human creativity in a sense of time and space that begins and ends with the expectations of the individual. This kind of anthropocentric thinking continues to be supported by leading critical theorists such as Henry Giroux, Paulo Freire, and Peter McLaren among others. While such a dialectical conception of Self is useful to the discourse of emancipatory social praxis, it is less central to the enterprise of seeing the interconnectedness of reality, the fundamental unity of the universe, and the development of more ecologically responsible forms of social organization.

Constructive postmodernism places the person within a continuum where an awareness of past and future generations helps to define what constitutes meaningful knowledge, values, and responsibility. The practice of Native-American cultures making decisions with the seventh unborn generations in mind captures this sense of life as part of a continuum. Specifically, their work has focused on the development of forms of community, agriculture, work, and art that improve the quality of human life (and cultures) by living more in dynamic harmony with the earth's everchanging ecosystems.

*The Sacredness of Nature.* The view of nature as transformative and sacred, and the search for the key to "the reenchantment of nature, life, and art" does not have to mean something "cosmic," "transcendent," or "otherworldly"—it emerges quite naturally when we cultivate compassionate, caring, responsive modes of relating to our natural ecosystems and cultural environments and to each other. With the realization that all life is sacred, we begin to radically alter our idiosyncratic value systems and our consumer-driven exploitative lifestyles. The underlying ethos of constructive postmodern thought in regard to the sacredness of all life is perhaps most clearly stated in the "Declaration of the Four Sacred Things" written by Starhawk (1993):

> To call these things sacred (earth, fire, water, and air) is to say that they have a value beyond their usefulness for human ends, that they themselves become standards by which our acts, our economics, our laws, our purposes, must be judged . . . all people, all living things are part of the earth, and so are sacred. No one of us stands higher or lower than any other . . . only ecological balance can sustain freedom. . . . To honor the sacred is to create the conditions in which nourishment, sustenance, habitat, knowledge, freedom, and beauty can survive.

While it is easy to dismiss (or mistake) such statements about the sacredness of nature as the return to an overly naive premodern form of tribal spirituality, one should consider that recently some well-known scientists (among them Carl Sagan and Stephen Gould) recently issued a collaborative statement proclaiming the ethical responsibilities of the scientific community in words strikingly similar to those of Starhawk:

> As scientists, many of us have had profound experiences of awe and reverence for the universe. We understand that what is regarded as sacred is more likely to be treated with care and respect. Our planetary home should be so regarded. Efforts to safeguard and cherish the environment need to be infused with a vision of the sacred (in Bowers, 1995; Suzuki & Knudtson, 1992).

*An Ecological View of Emancipatory Pedagogical Praxis.* Constructive postmoderns have also argued for a different view of intelligence, what they refer to as "ecological intelligence" (Bowers, 1995, 126ff). Combining the more culturally grounded view of intelligence employed by the critical theorists with the ecological view of intelligence of the constructive postmoderns would lead to a more inclusive approach to social praxis. For example, such an alliance would place at the center of the curriculum process the more ecologically problematic aspects of the dominant culture. Helping students to understand how the dominant culture has achieved social progress only at the expense of the degradation of both our natural systems and our indigenous cultures would be central to the teacher's responsibility.

David Orr and C. A. Bowers are the foremost holistic educators working within this constructive postmodern paradigm. Together they have produced an extraordinary corpus of scholarship on the theme of "ecological literacy" that has comprehensively worked out both the theoretical and practical aspects of such programs (Orr, 1992, 1995; Bowers, 1987, 1993a, 1993b, 1995). For example, Orr's curricular pedagogy brings together school communities in a critical study of all it consumes and wastes. Orr's pedagogy does not address these questions in the abstract discourse and difficult terminology so familiar to critical postmodern educators but, rather, depends on a "hands-on approach" for transforming the daily life of the educational community. He also leads the way in his attempts to combine holistic ideals with authentic praxis in actual local communities and schools. In this way, he demonstrates how our communities and schools can become an important part of the transformation toward more sustainable, human-scale, postmodern communities. "Think globally, act locally" is rediscovered and enriched by this new paradigmatic webbing of cultural critique with ecological praxis.

The constructive postmodern movement has recently been criticized as a white, middle-class endeavor with an exaggerated interest in flora and fauna and distant indigenous peoples. However, Jim Schwab's new book, *Shades of Darker Green: The Rise of Blue Collar and Minority Environmentalism*, focuses on a more recent development with the postmodern movement that has important implications for both critical theory and holistic educators (Schwab, 1994). Schwab writes of the birth of ecological community activism here in the United States among those most ignored by most environmental groups—blue collar whites, Native Americans, and people of color. Schwab's focus is on impoverished inner cities, poor rural communities, and isolated Native-American reservations. The common enemies here are industry, with its dreadful plans for toxic waste dumps, carcinogenic get-rich-quick schemes. His book reveals the extent to which our real constructive postmodern heroes and heroines are, literally, average citizens—housewives and ministers, small business owners and practitioner-based academics—who discover the power of working quietly in small groups to accomplish extraordinary social transformations in their simple, ordinary, everyday lives. I suspect that such a collaborative praxis/discourse between critical theorists and holistic educators would address some of the concerns recently raised by scholars about the seeming lack of any transformative power in critical theory formulations pedagogy (Pignatelli, 1993; Senese, 1991; Thompson & Gitlin, 1995). It is also the kind of collaborative social activism that Ron Miller has been so persuasively and passionately advocating for holistic educators in the last few years (Miller, 1990, 1991, 1993).

In his most recent book, *Sex, Economy, Freedom and Community*, Wendell Berry, one of our important postmodern commentators, decries the devastation of the American small farm and small town, in the words: "A nation will destroy its land and therefore itself if it does not foster in every possible way the sort of . . . households and communities that have the desire, the skills, and the means to properly care for the land they are using" (Berry, 1994, 21). That's why for him, words such as "globalism" and "international development" are worse than abstractions; they promote the idea that our really important work will be some kind of "big deal" in the "global strategy." They function, he tells us, as some kind of environmental and commercial Star Wars. By contrast, Berry argues:

> The real work of planet-saving will be small, humble, and unrewarding, and (insofar as it involves love) pleasing and rewarding. Its jobs will be too many to count . . . too small to make anyone rich or famous. (Berry, 1994, 24)

Ultimately, for Berry, we must learn to grow like a tree, not like a fire: "to go down and down into the daunting, humbling, almost hopeless local presence of the problem" (Berry, 1994, 24). It is here that ecology meets consciousness; critical theory meets holistic education.

Pedagogical Implications for the Postmodern Teacher

Metaphors help shape the way we view the world and enable us to more clearly envision new ways of understanding ourselves, especially during times of rapid social change. Metaphors of American classrooms have of course changed along with our evolving perspectives on our relationship to the world around us. There are, of course, a wide variety of metaphors current in today's educational literature. In everyday educational discourse, one frequently hears life in classrooms compared to that in prisons, factories, shopping malls, war, and drugstores, as well as families, gardens, and streams. In many of these metaphors, there are dramatic contradictions and tensions that reflect the competing visions and priorities that different social groups have for the American public school system. One metaphorical image that postmodern classroom teachers might employ to begin the process of revisioning for themselves what life in a postmodern classroom might entail is that of the classroom as a living ecological web of relationships. Teacher educators can learn, therefore, a great deal about themselves and their relationships to their students by exploring this metaphorical image.

The image of the classroom as a living ecological web of relationships is a favorite metaphor used to describe the structure and functioning of the American public schools. This metaphor is grounded in the image of caring, sharing, and of mutual coexistence; the implication here is that since we are all connected, we should all act cooperatively to maintain and preserve our collective work environments. Here, one sees oneself and others as part of a collective whole, an organic "Gaia," a universal classroom, a part of an interconnected bioregionally based web of community alliances and obligations. At its core, then, the living ecological web metaphor resonates with a concern for the delicacy of the strands that connect us and provide us with sustenance—it dramatically captures the theme that we affect everything and everything affects us. Perhaps Teilhard de Chardin expressed it best when he wrote:

> The farther and more deeply we penetrate into matter, by means of increasingly powerful methods, the more we are confounded by the interdependence of its parts. Each element of the cosmos is positively woven from all the others. . . . It is impossible to cut into this network, to isolate a portion without it becoming frayed and unraveled at all its edges. All around us, as far as the eye can see, the universe holds together, and only one way of considering it is really possible, that is, to take it as a whole, in one piece. (Chardin, quoted in Miller, 1993a, 76)

The critical postmodern educator, however, is also aware that this web can entrap and ensnarl its prey as well as nurture and protect its allies. For example, most American public school teachers must work under conditions largely beyond their control, implementing national and state-mandated standards, curriculum, textbooks, evaluation, and testing in which they have little or no input (Miller, 1995). Not unexpectedly, this sort of top-down "colonization" of teachers and students has resulted in myriad forms of teacher and student subservience, passivity, and acquiescence, as well as disruption, resistance, and revolt.

The development of a critical classroom pedagogy, therefore, rests on the difficult and demanding task of becoming familiar with the new "language of critique." Words such as: boundary crossing, commodification, discourse, counter-discourse, counter-hegemonic practices, critical consciousness, demystification, cultural capital, cultural reproduction, cultural worker, deconstruction, deficit model, dialectics, domesticate, dominant ideologies, false consciousness, grand/totalizing/master narratives, hegemony, hermeneutics, hidden curriculum, historical amnesia, internalized oppression, logocentrism, marginalize, metanarrative, objectification, political awareness, positionality, positivism, postcolonialism, postmodernism, poststructuralism, praxis, problematize, resistance, oppositional identity, subordinated cultures, technocratic, telecratic, and voice must become woven into the very fabric of how teachers construct and make meaning out of even the most mundane, ordinary, everyday classroom events and practices. It is this new "language of critique" that can assist postmodern educators in their daily classroom struggles to ensure that equality, social justice, and tolerance for diversity are the strong supporting strands that form the foundational core in everyday classroom processes and practices.

The metaphor of "the classroom as an ecological web" is one that the constructive postmodern teacher can successfully employ to counter the top-down, control-oriented modes of "democratic" restructuring that have resulted in the decline of local schools and communities as repositories of local commitment, loyalty, and obligation. In her book, *African American Mothers and Urban Schools: The Power of Participation*, Winters tell us that "communities [as well as classrooms] should be a place where compassion abounds and where individuals are valued for their uniqueness" (Winters, 1993, 110). It is only by a revival of such intimate school-community relationships that authentic local traditions and values can flourish, be reinforced and celebrated. In recent works John Miller (1985, 1993a, 1993b, 1994) has been carefully working out the dimensions of a new transformational "holistic" approach to classroom practice that is grounded in a rich network of human-scale, community-based, ecological webs. He writes:

> The focus of holistic education is on relationships . . . the relationship between linear thinking and intuition, the relationship between mind and body, the relationships between various domains of knowledge, the relationship between the individual and community, and the relationship between the self and the Self. In the holistic curriculum, the student examines these relationships so that he/she gains both an awareness of them and the skills necessary to transform the relationships where it is appropriate (Miller, 1993a, 73).

The postmodern classroom teacher is intuitively aware that this web of relationships begins with the internal web of relationships that each child weaves within. The cultivation of such awareness, of the intimate web of relationships that connect us all, lies at the heart of Buddhism, Taoism, and other Eastern philosophies and is also embedded deeply within the Native-American wisdom traditions, the African-American folk cultures, as well as the American Transcendental movement (Katagiri, 1988; Miller, 1967; Suzuki & Knudtson, 1992; Suzuki, 1970; Thich Nhat Hanh, 1975, 1987).

Most of us get so busy teaching the "required" curriculum that we forget to ask ourselves what a real education (and person) should really be? Try asking yourself from time to time in the classroom: Am I awake right now? Am I aware of the creative possibilities in this moment for myself and my students? The postmodern classroom teacher is attuned to the unique opportunities that each moment presents for connecting and weaving new webs of relationships within the local school-community nexus. Parents are welcomed guests and volunteers in the postmodern classroom. Teachers and students share tasks and conegotiate learning options in educational cultures that are collegial, respectful, and collaborative. In making the metaphorical imagery of "the classroom as a living ecological web of relationships" come alive in one's spirit, postmodern classroom teachers can (re)envision for themselves and their students how local schools can become rich resources for exploration, adventure, and discovery as well as joyful places to grow in strength, wisdom, and compassion.

## SUMMARY

Still marginal to mainstream academic conversations, this emerging revisionary constructive postmodernism is struggling to move us beyond the modern world's drive toward greater mechanization, economism, nationalism, consumerism, militarism, rugged individualism, and patriarchy. It is uniquely suited to help us (re)envision ecologically viable postmodern ways of relating to self, community, nature, and the cosmos. The scope of the present crisis underscores the powerful need for a collaborative praxis/dialogue between critical poststructural postmoderns and constructive, (re)visionary postmoderns.

## NOTE

1. The author is grateful for conversations with Paul Gallimore, Director of the Long Branch Environmental Center in Leicester, NC, for helping her conceptualize the themes upon which this section is premised.

## REFERENCES

Aronowitz, S., & Giroux, H. A. (1985). *Education under siege: The conservative, liberal, and radical debate over schooling.* South Hadley, MA: Bergin & Garvey.

Berry, W. (1994). *Sex, economy, freedom, and community.* New York: Pantheon.

Bertens, H. (1995). *The idea of the postmodern: A history.* New York: Routledge and Kegan Paul.

Bowers, C. A. (1987). *Elements of a post-liberal theory of education.* New York: Teachers College Press.

Bowers, C. A. (1993a). *Education, cultural myths, and the ecological crisis: Toward deep changes.* Albany, NY: SUNY Press.

Bowers, C. A. (1993b). *Recovery of the ecological imperative in education and social thought: Critical essay, 1977–1992.* New York: Teachers College Press.

Bowers, C. A. (1995). *Educating for an ecologically sustainable culture.* Albany, NY: SUNY Press.

Callinicos, A. (1989). *Against postmodernism: A marxist critique.* Cambridge, MA: Polity Press.

Deleuze, G. (1988). *Foucault.* Minneapolis: University of Minnesota Press.

Dewey, J. [1916] (1929). *The quest for certainty.* New York: Minton, Balch.

Fox, W. (1990). *Towards a transpersonal ecology: Developing new foundations for environmentalism.* Boston: Shambhala.

Frankel, B. (1987). *The post-industrial utopians.* Cambridge, MA: Polity Press.

Gabbard, D. A. (1994). Ivan Illich, postmodernism, and the eco-crisis: Reintroducing a "wild" discourse. *Educational Theory* 44(2).

Giroux, H. A. (1991). *Postmodernism, feminism, and cultural politics: Redrawing educational boundaries*. Albany, NY: SUNY Press.

Gough, N. (1994). Playing at catastrophe: Ecopolitical education after poststructuralism. *Educational Theory* 44(2).

Griffin, D. R. (1992). Introduction to SUNY series on constructive postmodern thought. In *Ecological literacy: Education and the transition to a postmodern world*, ed. D. Orr. Albany, NY: State University of New York Press.

Habermas, J. (1987). *The philosophical discourse of modernism*. Cambridge, MA: MIT Press.

Jameson, F. (1991). *Postmodernism, or the cultural logic of late capitalism*. Durham, NC: Duke University Press.

Karier, C. J. (1973, April). Ideology and evaluation: In quest of meritocracy. Paper prepared for the Wisconsin Conference on Education and Evaluation. Madison, WI.

Karier, C. J. et al. (1973). *Roots of crisis: American education in the twentieth century*. Chicago: Rand McNally.

Katagiri, D. (1988). *Returning to silence: Zen practices in daily life*. Boston: Shambhala.

Lather, P. (1991). Deconstructing/deconstructive inquiry: The politics of knowing and being known. *Educational Theory* 41(2).

Leistyna, P., Woodrum, A., & Sherblom, S. (Eds.). (1996). *Breaking free: The transformative power of critical pedagogy*. Cambridge, MA: Harvard Educational Review.

Lyotard, J. F. (1984). *The postmodern condition: A report on knowledge*. Minneapolis: University of Minnesota Press.

Miller, J. (1985). *Curriculum: Perspectives and practices*. New York: Longman.

Miller, J. (1993a). *The holistic curriculum*. Toronto: OISE Press.

Miller, J. (1993b). *The holistic teacher*. Toronto: OISE Press.

Miller, J. (1994). *The contemplative practitioner: Meditation in education and the professions*. South Hadley, MA: Bergen & Garvey.

Miller, P. (1967). *The transcendentalists: An anthology*. Cambridge, MA: Harvard University Press.

Miller, R. (Ed.). (1991). *The renewal of meaning in education: Responses to the cultural crisis and ecological crisis of our times*. Brandon, VT: Holistic Education Press.

Miller, R. (1992). *What are schools for? Holistic education in American culture*. Brandon, VT: Holistic Education Press.

Miller, R. (1993). Holistic education in the United States: A "new paradigm" or a cultural struggle? *Holistic Education Review* 6(4).

Miller, R. (Ed.). (1995). *Educational freedom for a democratic society: A critique of national goals, standards, and curriculum*. Brandon, VT: Resource Center for Redesigning Education.

Natoli, J., & Hutcheon, L. (Eds.). (1993). *The postmodern reader*. Albany, NY: SUNY Press.

Nicholson, C. (1989). Postmodernism, feminism, and education: The need for solidarity. *Educational Theory* 39(3).

Oliver, D. W., & Gershman, K. W. (1989). *Education, modernity, and fractured meaning: Toward a process theory of teaching and learning*. Albany, NY: SUNY Press.

Orr, D. (1992). *Ecological literacy: Education and the transition to a postmodern world*. Albany, NY: SUNY Press.

Orr, D. (1995). *Earth in Mind*. Albany, NY: SUNY Press.

Peters, M. (1989). Techno-science, rationality, and the university: Lyotard on the postmodern condition. *Educational Theory* 39(2).

Pignatelli, F. (1993). What can I do? Foucault on freedom and the question of teacher agency. *Educational Theory* 43(4).

Poster, M. (1984). *Foucault, Marxism, and history*. Cambridge, MA: Polity Press.

Prakash, M. S. (1994). What are people for? Wendell Berry on education, ecology, and culture. *Educational Theory* 44(2).

Rosenau, P. M. (1992). *Postmodernism and the social sciences: Insights, inroads, and intrusions.* Princeton, NJ: Princeton University Press.

Ross, E. A. (1912). *Social control.* New York: Macmillan.

Schwab, J. (1994). *Shades of darker green: The rise of blue collar and minority environmentalism.* San Francisco: Sierra Club Books.

Senese, G. B. (1991). Warnings on resistance and the language of possibility: Gramsci and a pedagogy from the surreal. *Educational Theory* 41(1).

Shea, C. M. (1980). *The ideology of mental health and the emergence of the therapeutic liberal state: The American mental hygiene movement, 1900–1930.* Ph.D. diss., University of Illinois, Champaign-Urbana.

Spencer, L. (1996, February 26). Multiculturalism and oppression: A framework for analysis. Class presentation given to FED 251 students, College of Education, Georgia Southern University.

Starhawk. (1993). *The fifth sacred thing.* New York: Bantam.

Suzuki, D., & Knudtson, P. (1992). *Wisdom of the elders: Sacred native stories of nature.* New York: Bantam.

Suzuki, S. (1970). *Zen mind, Beginner's mind.* New York: Weatherhill.

Thich Nhat Hanh. (1975). *The miracle of mindfulness: A manual on meditation.* Boston: Beacon Press.

Thich Nhat Hanh. (1987). *Being peace.* Berkeley, CA: Paralux Press.

Thompson, A., & Gitlin, A. (1995). Creating spaces for reconstructing knowledge in feminist pedagogy. *Educational Theory*, 45(2).

Turkle, S. (1979). *Psychoanalytic politics: Jacques Lacan and Freud's French revolution.* London: Burnett Books.

Winters, W. G. (1993). *African-American mothers and urban schools: The power of participation.* New York: Lexington.

# 23
▼▼▼▼▼▼▼

# Social Transformation and Holistic Education: Limitations and Possibilities*

David E. Purpel

I believe that the term "educators" has had a misleading and problematic effect, for it has enabled us to participate in the fiction that educational issues have a reality of their own apart from their social and cultural context. At its most distorted, the term "educator" can mean a person who is an expert on what and how students learn, i.e., a skilled technician or craftsperson who specializes in what happens in the classroom. This distortion has at least two important troubling dimensions: first, there is the myth that the educational process can be separated from the historical and social context, and second, there is the absurdity that educators are primarily, if not only, educators.

Educators, like everyone else, are responsible for the creation, preservation, and/or re-creation of a social system or, if you prefer, a community. Whatever else people are called upon to do, they have the inevitable, agonizing, and exhilarating task of constructing ways in which we are to live with each other. Each of us participates willy-nilly in this extraordinarily vital process, however unaware we might be, however tiny or major our impact, however beneficial or destructive the contribution.

Some people (e.g., educators) are lucky enough to be in positions where they are explicitly called upon to articulate and act upon a vision of the good life. I often tell my students that there are no such things as educational issues, there are instead a number of moral, spiritual, philosophical, psychological, social, and cultural issues that get expressed and acted out in educational settings. In that same spirit, let me add that there are no educators per se, but more profoundly, there are moral and spiritual leaders who exercise their responsi-

*Purpel, David. "Social Transformation and Holistic Education: Limits and Possibilities." From *Holistic Education Review*, vol. 9, no. 2 June 1996, (pp. 26–34).

bilities in the context of educational settings. These moral and spiritual educators presumably have some strong ideas as to what is involved in imagining and developing a life of individual and communal meaning and their particular work has two aspects: 1) the creation of an educational community that in critical ways reflects that broader vision; and 2) the creation of teaching and learning activities that can nurture and nourish that vision. The real issue is clearly not what specific term we use to call ourselves but more importantly, how we name our work, and I would suggest that the naming must reflect our awareness of our deep and intense involvement in the inevitable, awesome, and continuous process of creating community. Indeed, John Dewey has defined education as "the making of a world."

Certain processes and institutions are inevitable in developing community, most notably a moral framework that informs a political and economic system that creates and distributes the rights, responsibilities, and rewards of citizenship, i.e., a system of justice. However, what holistic educators know only too well is that these political and economic policies and institutions interact with other important dimensions of our lives and, moreover, we must insist on an education that seeks to integrate *all* facets of human life, being sure to avoid a one-sided or distorted vision of human being.

There is, of course, some intended ironic criticism here since it has been my view that, by and large, holistic educators have tended to focus much more on the personal and spiritual than on the social and moral dimensions of education. This is ironic to me because I believe that in their zeal to rightfully point out how conventional educators have a truncated vision of learning, holistic educators tend to substitute an equally truncated, albeit more aesthetically satisfying, vision of learning. It is quite true that holistic educators are making an enormously important contribution to our society and culture by emphasizing such neglected areas as the intuitive, the artistic, the creative, and the mythopoetic and for that they deserve our thanks and approbation. What is spectacularly exciting is that the conceptual framework of the current holistic education movement provides for the possibility of a *truly* holistic education—one that seeks to integrate the inner self with the outer self and thereby connect the personal with our social, cultural, moral, political, and economic contexts.

Not only must we be wary of a narrow professionalism that renders our work as being in "the field of education," we must also be suspicious of formulas that proclaim the importance of "keeping politics out of education," as if that were even possible. We must also guard against the preciousness that seeks to keep us all shielded from the harsh realities of social injustice and political oppression. Perhaps most importantly of all, we must have the courage to confess to and witness the ways that we and the educational system are part of a system that has created, sustained, and legitimized this injustice and oppression. Not only must we be fully aware of our political, economic, and social contexts, but we must reaffirm and renew our commitments to our social vision of the just, loving, and joyous community.

To be an educator without a social vision is like being an artist without an aesthetic and to be a holistic educator without a social vision is to be like an artist without a soul. However, it is not that easy since what we want is not any old social vision but one that enables us to transcend to a consciousness of beauty, love, and compassion. Indeed, it is vital to be reminded that conventional education does in fact reflect a social and cultural vision and in so doing, it serves a particular political and economic ideology. Let us then take a look at the relationship between the dominant educational discourse and how it is related to social, political, and economic considerations.

The dominant ideology puts an incredible amount of emphasis on the difficulty that the U.S. has had in maintaining its military and economic primacy in the face of foreign competition and that our prosperity depends on our reestablishing that supremacy. It is this ideology that drives the current reform movement that stresses so-called higher standards, greater mastery of knowledge, greater reliance on test scores, and more demanding instructional techniques. This orientation is neatly captured in President Clinton's 1994 State of the Union speech in which he said in the context of voicing support for alternative forms of schooling that such efforts are worthwhile "as long as we measure every school by one high standard: Are our children learning what they need to know to compete and win in the global economy?" This is hardly ambiguous and its bluntness and vulgarity should hardly be surprising since it represents, I believe, mainstream public opinion and the primary focus of professional energies.

In an increasingly global economy marked by extraordinarily intense competition, corporations are engaged in a frenzy of efforts to, if not gain an edge, at least survive. Mergers, buy-outs, downsizing, layoffs, union-busting are obvious manifestations of this hysteria spurred on by the fantasy of enormous wealth and power as well as the nightmare of being wiped out. This kind of vicious competition has contributed to a very significant reduction in the number of satisfying job opportunities and to incessant and cold-blooded efforts to reduce personnel costs. The result is a sense of unease and anxiety among us all as we become increasingly vulnerable to economic misfortune, threatening not only such material things as savings, medical care, and educational opportunities but also our hopes and dreams for peace and justice.

What *must* be understood is that these trends are reflected *in* and facilitated *by* current educational policies and practices, or at the very least, that is what most of our political and educational leaders are advocating. Schools, community colleges, and universities are all being asked to teach more technical and vocational skills, to be more selective and demanding with students, to test more, and to create closer partnerships with business. This is *not* about nourishing souls, it is not about individuation or even about encouraging learning. It *is* about harnessing educational institutions to the President's vision of "competing and winning" in the race to be the richest and most powerful nation of all.

The thrust behind the establishment of state-financed and state-controlled compulsory education in the 19th century (which was strongly resisted by a number of different groups for a variety of compelling reasons) was to require a common school experience for all children in an effort to create a common American culture. They would be required to pray and read the Christian Bible and learn the traits expected of the WASP middle class: piety, respect for authority, cleanliness, obedience, perseverance, hard work, civility, and delay of gratification. Such traits not only constituted the ethos of the dominant cultural vision but not surprisingly meshed with the requirements of the new industrial order with its insatiable demand for compliant and reliable workers. I would submit that this agenda still operates even though it is clear that the rhetoric has been somewhat altered in response to changes in the form in which these issues are currently framed. There is at least one major exception to this generalization and that, ironically enough, has to do with the emphasis on democracy, which had a very clear, strong, and urgent place on the agenda of 19th century advocates for compulsory common schooling. How different it would be if President Clinton had suggested that the one standard for schools be not "winning in the global economy" but instead nourishing and deepening the spirit of democracy.

## RESPONSE

If we have anything in common as professionals, citizens, and humans, we have responsibilities and we all have the ability to respond. If educational institutions do, in fact, have an effect on society, then presumably they can be a force for positive transformation as well as for the maintenance of the status quo. How then are we as educators to respond to the social, cultural, and economic crises of our time particularly if we are to accept the premise that we are inevitably involved in them whether we like it or not? To borrow from a familiar slogan—can we move from being part of the problem to being part of the solution?

I must necessarily begin with a confession that I take the tragic view of life, i.e., I see our lives as fated to involve heroic and virtuous struggles that ultimately end in failure. I resonate with the Sisyphean experience of meaning and dignity deriving from continuous and never-ending engagement in the task of creating a better world in the face of an awareness of its futility. This is based not only on my own perhaps impoverished inner spirit but on an analysis of the effects of various social movements for reform and political struggles for genuine revolution and transformation. The story of such efforts certainly contains many truly inspiring sagas of courage and determination as well as solid and enduring successes. Yet many of the gains are short-lived and even if some problems are resolved, new even more difficult ones appear. The story of public education in America is surely a case in point for, in spite of the imagination and perseverance of thousands of dedicated and talented educators and the availability of any number of wonderful ideas and programs, the sad reality of the matter is that, in general, schools are less creative, less playful, less joyful, and less stimulating than they were 10 or 15 years ago. We have made very little if any progress in reducing hostility, violence, racism, sexism, homophobia, and warfare. Poverty and homelessness persist while the standard of living and sense of security continues to erode even for the middle class. Our economists seem, in spite of their brilliance, unable to either understand or manage an economy that is cruel and relentless. Welfare programs seem to be counter-productive, pesticides turn out to be deadly to humans, and antibiotics produce even stronger, more dangerous viruses.

I do not see this view as necessarily cynical or despairing because for me it is very strongly tempered by the majesty of human persistence in the teeth of this storm of resistance to our earnest efforts. I joyfully join with those who would damn the torpedoes, light candles, or fight the good fight or who use any other cliché that celebrates the human impulse to participate in the covenant of creation. Indeed, I have to admit that I scorn the view that pessimism is an excuse for passivity and inaction. However, having said that, I need also to confess my parallel antipathy to sentimentality, i.e., a consciousness of mindless optimism that is a product of blindness, denial, wishful thinking, and fear. My position is that we must not be daunted by the magnitude of the task of creating a just and joyful community, but we must not add to its difficulty by underestimating what is involved. I am continuously energized by the Talmudic admonition that even though the task is not ours to finish, we are not free from the responsibility of engaging in the task.

Secondly, the task of creating cultural and social transformation is greatly magnified by two powerful, if not embarrassing, realities: 1) in spite of all our crises and fears, the dominant ideology of growth, achievement, success, privilege, individualism, and conquest is extremely alive and well and thrives in most if not all of us; and 2) relatedly, there are no broad alternative ideologies that are accessible to the public that could compete with the dominant ideology. The spirit of free enterprise and the sanctity of the concept of market are triumphant, virtually uncontested (especially with the collapse of the Soviet system and the weakening of the social democratic movements in the West), and venerated not only as ultimate truth but as a thing of beauty. There can be no greater indictment of our entire culture and particularly of our entire educational program than this shocking state

of affairs—that with all our knowledge and with all our creativity, imagination, and sensibilities, we find ourselves without a serious competitor to a
system that is killing us with its popularity. If nothing else, this speaks to
an immense failure in imagination but at a deeper level, it represents the
triumph of one set of spirits over another. The spirits of individual gain,
self-gratification, hedonism, competition, and possessiveness are beating the
pants off the spirits of interdependence, peace, joy, and love. Our culture
demands ever more products, thrills, innovations, titillations, scandals, sen-
sations, daring-dos, outrageousness; it is ever more mean-spirited and venge-
ful, increasingly paranoid, violent, and destructive. The dissenting elements
of the culture surely provide a great deal of criticism but precious little in
the way of affirmation. Ironically enough, one of the few groups offering
some alternative is the Christian Right, which, however, insists on wrapping
the banner of capitalism around the Cross. It, therefore, becomes an imperative that educators accept their responsibility to participate in the process of
not only providing and using the tools of cultural and social criticism but
nurturing and expressing the impulses of affirmation. Criticism without
affirmation not only is a contradiction in terms but carries with it the
destructive elements of sterility and paralysis. At the same time, let it be said
that affirmation without criticism is not only intellectually suspect, it is
fraught with the possibility of dogmatism and self-righteousness.

At this point, it is essential to temper my pessimism about the absence
of alternative social-political-economic paradigms by celebrating the enormous amount of energy and talent that is being expended in the effort to
make for a more just and peaceful society as expressed in innumerable
projects and movements. I have in mind comprehensive and ambitious programs as reflected in the ecology movement with its myriad projects in
recycling, consciousness raising, educational activities, legislative efforts, political lobbying, and activist campaigns. There are many parallel efforts in
other realms—concern for child abuse, civil rights, the handicapped, and
world peace, women's rights, liberation movements for any number of oppressed groups, the labor movement, gun control, concern for the homeless,
for refugees, for the starving, and, this is the main point, far too many to
mention and to know. The spirit of the sixties was not born in that era, it
was and *is*, a reenergized and renewed expression of the American and human
tradition of giving a damn, of responding to ancient and deeply felt impulses
to transcend existing limitations to a consciousness of love, joy, and peace
for all, and of the celebration of the mystery and beauty of life. That spirit
is very much alive in the 1990s as reflected not only in major programs like
the ones I have just mentioned, but also in the innumerable and unpublicized
daily acts of social responsibility, communal involvement, and personal
engagement such as doing volunteer work; political campaigning; comforting
the sick, the afflicted, and the wounded; speaking up at PTA meetings and

in legislative bodies for reform; writing letters to the editor; and, just as important, actively witnessing the pain and suffering in the land. Such efforts must be strongly recognized, joyfully celebrated, and widely disseminated for a number of very important reasons beginning with the necessity to provide support and encouragement for those involved. In addition, it is vital to resist the rising tide of understandable and somewhat justifiable despair that is being fanned into a consciousness of futility by a campaign of disinformation that claims that the 1960s was really about drugs, sex, and rock and roll and that the flower children of that era are now all stockbrokers. Those who want to hold on to the present paradigm want very much for us to believe that we have lost our sense of idealism, hope, and commitment and it is vital that we give the lie to that self-serving slander.

We must also be in touch with these positive movements and activities in order to join with them, to form coalitions, to learn from them, and to contribute to them. In a broader sense, what I am strongly suggesting is that educators need to align their work with other groups and movements as an important part of their involvement in and responsibility for the continuing development and creation of community, culture, and society. In this context, I want to reiterate my notion that we must work to broaden the concept of educator to go beyond someone skilled in classroom and school activities to one who connects classroom and school to a social and cultural vision. Educators are social leaders, cultural advocates, moral visionaries, spiritual directors who choose to do their leading, advocating, visioning, and directing in institutions labeled schools and universities. We must always be mindful that the public and most private schools were not and are not set up for deep social and cultural transformation; actually it's the opposite, for they function primarily as preservers and conservers, as forces of stability, continuity, and predictability. In this sense, we as educators are already aligned with particular social and political forces and if we want to teach "against the grain of history," it would make a great deal of sense to do so explicitly, consciously, and deliberately. It also makes sense for those of us interested in working for social transformation to team up with like-minded people who happen to operate in different but complementary realms. In this way, educators can participate in the dialogue, help shape the strategy, and develop the policies that provide for a far greater degree of articulation between educational and political, social, economic, and cultural matters. This makes sense for two other reasons—first, it would be more honest and forthright to acknowledge the inherent interconnections and, second, this process is going on anyway but without the significant proactive involvement of the profession. It is no accident, for example, that many if not most schools are now replete with computers for they are there because particular businesses and industries planned for them to be there. In other words, educators are usually called upon to figure out how to use their expertise to further the goals of certain others—politicians, economists, business leaders, and cultural leaders. I say that it is time that educators be involved in the process of which social, economic, political, and cultural goals need and ought to be furthered.

One very important implication of such an analysis for educators has to do with the significance and limitations of particular curriculum and instructional practices, especially those that are appealing, humane, imaginative, wise, and constructive, i.e., the good kind. Alas, I have concluded with many others that such wonderful ideas and programs as cooperative learning, peer teaching, whole language expressive writing, and nature walks will by themselves have little impact on social and cultural transformation unless they are integrated into a holistic concept in which the boundaries between education and society become very blurred. We must end the delusions of single variable research, namely that we can isolate and separate educational elements and that a limited amount of significant change on a small scope will ultimately lead to significant change on a grand scale. No, my friends, the answer is not more imaginative curriculum and more sensitive instruction when the question is how education can contribute to the creation of a more just and loving world. The answer lies more in seeing such work as absolutely necessary but clearly insufficient; in connecting our classroom to our spiritual and cultural visions; and in accepting the reality that our social, cultural, economic, and political structures are integral and inevitable elements of the school curriculum. If we insist, however, on using a discourse that posits a sharp distinction between society and education, then I would have to say that changes in the culture and society will come much before changes in the schools and not vice versa. There is yet another possibility and that is to be far more humble and modest about the significance of our work as educators, which seems always appropriate if not potentially liberating but nonetheless has the danger of being implicitly irresponsible and collusive. It is, however, possible to hold on to the requirements of both humility and responsibility by seeing ourselves as part of a larger struggle not only in collaboration with others but in connection with those who precede and follow us.

Having said all that, let me hasten to add that working to improve and enrich the lives of students within the school boundaries is a vital and necessary part of our work, and when we do so, we are striving to respond to our highest moral and spiritual aspirations. In fact, it must be said that life in the classroom *is* the real world in those moments; not only a preparation *for* life but *part of* life itself. We must therefore affirm, support, and honor those who have worked and continue to work courageously and creatively on a day-to-day, week-to-week, year-to-year basis for an education that is loving, nourishing, and stimulating. Such work sustains and warms us all and undoubtedly contributes not only to short-range gains but to longer lasting ones as well.

We can here again take a cue from holistic education by being mindful of the differences and connections between microcosm and macrocosm. In a very profound sense, every moment in the classroom is a sacred one and has within it the possibility of transcendence and connection. In that sense, the classroom itself becomes an arena for the struggle or, if you will, a place that invites the possibility of transforming the banal to the profound, the vulgar to the beautiful, and the profane to the sacred. Alas, it also provides the possibility within the power of the alchemy of education of turning gold into dross and innocence into savagery. Indeed I believe the stakes are that high, and if they are not, we needn't bother and fuss so much over our work, but the fact that they are endows our frustrations with the mark of tragedy and our perseverance with the glow of majesty.

## WHAT MORE CAN BE DONE?

I want now to speak more directly to issues regarding what we as educators might do to respond to our social, political, and economic crises (notice I did not say educational crisis) in addition to striving to connect enriching and life-giving classroom experiences with other complementary cultural and social movements. I especially want to address the matter of the particular contribution that those in holistic education could make to this effort. Before I get to that, however, I want to mention what I believe is perhaps the most important contribution all educators can make to the well-being of our society and culture and that is the matter of informing the public. As I have stressed, education in a democracy is ultimately a matter of public policy and, as such, its shape and content must be determined through public dialogue, debate, and decision. Our democratic principles require that this dialogue and debate be guided by reasoned, informed, and open-minded processes. Unfortunately, I find the quality of public discourse on education to be appalling in its simplistic and reductionist analysis as well as the dreariness and conventionality of its visions of change. This is not inevitable for there is good reason to believe that public discourse in general has deteriorated over time as evidenced, for example, in what appears to have been a very sophisticated and impassioned public debate in the mid-19th century over the issue of mandating publicly financed compulsory schooling. The current sad state of public discourse is by no means limited to cabs, barrooms, and talk shows but can be heard in legislative halls, the offices of government officials, the boardrooms of corporate America, and the towers of academe. The quote from the President's State of the Union speech that I cited is noteworthy not only for its crudeness and vulgarity but for its resonance with mainstream, middle-class public opinion. Indeed, when President Bush announced his mindlessly shallow Education 2000 program, the Democrats complained bitterly that the Republicans had stolen their ideas! I regret to say that this deplorable state of public discourse on education has been aided and abetted by our profession in acts of both commission and omission. Although it is not for the profession by itself to make public policy on education, it has a vital role in informing, shaping, and clarifying the dialogue and debate. It can do this by virtue of its expertise and experience by providing thoughtful, thorough, and critical reflections on the issues and by insisting that the public take these reflections seriously. In this way, the profession can act as the intellectual and professional conscience of the public. However, it is my experience that the profession withholds a great deal of its insights and understandings from the public and is more likely to provide material that is more technical than substantive, more sentimental than critical, and more distracting than candid. I see nothing to be gained and a great deal to be lost when the profession plays the role of enabler in the public's fatal addiction to avoidance and denial.

As educators and citizens, we may often feel overwhelmed by the magnitude of the transformative task to the point of despair and paralysis. Willis Harman, the president of the Noetic Institute, in response to the question of what individuals might do in the face of the enormity of what is required, has provided a useful and succinct framework for action. He makes three basic suggestions: 1) Each of us needs to engage in a process of inner transformation by reflecting on our identity, our inner struggles, our personal agenda, our individual denials and avoidances, and the way we mess up our best intentions; 2) Each of us should participate in some kind of worthwhile local activity such that we have a chance to make some kind of discernible difference and to get some clear and speedy feedback on our efforts; and 3) Each of us should confront the reality that our whole social system, including all its destructive and dysfunctional forms, is supported by beliefs that we individually and collectively choose, accept, and sustain. He says that it is his experience that the ability to admit that the beliefs that we have bought into (such as our enthusiasm for a consumer economy) are actually contributing to our crises is the most difficult of the three suggestions for people to adopt. This is probably because it requires us to face our own complicity in unnecessary human suffering and the exploitation of nature (Harman, 1991).

What I especially like about this elegantly simple model is the way it provides for an interactive, dialectical process that connects the inner self, the social persona, and the outside world, thus providing not only for the breadth of concern but for personal responsibility on a human scale. It allows us the space within which we can both do and be, reflect and act, and be decisive and contemplative; and to deal simultaneously with short- and long-term issues. I want to suggest that we add another dimension to Harman's framework, namely that which deals with the importance of grounding our work in a framework of ultimate meaning, that which integrates the inner being, social being, and the culture. This, of course, assumes the existence of meaning, of some force or energy that provides coherence and wholeness to our existence. Whether the search for such meaning is delusionary and quixotic is surely not clear, at least to me, but it is quite clear that we as a species continue to engage ourselves in this search with incredible energy, imagination, and passion. What we yearn for in this process is to relate and connect what we do on a day-to-day basis to that which has enduring consequence, for in so doing, we can avoid drabness, emptiness, and idolatry.

## THE ROLE OF HOLISTIC EDUCATION
## IN SOCIAL TRANSFORMATION

With this extended model in mind, we can now discuss the particular and critical ways in which the holistic education movement could significantly contribute to redemptive social and cultural transformation. The most important contribution lies at the very heart of the movement and that is its root metaphor of wholeness and interdependence with its rejection of dualism and alienation and its affirmation of connection and integrity. A passion for harmony, peace, and wholeness can only deepen the connections between our inner and outer selves, between individuals and the community, between the material and the spiritual, between humanity and nature, between Planet Earth and the universe, and all the other possible betweens and amongs. Peace, justice, love, harmony, and meaning are each and all indivisible—they are neither to be rationed nor circumscribed; none of them individually sufficient, all of them necessary, each of them identifiable, and all of them blurrable with each other.

I am convinced that a key, if not central, educational element to the possibility of social and cultural transformation is the nourishment of imagination. One way of regarding our current crises is to see them as failures of imagination, as an inability to envision, for example, an economy without poverty and where there can be meaningful work for everyone, or an international order that can be maintained without recourse to violence, or a social system based on sufficiency for all rather than luxury for a few. Holistic educators need not be convinced about the importance of imagination for not only have they continuously and passionately argued for the necessity of encouraging the creative process but they have also demonstrated their faith in the extraordinary and untapped genius that resides in human imagination. It is time to direct the incredible power of fantastic, fanciful, and daring flights of imagination not only to the arts and letters but to fresh new social and economic visions, to developing more aesthetically pleasing ways of living together, and to designing more creative and life-giving social institutions.

However, when we consider the connection between the elements of holism and imagination, it becomes time to exercise extreme caution and to be in touch with our requirement of humility. What I mean here is that the impulse to image and create a coherent and whole vision of meaning, purpose, and destiny is as irresistible as it is dangerous, inevitable as it is futile, and redemptive as it is idolatrous. Indeed, in our current intellectual climate we have come to see, for better or worse, all cosmological, social, even scientific formulations and visions as acts of human imagination and construal. In this perspective, we see narratives, paradigms, contexts, contingencies, and particularities rather than dogmas, truths, eternal verities, certainties, and grand theories. This orientation has been both liberating and harrowing in that it has helped us to renew the importance of human agency in its constructivist sense. However, it has also made it virtually impossible to fully and totally affirm a firm and sustaining framework and rationale for our cherished beliefs. The death of certainty cuts two ways—it undercuts both dogmatism and conviction, both rigidity and steadfastness, and in so doing, it sponsors both diversity and relativism. The incredibly powerful research on issues of race, class, culture, and gender has revealed not only that an immense variety and diversity have been lost, hidden, and/or suppressed but that our lives have been largely guided by a particular vision of particular and privileged groups. The good news is that this vision as a human construction, as an act of human imagination, is not inevitable and hence can be replaced. The bad news is that we don't seem to have a replacement of commensurable appeal and power. We are between a rock and a hard place for on one hand we see the necessity and feel the reality of a coherent worldview but on the other our intellect and history remind us of the dangers and foolishness of grand narratives. We value and revere the power of the human imagination but realize that it is able to produce evil and destructive designs. We see the necessity for boldness and transformation but recognize our limitations. We want to discover meaning and truth but recognize that there is extraordinary diversity in how they are named. We want to act but we are unsure and unclear as to what to do since everybody and everything seems to be right and/or wrong. We want to be sensitive to diverse views and perspectives but are fearful that we can be paralyzed by fairness. Is it possible to have strong convictions without being self-righteous, to be audacious without being grandiose, and to be imaginative without being idolatrous?

The theologian Walter Brueggemann has directly addressed such questions as they relate to Christianity in his book, *Texts Under Negotiation* (1994). Brueggemann insists that it is the church's role to preach rejection of our current materialist and present-oriented vision and to replace it with a worldview that accepts divine creation and ultimate redemption. However, he clearly recognizes the obstacles and offers a far more modest and humble process of change based on the metaphor of *funding*. "It is not," Brueggemann writes, "in my judgment, the work of the church . . . to construct a full alternative world, for that would be to act as preemptively and imperialistically as all those old construals and impositions. Rather, the task is a more modest one, namely, to *fund*—to provide the pieces, material, and resources, out of which a new world can be imagined. Our responsibility, then, is not a grand scheme or a coherent system, but the voicing of a lot of little pieces out of which people can put life together in fresh configurations."

He goes on to say that this new world is not to be given whole in one moment but, ". . . is given only a little at a time, one miracle at a time, one poem at a time, one healing, one promise, one commandment. Over time, these pieces are stitched together, all of us in concert, but each of us idiosyncratically stitched together in a new whole—all things new."

I believe that such a formulation can be applied to education and that we can be bold and visionary in our endeavors yet humble and modest in our expectations. As educators we certainly have pieces, poems, miracles, promises, and commandments to offer as part of the new collage and stand ready to stitch them together with offerings of other groups and individuals. Holistic educators have their own ways of contributing to this funding, feeding, nurturing, nourishing, and legitimating project, and it is vital to affirm them even as we are aware of their piecemeal quality. It is surely no small thing to be part of a quilt especially if we are talking of a new quilt of harmony, justice, and meaning.

How then might holistic educators contribute to the fund of pieces, materials, and patches that will constitute significant portions of that quilt in process? Let me count the ways. There is the matter of spirit—the concern for the soul, the divine, the mysterious, the inner self, the tacit, and the unconscious. There is the openness and insistence on legitimating diverse ways of knowing—aesthetic, intuitive, and kinesthetic. Holistic educators put special reliance on developing close and warm human relationships not as instruments of manipulation but as essential to human meaning and existence. Children, and for that matter people, become the center of concern not as in self-centered but as foci of connection to each other, the community, the planet, and the universe. Holistic educators are among the very first to affirm the ecological consciousness that stresses the vulnerable but vital interconnections among all forms of life and as such have much to contribute even further to the struggle to sustain and nourish Mother Earth. They are also unique in their insistent and heart-felt invitation to joyously celebrate the wonders of creation and the continuous miracle of life. This optimism, hope, determination, and energy is literally refreshing and renewing, a much needed antidote for the nay-sayers and grumps the likes of me.

I also urge holistic educators to extend another one of their unique capacities, i.e., the genius of being able to reach out and touch others. In this case to help break down the barriers among other educators committed to transformation, albeit with differing orientations, e.g., those in critical pedagogy, those in feminist groups, and those working in the area of curriculum criticism. Perhaps their concern for wholeness and their openness and optimism could enable them to be a principal catalyst for more harmony, complementarity, synergy, and integration among like-minded educators. The burden for this responsibility clearly does not rest only on the shoulders of holistic educators since other groups must come to move away from their positions of smugness and preciousness and have the sense to broaden and deepen their understandings in dialogue with those they have not really encountered.

Having said all that, please indulge me as I return to my previous condition of fear and foreboding. Even as I celebrate the optimism of holistic educators, I can't help but worry about the future. Do we have the time to rely on the emergence of a new collage, a transformed quilt, and a new whole? It is true that there have been dire predictions of calamity in all ages and it is true that we have survived any number of catastrophes. But it is also plausible that we may be running out of lives and that we ought to be extremely careful that we not be taken in by our resistance to wolf-crying. Many ecologists indeed have said that it is already too late to save the planet and many social critics see the inevitability of permanent violence and war created by the increasing gulf between haves and have-nots exacerbated by the population explosion and the depletion of the earth's resources. Our educational task surely includes providing a critical awareness of our condition but perhaps our most pressing immediate task as educators is the development of a pedagogy of hope and possibility. Each of us needs to wrestle with this task and to probe within ourselves for the source of renewing and reenergizing our own faith and hope without denying the magnitude of the dangers we face.

As for me, I find such energy in the prophetic traditions of the Bible and in its modern manifestations such as Liberation Theology. This tradition combines criticism and affirmation, anguish and hope, humanity and the spirit, this world and eternity. Reinhold Niebuhr (1935) has characterized the Biblical prophets as being able to "be confident that life is good in spite of its evil and that it is evil in spite of the good and in this way both sentimentality and despair are avoided." The prophetic tradition emphasizes a continuous collaboration between humanity and God in which both humans and God are free but interdependent and in which people are responsible to fulfill a divine destiny. I have to admit to some nervousness in using the G word, especially in an academic setting and given my own wavering agnosticism. Harvey Cox has helped me in this regard by suggesting this formulation: "God [is] whatever it is within the vast spectacle of cosmic evolution which inspires and supports the endless struggle for liberation, not just from tyranny but from all bondages. 'God' is that power which despite all setbacks never admits to final defeat" (Cox, 1973).

With that concept of God in mind, let me close with yet another quote from a theologian, this time the eminent Jewish scholar, Jacob Neusner. Neusner has translated and written a commentary on a book from the Talmud usually titled *Sayings of Our Fathers* but which Neusner translates as *Torah from Our Sages*. In a section discussing the insights of Rabbi Hillel, Neusner points to issues of hope as he examines Hillel's insistence that over time "God corrects the imbalances of life—pays back the evil and rewards the good." Although Neusner readily admits that this is hardly a description of reality, he goes on to say:

> We, for our part, must preserve that same hope for justice, even in the face of despair. We have to believe, despite the world, that God cares. . . . But part of the meaning of having faith in God is believing that there is justice when we see injustice, believing there is meaning when we face what seems an empty accident. Ours is not a time for complex explanation. We cannot appeal to how things come out right in the end. We have been through too much. Ours is an age that demands simple faith—or no faith at all. All the standard explanations have proved empty. But Hillel's, also was an age that gave no more evidence than it does now that God rules with justice. Yet Hillel said it, and so must we: against it all, despite it all. There is no alternative. (Neusner, 1994).

## REFERENCES

Brueggemann, W. (1994). *Texts under negotiation: The Bible and postmodern imagination.* Minneapolis: Fortress Press.

Cox, H. (1973). *The seduction of the spirit.* New York: Simon & Schuster.

Harman, W. (1991). Interview on audio tape, Noetic Institute.

Neusner, J., trans. and commentator. (1984). *Torah from our sages.* Dallas: Rossel Books.

Neibuhr, R. (1935). *An interpretation of Christian ethics.* New York: Harper and Brothers.

# TOWARD THE 21ST CENTURY:
# GLOBAL CATASTROPHE
# OR SOCIAL TRANSFORMATION?

# Beyond Liberation and Excellence:
# A Discourse for Education as
# Transformation*

David E. Purpel
Svi Shapiro

## THE CHALLENGE OF THE POSTMODERN:
## COHESION IN A WORLD OF DIFFERENCE

Although much of our own social and educational orientation has been
reflected in the first four chapters of this book, most of what we have said
has been in the nature of criticism and analysis of existing public and professional discourse. It is now time for us to be more direct and explicit about
our own point of view, fundamental assumptions, and particular recommendations. In this chapter, we set out a broad framework—or, if you will, a
credo—in which we provide a framework for an education directed at a
morally grounded social vision. The book concludes with a chapter that
deals with a political agenda that reflects that framework.

As we have indicated, our starting point is the critical pedagogy tradition;
however we intend to respond to a number of our criticisms of this movement,
particularly to its failure to articulate a political program, its failure to respond
to important psychological dimensions, its diffidence and wariness about
dealing with moral and spiritual issues, and its inability to extricate itself from
conflictual discourse. In writing this chapter, we have also had to directly
confront our own differing perspectives and to develop positions that were
truly integrative rather than merely complementary. We wanted to (and did)
experience the creative as well as the conflictful tensions between points of view
that differed in emphasis between the political and the moral, between short-
and long-range perspectives, between essentialist and pragmatic tendencies,
between optimism and despair, and between existential and historical out-

*From: BEYOND LIBERATION AND EXCELLENCE: RECONSTRUCTING THE PUBLIC
DISCOURSE, by Purpel & Shapiro. Copyright © 1995 by David E. Purpel and Svi Shapiro. Reproduced
with permission of GREENWOOD PUBLISHING GROUP, INC., Westport, CT.

looks. We believed that we accomplished more than most people thought we could and yet less than we had hoped for.

There is something that must be confessed at the outset of writing this chapter. Call it masculine hubris or intellectual arrogance perhaps. Our intention was to find and offer a language or vision for education that would express all aspects of our hopes and commitments for educational renewal and change. This discourse would tie together all of our concerns with a *single* thread. We felt capable of finding that one powerful, resonant image or representation of educational purpose and goals that could claim the allegiance, and capture the imagination, of the broad mass of citizens in this country. Indeed, we felt impelled to discern that unitary overarching demand for education that might unleash the political will and drive for educational reform—one that would connect changes in education to the impulse for changing our society in directions that are more socially just, democratic, and compassionate. It seemed to us that our combined visionary power and perspicacity would allow us to unlock the discursive secret for mobilizing wide public support and sympathy for transforming the nature and goals of education in the United States. As will become clear, our response to this challenge is more complex and rests less on a simple formula or clear-cut notions than perhaps we may have liked.

Perhaps our desire or our confidence in the possibility of finding such a language was the legacy of what has been called "totalizing" political thinking that, especially in the twentieth century, has promised to provide us with some key to social change.[1] This kind of thinking rests on a self-confident assumption that there is always an historically correct strategy that a group of committed political individuals can discern. On the political Left (with which we identify ourselves), this has meant, very often, the belief that there is a single, preeminent motive that, when galvanized, can bring a society toward its own transformation. Left intellectuals, in particular, have long operated under the assumption that, with the acquisition of a critical level of cultural, economic, and political understanding, it is possible to uncover the secret of social transformation; that, armed with their often prodigious knowledge of a society's nature and development, the mechanism of social change can be ignited and the quest for human emancipation will roar to life.[2] This belief has been one component of the often frantic intellectuality of Left intellectuals who are convinced that a final or complete grasp of the whole social situation is within their reach. The failures, losses, and unpredictability of events in this century—not the least of which have been the revolutionary changes in Europe at the end of the 1980s—have surely challenged this faith. These events have, or should have, tempered our belief in our capacity to know and steer the hearts and minds of the *masses* (a term itself that reeks of the separation between that privileged group who provide intellectual and moral guidance and the rest who may receive it).

Yet, and despite our own admission here, the difficulty of keeping faith with the promise of this book to provide some straightforward, clear, and evocative language by which to stir educational revolt or insurgency is a disappointment, even a bitter pill. Of course, this recognition is not ours alone. We are quite aware that it is no more than what a number of our thoughtful colleagues and comrades in struggles have also found. The pages of some of the most creative Left publications, such as *Tikkun* magazine, *Z* magazine, *In These Times*, and the *Utne Reader*, give testimony to this. The world is too complex, the range of views too wide, the diversity of concerns too differentiated, to imagine that there can, any more, be simple unanimity of goals or interests that unites all of us who desire deep political, social, economic, cultural, and educational change. Nor can we hold fast to the belief that all of those who are now apathetic, cynical, detached, or even hostile to social change can be mobilized around some all-embracing hope or that they can be won over to some transcendent image, representation, or vision of the future. Of course, as we have already noted, it is also possible to conclude, as some critical scholars have, that there is nothing left to unify us, no common human goal or vision, nothing for those of us who seek fundamental social change to attend to and support but the endless proliferation of different voices, each trying to find some justified place in the sun after imprisonment in silence, or exclusion. We in no way wish to diminish the recognition of the multiplicity of ways in which human beings have been oppressed, their dignity undermined, and the full realization of their humanity thwarted. For we have, at last, begun to enter a world where the multiple ways in which human beings suffer and are dehumanized is achieving its proper recognition.

Yet—and we will return to this later—something is lost in this radical discourse of difference. Where are the bridges that connect the suffering of one group of human beings to another? Where is the sense of commonality among different people—not just within the *particular* oppressed group itself?[3] If we all speak only from within our specific situations and identities (the sexually oppressed, native people, the old, the mentally disabled, women, and so forth), who speaks for humanity? While the socialist tradition of emphasizing working-class struggles may have arrogantly ignored or dismissed so many other forms of human pain and struggle, it did, at least, maintain some kind of universal human vision. We will need to decide whether such universal visions are part of man's megalomaniacal desire for power and uniformity or part of the deep failure of political nerve that now afflicts so many of those concerned with social transformation. The catastrophic failures of revolutionary social experiments in the twentieth century certainly can be seen as giving credence to either argument or position.

Such has indeed been the case with articulating an alternative radical discourse about education among what is undoubtedly a fragmented, divergent public. In this sense, we have come to accept the implication of what might be called our postmodern reality.[4] Our identities in the world are so complexly shaped that the "call to arms" to fight a clearly focused, unique opponent has become an outmoded discourse inapplicable to the particular social, cultural, political, and economic conditions that we now encounter in the United States.

More and more we have come to understand ourselves as "positioned" in the world in complex and contradictory ways with allegiances, concerns, and needs that are anything but given, static, or singular. Identities are not fixed by one or another sociological category, and people do not have predetermined ways of looking at or making sense of their world. Neither those whom we envisage as our "natural" allies in the struggle for our own survival nor those whom we come to see as our necessary nemesis or opponents is foretold by history. One only has to consider, for example, Elie Wiesel's assertion that today "all of us have become Jews."

Today all of humanity can be seen as victims living under the Damoclean sword of a world in the process of destroying its delicate web of life-giving resources. The carcinogenic effect of the pollution of water and food, the erosion of the ozone layer, and so forth, places even the wealthiest and most powerful among us at risk. In this sense, at least, much of humanity faces the death-dealing prospects of its own making. If it is self-interest that motivates collective action, then the spectrum of people who may be attracted to a socially transformative political—or educational—agenda could be very much wider than we often assume.

The sometimes surprising and unexpected nature of political commitment in the contemporary world is surely demonstrated in what is now frequently referred to as "green" politics. We have seen how such politics, as well as the closely related antinuclear and peace movements, have received their major support from the professional middle classes.[5] These relatively well-educated groups have what the German political thinker and activist, Rudolf Bahro, has termed "surplus consciousness," which allows them to consider, and be attentive to, far more than the immediate needs and imperatives of their existence.[6]

Such groups can be concerned about the destruction of the Brazilian or African rain forests because their consciousness (and conscience) radically expands the time and space coordinates that locate what is experienced as threatening or endangering to them. Humanity itself—not just a nation, a class, a race, or some other relatively circumscribed social entity—is under the gun, facing not just exploitation but global annihilation. The focus of struggle becomes the future of the earth itself; what is at stake is the continuity of our species. In this sense, there is a common human struggle—one which posits a common and shared human identity.

Bahro's analysis has taken on particular significance in the light of the successful uprisings against Stalinism and bureaucratic socialism in Eastern and Central Europe. The role of professional and white-collar middle-class groups, artists and intellectuals and their concern with issues of ecological deterioration, and peace and cultural freedom was obviously an important, even crucial, element in the transformation of the states in these countries. These concerns obviously were conjoined with working-class concerns for a poor and deteriorating standard of living and oppressive working conditions. In Western capitalist societies, the enormous growth of the state is both the product of, and the catalyst for, a vast expansion and proliferation of social struggles.

Traditional Marxist notions of class struggle at the point of production have been supplemented (if not replaced) with a multiplicity of popular movements that demand from government an expansion of their social, economic, political, and cultural rights.[7] AIDS, questions of abortion rights for women, consumer protection, the needs of senior citizens, financial support for students, and health care for those who cannot afford to buy it in the marketplace are among many such areas of struggle. Each organizes and mobilizes a distinct and different social entity; each need constitutes a different identity of want or deprivation.

However, while the range of political struggles expands to embrace more and more of our complex lives, the potential social fragmentation, divisiveness, and competition grows apace. Politics is paradoxically more pervasive and more insinuated in our lives and more particularistic, limited in its immediate concerns and mean-spirited as each constituency defines its objectives in highly parochial ways.

## MORAL IMAGINATION AND EDUCATIONAL DISCOURSE

As we come to perceive our place among other human beings, we develop what Douglas Kellner has called our "political imaginary."[8] This, he says, is the cognitive and moral mapping that gives individuals a vision of the existing state of their world and what it should or could become and that provides the sense of identification as to who does or does not share our needs and concerns in the world. The imaginary offers specific ways of seeing and interpreting the events and issues that people must deal with in their everyday lives. On the basis of what we have said, it is clear that the imaginary can be shaped and constituted in many diverse ways, though it is not infinitely elastic. It must, in some way, speak to people's needs, anxieties, tensions, feelings of insecurity, and so forth (though quite obviously these can be understood and made sense of in many different ways). Thus, for example, to see the world as threatened, and humanity itself as victims, makes it possible to see ourselves in a fundamentally different way and in a new kind of connection to others (and perhaps to nature itself). With the emergence of alternative ways of imaging our situation, different concerns are articulated, unrecognized or unfulfilled desires come to the fore, new voices are heard, and new forms of outrage and indignation are expressed.

The question of what kinds of discourse govern how citizens think of and define education belongs to this larger question of what kind of political imaginary—what kind of cognitive and moral map—governs our understanding of the existing state of our world and of what it should or could become. The question of the public discourse about education is then nothing less than the question of what kind of world we live in, what we wish it to become, and who are the innovators who may favor or obstruct such possibilities. Of course, as we have argued throughout this book, the relation of the public discourse about education to the larger questions of culture and society have typically been treated with varying degrees of obfuscation, denial, and mystification. Its dominant tendencies have ranged from the assertion by some of the need for education's moral and political neutrality (obviously something that we think is impossible) to the overwhelming centrality of an economic rationale for education (the "human capital" view of the purpose of schools), to the Right's demand that education act as a brake on the moral and cultural disintegration of the nation.[9]

While we disagree with the prescriptive nature of the latter's claims—its coercive, parochial, and chauvinistic view of education—we believe nonetheless that it appropriately argues for a moral/cultural vision of the purpose of education. The Right's prescription places education on what is for us the correct and most desirable discursive terrain: Education must primarily be defined in terms of its relation to the community's moral vision. Education must be seen in the context of the crucial social and human condition of our time, and it must be rooted not only in a prophetic commitment to raising social awareness about the dangers and suffering of our world but also in the praxis of deep personal and social change. More specifically, it is our belief that the struggle for a genuinely new public discourse of education depends on our capacity to offer a cognitively convincing and, more especially, a morally compelling vision of our possibilities as a culture and a society. The struggle for transformative social change—whether about education or anything else—depends now on a politics that is ready and able to articulate the future in the framework of a compelling moral vision rooted in the material, emotional, and spiritual needs of our lives.

This is one of the lessons of the political success of the Right in the 1980s and 1990s. This argument has been eloquently and forcefully made by *Tikkun* editor Michael Lerner, who notes that the thirst for moral meaning is one of the deepest in American life. Moral vision, he says, far from being a "soft issue" is potentially the guts of American politics.[10] It powerfully fuels the "traditional values" crusade of the Right that continues to haunt and obstruct attempts at a more progressive politics. Failing to grasp this fact (by staying away from the moral needs of the people), the Left in America has been unable to mobilize a strong sense of commitment.

The power of the Right's discourse has been that its moral language addresses the psychological deprivation that has grown out of the failure of communal life in the United States. While liberals and the Left have championed the poor and those who face overt racial and sexual oppression, they have ignored the pain that many others, especially middle-class people, have experienced in the not strictly legal or economic arenas—in their families, in the absence of community and an ethical frame to life.

Implicit in conservatives' "profamily" and "traditional values" politics, argues Lerner, is a compassion that counteracts the self-blaming that dominates personal life today. Whether it be personal happiness, economic well-being, or social success and recognition, everything is supposedly in the hands of the individual. The pop-psychology formulation of "Take responsibility for your own life" and "You can make it if you really try," he says, reinforces in new ways the cornerstone of American ideology, namely, the belief in meritocracy. If you want happiness, you will get it; if you don't have it, you have only yourself to blame.

Lerner argues that conservative politics depends not on the specifics of its program but on the way in which it acknowledges the crisis in personal lives while pointing the finger at a set of social causes (feminism, gays, "liberal permissiveness") that are not the fault of individual Americans. Lerner continues:

> While strongly rejecting the conservatives scape-goating, we can also see that by encouraging people to find a social cause for family crisis they decrease self-blame and increase self-compassion.
>
> This analysis helps us to understand the popularity of Reagan in the first six years of his presidency. Reagan's picture of an America in which people could find true community and pride in their lives offered a seductive alternative to self-blaming. We need not adopt or accept a similar patriotic chauvinism, but we do need to be able to understand the seductiveness of such an appeal.[11]

It is easy to see similar factors at work in the Right's educational agenda—the homogeneity and uniformity of a core curriculum and a common standard of cultural literacy, the question of prayer in school or the demand for an end to busing, a return to neighborhood schools and the explicit inculcation of "traditional" moral values in schools. The conservatives' moral language is a call for a communal life that would buffer the insecurities and uncertainties of daily life.

Paradoxically, of course, this desire for security is undermined by the very economic system that the Right trumpets unquestioningly. While, as Lerner notes, decent human relationships depend on trust, caring, and the ability to give to others, today the "successful" American spends much of his or her day manipulating and controlling others. The kind of people who will be rewarded with promotions, clients, and customers must learn to continually manipulate and sell themselves. They must develop personalities in which their own feelings and emotions become distant and alienated, which precludes authentic and deep relationships with other human beings, whether in families or in friendships. The conservative philosophy of selfishness and individualism expressed in a worship of the capitalist marketplace and its disdain for the poor contradicts relationships that are open, loving, and caring—the cement of a compassionate and supportive communal life.[12]

Notwithstanding the distortions of conservative discourse and the phony remedies, there are important lessons here for those of us committed to the possibilities of a more just and equitable society. Not the least of these lessons is the power and importance of rooting our concerns in a vision that speaks to our moral and spiritual needs as a community. Without this vision, progressive politics becomes what it so often is, namely, a laundry list of worthy but disparate issues (health care, equal pay, day care, environmental protection, tax reform, etc.)—a set of unquestionably important concerns but without the moral and spiritual vision that moves people and in which people find themselves affirmed.

The Left's current preoccupation with "difference" reduces politics to the clamor of a warring tribalism. Instead of a communal moral and spiritual vision, the Left offers an image of a world balkanized into an endless proliferation of those who can claim some history of oppression and exclusion. Such oppression becomes a jealously guarded experience about which no one outside of it dare speak (without the accusation of acting imperiously and arrogantly).

Again, our goal here is not to disregard difference or to deny the experience, language, and distinctiveness, of people's lives. The world, as we know too well, has been hideously deformed by the way in which whole groups of human beings have been silenced and made invisible through the power of other people's discourse. While the validation of these disregarded voices is necessary, it is not a sufficient condition for radical social change. It too easily becomes a politics that divides people, excludes, and emphasizes our separation. It becomes a holier-than-thou sectarianism, very far from the image of a world in which we can all see ourselves valued and loved.

While we emphasize irreducible differences and distinctiveness, the Right and the religious fundamentalist will bludgeon us into a "recognition" of our common heritage, tradition, and values. Perhaps the image of the "quilt" with its validation of the distinct patches whose singularity is enhanced by their contiguity with others and the richness of the whole is the metaphor for a liberating communal life that we like the best and think appropriate for our time. Despite the multiplicity of identities in modern society and the complexity of demand, claims, needs, and wants, we should not imagine that this lessens the power or significance of a morally and spiritually rooted communal vision as the leitmotif for a renewal of a politics of progressive social change.

## THE POLITICS OF EDUCATIONAL TRANSFORMATION

Of course, the struggle for a different definition of the purpose and goals of education in many ways turns on the matter of social agency: Who will support and respond to an alternative language or vision of educational concerns?[13] Yet the world we have entered—the postmodern world as it is sometimes called—makes it harder than before to identify some kind of "natural" progressive constituency.[14] For example, who is to identify with the victims of oppression and who with the perpetrators? Who will respond with enthusiasm for an alternative educational discourse agenda that concerns itself, say, with issues of social justice, social responsibility, and democratic empowerment? The shifting, more fluid nature of identity in today's culture and the multiple forms of suffering, indignity, and deprivation felt by human beings in the world makes the ground on which we struggle to banish or at least mitigate oppression and pain a slippery one, without a secure or stable point in which we may situate ourselves and understand who we are in relation to those around us.

The human catastrophes of drug addiction or emotional illness, for example, create new forms of solidarity among people separated in other ways by social class, race, or other forms of identification. Within this context in which human beings find themselves united in shared desperation and need, different kinds of politics can emerge that pose questions about society, its compassion, and its supportiveness. Addiction and emotional illness reflect deep veins of suffering and need that run through the society; these forms of indignity and exclusion criss-cross the culture. Like the crisis of the environment, this represents a context of human experience that lends itself to new forms of shared concerns and expectations and, thus, to new languages and images that may reorient the larger vision for our society and our expectations and hopes for education.

While we wish to emphasize the fluid and relatively open way in which political struggles—including those around education—might be constituted, it would be foolish to suggest (as some have) that the lines that distinguish oppressor and oppressed have lost all meaning or relevance and that we are all, for example, equally culpable for the ills and injustices in the world. The exploitation of labor by capital continues to be readily discernible. Corporate greed and disregard for the needs of the working and middle class is all too visible. Military and political elites in this country support and supply ma-

terial to Third World authoritarian governments that continue to suppress
those who call for more equitable and democratic social and economic
systems. At home, women suffer the structural violence of poverty and
economic injustice, as well as personal violence at the hands of men, for
whom there are real social, cultural, and economic advantages in the existing
gender arrangements. While in some ways we may all be responsible for the
current degradation of nature, this must not be confused with the guilt of
those powerful political and economic interests who plunder the earth's
limited resources.

Yet know that none of us operate in sealed and unidimensional social
spaces. We slide quickly from roles in which we exploit and dehumanize
others to those in which we ourselves are the object of others' instrumental
attitudes and exploitative treatment. In the complexity of the contemporary
world, we occupy, at once, positions where others are targets of our prejudice,
venality or manipulation, and places where we are objects of manipulation
by others. In the loose and shifting sands of our world, few of us are unscarred
by the indifference, callousness, and indignity endemic to our private and
public worlds. For some, this psychic and spiritual wounding is more visible,
more unrelenting, and sometimes more total. For people of color, women,
gays and lesbians, the handicapped, the aged, the mentally ill, the poor, and
all of those who come to be, in our society, designated as "other," the pain
of exclusion and abuse is obviously palpable. Even domination, however,
exacts its price in suffering. Robert Bly and others have, for example, begun
to make the case for a male liberation from the drivenness and emotional
stuntedness of masculine middle-class life, the consequences of which is male
rage that more and more seems to explode on our streets and in our homes.[15]

Again, we do not wish to suggest that all of the suffering is on a par. The
deprivation of homelessness, poverty, racism, or sexual abuse is certainly
more brutal and more terrible than other forms of human suffering. The
issue here is not whether we may find equivalence in the forms of pain and
oppression. For some, oppression and victimization are unrelenting, wherein
survival itself is a matter of unrelieved struggle. Rather, we wish to recognize
that there is no "privileged" bearer of oppression or suffering in our society.
There is not a simple duality that distinguishes people as *either* those who
dominate, exploit, or inflict pain on others *or* those who are the recipients
of the same. Political topographies that categorize the world in this way end
up with rigid, predetermined images of "us" and "them" or "us" versus
"them." They lead us to the reassuring simplicities of "enemy thinking."
Demographically these maps have carved up the population so that it is clear
from the outset who is politically "progressive" and who is not. The political
images and understandings that people adopt are, from this point of view,
merely waiting in the wings for the curtain to rise before making their
appearance according to an already rehearsed dramatization.

Yet such interpretations, in their rigidity and dogmatism, start by ignoring the complexity of human experience and identity and the increasingly problematic nature of our political affiliations and the preferences that confront us. As Sharon Welch courageously acknowledges, we may assume concurrently the roles of both oppressor and oppressed. She writes as both a woman in a patriarchal culture and as a professor at an elite university that is a cornerstone of the system of class privilege in the United States. Such contradictions are not uncommon. We may move routinely between positions that seem privileged and offer us authority and status to situations in which we are degraded, disempowered, and victimized. Such is the routine character, for example, of many women's lives.[16]

To understand all this is to appreciate the importance of Michel Foucault's critique of the Marxian concept of power and categorization.[17] There is no *single* axis around which all relations of power and domination, struggle and resistance are plotted. There are, instead, a multiplicity of fields in which human beings struggle for freedom, justice, dignity, and a fuller realization of their lives. These fields overlap and cut across one another, thus producing a complex social map of human aspirations and struggles. Such struggles have their own dynamic, character, and set of possibilities. Families, schools, religious communities, neighborhoods, workplaces, cultural institutions, state institutions, and so forth, sustain and focus deep, even explosive, tensions. While such tensions are fueled by the unrealized aspirations and disappointed hopes generated from within the culture, these tensions cannot easily be assimilated within one another, reduced to one overarching problem that, if resolved, would herald a utopian transformation of the world—solving at one stroke all our problems and concerns.

Relinquishing such an apocalyptic tale of revolutionary change may be disappointing to those who hunger for the simple, the universal, and the either/or explanation of events. However, it does not diminish our sense of radical possibility and the hope of human transformation and social change. Quite the opposite! Released as we are from the old Left fixation on finding the historically "privileged" agent of social change or revolution, or the one real focus for radical struggle, we can now open our eyes and see a world replete with human aspirations for fulfillment, plenitude, dignity, justice, compassion, love, and spiritual significance and replete with the struggles to realize such possibilities in modern society.

Of course, our different situations inflect our hopes and struggles in different ways. The possibilities for change are shaped and delimited by their multiple discourses. Even within the life of one person, relative satisfaction at work, might give way to fury and agitation at the inability to be safe from harassment on the streets; economic well-being might be accompanied by the fear of family disintegration or the despair of a spiritual emptiness, and patriotic sentiments might coexist with a religious faith that impels one to

work for the sanctuary of those who are the victims of U.S. collusion with
fascist governments in Central or South America.

The politics that emerge from the fluidity and complexities of identity in
contemporary America do not, it must be emphasized, negate those historically important social struggles. We, in no sense, wish to underestimate, for
example, the long and difficult struggles by labor in this country to ameliorate
exploitative economic relations or to advance the welfare and occupational
conditions of working people. Nor do we wish to detract from the crucial value
of movements like those for racial justice, for peace, or for sexual equality. Our
goal is, however, to offer an educational language—and later, an agenda—that
can be as inclusive in its appearance as possible, able to recognize the fullest
possible range of human struggles and concerns at this juncture in time.

## EDUCATIONAL DISCOURSE AND THE CRISIS
## OF MEANING

We believe that life in the United States at this time has become so painful,
alienating, ethically compromised, and spiritually impoverished, that education must speak first and foremost to this human and social crisis. The crisis
is pervasive and multidimensional in its effects: sometimes material, sometimes
psychological and emotional, and sometimes spiritual (and often all of the
above). The crisis reaches into the very corners and crevices of our society,
producing the pauperization of some and the miseration of many.[18] Its
consequences are in the form of shame, deprivation, indignity, and psychic
distress.

The desperate need for a transformative politics and an educational vision
and language commensurate with this leads us to attempt to construct a
discourse and an agenda that can speak to the widest range of people who
might be responsive to the need for deep social change and who might
recognize that our present cultural, moral and economic path as a nation
(and as a planet) is destructive and dehumanizing. This is not a time to speak
to the converted (as, sadly, so much of critical educational scholarship tends
to do) or to stay within predictable and expected social constituencies, or to
seek what is ideologically "correct" but politically ineffective.[19] Our struggles
here are not ours alone. They belong to all those who are sincerely attempting
to renew a socially transformative vision and language.

Such a renewal requires questioning seriously the tried and traditional
language of Left and liberal politics and the subjects of such politics.[20] We
are convinced, for example, that an "economic" discourse alone—that is,
the question of how wealth is to be divided between classes—is necessary
but insufficient to mobilize the kind of support that is needed. Nor is it
enough to attach the politics of transformation solely to the language of

political, civil, or social rights or to the expansion of a democratic culture. As important as this is, such an emphasis does not speak clearly enough to the emotional distress and spiritual despair of a world that does not offer the support, solidarity, and compassion of a loving community.[21] As important as is the language of economic justice, it implies, in and of itself, little about how we should break out of the ecodestructive conditions of industrial societies that currently bind both working class and the captains of industry to a global path that is suicidal.[22]

Nor can we find convincing anymore the equation of a radical vision of a world that is thoroughly rational and, therefore, fully engineered. For many of us, especially the young, what seems especially attractive is rather a world in which the spontaneous, the unpredictable, and the ecstatic flourish and in which individualism and freedom find deep and vibrant expression. What has been called the post-Fordist phase of capitalism, with its computerized capacity for unprecedented novelty, diversity, and creative fluidity, has made the old heroic production-oriented images of socialism seem repressive and archaic. In such conditions, the demand for diversity and pleasure in everyday life cannot be derided as purely romantic escape or capitalist excess.[23] Nor is there much attention to the Marxian promise of a society wherein everything is fully transparent and accessible to reasoned intellect. Such a vision seems positively perverse in its denial of the mysterious, the unfathomable, and the wondrous. While, for example, we might insist on women's reproductive rights, we need also to acknowledge the difficulties and dilemmas that do indeed surround the question of how and when the precious phenomenon of human life comes into being. As our life-world is corroded and subjugated by the technocratic order, with its depersonalization and abstract rationalities, men and women understandingly turn to the religious, the spiritual, and the mystical as means of asserting the ineffable qualities of human life and experience.[24]

The Left's long marriage to modernism, with its narratives that are so determinedly secular, rationalistic, and instrumental, has wrought a vision at odds with many of the most powerful and moving discourses of human freedom and resistance in the world today.[25] But to accept and include such discourses in a language of transformation means to shed any remaining illusions about our capacity to describe the world as it really is, rather than in metaphors that offer resonant and evocative images concerning human existence and possibilities. Perhaps the difficulty of doing this is reflected in the reluctance of critical intellectuals in the United States to fully embrace the languages that have emerged from Liberation, Feminist, and Creation theologies—surely some of the most moving and powerful revolutionary discourses in existence today.[26] To include the spiritual and the religious in our language of social or educational change is to acknowledge that political struggle is not so much about "truth" but about how we and others can image or re-image the world. It is about the way we can envision human possibility, identity, and a meaningful existence.

Just at the moment when the Left has come to recognize so clearly the mass psychic impoverishment that both capitalism and bureaucratic socialism have wrought, it has been captured by a sensibility that makes it both increasingly cynical and increasingly reluctant to articulate the value of universal human rights, liberation, community, and social justice.[27] Such notions are dismissed by critics as but part of the metaphysics of modernity and so-called enlightenment. What is offered instead is nothing but the endless transgression of cultural limits and the proliferation of differences among people. Yet, for many people, this "postmodern bazaar" is repulsive and terrifying. It is part of the problem, not the solution. It offers little that validates tradition, it provides little that connects us across time and space, and it says little about what might transcend the particular, the local, and the contingent and about what might speak to the whole human condition.[28]

## EDUCATIONAL DISCOURSE AND THE POLITICS OF INCLUSIVENESS

Therefore, we want to offer the elements of a public discourse for education that privileges no one group of people and that tries to speak to and include the experiences, needs, and hopes of a broad spectrum of individuals. Together, these constitute what Stuart Hall referred to as a "popular bloc," a political movement composed of a diverse set of social groups who might favor deep social and educational change.[29] The language that we offer here is broad, inclusive, and rooted in aspects of our national culture. It seems to make possible the articulation of the multiple concerns of human beings who in obviously different ways might be moved by a vision of education whose overriding task is what has been called "tikkun olam"—the healing and repair of our society and world. In this sense, we seek here to offer a discourse for education centered in a moral language that can embrace and express the variety and complexity of wounds, indignities, and exclusions that are the experiences of our fellow citizens.

To construct this bloc means finding ways in which dissimilar people with distinct, sometimes divergent, interests can come together and find common ground. It means to seek a language—and an agenda—for education that reflects the particular struggles and aspirations of social groups and that can reconcile their differences without denying or subordinating any of them. A transformative educational discourse requires a language and an agenda for educational reform that insists on educating the young for a socially just, socially responsible, democratic, and compassionate community. Proposing that the work of education be conceived of in these terms means, on the one hand, to envisage an education that works for the transformation of our culture in ways that emphasize the overarching moral imperative of a compassionate, solidaristic, and participatory society. Yet, at the same time, this vision must not turn into some monolithic moral straitjacket that dictates educational concerns in narrowly defined ways.

The struggle for a fuller, deeper, and more humane community may, in some set of circumstances, mean that education be about ensuring literacy; elsewhere, the possibility of jobs; and in some other places, political participation and empowerment. Given the complex nature of identity and the diversity of ways in which people may conceive of a humane transformation of our world, our educational language and agenda must not be confused with the dead hand of some programmatically "correct" instructional curriculum or form of pedagogy. Our overriding concern is quite distinct from questions of exactly what and how we teach in the classroom (even when this is conceived in the radical forms of critical or feminist pedagogy). Although this is not irrelevant to reshaping education, it should not be confused with our present task, which is to formulate and offer a broad and inclusive discursive framework through which a diversity of people can see the concerns and hopes that they have for themselves and for their children given expression and related to the purposes of education in this country.

The struggle here is not about pedagogy as much as it is about education's place in what we earlier referred to as the political imaginary. It is about how to reconceive the purpose and goals of education so that it is explicitly linked to the transformation of the social and cultural realities that we live. Notwithstanding the obvious importance of classroom methodologies, modes of teaching, and so forth, we do not want to be caught in the trap of technique, of an obsessive focus on matters of practice, or of questions about how to do things in the classrooms. To avoid this, it is worth running the risk of urging a different kind of conversation—one that might be dismissed as removed from real school concerns—but that insists on referencing the larger human, cultural, moral, and spiritual vision within which we wish to educate our children. It does not aim to displace matters or questions of practice, but only to act as the referent point (or points) for how we are to conceive of the value and purpose of what education ought to be in this society at this time.

Educational work is made more meaningful and vital by its situatedness in this vision. The political effectiveness of this vision (i.e., the extent of its appeal and support) depends on how well it is capable of drawing in and articulating the diverse and divergent needs and concerns of ordinary people. It depends on how well an education oriented to this vision can be seen as speaking to people's lives and, more important, to the lives of their children. The danger of ignoring this is apparent in the emphasis today in radical educational circles on critical or feminist pedagogies, or on defining educational change as a revitalization of what it means to be a citizen and pursuing what has been called a critical democracy. The issue is not that these are not valuable and valid aspects of what we on the Left have to offer education in the present situation. It is that they are too limited in emphasis, too circumscribed in whom they address, too one-sided in their definition of what constitutes educational renewal.

The result is—as is quite clear from the limited enthusiasm or acceptance of the whole critical pedagogy project—an agenda for education that is simply not sufficiently resonant with the concerns of many people.[30] That is glaring in its disregard for a whole range of human concerns, like the role of the traditional, the spiritual, community and obligation, responsibility and discipline. Making the expansion of democratic life the leitmotif of radical change in contemporary society[31] strikes us as a necessary but insufficient way to image our future social reality. Radically extended popular empowerment in economic, cultural, and political life is certainly a crucially important goal of a society more and more subject to a quality of existence emptied of any meaningful democratic experiences. Reform or changes in education directed toward a deepening of the meaning of democratic rights and responsibilities in the public sphere is certainly a crucial concern for progressives.

However, the discourse of an education that can speak to a healing and a repair of our world must say more than this if it is to be heeded. It must touch people's spiritual and emotional lives through what have been called the feminine moral images—of wholeness, compassion, care, and responsibility. This the discourse of social rights and democratic empowerment cannot do: These concerns are necessary but insufficiently evocative for a transformational politics in the closing decade of this century. The politics of radical change in these years will belong to those who can successfully articulate the postmodern—or antimodern—impulses that are increasingly being unleashed in the world.[32] In the case of education, the Right and the religious fundamentalist have, for the most part, been more adept at this task. They have been (for obvious reasons) both more successful and the more ready to use this kind of language. They have been able to step into what we know from our work with teachers and community groups as the discursive emptiness of the present moment—where educational talk is conducted without reference to some prophetic vision of society or human life, a discourse bereft of the mobilizing power of a moral focus that links the work of education to the needs, hopes, and possibilities of the larger culture. Such a focus would link our educational concerns, policies, practices, and goals to the question of the quality and character of our personal and communal lives. It would insist that educational questions are always, at the same time, questions about what it means to be human and about how we as humans ought to live together.

EDUCATION AND THE HUMAN STRUGGLE:
A VISION QUEST

In the following pages, we respond to the necessity as educators to affirm the basic beliefs and commitments that ground our work as professionals and citizens. We do so in the recognition that such a process is a necessity that also yields limitations, possibilities, and problematics. We have endeavored to provide a framework that attempts to be inclusive; and though knowing that it cannot possibly accommodate all positions and orientations, we will offer a discourse that endeavors to be rational and rigorous but that nonetheless includes a language of a more elusive and evocative nature. Our orientation is rooted in both history and myth, in both the nightmare of contemporary realities and the dreams of the ages, and in both the promise and violation of our social and cultural covenants. We offer these views in the light of our preceding analysis, which proposed an educational vision in the postmodern world that recognizes the perils and problematics of both righteousness and moral evasion, of both dogmatism and inanity, and of both certainty and relativism. We are quite clear that educational discourse *must* reflect significant moral and political concerns, although we welcome further debate and dialogue on the particulars of our moral and political orientation. It is imperative that educators strive to engage in a continuous process of reflection and practice that helps to illumine our historical aspirations and our continuing response to them.

In this spirit, we associate ourselves with some of our culture's most treasured traditions. We affirm and celebrate with others the recognition of the mystery and the belief in the sanctity of life and its corollary, the significance of all life and the worth of all individuals. We celebrate the incredible energy and imagination that humans have across time and space devoted to developing processes and institutions that impel us to make these beliefs palpable and vital. Over the centuries, human genius has provided us with extraordinary ideas, including the very basic notions that life is to have meaning and that we as a people have the capacity to conceive and create a better life. We are heir to a wealth of ideas on what constitutes a better life, on how we can better understand the complexities involved in creating a better world, and on how we can attain these goals. These processes have produced brilliant and dazzling ideas and have led to extraordinarily ambitious human endeavors. We have available to us powerful religious texts (the Bible, the Koran, numerous liturgies and theologies) and enormously influential political documents (the Rights of Man, the Declaration of Independence, the Bill of Rights). We also have been enriched by magnificent philosophers, theologians, and teachers like Moses, Jesus, and Socrates, who have provided us with the intellectual and spiritual energy to conceptualize and actualize these visions.

We also sadly must confront the failures of such efforts in the face of other, darker human impulses—those forces that impel oppression, greed, cruelty, hatred, and callousness. These failures have produced incredible suffering, pain, anguish, and misery over the centuries in the form of any number of human inventions—war, poverty, racism, sexism, hierarchy, classism, privilege, and slavery.

We also acknowledge the powerful contribution that great minds have made in providing us with ways of understanding, conceptualizing, and responding to the immense chasm between our vision and our realities. Thinkers like Freud, Marx, Dewey, Locke, and Rousseau have provided us with modes of recognizing and naming that which divides us within and among ourselves.

We are witness, therefore, to amazing stories of our existence as a people. These stories of conflict and struggle, in which great nations and notions have risen, reveal an incredible range of human responses—sacrifice as well as greed; pacifism *and* violence; cynicism *and* transcendence; vulgarity, crudeness, and primitiveness, along with beauty, grace, and sophistication. Our history is about the Sermon on the Mount and Auschwitz, is rife with slavery and liberation, is about war and peace, and is witness to penicillin and the hydrogen bomb. We have put people on the moon and made hell on earth, and our heritage includes both the Golden Rule and the principle of the survival of the fittest.

As educators, we locate ourselves, therefore, as both heirs to and participants in this continually disheartening, turbulent, and exhilarating struggle to create a world of peace, justice, love, and joy. We recognize that as participants what we and our colleagues do will, for better or worse, have an effect not only on our lives, but on those that come after us. We also reaffirm our faith in the belief that careful, thoughtful, and reasonable reflection and inquiry can significantly help to clarify the struggle, as well as help provide direction for the amelioration of, if not the solution to, our problems.

As educators, we must stand fast in our faith that understanding and insight are vital to the struggle for liberation and that the development of intellectual capacities for this purpose remains a central concern. However, our view of education is that its processes must extend beyond the intellectual realm since it is clear that humans do not learn to live and love by intellect alone. We as a people respond also to the rhythms of the body, the light of the soul, and the voices of the spirit. We are also mindful of human psychology and, hence, of the tyranny and distortion that can emerge from our propensity to evade, deny, and rationalize in the service of self or group. Therefore, our commitment to education for social justice and personal fulfillment must at all times be informed by the imperative of remaining critical, skeptical, and humble.

## EDUCATION AND THE HISTORICAL MOMENT

We have in other places sketched out a broad framework for an educational orientation specific to the particular struggles of our time.[33] It is a framework that posits our historical moment as incredibly perilous, dangerous, and unconscionable. Our view is that educational planning and theorizing must have, as its most crucial point of departure, the harsh realities and extraordinary possibilities of our present existence. The dominant text for educators must clearly and explicitly reflect recognition of the enormous dangers and opportunities that define our historical moment. The planet is at risk because the environment has been plundered. The world is at risk because intense national rivalries have produced weapons with immensely destructive capacities. Our civilization is at risk because we have produced and tolerated untold human misery, poverty, and degradation. We, as a people, are at risk as a consequence of a consciousness of alienation and meaninglessness that seeks solace in drugs, hedonism, violence, and materialism.

We recognize, with others, the volatility, ambiguity, and danger of addressing such questions. What is less recognized and affirmed is the enormous risk involved in not addressing them. Fundamentally, human history is about trying to define and act on what is good and, simultaneously, trying to examine and overcome the resistance to that impulse. At this moment in time, we note with pain and bewilderment that we live in a world of unnecessary human suffering that can only be described as barbaric, if not demonic. So much so, that all people—including, of course, educators—must ground their work in the responsibility to participate in healing the pain of this suffering by joining in the effort to liberate us from oppression and the impulse to oppress, thereby engaging in the tasks of creating a more just and peaceful world.

Our educational and social orientation is broadly based on powerful themes of Western culture, with particular reference to the tradition of Socratic critical reflection; prophetic moral outrage and poetic inspiration; and the religious, moral, and political traditions that speak to the centrality of justice, love, community, peace, and joy. Those traditions recognize that humans are flawed and fully capable of inflicting pain and misery but also have the capacity to transcend a consciousness of savagery. There is also a recognition that this transcendence is not a matter of choice or destiny but of will, requiring the concerted efforts of human agency.

Vital to this orientation is the recognition that democratic processes represent the most resonant political model of working toward these goals. We, therefore, join with others in demanding that educators work diligently with others to renew and revitalize our democratic traditions and sensibilities. Ironically and tragically, our present educational system, for the most part, erodes democratic traditions in ways that are both highly visible and marked.

Clearly, concerns for the development of democratic processes is no longer central in even the rhetoric of dominant educational ideology.

Competition (masked as excellence) and authoritarianism (masked as effective schools) have replaced democracy as the chief rallying calls of educational practice. At a deeper level, the corrosive force of grades, tests, and tracking act even more fiendishly to weaken the basic moral commitment to human dignity. We find ourselves anguished and captured by a consciousness in which our worth and dignity are not inherent and self-evident, but instead are to be "earned." Schools are part of an institutional arrangement in which dignity is awarded, parceled out, and distributed. Our moral traditions urge us to exercise the Golden Rule and to love our neighbor, but the Iron Rule of schools is to love, if not envy, only those neighbors who achieve.

The harshness and severity of social competition that is so vividly acted out in educational institutions is root and symptom of the increasingly dangerous tendency to promote what Dorothee Soelle calls "hyper-individuality." Robert Bellah and his colleagues have poignantly and eloquently documented how community is perhaps our most significant "endangered species." However, ironically enough, community is threatened not only by concern for self but also by the polarization engendered by the proliferation of narrowly focused communities.

The poison that has produced the epidemic of distrust and division is the competition that is embedded in our structural inequality. Our system of social justice continues to produce a harsh economic class system in which the benefits of life are immorally distributed. This system demands intense competition for the available rewards under the guise of a free system open to anyone willing to work hard. Schools add fuel to class division as well as to the internecine warfare within classes by legitimizing this gross and debasing warfare as meritocracy, presumably an equitable way to achieve the American Dream.

What our society and schools irresponsibly and unconscionably fail to make clear is that the American Dream involves success at the expense of others. In this sense, the American Dream becomes the moral nightmare of those forced to pursue individual rather than communal fulfillment by rejecting the vision of an America with liberty and justice for all. Competition American style, provides a winner-loser consciousness in which individuals and groups are pitted against each other in a game of very high stakes.

We have also come to see that a major element of oppression is one in which certain people are seen as objects to be manipulated and directed in the interest of those who are subjects. This same subject-object relationship, in which people are seen as resources to be utilized, has also had disastrous effects upon our environment, resulting in the very real possibility of global extinction. Moreover, this consciousness reflects not only greed, rapaciousness, and stupidity, but also poignantly demonstrates the tragedy and horror of a people unable to develop a sense of their connection to each other, to the planet, or to the universe. The pollution and plunder of the planet indicates little or no sense of how we are connected to the awesomeness and mystery of our origins and destiny. To educate must involve consideration of who we are in relation, not only to each other, but to the environment, the globe, and the universe.

The history of human existence reveals a persistence, therefore, of paradox and dialectic—of progress and retrogression, of hope and despair, of a series of "the best of times and the worst of times." This is not to be taken as a reason for complacency and serenity, but rather as a reminder of our responsibilities as citizens and educators to be alert to the continuous possibilities of danger and liberation. Our history is, as we have said, replete not only with horror and misery but also with the consciousness that such experiences are not inevitable: Indeed, human genius has enabled us to resist and overcome such experiences. The American experience includes slavery and emancipation, the Ku Klux Klan and the civil rights movement. Its history encompasses women's exclusion and the women's movement, robber barons and muckrakers, jingoism and pacifism, labor bashing and the labor movement. Our icons include Simon Legree and Sojournor Truth, Lincoln and Booth, Ivan Boesky and Ralph Nader, David Duke and Martin Luther King, Jr., the Grand Inquisitor and Dorothy Day.

We see the task of educators as that of nourishing a consciousness that would facilitate a significantly more just, peaceful, and harmonious world. Basic to such a consciousness would be an awareness of both our individuality and our dependence on each other, our culture, society, planet, and universe. As people who grapple with the clear and present demands of life (work, family, relationships, shelter, food, health), such dependence is required, necessary, sensible, and pragmatic. As people who wrestle with meaning and fulfillment, interdependence is integral and inevitable. It is, however, not enough to recognize our oneness with nature and the reality of our human solidarity. We also must affirm a moral commitment to that connection. It is one thing to say that we are in fact connected to each other and quite another to figure out how to respond to that reality.

Surprisingly enough, there is a very high degree of agreement on what should ground this response. Our traditions and instincts urge us to seek harmony, peace, and justice and to conduct this task with a sense of care, love, and compassion. Language and images surely differ, as do interpretations and understandings of these notions, but we cannot but be sustained by the persistence of these commitments. Even if we suspect that this rhetoric can and has been used cynically and manipulatively, we can take solace from the fact that it is relied on so heavily, for as La Rochfoucault put it, "Hypocrisy is the tribute that vice pays to virtue."

A consciousness of caring, compassion, and justice is related to notions of the beauty and sacredness of life itself—and with that comes the centrality of the idea of dignity for all. The mystery, awareness, and drama of life are acted out in and within all life-forms. Every life becomes precious and invites us to become ever more aware of that which endows us with the energy to seek meaning. Within such a view, humans have pursued the possibilities of fulfilling the promises of human destiny by creating institutions designed to support the struggle for human dignity and meaning. Fundamental to such institutions is the principle of democracy, the spirit of faith in the human capacity to be free. Democratic procedures are more than benign techniques for facilitating decision making. They are also concrete manifestations of the affirmation that life is sacred, and therefore our greatest responsibility is to pursue liberty and justice for all.

## AN EDUCATIONAL CREDO FOR A TIME
## OF CRISIS AND URGENCY

Educators are primarily moral, political, and cultural agents charged with the responsibility of grounding their specialized insights in a cultural political, and moral vision. An educator without some kind of moral and cultural grounding is either tragically alienated, cynically deceptive, or naively shallow. John Dewey reminds us that education is about learning to create a world and that our most vital and demanding task as educators is to be mindful of the kind of world that we want to create. Absolutely essential, therefore, in the ethics of education are the twin pillars of freedom, namely, responsibility and choice. As educators, we are required to respond to the challenges of life and to choose among the many moral, political, and cultural possibilities open to us.

*We Choose, Celebrate, and Affirm These Propositions:*

1. *We recognize the wonder, mystery, and awe that surrounds our life and that beckons us to contemplate, examine, and make meaning of it and of our part in it.* As educators, we must encourage and help students to separate mystery and awe from ignorance and superstition, but we must be careful to witness and be informed by what is beyond our present human capacity to comprehend. As educators, our responsibility is to present with respect varying interpretations of life's meaning. But our most compelling responsibility is to renew and reenergize the commitment to pursue lives of individual and communal meaning.

2. *We renew our faith in the capacity to celebrate diversity and difference while working to create a world of harmony, peace, and justice.* As educators, we must avoid the perils of pride and arrogance that emerge from a posture of cultural superiority. We recognize that meaning and fulfillment derive, in part, from cultural identity, and we must therefore

strive to revere and respect, not patronize and romanticize, the ethos of particular cultural, racial, and ethnic groups. This consciousness requires basic trust in the recognition that harmony is not synonymous with homogeneity, that peace is not to be equated with control, and that justice is not to be blurred with freedom.

As educators, we must move from a consciousness of mastery, domination, submission, and docility in which some persons are subjects and others are objects. As educators, we must strive to see our students not as black boxes, not as clay to be molded or minds to be trained, but as sentient beings deserving of dignity, love, and fulfillment. As educators, we must not require people to earn their dignity, but we must strive to celebrate the sanctity, miracle, and preciousness of life. This consciousness does not bring us to punishment, tracking, grading, and honors programs, but to an education that reveres life as sacred and inviolate. Such a consciousness does not urge us to get ahead, but to stand with; does not idealize competition, but venerates dignity; does not legitimate privilege and advantage, but rather seeks to heal the deadly quarrels that divide the human family.

3. *We renew our faith in the human impulse to seek to create a world of justice, compassion, love, and joy, and in the human capacity to create such a world.* As educators, our responsibility is to nurture these impulses that have permeated human history not only by increasing awareness and understanding of them but by confronting the equally human impulses to oppress, dominate, and objectify. As educators, we can be guided and comforted by the immensity of human intellectual, creative, and intuitive potential to re-create our world; and at the same time, we should be sobered by the human capacity to be destructive, cruel, and callous. We speak to an education that is grounded in our strongest and deepest moral traditions, which urge us to love our neighbor, to seek justice, and to pledge ourselves to a nation committed to liberty and justice for all and a government of the people, by the people, and for the people. We speak to an education based on traditions that urge us to beat swords into ploughshares, not to develop more deadly swords; a vision in which lions lie down with lambs, not one in which we train lambs to be lions; and a universal dream of milk and honey for all, not the American Dream of champagne and caviar for a few.

4. *We reaffirm our commitment to the joys of community, the profundity of compassion, and to the power of interdependence.* As educators, we must become aware of the spiritual disease of alienation, loneliness, fragmentation, and isolation and must act to reduce the perilous effects of an education directed toward success, achievement, and personalism. As educators, we have the responsibility of nurturing the impulse for meaningful and cooperative relationships and for exposing the myths

and dangers of individual achievement. Education must not act to convert the uncivilized, but neither should it serve to create a myriad of individual universes. Compassion serves neither to distance nor to blur or annihilate differences, but rather seeks to share the struggles, pain, and joys that are common to us all. If we are to compete, we as educators need to confront the significance of the race not only for the winners but also for the losers. If we are to be committed to individual excellence, then we must know if it is achieved at the expense of others. More important, we as educators must participate in the process of creating a society in which people are more united than divided, where differences are not translated into hierarchy, and where pain and anguish are occasions for neither pity nor exploitation but for compassion and solidarity.

5. *We affirm the central importance of nourishing a consciousness of moral outrage and social responsibility.* As educators, we must go far beyond informing, describing, and analyzing and must free ourselves from the destructive force of moral numbness. We must help our students to become aware of our failures to meet our moral and cultural imperatives and to help them inform their intellectual understanding with moral judgments. An education that engenders a posture of promiscuous tolerance, scholarly detachment, or cynical weariness toward unnecessary human suffering is an abomination! We must avoid the temptation to teach only what makes one feel good or to teach that social problems are only "interesting." Education is not about finding out things, but about finding ourselves. It is not enough to say further research is needed when what is needed is not more information but more justice. To know without a sense of outrage, compassion, or concern deadens our souls and significantly eases the struggle of demonic forces to capture our consciousness. We need an education that produces moral indignation and energy rather than one that excuses, mitigates, and temporizes human misery. Heschel reminds us that although only a few are guilty, all are responsible. Our task as educators is therefore to teach students to identify the guilty, to have compassion for the victims, and to exercise their responsibility to reduce, if not eliminate, injustices.

## POSSIBILITIES AND PROBLEMATICS OF THE DISCOURSE: FROM EDUCATIONAL RHETORIC TO POLITICAL DIALOGUE

We therefore offer a discourse that is unapologetically moral, spiritual, and political and that is rooted in imagery of justice, freedom, joy, and peace. Although our commitment is deep, we are not unmindful of at least some of the problematics of such a discourse. We are aware of the dangers of self-righteousness and of moral zealotry, and we recognize that tyranny and oppression often are associated with political movements grounded in such visions. Our discourse has its share of inner tensions and paradoxes—affirmation of both criticality and commitment, of firmness and flexibility, community and individuality, freedom and equality, harmony and diversity. As intellectuals, we cannot but be wary, skeptical, and critical of any creed, formulation, or manifesto; but as moral agents, we cannot be paralyzed by complexity and tolerance. Our discourse, therefore, needs to be enriched by considerations of promoting serious dialogue on how to sophisticate and enlarge our vision. We must also take seriously the existence of other vital discourses, orientations, and visions, and we must be mindful of the necessity of developing sufficient consensus among these groups in order to constitute a coherent and significant political movement.

It is important to reiterate that we are speaking to public as well as professional discourse on education. A sophisticated and informed public dialogue on education is absolutely required for both ideological and strategic reasons. Because our nation was founded on the moral and political traditions of democracy, it is essential that our educational policies emerge from a well-informed and energized public will. Moreover, it is clear that significant educational changes can happen only when there is strong social and cultural demand, understanding, and support for them. Professionals have a special responsibility in this process. So also do those who do not consider themselves to be professional educators but who seek to participate actively in educational debate.

This responsibility (in addition to others, such as research, teaching, and consulting) involves the profession in helping to frame the public dialogue in a more sophisticated and textured manner. While it is the public who has the responsibility and the power to determine cultural, social, and political matters—and, hence, educational policies—the public looks to the professional for guidance in determining the nature and scope of the issues. In a word, professionals have particular and special responsibilities in the critical task of problem posing. By this, we do not mean that the public should be totally dependent on just another kind of expertise—"We'll tell you the problems, and you solve them." What we do mean is that our leadership responsibilities involve seriously engaging the public in the process of framing and posing important questions and issues. Such responsibility is merited to the extent that the profession exercises its critical capacities and its understanding of the social, cultural, political, moral, economic, and religious context and the significance of more technical matters. This is to move away from a notion of a professional rooted in narrowly conceived pedagogical and technical matters to one inevitably and intimately involved in major political and social concerns.

Those of us interested in significant educational change must be committed to significant cultural and social change. If educators are concerned with not only understanding but also changing the world, then they must integrate their work with political and social movements. This requires, among other things, overcoming the insularity of educational theorists as well as the divisions within their ranks. Thankfully, there has been a considerable discussion of this process as expressed in the exposition and analysis of the concept of *inclusiveness*, meaning a movement that seeks to include and involve rather than to exclude and alienate.

## Enemies: A Love Story

Inclusiveness is meant not simply to convert more people but rather, or in addition, to validate and incorporate beliefs from the previously excluded or ignored. It is not a marketing or promotional endeavor, but the exemplification of the intellectual and democratic processes of free, open, and good-faith exchange. Chief among the challenges involved in attempts at inclusiveness are, on the one hand, clarifying the difference between deepening commitments and distorting them, and on the other, developing the ability to distinguish potential colleagues from closet adversaries.

Indeed, a major dimension of radical discourse of both Right and Left has been the use of the metaphor of "enemy," which emerges as oppositional language rich with references to "class warfare," "social conflict," and "the battle between the Right and the Left." There are at least two major issues here. The first has to do with how we should regard those who seem to support ideas that we feel are clearly inimical to a just and peaceful world; and the second, with how we can maintain our principles and commitments in the face of plausible, if not persuasive, resistance.

The first question involves the matter of how to name those who seem bent on reactionary policies and practices. Are such people wicked and evil? Perhaps they are not evil, but sick or neurotic, or emotionally unbalanced. In any event, as we have already discussed, we would be naive to believe that critical analysis and rational persuasion can, by themselves, significantly alter neuroses or conquer evil. Perhaps then it would be better to consider them misinformed, if not ignorant. In this case, we can have more confidence that traditional educative processes can be enlightening and efficacious. There are, of course, many other explanations for destructive behavior and attitudes, including sociological (upbringing, subculture, class origins, etc.) and biological ones (genetic disorders, brain abnormalities, etc.). In any case, shall we name those who are misinformed, deformed, and/or possessed as "enemies"? What are we to do with enemies? Normally, enemies are to be battled and vanquished and perhaps, if we are gracious, eventually rehabilitated.

Others, of course, have suggested another response to enemies—to turn the other cheek and even to love them. Despite the heroics of martyrs and the efforts of the churches, this formulation, although extraordinarily attractive and popular, has not exactly caught on. For one thing, it seems well nigh impossible to juxtapose the concepts of love and enemy as anything but a psychological oxymoron. In addition, to love thy neighbor is to invite the possibility of weakness, wishy-washiness, and appeasement. Can we passionately observe and adequately protect our covenants and still stoutly defend the faithful through such passivity, weakness, and naivete? Should we love a neighbor who does not do these things? How are we to regard neighbors who dishonor our parents or covet our spouses; who lie, steal, ravage, despoil, and violate? Are there no principles that we will not passionately oppose? No outrage that we will not tolerate? No ideas that we reject? Are there not monsters out there who are beyond the confines of sanity and safety?

The paradox of being wholeheartedly committed to principled decision and just as firmly committed to tolerance, diversity, and openness is as knotty as it is crucial. Our intellectual and moral energies direct us to confront the enormity of human malice, arrogance, and stupidity and to feel a sense of moral outrage. The evidence of unnecessary human suffering brought on by unnecessary human stupidity or intolerable evil is overwhelming. However, what is not so clear is its etiology and treatment. Who, if anyone, is to blame? Who and where are the culprits and what should we do to them? The paradox is intensified by our own consciousness of fairness, rationality, careful analysis, and skepticism—we become hoist by the petard of our commitment to reasonableness. We have come to see the horrors that emerge from ideological, philosophical, and theological certainty and dogma. We have learned about the contingencies of knowledge, how our beliefs are shaped by history, interests, circumstance, culture, family, and so forth. We are very much aware of the power of rhetoric, of how language can frame the debate, and of the endless narrative possibilities open to us.

Yet, as moral uncertainty and intellectual ambiguity grow, so does our fear about them. We note that the forces of oppression, greed, and privilege seem not to be deterred by theoretical misgivings or professional concerns for fairness. We are very much aware of how uncertainty feeds into existing and rampant apathy, indifference, alienation, and powerlessness. We are increasingly frustrated by the failure of progressives to ground their movement in a discourse of passion and faith.

## Converting the Enemy

In this time of peril, we must risk not only a strong affirmation of a vision of justice, peace, and freedom but also a full-hearted commitment to the struggle to make this vision real. We urge, however, that we inform and infuse this struggle with a deep sense of humility and compassion. When we speak of humility, we do not speak of abasement or false modesty since we have ample reason to celebrate what we as a people already have learned and accomplished. Rather, we need to accept that whatever talents we as people might possess have come to us undeserved and unearned. In addition, we speak to the humility that comes from the recognition of the awesomeness of the mystery of life, the extraordinary complexity of human beings, the incredible diversity of human expression, the yet-to-be determined nature of human possibilities, and the unbelievable richness of human experience.

When we speak of compassion, we do not speak of pity, sympathy, or even empathy alone, but rather to a sharing of the burden involved in the struggle for meaning and dignity. To suffer with others is not only to empathize with the difficulties, paradoxes, and conflicts involved with the struggle, but also to participate in it in solidarity. We are both united and divided by our differences, with good reason to believe that differences within people mirror those between them. To act in good faith is to assume that we all seek improvement, amelioration, progress, even as we disagree on what this means and indicates. Acting in good faith means that we allow for the possibility of error, distortion, and misinformation in all of us and that failures to agree are matters of regret and sadness rather than rage and dismay.

By definition it would seem that it would be extremely difficult to act in good faith with "enemies." Perhaps it is time to deconstruct the concept, or at least to examine the value of the term. Does it really help to maintain the dualism of enemy/ally or friend/foe? What is the source of this distinction that is so prevalent, so deep, and so destructive? Indeed, it runs so deep in our consciousness that even Jesus seems to affirm it by contributing to its reification, since he does not urge us to reconceptualize the concept of "enemy," but only to change our attitude toward the enemy.[34] It has been suggested that the concept of enemy is an atavistic one, rooted in a primordial but now anachronistic consciousness in which the species had literally to fight for survival. Perhaps our most compelling educational responsibility is to move our consciousness away from one in which people must be in conflict because of scarcity to one in which a consciousness of sufficiency obviates the need for deadly conflicts. We must learn not to fight fire with fire but with warmth; to cool passion, not with ice but with compassion; and to seek to understand, rather than vanquish, those who differ with us. Such a task is obviously not easy, and it has within it the danger of sentimentality and the denial of real differences of enormous consequences. However, it seems a manageable enough task to reduce rather than increase our "enemies," or at least to diminish our contempt for them.

At the risk of oversimplification, it is clear that educators lack the particular conceptual tools that can help us understand the psychological mechanisms involved in the impulses to oppress and to liberate. Notwithstanding our faith in critical rationality, we must admit that a pedagogy that relies primarily on rational analysis and critical reflection for transformation of consciousness is bound, at best, to have limited effect. As educators, we must have the courage to look unblinkingly at what seems to be as real an educational fact as there is, namely, that even very bright, intellectually able people are significantly involved in developing and administering policies directed at preserving inequality, hierarchy, and oppression. We must examine ways in which we can add to the texture of a pedagogy of critical rationality rooted in the commitment to social justice and personal liberation. It surely is clear by now, and perhaps gratuitous to mention again, that humans are extraordinarily complex, contradictory, and paradoxical beings, capable of acting divinely and/or demoniacally.

## Confessions of a True Professional

Education theorists also must do again what would seem obvious—that is to see ourselves and our colleagues as human, finite, and fallible people subject to conflicting and questionable impulses. In so doing, we act not only in an intellectually and morally honest way but also in a way appropriate to our responsibilities to provide leadership to the public. This responsibility includes being much more open and candid with the public about our strengths and limitations, which can help us to avoid the dangers of professional hegemony and can also help liberate all of us from the fantasies of certainty, perfection, and objectivity. We must seek for similar reasons to escape the prison of narrow professionalism and the chains of the academic ethos. This ought to be relatively painless for those who, on intellectual grounds, reject the posture of detachment and objectivity as misinformed or pompous or both. It would seem that the writings and talks of at least these people ought to reflect more subjectivity and personal reflection. The risk in such an endeavor, of course, is increased personal vulnerability and the possibility of being intellectually discounted.

This risk is heightened and made real by virtue of the intensely competitive nature of professional and academic life. Ironically enough, cultural criticism is a kind of growth industry in academia, and we are witness to the absurdity of people gaining power, privilege, and status as a consequence of pointing out the evils of power, privilege, and status. We must find ways to resist the forces that impel us to attack others in the guise of critique and the temptation to establish our professional identities at the expense of our colleagues. We must recognize in our own dialectical wisdom that this professional ethos of competition, hierarchy, and self-servingness emerges from the intersection of institutional demands and personal intentions.

We must therefore be prepared to be more understanding, honest, forgiving, empathic, and compassionate not only about others but also about ourselves. There certainly are powerful intellectual reasons for significant self-examinations—never mind the moral and psychological requirements for honesty, openness, and candor. Within a context of the blend of affirmation and humility that we have been discussing, we suggest that the concept of confession might help. By confession, we mean simply the process of continuous, candid self-reflection, self-criticism, self-affirmation, and self-renewal. It is a process that is grounded neither in our sinfulness nor in our purity, but rather in an understanding that we are sentient beings constantly engaged in a struggle within and among ourselves. Such a process would enable us to affirm and reaffirm; to remind us of our strengths, weaknesses, predilections; and to go on with our individual praxis as we acknowledge and forgive our weaknesses and affirm and celebrate our strengths. Confession to us is not about guilt but about responsibility, that is, about becoming more aware of our ability to respond to our commitments. It is a process that must happen within and among us, for we need the support and insights of each other to strengthen both our individual selves and our sense of solidarity. Professional community cannot help but be divisive, if it continues to be firmly rooted in individual achievement, discipleship, and ideological loyalty. Collegiality, if we are to be intellectually honest and morally responsible, must extend to concerns for the problematics of being human. Since our work is to heal and liberate, our task can only be made easier when we learn to heal and liberate ourselves from the doubt, envy, scorn, fear, and hostility that haunts and has the capacity ultimately to destroy us.

To affirm our commitments with humility, we must consider the possibility of letting go of some basic elements of our consciousness—for example, enemies, competition, hierarchy. We believe that it is very difficult and problematic simply to will greater openness, but that a consciousness of affirmation, humility, and confession will lead us to a much greater degree of openness. If we are to engage the public in a dialogue on the moral and political dimensions of education and in a discourse that involves the problematics of human agency, then we ourselves must engage in this very praxis. In this way, we celebrate both the particularities of our work and our solidarity with the public.

We see, for example, very real possibilities for developing significant openings to groups and orientation now marginal to radical educational theorists. These groups and individuals include, among others, those who believe that rationality does not exhaust the possibilities of knowing and that intuitive and esthetic experiences also can provide insight and understanding. Moreover, there is powerful evidence that the human experience has always involved and continues to involve religious and spiritual aspirations and sensibilities. We must, at the very least, learn not to deny and discount such widespread and deeply felt convictions since it would be infinitely more constructive and healthy to be responsive and open toward them. Do we seriously believe that those who value intuition, the body, and self-reflection are entirely primitive, naïve, and narcissistic? If so, then do we really believe anything is gained by urging these people to consider that their lives are shallow and meaningless? Do we really believe that the millions of people who are grounded in religious faith are ignorant and superstitious and that we should ask and expect them to deny that which has given them meaning, fulfillment, and solace? Is it not also possible that important insight and wisdom is contained within the consciousness informed by esthetic, subjective, and spiritual sensibilities?

In a parallel way, we also must learn to affirm those colleagues who have taken on diverse and varied roles, functions, situations, and projects. We indicated before that the highly competitive ethos of academic and professional life tends to encourage a great deal of dismissiveness and discounting of the work of others. Radical theorists, in particular, tend to be very suspicious of so-called moderates or liberals who work on making relatively modest changes within the existing school system—because they do not see the big picture or, worse, will become dupes of the power structure. We confess to sharing the fear that such so-called realistic efforts can, at best, distract us from more basic considerations and, at worst, deceive us into blurring change with transformation.

We are more persuaded, however, that while it is probably desirable to maintain this skepticism it is also important to affirm and celebrate efforts that are simultaneously modest and significant. For example, tutoring children in a working-class neighborhood on the SATs may be modest, in that only relatively few children are involved, and also may tend to perpetuate hierarchy and monitoring. However, in the short-run and in the context of other more fundamental projects and given the particular circumstances of the particular children, it would seem that such a project has important redemptive dimensions, that is, doing well on the SAT probably and very likely will help to empower these children by giving them the intellectual skills and cultural capital necessary to participate in cultural politics.

We must demonstrate our awareness of and learn to respond to the reality of a culture that operates on several levels. There is the continuum of time (e.g., immediate, short range, middle range, longer range, ultimate, etc.) and there are the varieties of important contexts (e.g., changes within individuals or within culture/society/institutions; change of consciousness, outlook, paradigms; transformation of institutions, etc.). As individuals, we constantly move between, within, and among these levels, usually at a very rapid and dizzying rate. Shall we change our cereal, our diet, or our total outlook on food? Do we see family traditions as generally satisfying, as bourgeois artifacts, or as vital and enduring elements of tradition? Responses to such questions inevitably involve our own individual existential circumstances. How do we respond to questions about education for liberation when our teenage children want to drop out of school and get married? How do we handle our disgust and outrage at grades when our students write poor term papers? What do we do when our colleagues with heavy financial obligations are too terrified to protest?

Again, within the context of a consciousness of confession, we must show compassion for others and for ourselves when we find ourselves in contradictory and paradoxical situations. Although it is surely possible to significantly reduce the degree of contradiction through reflection and analysis, it is also likely that many contradictions emerge from the necessity to operate simultaneously in several of these levels—to have to deal with both short- and long-range issues—to deal with the preservation of institutions simultaneously with the necessity of totally transforming them. There is, indeed, extremely important work to be done in the name of justice, peace, and freedom in all of these levels and contexts.

There are risks and problematics involved, but here again we can have confidence in our capacity to be critical and compassionate within a context of good faith. We need to learn that there are always possibilities and limitations involved in the particular work that we do. This requires both intellectual and moral considerations. Intellectually, it is clear the boundary sites and areas of cultural politics are fuzzy, unclear, overlapping, discontinuous yet interconnected. From a moral perspective, we surely can have compassion for those who struggle earnestly in their particular ways and varied situations and, at the same time, insist that these struggles be grounded in a quest for peace, justice, and freedom.

Within a consciousness of confession and humility, we must come to accept the limitations under which we all work. Healing and transforming the world will not be the result of the work of one or a few giants. Nor will it emerge from one or a small number of strategies. It will emerge from the cumulative and continuous efforts of a great many people working in a great many arenas, albeit generated by a few basic moral and political principles and commitments. We need the courage and confidence to continue our work while realizing its insufficiency and incompleteness, and we need the humility to celebrate the contributions that our colleagues working very differently from us can make to our common quest. However, we must avoid the sentimentality of nostrums that ease the pain and anguish of our insufficiency, such as the piety of "Everything works out for the best," the narcissism of "Aren't we all wonderful," and the preciousness of "the solidarity of the marginal and oppressed."

Within a consciousness of critical and skeptical rationality, therefore, we must be wary, if not suspicious, of glibness, wishy-washiness, and evasion. We need to be particularly wary of being captured by the tyranny of trying to be politically correct and of being held hostage by doctrinaire ideology. Along with the struggle to rid ourselves of the consciousness of "enemy" should come the capacity to be more discerning about the meaning and significance of our highly diverse social movements and ideas. Our society grows increasingly diverse, but our dominant culture is reluctant to cede its canons of judgment. We must persist in our determination to be affirmative and flexible in the realization that there are psychological, intellectual, and moral barriers to being nonjudgmental. Furthermore, we must recognize the depth and significance of the impulse to affiliate with particular groups, cultures, and movements.

A compassionate, humble, yet penetrating criticality can help us see more deeply into the paradoxical and complex consciousness of both "good" and "bad guys." For example, people who resist affirmative action may be misguided and misinformed, but they also are likely to be responding, however inappropriately, to genuine and legitimate fears. People who demand, on the other hand, such commendable and legitimate aspirations as community participation in the schools may very well have extremely limited and conventional ideas on curriculum and instruction. Teachers are surely oppressed, underpaid, and overworked, but some are also capable of cruelty, inconsiderateness, and stupidity. Radicals who provide moral energy and conceptual breakthroughs can also have quite conventional and narrow notions of scholarship.

Oppressed and marginal groups and individuals have a right to demand to be heard, and those in power have a responsibility to at least ease, if not remove, mechanisms of silencing. We need at the same time to learn not to patronize such groups and individuals by endowing them with special powers or sensitivities or to exclude them from the responsibility to pursue the reduction, rather than the exploitation, of divisiveness. Camus has said that we are all murderers, Welch confesses that she is both oppressor and oppressed, and Freud can help us understand why this would be so. This understanding is surely vital, but it is an understanding that should inform and not paralyze judgment and will. Our critical consciousness can help us become more aware of the ramifications and implications of what we are doing and why, but it is our moral consciousness that helps us determine what we should be doing.

We therefore return to our concern about how we are to participate in the great continuous human drama that shapes and directs our lives. As educators, we have special responsibilities to engage in the human enterprise of creating a life of dignity, justice, peace, joy, and meaning for all. We must ground our expertise in this endeavor and put our special knowledge in the service of this project. We are not merely experts, but first of all human beings who respond to the call for cultural, moral, and political leadership from the perspective of those who work in educational institutions. We have faith in the human capacity to create a just world and confidence that this capacity can be further enriched by deepening awareness and possibility through the nourishment of our intellectual, critical, esthetic, and moral sensibilities. We are intolerant of and outraged at unnecessary human suffering and the oppression of the human spirit. We are dedicated to using our energies to transform that which enables oppression and inhibits transformation. We do so humbly but with determination and in the faith that our work is neither sufficient nor unnecessary. We must avoid the triviality and banality of professionalism, the smugness and arrogance of scholarship, and the suffocation of self-righteousness. We also, however, must celebrate the energy of a professional ethic that is grounded in democracy and justice, the liberation that comes from critical rationality, and the meaning that emerges from a moral vision.

We have attempted to lay out the dimensions of an agenda for educational reform. We found it difficult, however, to separate in any neat way the concern with, and the pursuit of, an alternative discourse for education from the issue of an agenda. Perhaps in our fixation on language, we are victims of the current preoccupation with the text in academic life. Yet, what is clear to us is that there really is no way in which the struggle for a deep change in our educational concerns can be separated from a focus on the terms, meanings, and definitions of educational work. Not to do this consigns us quickly to the limited—and, for us, ultimately unacceptable—parameters of prevailing educational policies and practices.

In making this point, we do not wish to ignore or denigrate important ongoing struggles that are part of a progressive reform agenda in education. These include attempting to win equitable funding for schools and school systems; giving more managerial power to teachers and improving the status and conditions of their work; ensuring wide access to early childhood programs of high quality; fighting class, race and gender bias in the evaluation and assessment of students; reducing or eliminating tracking or other forms of separation in schools and school systems that stigmatize or exclude students; providing broad opportunities for meaningful sex education; resisting censorship of books in classrooms and school libraries; and supporting efforts to make curricula fully embody multicultural and multiethnic and nonsexist approaches to teaching, and so forth. Yet, if we are to go beyond this and "unpack" educational goals and concerns in some more fundamental way, we will need an agenda that stays in touch with—indeed, continually refocuses—our energies on the underlying motives and impulses of the educational enterprise itself.

While we might disappoint some by not offering a sufficiently systematic, point by point, series of proposals for reform, we believe we have stayed true to our project of trying to shift the ground on which educational work and effects are ultimately predicated. Clearly for us, too, there is no easy separation between words and deeds. The struggle to redirect how we analyze the nature and purpose of education is as real and as practical a task, we believe, as any true policy objective might be.

## NOTES

1. The assertion of "totalizing" political thinking and its inherent dangers has been central to the critique of Marxism by both postmodern and feminist writers. See, for example, David Kolb, *The Critique of Pure Modernity* (Chicago: University of Chicago Press, 1987); Jean-Francois Lyotard, *The Postmodern Condition* (Minneapolis: University of Minnesota Press, 1984); Michel Foucault, *Power/Knowledge* (New York: Random House, 1981); Linda Nicholson, ed., *Feminism/Postmodernism* (New York: Routledge, 1990).
2. Alvin W. Gouldner, *The Two Marxisms* (New York: Seabury Press, 1990); Martin Jay, *Marxism and Totality* (Berkeley: University of California Press, 1984); Russell Jacoby, *Dialectic of Defeat* (Cambridge, England: Cambridge University Press, 1981).
3. A growing concern with the emphasis on "difference" in left political thinking at the expense of a notion of community is found in a number of writers. See, for example, Marshall Berman, "Why Modernism Still Matters," *Tikkun* 4, no. 1 (January/February 1989), pp. 11–14, 81–86; Barry Kanpol, *Towards a Postmodern Theory of Teacher Cultural Politics* (forthcoming); Wendy Kohli, "Postmodernism, Critical Theory and the 'New' Pedagogies: What's at Stake in the Discourse?" *Education and Society* 9, no. 1 (1991), pp. 39–46; Suzanne Moore, "Gender, Post-Modern Style," *Marxism Today* (May 1990), p. 91; Henry Giroux, *Border Crossings: Cultural Workers and the Politics of Education* (London: Routledge, 1992).
4. See, for example, Steven Connor, *Postmodern Culture* (New York: Basil Blackwell, 1989); David Kolb, *Postmodernism Publication* (Chicago: University of Chicago Press, 1990); Douglas Kellner, *Jean Baudrillard, From Marxism to Post-Modernism and Beyond* (Oxford: Polity Press, 1988).
5. Fritjof Capra and Charlene Spretnak, *Green Politics* (New York: Dutton, 1984); Carl Boggs, *Social Movements and Political Power* (Philadelphia: Temple University Press, 1986).
6. Rudolf Bahro, *The Alternatives in Eastern Europe* (London: NLB, 1978).
7. See, for example, Richard A. Cloward and Francis F. Piven, *The New Class War* (New York: Pantheon, 1982); Boggs, *Social Movements and Political Power* (Philadelphia: Temple University Press, 1986); Jurgen Habermas, *Legitimation Crisis* (Boston: Beacon, 1975); Richard Flacks, *Making History: The Radical Tradition in American Life* (New York: Columbia University Press, 1988).
8. Douglas Kellner, *Critical Theory, Marxism and Modernity* (Baltimore: Johns Hopkins University Press, 1989).
9. See, for example, H. Svi Shapiro, *Between Capitalism and Democracy: Education Policy and the Crisis of the Welfare State* (Westport, Conn.: Bergin & Garvey, 1990); also, Stanley Aronowitz and Henry Giroux, *Education under Siege* (South Hadley, Mass.: Bergin & Garvey, 1985); Ira Shor, *Culture Wars: Schools and Society in the Conservative Restoration* (Boston: Routledge, 1986).
10. Michael Lerner, "A New Paradigm for Liberals: The Primacy of Ethics and Emotions," *Tikkun* 2, no. 1 (1987), pp. 22–28, 132–38.
11. Ibid., pp. 24–25.
12. Ibid. See also Christopher Lasch, "What's Wrong with the Right," *Tikkun* 1, no. 1 (1986), pp. 23–29; and Robert Bellah et al., *Habits of the Heart* (Berkeley: University of California Pres, 1985).
13. For an analysis of the question of social agency in the quest for radical school reform, see H. Svi Shapiro, "Beyond the Sociology of Education: Culture, Politics, and the Promise of Educational Change," *Educational Theory* 38, no. 4 (Fall 1988), pp. 415–30; see also Geoff Whitty, *Sociology and School Knowledge* (London: Methuen, 1985).
14. There is now a large literature that attempts to address this issue. See, for example, Stanley Aronowitz, *The Crisis in Historical Materialism* (Minneapolis: University of Minnesota

Press, 1990); Stuart Hall, *The Hard Road to Renewal* (London: Vergo, 1988); Raymond Williams, *The Year 2000* (New York: Pantheon Books, 1983).

15. R. Todd Erkel, "The Birth of a Movement," *Networker* (May/June 1990), pp. 26–35.
16. Sharon Welch, *Communities of Resistance and Solidarity* (New York: Orbis, 1985).
17. Foucault, *Power/Knowledge*; see also, Nancy Hartsock, "Foucault on Power: A Theory for Women," in *Feminism/Postmodernism*, ed. Linda J. Nicholson (New York: Routledge, 1990), pp. 157–75.
18. The list of authors who have contributed to our view of the ethical and spiritual crisis of the nation is a long one. It includes Cornel West, Michael Harrington, Robert Bellah, Barbara Ehrenreich, Theodore Roszack, Matthew Fox, Beverly Harrison, Maya Angelou, Michael Lerner, Philip Slater, Richard Sennett, Sharon Welch, Dorothee Soelle, Harvey Cox, Peter Clecak, and Sallie McPhague, among others.
19. This criticism must not be interpreted in a personalized manner. In no sense is this statement meant to invalidate the overall powerful and important work of critical educational theorists that has been, and continues to be, done. It concerns accessibility of what has been written and the need for a discourse about schools that can go beyond the limited constituencies that are now its primary audience.
20. Among these are Michael Lerner, Cornel West, Dorothee Soelle, Isaac Balbus, Stuart Hall, Douglas Kellner, Stanley Aronowitz, Sheila Rowbottom, Andre Gorz, Murray Bookchin, Jean Cohen, Terry Eagleton, bell hooks, and others.
21. See, for example, Sharon Welch, *A Feminist Ethic of Risk* (Minneapolis: Fortress Press, 1990); Beverly Harrison, *Making the Connections* (Boston: Beacon, 1985); Matthew Fox, *A Spirituality Named Compassion* (Minneapolis: Winston Press, 1979).
22. See, for example, Andre Gorz, *Ecology as Politics* (Boston: South End Press, 1980); Murray Bookchin, *The Modern Crisis* (Philadelphia: New Society Publishers, 1986); Petra Kelly, *Fighting for Hope* (Boston: South End Press, 1984).
23. See, for example, *Marxism Today* (October 1988), special edition on "New Times"; see also Alvin Toffler, *Powershift* (New York: Bantam Books, 1990).
24. See, for example, Peter Gabel, "Creationism and the Spirit of Nature," *Tikkun* 2, no. 5 (1987), pp. 55–63; Michael Harrington, *The Politics at God's Funeral* (New York: Holt, Rinehart, 1983); Harvey Cox, *Religion in the Secular City* (New York: Simon & Schuster, 1984); see also the work of Marion Woodman, Dianne Stein, Theodore Roszak, or Fritjof Capra.
25. See, for example, Isaac D. Balbus, *Marxism and Domination* (Princeton, N.J.: Princeton University Press, 1982). See also, Terry Eagleton, *The Ideology of the Aesthetic* (Oxford: Basil Blackwell, 1990).
26. See, for example, the work in this country of Sharon Welch, Beverly Harrison, Dorothee Soelle, Matthew Fox, Walter Breuggemen, Starhawk, and Judity Plaskow.
27. This is perhaps best reflected in the wave of admiration for the work of the French guru of postmodern social theory Jean Baudrillard, with its cynical, self-indulgent assertion of the meaninglessness of social and political struggle. For an excellent discussion of the phenomenon, see Douglas Kellner, *Jean Baudrillard: From Marxism to Postmodernism and Beyond* (Oxford: Polity Press, 1988).
28. Of course, it is this which is embodied in the fearful conservatism of intellectuals like Allan Bloom, Daniel Bell, E. D. Hirsch, William J. Bennett, and others.
29. See, for example, Stuart Hall, "Blue Election, Election Blues," *Marxism Today* (July 1987), pp. 30–35.
30. See, for example, H. Svi Shapiro, "Educational Theory and Recent Political Discourse: A New Agenda for the Left?" *Teachers College Record* 89, no. 2 (Winter 1987), pp. 171–200.
31. Chantal Mouffe and Ernest Laclau, *Hegemony and Socialist Strategy* (London: Vergo, 1985); see also, Samuel Bowles and Herbert Gintis, *Democracy and Capitalism* (New York: Basic Books, 1986).

32. See, for example, Cox, *Religion in the Secular City*.
33. David Purpel, *The Moral and Spiritual Crisis in Education: A Curriculum for Social Justice* (Granby, Mass.: Bergin & Garvey, 1988).
34. We are indebted to Dr. Marshall Gordon for this insight.

# Author Index

# Subject Index

childhood, 92–94, 165–167, 188
school failure and, 164–165
Poverty rate, 92–94, 102, 188
Power in education, 342–343, *see also* Authoritarianism
Private school, Jewish, *see* Jewish *vs.* public education
Public policy, *see also* Clinton, Bill; Government funding for achieving sustainable livelihoods, 77–79
disabilities and, 104–105
ineffective, 70–75

# R

Race
*vs.* citizenship, 159
classification, history of, 58–59
"multiracial," 161–162
politics of, 182–184
poverty and, 162–167, 173–174, 188
Racial attitudes, 181–184
classroom racism, 110–116
segregation, 112–116
during desegregation, 262–263
"White panic," 184–186
White supremacist, 181–184, 263, 393
Reform, 80, *see also* Educational reform
Religion, *see* Christianity; Jewish *vs.* public education; Spirituality
Responsibility, community and social, 3, 51–54, 80, 178, 238, 396
teaching of, 52–54

# S

Schools, *see also* Education
as microcosm of society, 105, 116, 365, *see also* Holistic education
Self-esteem, educational concerns about, 253
Sexual orientation, *see* Homosexuality
Sexuality curriculum, 178, 219–220
on sexual diversity, 220–223
Smith, Adam, 5
Social change, *see* Education, goals of; Holistic education
Social Darwinism, 275
and differentiated education, 132, 139–140
Social economy
restoration of, 76–77
undervaluation and destruction of, 73–77
Social programs, *see also* Clinton, Bill; Government funding; Public policy opposition to, 20–24
Social responsibility, *see* Responsibility
Society, breakdown of, 6, 18–20
Socioeconomic status, *see* Students, working class

Special education, 241–242
denial of dignity and, 245–253
labeling and, 245
lowered expectations in, 247
Spirituality in education, 51, 322–327, 330–335, 355–356, 385–386
teaching and, 331–335
Sputnik, 273, 331
Student culture, 117–119
Student interaction, and performance, 315–316
Students, *see also* Teacher-student interaction
grouping of, 112–116, 128
by ability, 85, 113–116, 128–130
*vs.* democratic initiative, 65–67
disabilities and, 114, 115
by IQ tests, 67
by race, 112–113, 115–117
inability to think
authoritarian education and, 60
passivity encouraged by schools, 59–64
powerlessness of, 65
working class, inferior education of, 50–51, 60–61, 281–282
Sustainable livelihoods, 50, 52, 69, 77–79

# T

Taxation, opposition to, 20–24
Teachers, as authority figures, 118
Teacher-student interaction, 117–118
gender patterns of, 109, 110
Teaching, *see also* Education
as a mission, 331–333
styles of
learning styles and, 107–109
Testing, 67, 141
emphasis on, 3, 48–49, 60, 141, 282
labeling and, 247
special education, 247, 248
Tracking, educational, *see* Students, grouping of
"Trickle-down" principle, 136–139, 145

# V

Video games, cultural influences of, 300–302
Violence, *see also* Culture, wilding
domestic, 11–13, 100
prevalence of, 10–11
Vocational education, 280

# W

Welfare
attitudes toward, 169–170, 172–174
Bill Clinton plan, 171–172, 174
Women, *see also* Gender
role in educational thought, 203
Worker vulnerability, 40–41

7210